KU-030-855

An Infinity of Things

AN
INFINITY
OF THINGS

How Sir Henry Wellcome
Collected the World

FRANCES LARSON

OXFORD
UNIVERSITY PRESS

OXFORD
UNIVERSITY PRESS

Great Clarendon Street, Oxford OX2 6DP

Oxford University Press is a department of the University of Oxford.
It furthers the University's objective of excellence in research, scholarship,
and education by publishing worldwide in

Oxford New York

Auckland Cape Town Dar es Salaam Hong Kong Karachi
Kuala Lumpur Madrid Melbourne Mexico City Nairobi
New Delhi Shanghai Taipei Toronto

With offices in

Argentina Austria Brazil Chile Czech Republic France Greece
Guatemala Hungary Italy Japan Poland Portugal Singapore
South Korea Switzerland Thailand Turkey Ukraine Vietnam

Oxford is a registered trade mark of Oxford University Press
in the UK and in certain other countries

Published in the United States
by Oxford University Press Inc., New York

© Frances Larson 2009

The moral rights of the author have been asserted
Database right Oxford University Press (maker)

First published 2009

All rights reserved. No part of this publication may be reproduced,
stored in a retrieval system, or transmitted, in any form or by any means,
without the prior permission in writing of Oxford University Press,
or as expressly permitted by law, or under terms agreed with the appropriate
reprographics rights organization. Enquiries concerning reproduction
outside the scope of the above should be sent to the Rights Department,
Oxford University Press, at the address above

You must not circulate this book in any other binding or cover
and you must impose the same condition on any acquirer

British Library Cataloguing in Publication Data
Data available

Library of Congress Control Number: 2009928977

Typeset by SPI Publisher Services, Pondicherry, India
Printed in Great Britain
on acid-free paper by
Clays Ltd, St Ives plc

ISBN 978–0–19–955446–1

For my parents

CONTENTS

PART IV. LEGACIES

LIST OF ILLUSTRATIONS

All illustrations, unless otherwise identified, are reproduced by kind permission of the Wellcome Library. More pictures of Henry Wellcome and his collection can be found at http://images.wellcome.ac.uk/

In-text Illustrations

Colour Plates

ACKNOWLEDGEMENTS

This book began life as my doctoral thesis in 2000–3. I would like to thank the following people for their advice during that time: Jeremy Coote, Michael O'Hanlon, Danielle Olsen, Michael Rowlands, and John Symons. My thanks to the Wingate Foundation, whose generosity allowed me to return to the project three years later and embark on a new phase of study and writing. I am indebted to all the staff who assisted me at the Wellcome Library, the Bodleian Library, the Pitt Rivers Museum, and Liverpool University Special Collections. Thank you to Ken Arnold, Jude Hill, Ross MacFarlane, Alison Petch, and William Schupbach for reading the manuscript, or parts of it, and giving their judicious advice. The Wellcome Trust has provided the illustrations for this book and has met the costs of the colour plate section, for which I am very grateful. Anna Smith, at Wellcome Images, helped to organize the illustrations. The Wellcome Library provides an outstanding resource for researchers, and the staff there have been extremely helpful to me; however, the opinions expressed here are based on independent research funded entirely by the Wingate Foundation. Any shortcomings in the text are my own. Rupert Cousens, Seth Cayley, Kate Hind, and the team at Oxford University Press have been fantastic. The comments made by an anonymous reviewer for Oxford University Press were valuable and constructive. My greatest thanks go to Chris Gosden, who first suggested that I work on the Wellcome Collection, guided my research thereafter, and lugged the manuscript with him to Borneo to read; and to my parents and my husband, who have read and critiqued my words and supported me throughout. This book is dedicated to my parents, with thanks.

A NOTE ON MONEY

Changes in the relative value of goods, services, and property make it extremely difficult to convert late-nineteenth-century and early-twentieth-century prices into contemporary ones. As there are references to people's salaries and the price of various objects in the chapters and notes that follow, I have decided not to try and calculate their value today. More information, and various methods for calculating relative worth, can be found at http://measuringworth.com/calculators/ukcompare/

CHAPTER ONE

QUITE INDESCRIBABLE
DISORDER

In the autumn of 1943, the Conservator at the Wellcome Historical Medical Museum sat down to write a report on the state of the collection in his care. It is an astonishing document. The Museum was in the process of consolidating its holdings; staff were trying to streamline the mass of objects left behind by the collection's creator, Sir Henry Wellcome, after his death in 1936. The Conservator explained that several auction sales had already taken place to this end. In fact, more than £30,000 had been made through the resale of Wellcome's artefacts in the seven years since he had died. Wellcome, it would seem, had collected far too many objects for the Museum to cope with. Just how many becomes clear on reading the Conservator's report.[1]

The weapons and armour had proved particularly problematic. There were so many weapons in the collection, from 'practically every country in the world', that storing them had long ago become 'an embarrassment' to staff at the Museum. So, steps were taken to dispose of them. Already, upwards of 6,200 weapons had been sold at auction by Sotheby's. Donations of serviceable arms had been made to the Royal Artillery Institution, the Armouries of the Tower of London, the Honourable Artillery Company, and the Home Guard. But even so, there remained 'a considerable quantity' which was only fit for scrap. A 'considerable quantity' turned out to be 'approximately 3½ tons of swords and 2½ tons of guns, cannon, helmets and shields', which were taken away for disposal by the Ministry of Supply.

But Wellcome's weaponry was just the start. Over the years the Museum stores had become clogged with a 'considerable quantity' of other kinds of junk, too. No less than three tons of worthless metal—'old steel safe doors, obsolete lifting tackle, including chains and blocks, and a large quantity of useless tools'—that Sir Henry had bought for archaeological excavations and other projects, had to be sent to the scrapyard. A further five tons of 'old photograph albums and waste paper' had to be disposed of because they had degraded hopelessly after decades deep in storage. Some two tons of 'wooden boulders', which had been bought with the intention of making furniture and display cases for the Museum but were now 'more or less rotten', were thrown out. However, all was not lost, for three tons of wood was salvaged from the Museum stores and sent to the scientific research laboratories Wellcome had established in Kent, where it might be put to good use.

Despite the efforts that had already been made, the Conservator knew, as he drafted his report, that he presided over a collection so colossal and so amorphous it would take years, if not decades, to sort through. There is, unsurprisingly, a measured weariness, a sense of stoicism, to his tone. His report subsides into a cursory list of the remaining artefacts in storage: 1,100 cases of ethnological objects, 110 cases of Graeco-Roman and other classical objects, . . . 80 cases of miscellaneous small arms, 150 cases of prehistoric objects, 300 framed pictures, . . . 85 cases of surgical instruments, . . . 60 cases of pestles and mortars, 170 cases of Peruvian objects, . . . 74 cases of weights and measures. And so it goes on. Small wonder if the author felt a little defeated at the prospect of writing a 'Report on the steps which have been taken to dispose of surplus material' in Wellcome's collection.

It took another forty years to organize and re-home the objects Henry Wellcome had devoted his life to acquiring. As they worked through the collection, staff at the Museum dealt not with one or two packing cases of his artefacts at a time, but with one or two *hundred* packing cases at a time. One unsuspecting gentleman answered a newspaper advertisement, placed by the Museum staff in 1945, offering a collection of European and Asian armour for sale by public tender. When he arrived to collect his goods he found himself the proud owner of an entire 'warehouseful, in quite indescribable disorder'. Such scenes had presumably become commonplace for staff (even then, one estimate put the number of remaining non-mechanical arms in the collection— spears, clubs, shields, arrows, and the like—at a mind-numbing 50,000).[2]

Since Wellcome's death, entire museums have been founded on a fraction of his collection's treasures. Indeed, all the major museums in Great Britain, and many of the lesser known ones, now have Wellcome material in their care, with some looking after tens of thousands of items. In the late 1970s, after forty years of sorting, selling, gifting, and getting rid of Wellcome's artefacts, the residual hub of the collection—a not insignificant hoard of 100,000 objects relating to the history of medicine—was transferred to the Science Museum in London on permanent loan. Some of it can be seen there today, by people who take the time to ascend to the top two floors of the building. These galleries, and the Wellcome Library on Euston Road, where the core of Sir Henry's magnificent collection of books, manuscripts, and paintings can still be consulted, are the rich and orderly residue so painstakingly lifted from a life of ceaseless explorations into the history of science.[3]

What led a successful, self-made businessman, head of a leading international pharmaceuticals firm, to spend his fortune filling a series of warehouses with artefacts and books that he never saw, and that were destined to gather dust in the darkness for years to come, unseen and unknown? Paradoxically, it was because Wellcome was so organized in his pursuit of the perfect museum that his collection rapidly devolved into a state bordering on chaos. He took to employing a team of collecting agents, who scoured the markets and salesrooms of Britain's towns and cities week in and week out, and who searched for objects across Europe, Africa, and Asia. Wellcome was determined that nothing should be missed. Acquisitions poured in from all corners of the globe, and he leased a string of warehouses to store his growing cache, but the inescapable compulsion of collecting had taken hold: however much he acquired, there would always be more; and all the things he had yet to find promised to be considerably more interesting than all the things he already owned. The means overshadowed the end. Collecting became a way of life.

The acquisition process was intensely sociable. Gathering objects on this scale also necessitated a gathering of people—agents, assistants, researchers, caretakers, workmen—and their personalities became bound up in the growing collection, as their relationships with Wellcome unfurled in its midst. Wellcome's desire for things stirred him to travel the world, and to forge friendships and professional associations, just as it led him, sometimes, to terminate these alliances abruptly. For if a passion for collecting has the power to weave lives together, it can also pull them apart. And so, through all these relationships, Wellcome and his collection emerged concomitantly. Their fates were intimately entwined. Collecting permeated Wellcome's existence. His wealth placed few limits on its power to shape him. This was not a man who simply projected his inner character through his purchasing power; this was a man who was drawn into the world through his desire for objects.

'One of the things about Sir Henry', an employee later wrote, 'was that he never thought he would die.'[4] And because of this, perhaps, Wellcome ran out of time. The story that might have emerged from all his frantic collecting—the great history 'of the art and science of healing' that he intended to depict through his rarities—was never finished. The collection was never exhibited *en masse*, polished and consistent as he intended it to be. This failure means that we are left with the same impression of Wellcome's collection that his immediate successors were left with: overflowing warehouses, mountains of packing cases, little concrete information, disarray. And not without good reason, for the story of the collection is often a story of insecurities, resentments, and questionable convictions. But there is also a lesson in the incompleteness. The collection's perpetual state of imperfection—the trash and the tangents and the hidden treasures—remind us that life too is lived incomplete, and always projected towards an unknown future.

Wellcome was too busy collecting, too busy living, to interpret the significance of all the things he had acquired. Each new acquisition promised great things: fresh understanding, intellectual opportunities, the possibility of discoveries and diversions and new interests. And so he was drawn ever onwards, and by the time he stopped to look back it was too late. Every collection—every life—opens up infinite possibilities and paths that might be struck, Wellcome's, perhaps, more than most.

This, then, is the biography of a collection. Like all biographies, it seeks to distil some pattern and purpose from the 'indescribable disorder' that threatens to complicate every life. The book falls into four parts: the first part traces the deepest roots, and the earliest phase, of Wellcome's collecting instinct in the late nineteenth century; the second part charts the major expansion of his collection during the early twentieth century when he began to employ other people to buy things for him and he established the systems upon which the collection would continue to grow; the third part assesses the immediate outcome of all this collecting activity—the Wellcome Historical Medical Museum, opened in 1913—and goes on to explore Wellcome's, often difficult, relationships with key members of his Museum staff; the fourth part looks at the fate of the collection in the final years of Wellcome's life, and beyond, and reflects on the broader implications of this man's great, and little known, material legacy.

I focus on the period up to Wellcome's death, in 1936. After this, the story splinters, to be taken up again by the Wellcome Library and the other institutions that absorbed portions of Wellcome's collection into their own.

There are numerous success stories, telling of exhibitions, publications, academic research, publicity, education, and outreach programmes, each inspired by Wellcome's artefacts. When Wellcome died, however, these achievements lay many years ahead, and, even today, there is still work to be done before all his possessions can be studied and admired as he had hoped. Hundreds of books could be written about the Wellcome Collection, such is its richness: this one begins to explore how it all came together in the first place. Just as it was a starting point for Wellcome's curiosity about the world around him, today, as an historical entity, it provides a starting point for exploring his own hopes and fears, his failures and successes, his ideas and his interests, as well as those of the people who were drawn into his collecting world with him.

Wellcome was secretive about his plans for his collection: he hardly published anything about it and he rarely spoke of his intentions for it. Comments in his personal letters are relatively rare, but perhaps this has more to do with the fact that collecting was not unusual at the time. Today we tend to think of collecting as an eccentric pastime that suggests a need for psychoanalysis, but one hundred years ago, as we shall see, many people had a collection. Collecting things provided entertainment, education, social opportunities, and an outlet for creative expression in the home. Wellcome's desire to collect was not unusual, but his ability to pursue that desire so zealously set him apart. His skills and his success as a businessman contributed directly to his tactics as a collector. He became a collecting tycoon, making money and spending it at an enormous rate. His fortune rested, in part, on the forces of mass production transforming the pharmaceuticals industry, and he expressed his intellectual interests as a consumer on a massive scale. Wellcome was a businessman seeking recognition in an academic world, and he sometimes found it difficult to reconcile these spheres of interest. His collection belonged to the commercial world and to the world of scholarship, and these overlapping arenas brought challenges as well as rewards.

Although the collection sheds light on Wellcome's character, it was so large, and so diverse, and so thoroughly collaborative in conception that it is impossible to see it as the physical manifestation of a single mind at work. The history of the collection constantly draws us away from Wellcome and towards the other people who collected for him. Wellcome's collection, and, by extension, his life, like all lives, was an emergent, negotiated entity. This book is my attempt to 'portray a more open, less complete, person, and thus to create a less centred biography',[5] by tracking Wellcome's social relationships rather than trying to mine his mental state. The analysis of museum collectors and collections, and the practice of life writing have much in common. Both require a balancing act to keep their subject at the centre of the frame, while exploring the ways in which that subject is constituted through a peopled material world largely beyond their control. This is no small achievement, but then, it is something that each of us achieves every day, as we live out our lives.

All the stories that follow have their origin in objects: in a man's insatiable desire for *things*, and in the wealth of knowledge and the prestige that those things promised to impart. Objects hold together all the characters in this book. Wellcome's social world was stitched together by objects, and objects seemed to render his world more manageable and meaningful. They were something that he thought he could control, but now it seems clear that they had been controlling him all along.

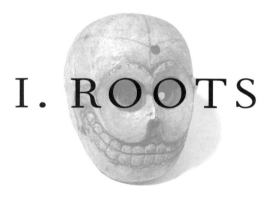

I. ROOTS

Little is known about the earliest years of Henry Wellcome's collection. He collected artefacts throughout his life, but it was only in middle age, when his private hobby became focused on a public goal and he began to plan an historical medical exhibition, that systematic records were first kept. So, before the early 1900s, before Wellcome's fiftieth birthday in 1903, the story must be pieced together from a small number of letters and documents. What is clear, however, is that from the beginning Wellcome bought artefacts for business purposes, and his ever-present interest in the history of science influenced his work as the owner of an international pharmaceuticals firm.

Wellcome's collection permeated four important areas of his life: his business, his intellectual interests, his philanthropic ventures, and his domestic environment. All were intertwined, and it was only later on that he tried, rather unsuccessfully, to disentangle his business interests from his museum work. It is in the papers of Burroughs Wellcome and Company that Wellcome's long-standing curiosity for artefacts first emerges, and his work at Burroughs Wellcome also inspired his first major intellectual project, investigating the history of animal products used in medicine. Collecting may have been a natural facet of Wellcome's professional world, but it seems to have caused tensions in his marriage, which is the subject of the final chapter in this section.

It is easy to forget that for the majority of Wellcome's life collecting was a private, and relatively modest, occupation. He did not marry until he was forty-seven years old, but his marriage coincided with the steady expansion of his collecting work. The story of Wellcome's marriage to Syrie Barnardo offers a different perspective on the elaborate collecting enterprise that dominates later chapters. Despite all the bureaucracy it generated in later years, Wellcome's collection was borne of a deeply personal fascination with artefacts, and it was a fascination so intense that it had the power to exclude the people around him.

CHAPTER TWO

HEREWITH PLEASE
FIND THREE ROLLS
OF CHOCOLATE FOIL

In the summer of 1880, Henry Wellcome arrived in London to join his friend, Silas Burroughs, in partnership selling pharmaceuticals. Wellcome was 26 years old, almost 27, and had left behind a promising career as a salesman for one of America's largest drugs companies in New York. He had no capital, and would have to borrow heavily from his new partner in order to establish himself. It was a risky venture, but Burroughs had been in England for two years already and knew that with superior American products and a creative approach to marketing they could effectively exploit the lacklustre British market. The two young Americans were ambitious: Wellcome would consolidate and expand their business in Britain, while Burroughs planned a world tour to launch the company abroad.

As he settled into life in England, Wellcome relished the intensity of his work, and he enjoyed London society. He took rooms near St James's Square, before moving to Marylebone Road in the summer of 1881. Here, as if confirming his commitment to his new home, he installed his private collection and enjoyed showing it off to his guests:

My collection of curiosities, Indian relics etc. tally admirably with the house, and so everybody seems rather fascinated with the effect, and in fact I rather like it myself. Some call it 'Aesthetic', some say 'Heathenish', some 'Bohemian', 'Ideal', 'Artistic', etc.

etc. . . . All in it is very cheerful: I brought my library and museum from America last Winter.[1]

Gathered from a frontier childhood in Minnesota, lived, for much of the time, in friendship with neighbouring Native American communities, and from six years based in New York, navigating the antiquities market when time and money allowed, the objects in Wellcome's collection belied his young age. During his travels through North and South America for his previous employers, McKesson and Robbins, he found time, when not drumming up sales, to spend his money on local curiosities: alabaster amulets from Mexico; carved and painted gourds from Guatemala; 'shells picked up by Mr Wellcome on the coast of Panama'; two wooden animals carved by Quichua Indians at Quito; a silver mirror; and a bamboo comb 'excavated from the Inca tombs by Mr. Wellcome'.[2]

The deepest roots of Wellcome's private collection are hard to trace. Few records of his earliest acquisitions survive. In the 1920s, a type case specimen set with the letters 'H. S. W.' was located in Wellcome's storehouses along with a note that he had acquired it as a boy, sixty years earlier, during a visit to a type foundry. It was listed with a 'Piece of the doorstep of the stable in which the Fire of Chicago broke out. Obtained by Mr. Wellcome on the spot.' Wellcome must have acquired this shortly after arriving in Chicago, aged nineteen, to study at the College of Pharmacy, a few months after the Great Fire of 1872.[3] He continued to collect during the 1880s and 1890s, acquiring, amongst other things, handmade birch bark canoes, paddles, and wigwams from Canada, and a bas relief by the American sculptor Francis Elwell, as well as Indian rugs, Chinese prints, and naval memorabilia.[4]

Besides rarities like these, much of Wellcome's collection consisted of old medical paraphernalia. In 1880 he showed a group of 'curiosities' at the American Medical Convention that was deemed to be 'the finest display at the Hall', and drew the attention of all the attending physicians.[5] His interest in the history of medicine dated back to his days as a student of pharmacy when he had 'sought in vain for historical, medical and surgical objects in all the great museums',[6] but the collection he displayed at his home on Marylebone Road was not intended to be primarily educational. Wellcome said that his visitors thought his collection heathenish, bohemian, ideal, and artistic, and he seemed to enjoy the different reactions it provoked. His rooms had been occupied and decorated by an Indian rajah, 'but as barbaric decoration is now the rage it is in perfect accord with high art of the day',

Wellcome noted when he moved in, and he tried to complement the 'general style and quaintness'.[7] People did not know quite how to categorize the unusual things he kept in his home. Perhaps, in a world increasingly filled with cheap manufactured goods and imitation furnishings, it was striking to find authentic artefacts from America and scientific relics decorating a young businessman's lodgings.

Wellcome's collection may have caused a stir amongst his house guests, but his hobby was by no means unusual. After all, fashioning a collection of choice curiosities, to adorn the mantelpieces and fill the cabinets in one's drawing room, ensured the admiration of one's guests as well as providing them with some entertainment. Home furnishing had become a national pastime in Britain by the 1880s, one catered to by a growing array of advice manuals, catalogues, department stores, and, at the end of the century, interior decoration magazines. For those who could afford it, shopping became a pastime in itself, and owning things—particularly things that were rare or old or exotic, and preferably quite a few of them—conferred a certain prestige: 'How a person spent his money was as important (if not more so) than how he had earned it.'[8] A person's home came to be seen as an expression of their individuality rather than simply a statement of social status, and the ubiquity of new products and styles led discerning shoppers to focus their efforts on antiquities which would convey their good judgement and taste. Indeed, collecting art, books, or antiques was advocated for all homeowners as an informative hobby that cultivated good taste, need not be expensive, and might prove to be a prudent investment.

Even commentators, like the Revd W. J. Loftie, who disapproved of homes transformed into private museums filled with curiosities, advocated a little collecting as a moral duty, for it brought beauty and order to the home, and provided a wholesome family environment.[9] So craftsmen were kept busy constructing cabinets and dado rails and alcoves, and mantelpieces were heavy with velvet-lined recesses and extra shelves, to be filled with china, pewter, glass, or a motley assortment of bric-a-brac. Those who could show off a private collection at home tended to be well travelled, well read, well connected, and well to do, or at least that was the impression they wanted to give. As a young American arriving in London, Wellcome's collection helped to establish his social credentials. He started to collect before he became wealthy, when the majority of his income was spent on providing for himself and his parents back home in Minnesota. The collection he displayed in his new home on Marylebone Road was not so much created by a gentleman as it was helping to create one.

Before long, Wellcome's professional status began to catch up with his domestic style. Burroughs Wellcome and Company started to thrive. They had established themselves as sole overseas agents for two major American pharmaceuticals firms: the Philadelphia company of John Wyeth and Brother, where Burroughs had worked as a sales representative, and Wellcome's previous employer, McKesson and Robbins in New York. Both companies produced a range of compressed tablets and capsules practically unknown to the British industry at the time. But for Burroughs Wellcome and Company success rested, not so much on the novelty of preparations they sold, as on the way in which those products were designed and marketed.[10]

The vast majority of drugs available in the 1870s and 1880s were little more than dietary supplements: syrups, salts, oils, and extracts that claimed to restore a healthy balance and, more often than not, were prescribed for a range of bodily complaints. Burroughs Wellcome sold products like malt and beef extract, cod liver oil, soda mint (sodium bicarbonate, to regulate stomach acid), citrate of caffeine (for headaches), and Fellowes syrup (an all-purpose American remedy), but they offered these prescriptions in a form that was both more convenient to administer and more palatable. They worked hard on improving their recipes, and insisted on the highest possible quality controls. Nevertheless, it was the compressed tablets, some made on Wyeth's patented rotary production machines and others gelatine-coated by McKesson and Robbins, that really got them noticed. Many British commentators reported how attractive their little pills were. 'They are beautiful preparations, and form by far the best and most convenient mode of administering many drugs in common use', one reporter noted. He thought the tablets were 'ingenious' and 'so attractive in appearance that they might almost be mistaken for sweets'.[11] The 'simplicity' and 'efficiency' of these 'beautiful' pills drew comment year after year in the medical press.

Burroughs Wellcome also brought a fresh and energetic approach to marketing their products. Silas Burroughs had carved out a British niche for American pharmaceuticals in the late 1870s. He arrived in London in the spring of 1878 with a twofold business strategy. Firstly, he sent samples to individual doctors and pharmacists, and, crucially, followed up these promotional gifts with personal visits and briefings held in hospitals. This direct approach was unheard of in the passive British market. Secondly, Burroughs invested in an intense advertising campaign, but he restricted his advertisements to established medical journals, like the *Lancet* and the *British Medical Journal*, directing his attention towards medical professionals rather than the public. Meanwhile, suitably 'gentlemanly' representatives were chosen to maintain the firm's 'scientific' image.

Wearing frock coasts and silk hats and carrying sample bags of real crocodile skin they used to present an impressive spectacle. The most senior of the staff wore the same attire except in hot weather when even Mr Sudlow [the General Manager] would relax and appear at the office in a loosely fitting lounge suit surmounted by a somewhat ancient straw hat decorated with a blue and white hat band.[12]

The company's client lists were constantly reviewed, and each of the firm's representatives had his work and quotas regularly re-evaluated. This marketing strategy formed the basis for the company's huge success in later years.[13]

Wellcome essentially systematized and broadened the business approach initiated by Burroughs, and his meticulous attention to detail, coupled with his flair for advertising, ensured the company's impeccable public profile over the ensuing decades. Wellcome was more cautious and meticulous than Burroughs, who tended to act impulsively; he grounded Burroughs's enthusiasm in commercial rigour. He insisted on quality at every level of the business, and he took personal responsibility for the firm's accounts, advertising strategies, and product development while Burroughs worked overseas. He kept their growing staff to high standards and established the firm's working protocols. In 1883, Burroughs Wellcome began to manufacture their own products, freeing them from the heavy stamp duties on American imports. Soon afterwards, they moved into imposing premises on the corner of Snow Hill and Holborn Viaduct in the City (Figure 1).

The company's new offices were large, and a little beyond their means when first acquired, but Wellcome nonetheless took great care designing and arranging the fittings in consultation with the industrial designer Christopher Dresser (Burroughs was abroad at the time). Wellcome's fastidious interest in interior design was recalled by later employees, who remembered him ordering thirty successive coats of paint to be applied to one room at his home until just the right shade was found, and, on another occasion, carrying around a horse chestnut in his waistcoat pocket to check that the new paintwork matched exactly. 'He disliked sharp corners on furniture and usually wanted corners to be exact curve of a sixpence, and always tested with a coin on first inspection.'[14] In this respect, he was a man of his times, entering into the late Victorian mania for interior decorating with aplomb. In

Figure 1. The Burroughs Wellcome building at Snow Hill in the early 1900s.

fact, Wellcome's enthusiasm for good design influenced many of his business ventures and his earliest collecting work. It is a theme that recurs throughout the story of his collection.

The work at Snow Hill was no easy task since there was 'not a single right angle in the whole building'. The new offices occupied a promontory site formed by the curve of Snow Hill up to Holborn Viaduct. A press description, from 1888, gives some idea of the atmosphere of the place and an insight into Wellcome's personal taste. The semicircular premises were fitted in dark, unpolished American walnut, moulded and carved 'in straw-plait style'; chairs and settees were upholstered in alligator hide; the door plates, handles, and office accessories were fashioned from hammered copper; the curtains were plush. 'The whole appearance of the office is rich and artistic.' The vestibule, which was similarly fitted, had a mosaic floor 'with pictorial insertions representing Commerce and Industry', and a large screen of unpolished plate glass (Figure 2). The walnut screens in the windows were 'quaintly carved on the lower part, and composed above of intricate Moorish or Baghdad spindle-work'. All the furnishings were designed to coordinate.

Figure 2. The interior of the Burroughs Wellcome building at Snow Hill in 1885.

The decoration in Wellcome's own office was 'of a highly artistic character, but quiet in tone'.[15]

But it was probably not the furniture that caught the visitor's attention on entering Wellcome's room at Snow Hill, for, unlike his partner's office next door, it was filled with far more interesting accoutrements: '[It] is furnished as a library, although hunting trophies, works of art from countries visited by the occupant, a striking statuette of Henry Ward Beecher, and a varied selection of general literature give it less the look of a commercial room and more the appearance of a bachelor's den.'[16] So Wellcome had surrounded himself with a gentlemanly assortment of exotic treasures at work and at home. And some of the books and artefacts he kept in his office had been acquired for business purposes, because as a young executive Wellcome was now collecting in the course of his research into new or improved products and business ventures. Indeed, his office had the appearance of a bachelor's den because his collecting instincts merged the two spheres of his life, professional and private, inextricably together. Objects—the books, prints, prototypes, and historical artefacts he acquired—came to shape his commercial projects as well as his personal taste.

Burroughs had cause to grumble that Wellcome had spent more time and money on his 'antiquarian studies' than his business interests while on a trip to Spain in 1894,[17] and the truth is that a great deal can be learned of Wellcome's innate interest in material culture from his professional dealings during these years. Acquiring things was so deeply ingrained in Wellcome's psyche that he turned to objects as inspiration for his work as well as for pleasure. Wherever he went, he scrutinized artefacts in shops and markets that might prove helpful for product designs, advertising, or trade exhibits. Collecting things was, for him, a way of thinking through problems and ideas, and so his acquisitive instincts became directed towards commercial gain.

This is most clearly illustrated in Wellcome's correspondence regarding the range of Burroughs Wellcome medicine cases launched during the 1880s. Wellcome began to design medicine chests for travellers around the time the company moved into the new Snow Hill building. It was Burroughs who first had the idea of producing medicine cases, while travelling abroad, and instructed Wellcome to develop a prototype.[18] They were the perfect vehicle for showing off the firm's products. The new compressed medicines sold by Burroughs Wellcome meant that many remedies no longer had to be measured out, crushed, mixed, or dissolved every time they were administered. Gone were the days of hulking wooden chests filled with fat glass bottles, basins, and flasks; now all that a traveller or country doctor needed were a few little tubes of tablets and tinctures, kept in a stylish pocket case. Wellcome began researching possible materials and containers by gathering together a range of prototypes.

In June 1883, he reported to Burroughs: 'The Medicine Cases. We have had a great deal of difficulty in having these made, but finally an assortment of them has been completed, which we will send you. We have not yet been able to get anything satisfactory in the way of Medicine Chests but we will have it in hand.'[19] Wellcome was determined to produce a range of containers that were portable, robust, and elegant. The choice of materials and the structure of the fittings were crucial. And his efforts were soon rewarded. One of the first customers to order Burroughs Wellcome cases was Henry Morton Stanley. ('Stanley has been very agreeable I have made a very pleasant social acquaintance with him', Wellcome informed Burroughs in 1885.[20]) The famed Welsh explorer was effusive in his praise of the 'nine beautiful Chests' Burroughs Wellcome had made for him, 'replete with every medicament necessary to combat the epidemic diseases peculiar to Africa'. 'Every compartment was well stocked with essentials for the Doctor and Surgeon', Stanley later wrote in *In Darkest Africa*. 'Nothing was omitted, and we all owe a deep debt of gratitude to these gentlemen, not only for the intrinsic value of these Chests and excellent medicines but also for the personal selection of the best that London could furnish.'[21]

With such accolades it is little wonder that during the course of the next decade Burroughs Wellcome pocket cases and chests came to dominate the market. Adventurers like Roald Amundsen, Ernest Shackleton and Robert Scott, Louis Blériot and Calbraith Rodgers, joined the roll call of eminent Victorians and Edwardians who relied on Burroughs Wellcome equipment.

Wellcome continued to work on improving the design of the cases well into the twentieth century, which resulted in a steady stream of tins and tubes and bottles and boxes sent back to headquarters whenever he travelled for business. His hastily scribbled instructions often accompanied the sample specimens, and were passed onto relevant staff by Wellcome's secretary in London. A pen case, bought in Zurich, arrived with the message: 'We need some such steel work for shells of cases to cover with leather instead of wood. Find out where this work is done, and show me specimens on my return.' Wellcome sent a silver box to 'illustrate good shoulder for closing and good hinge at back', with a small technical proviso: 'Mr Wellcome believes that this shoulder could be produced without an extra piece of metal', his secretary wrote.[22] A tube of liquid ammonia picked up in Switzerland, and intended for soothing insect bites, might be 'very handy, but would it not be better smaller stopper and friction instead of screw?' Two metal cases Wellcome had found, either 'German or Swiss...close so admirably, and are well joined. The catch...is excellent,' but, if adapted for use as a medicine case, he added, the 'edge and corners would be more squared...and the cover come closer to the edge.'[23]

Wellcome was endlessly attentive to each object's construction. Even the most mundane objects inspired him and enabled him to communicate efficiently with his staff. 'Herewith please find three rolls of chocolate foil,' one internal memo explained, 'which Mr Wellcome has sent for you as illustrations of how certain drugs for mixtures etc. might be compressed or moulded and rolled.'[24] Pencil tins, cigarette cases, and biscuit boxes all played their part in improving the company's products. And he was tireless in this work. While he was abroad, his staff received shipments of objects and notes almost every week. In response, they researched costs, sourced materials, and trialled manufacturing techniques. They learned 'to pay special attention to minute detail',[25] but Wellcome was not an easy man to please. When a copper riveted case, covered in cowhide and, 'made in accordance with your instructions', was sent to Wellcome for approval before full-scale production began, his team were sent back to the drawing board with a flourish of their employer's pen, for he found the case to be 'Badly riveted and badly cut out and [with] carelessly stained edges'. 'It would cost no more labour to do it properly and carefully', he admonished.[26] Wellcome knew that consistency and quality were crucial in the pharmaceuticals industry. He was still sending bottle caps back to his manufacturing manager in the late 1920s, on account of the 'improved uniform moulded screw neck and metal cap' and the new air- and damp-proof disc inside.[27] Clients, whether they were doctors or explorers or members of the public, had to trust in the Burroughs Wellcome brand.

The second most important company attribute for Wellcome, after quality, was style. As far as the medicine cases were concerned, this meant that they had to be available in a range of light, durable, and luxurious finishes. The case itself might be made of aluminium, nickel-plated metal, or even silver (larger chests were made of sheet iron), others were finished in crocodile or morocco leather, pigskin or seal hide. Many were then protected by a fine doeskin or leather envelope, like a precious gem. Indeed, the smaller medicine cases were designed to appeal to clients in much the same way as jewellery might: part medical necessity, part fashion accessory, these smooth metal compacts were status symbols intended for a doctor's waistcoat pocket.[28] Of course, an expensive finish hinted at the superiority of the items that lay within. Quality and presentation went hand in hand, and it is no coincidence that Wellcome involved himself in the firm's public image at every level, whether by researching materials for medicine chests, or designing letterheads and logos, or supervising the layout for company advertisements.

The collection of books that lined the walls in Wellcome's London offices constituted a reference library for his ongoing work on advertisement designs. He bought almanacs and old atlases, albums on penmanship and typography, and volumes filled with monograms, embroidery patterns, engravings, and architectural motifs, and by the late 1890s and early 1900s these books formed the core of the company's library, which grew steadily under Wellcome's charge.[29] In December 1898, he made his first major purchase of books at auction, when he spent £1,843 9s 6d on 482 lots at the sale of William Morris's library by Sotheby's. The haul included books on dyeing, architecture, textiles, printing, and bibliography: there were a handful of books of scientific interest, but Wellcome's fascination with design most clearly guided his choices at this early sale.[30] He wrote in the sale catalogue, next to a very rare book, *The Orcharde of Syon*, dated 1519, 'Superb must have inspired Morris Stick high.'[31] Perhaps the books that had inspired Morris as a designer were to serve a similar purpose for Wellcome and his staff.

Wellcome had a talent for advertising, and it was a talent informed by his passion for collecting. Burroughs Wellcome advertisements were striking, and he spent a significant amount of his time checking proofs, deliberating over images, choosing layouts, and reviewing text for posters, leaflets, and promotional publications. As with the medicine cases, his standards were exacting. In fact, he was remembered as 'a fanatical perfectionist where print was concerned, examining with a magnifying glass everything . . . and rejecting an item with even a broken serif on a single letter'.[32] This is clear from the meticulous notes he scribbled in the margins of his staff's reports. In November 1901, for instance, he found a number of the company's efforts very pleasing: the annual promotional leaflet *This Year's Progress* was 'splendid, you have quite caught the spirit and idea I wanted to convey it is neither dead nor sleepy'. But other publications had failed to impress him. A recent trade list for Wellcome brand chemicals was 'a dismal failure and not as I indicated the whole appearance is lead—the border is most inappropriate the crowded text is ineffective and the fine crystals [in the picture] not well rendered, but against that text the crystals have no show'. Another advertisement was 'good but antique [font] next size smaller for foot note wd be better it ought not to be same style type as text of notice'.[33]

Wellcome's interest in history increasingly influenced the company's advertising style. Inspiration was often found in the stories of classical gods or ancient myths. An image of the Roman god Vulcan provided a fitting display of fiery power for the Burroughs Wellcome Beef and Iron Wine advertisements; while the firm's 'Kepler' brand cod liver oil and malt products were promoted in a series of advertisements inspired by the ancient history of Greece. Historical accuracy became another sticking point during the design process. One group of advertisements drew on the Chaldean mythologies of ancient Sumer, Akkad, Assyria, and Babylonia, and debates on the historical accuracy of the selected images ensued. Wellcome's research staff informed him that 'there is no winged sun in Assyrian design . . . it does not appear until the Egyptian period, we are inserting a sun without wings, and shall be glad to know if this has your approval'. A few days later, the design team were 'fortunate enough to find a good Assyrian Sun and it has been thought better to substitute it for the rayed emblem which consists of a couple of outspread wings supporting a deity and which Mr C. J. S. Thompson [the company researcher] thinks does not refer to the sun'.[34]

Wellcome frequently forwarded books he had recently acquired to his staff on account of their illustrations or historical information. Another long-running promotional series was styled on the signs of the zodiac: 'Referring to the very old atlas which you sent over to us from Paris,' his secretary wrote in November 1901, 'Mr Linstead's and Mr C. J. S. Thompson's attention has been called to the Zodiac in the first illustration. Enclosed we have pleasure in handing you a rough sketch showing how they consider the Zodiac could be used in the Zodiac series. Kindly favour us with your views.'[35] Once the books and manuscripts had served their commercial purpose, they were added to the company's library. Artefacts in Wellcome's private collection no doubt proved useful from time to time also: a couple of years earlier he had been on the trail of a set of Ghanaian weights, used to measure gold dust, and asked an acquaintance who was visiting the region to try and secure some for him:

The little weights, I believe, bear some extraordinary hieroglyphics which, in some cases, resemble the signs of the Zodiac. If you could, besides obtaining specimens of the various sizes of weights and measures also find out and make a record of the significance of the signs or symbols, it would add materially to the interest of the collection.[36]

So it was that Wellcome's collecting impulses shaped many of the firm's advertising ventures, and his business projects shaped his early collection. Points of language, style, colour, and layout were constantly batted back and forth between Wellcome and his staff, who busied themselves researching potential images and checking on the historical accuracy of favoured designs. Meanwhile he supplied them with a steady flow of new, or rather newly acquired but generally antiquated, material to work with.

If Wellcome's habits as a collector were informing the company's product design and advertising agenda, his talents as an exhibitor were also put to good use organizing the firm's displays at trade fairs. As Burroughs and Wellcome carved out a niche for themselves in the pharmaceuticals industry during the closing decades of the nineteenth century, trade exhibitions were vital to the market. In 1881 alone, Burroughs Wellcome exhibited their products at the International Medical and Sanitary Exhibition at South Kensington; the International Temperance Exhibition, at the Agricultural Hall in Olympia; Brighton Health Congress and Domestic and Scientific Exhibition at the Royal Pavilion in Brighton; the Eastbourne Exhibition of Sanitary Appliances and Articles of Domestic Use and Economy; and the Exhibition at the Annual Meeting of the British Medical Association.[37] Temporary exhibitions provided essential promotional space, but they also gave companies the opportunity to scope out the competition, court potential clients, and generally keep abreast of the market, and they invariably produced a good show, as each exhibitor tried to outdo his neighbours.

In the early 1880s, the newly formed partnership of Burroughs Wellcome and Company joined the ranks of established pharmaceuticals firms—among them, Allen and Hanburys, Beecham, Duncan Flockhart, and Thomas Morson and Son—on the trade fair circuit, hoping to make an impact and reap the rewards. They succeeded. Almost immediately, Burroughs Wellcome exhibits caught people's attention, and started to win awards. And it was Wellcome, initially working in his partner's absence, who was behind their success.[38]

A good deal of the interest in the Burroughs Wellcome trade exhibits was due to their novel merchandise, but Wellcome also understood how to construct an eye-catching display. His general approach seems to have been to pile as many products as physically possible into the space available. An early photograph shows tier upon tier of bottles, boxes, and glass phials, proudly displayed under the banner, 'American Improvements in Pharmacy. Burroughs Wellcome and Co. 7 Snow Hill. London. Importers, Exporters and Manufacturing Chemists.' But Wellcome did not rely solely on the quality of his merchandise to make an impact. He used other clever tricks to draw his audience in. Microscopes were made available at Burroughs Wellcome counters, so that passers-by could examine the company's cod liver oil and extract of malt for themselves under magnification, and 'a great number of medical men availed themselves of the opportunity'.[39] Wellcome also understood the power of celebrity endorsement, and at the 1886 annual meeting of the British Medical Association he decided to display a medicine chest that had been made for Stanley, who was soon to depart on the famed Emin Pasha Relief Expedition up the Congo River to rescue the besieged Governor of Equatoria.[40] When the International Medical Congress came to London in 1895, Wellcome went a step further and resolved to exhibit a large group of medicine cases, giving centre stage to those 'which have been brought back from exploring expeditions etc by great travellers, especially if they are well battered and show sufficient wear and tear and particularly show that the contents have stood the test of climate and rough usage'.[41]

By this time, Wellcome's attention-grabbing schemes had become more ambitious. For the 1896 annual meeting of the British Medical Association, he decided to exhibit a live sheep and a tank of live cod, to draw attention to the company's lanolin soap and cod liver oil products. Transporting live cod to Carlisle proved challenging. One of the firm's representatives, George Pearson, who was later to become General Manager, was sent to Grimsby to fetch the cod, where he chartered a tug boat to take him 20 miles out to sea for suitable water to fill a fish tank. Six cod were placed in the tank, which was six feet long and four feet wide and aerated by a bicycle pump, and were transported in a special wagon by train to Carlisle. Despite all Pearson's efforts, one fish expired at Manchester, and another between Manchester and Carlisle, but the remaining four were exhibited successfully at the Burroughs Wellcome stand, along with the sheep, much to Wellcome's satisfaction and the audience's amazement.[42]

Long before Wellcome had any plans to organize his own museum exhibition, the firm's profile was honed through regular exhibitions and fairs not dissimilar to museum displays (the British Medical Association's fair was known as the 'Annual Museum'), and trade exhibitions frequently included displays of artworks, books, and prints alongside the latest laboratory equipment, drugs, surgical implements, and sanitary appliances. Burroughs Wellcome did not always limit their exhibits to medicinal products. A photograph of their stand at the Chicago Exposition in 1893 shows an array of vases, a decorative metal tray, an elaborate allegorical sculpture, and Wellcome himself flanked by a group of unnamed Native Americans in traditional costume, who may have been appropriated for the benefit of the camera, or perhaps to help draw the crowds (Figure 3).

To the end of his days, Wellcome encouraged his staff to be innovative in their exhibition designs, and they constructed display cases that were larger, stronger, and more elegant than ever before for trade fairs. He experimented

Figure 3. Burroughs Wellcome exhibit at the Chicago Exhibition of 1893. Wellcome, wearing a hat, is on the left.

by suspending exhibits from the roof of exhibition cases, so that more objects could be seen, unobstructed and without overcrowding; and he used lantern slides to draw attention to the firm's products. Again, he was inspired by his interest in history, and sometimes the boundaries between business and scholarship were blurred. At the 1904 St. Louis Exposition, 'It was an entirely original idea of Sir H[enry] to take the beautiful shapes evolved by the ancient Greeks for their many earthenware vessels and have these shapes produced in glass to contain specimens for display.'[43] Wellcome's interest in design, which was unusual for a manufacturing pharmacist in Britain at the time, came into its own on occasions like these. And his perfectionism was in evidence, as he poured over colour shade cards, insisted that descriptive labels were tilted to correspond with the viewer's eye level, arranged for the text to be printed in a larger type when it was further away, and even ensured that his workmen use screwdrivers that exactly fitted their screws so that they would not slip or burr the edges as they worked.

By the mid-1890s, Wellcome could draw on fifteen years of professional exhibiting expertise when planning these shows. Indeed, in certain important respects, his success in the pharmaceuticals industry was interwoven with the deep appreciation he had felt for the material world since childhood, for his inclination to collect things and surround himself with unusual artefacts infiltrated his achievements as a businessman.

Years later, Wellcome traced the origin of his life as a collector back to the age of four. His story, although short, was imbued with romantic nostalgia for his childhood and the strong sense of personal destiny that can only emerge with hindsight. He remembered that, while playing near the family home—one of the first houses built in the tiny settlement of Almond in Wisconsin's empty central plains, where he lived until he was four years old—he had found an oddly chipped stone. He took a fancy to it, picked it up, and showed it to his father. The stone prompted Henry's first 'object lesson', as he described it, for his father then talked to him about its history and purpose. It was an ancient tool, shaped by human hands thousands of years ago; perhaps it had been used for crafting weapons or for slicing meat. Wellcome's father, he recalled, 'explained to me that the perfecting of that late Neolithic implement meant more to those ancient peoples for their protection and as a means of gaining their livelihood than the invention of the electric telegraph or the steam railway engine meant to us. That excited my imagination and was never forgotten.'[44]

Even the plainest of things, the little boy discovered, had stories to tell. And it was this knowledge that sustained his interest in old atlases and foil wrappers and pencil tins when he found himself managing a growing pharmaceuticals company three decades later. Wellcome had an eye for identifying 'object lessons' in the unlikeliest of material. Moreover, he understood that simple innovations—like sharpening the edge of a flint tool, or producing a smaller, lighter, and more robust style of a medicine case—could have significant implications for the way people lived their lives. So he carefully attended to each object's qualities of form and structure. He had an intellectual affinity for things, and 'he always found time to be thorough'.[45] He looked to objects to help him think; to refine his vision of the world and how it worked; and to communicate effectively with others. An ancient manuscript might provide the inspiration for a new advertising design; an unusual cigarette case might suggest a better clasp mechanism for the latest pocket medicine case; a set of Swiss metal bottles might be adapted to keep Burroughs Wellcome tablets fresher for longer; an ancient Greek vase might provide inspiration for a trade fair exhibit and help to ensure the company's continued dominance in the market.

The roots of Wellcome's great historical medical collection and of his commercial pre-eminence are thus enmeshed. It is impossible to say, for example, whether Wellcome's professional interest in medicine chests spawned his curiosity in them as historical relics, or vice versa. He collected them for his trade exhibits, for his research into the firm's own product range, and simply because he was interested in their history. Whatever the reasons, by the early 1900s, he had gathered together such a number that when accepting a medicine chest for his collection that had been used by Edward James Glave—a protégé of Stanley's, who had discovered the final resting place of David Livingstone's heart, under a tree in Ilala, in 1895—he was able to assure the donor that he would 'regard this as one of my most valued relics', adding, 'it shall find a permanent place in my museum of historic medicine chests'.[46]

Medicine chests, a library of old manuscripts and books, an assortment of decorative vases, pieces of art and sculpture, a collection of Native American objects, some rugs and naval memorabilia: these are the beginnings of Wellcome's collection. His 'antiquarian studies', as Burroughs had described them, were varied, but they shaped his success as a businessman and played their part in his domestic life too. As the new century dawned, Wellcome's collection had grown so large that it not only amused his guests at home and impressed his visitors at work, it warranted a staff of its own. In the closing weeks of 1899, Wellcome employed a librarian to care for his ever-expanding collection of books, and so began a new, collaborative era in his life as a collector. Not until he reached his mid-forties did Wellcome really begin to exercise his latent intellectual ambitions and collect in the name of academic research. And it may have been no coincidence that another event left its mark on his financial and philosophical outlook in the late 1890s with implications for his work as a collector. In 1895, Wellcome's business partner, Silas Burroughs, died unexpectedly at the age of 49.

CHAPTER THREE

A VERY FULL AND
COMPLETE VOLUME

Burroughs Wellcome had steadily expanded their range of products. During the 1890s their price lists filled more than thirty pages. Clients could choose from a variety of photographic chemicals, cosmetic creams and soaps, sweeteners and compressed tea, as well as bandages and gauzes, medical preparations like chloroform and ether, hypodermic needles, sanitary towels, menthol snuff, and an extensive series of remedial solutions, tablets, and powders. Silas Burroughs and Henry Wellcome had created strong brands, most notably their 'Soloid' and 'Tabloid' ranges, which they defended fiercely. The firm now manufactured its own products at a large factory site at Dartford in Kent, which housed patented machines capable of producing 600 tablets a minute. Lucrative government contracts for supplying medicines and equipment to the armed services and some colonial offices guaranteed profits, and, ever innovative, Wellcome and Burroughs had established a tradition of experimental work for the development of new drugs. By 1893, they could boast a laboratory for product testing that 'would do credit to a university'.[1] But success had come at a price. Their personal relationship was in tatters.

Such was the state of their friendship, after ten years in partnership, that by 1890 Burroughs and Wellcome no longer spoke to each other directly, preferring to communicate through their General Manager, Robert Sudlow, and, increasingly, through their lawyers. They had come to disagree on almost everything, from hiring staff to shaping the long-term development of the business. Wellcome wanted to invest in private research programmes, while Burroughs pushed to purchase the rights to existing products made by other companies. They began to distrust each other; suspicions and resentments surfaced between them. Burroughs tried to alter the balance of power by proposing a third partnership, which twice proved futile, and then attempting to create a limited liability company, a scheme that also failed more than once. In 1889, he had made an ill-advised attempt to dissolve the partnership through the courts, claiming Wellcome had neglected the business, but his accusations were baseless and he was roundly defeated. The two men became locked in endless disputes, which benefited no one but their lawyers, as neither man could agree terms on which to disband their partnership.

Temperamentally, Burroughs and Wellcome could not have been more different. Burroughs was self-confident and frequently impetuous; Wellcome was methodical and could be painfully vigilant. John Wyeth, who supplied the drugs Burroughs first sold when he arrived in London, had greeted their partnership in 1880 with approval, knowing Wellcome would keep Burroughs's sometimes wilful attitude to business in check. But Burroughs thought of himself as the firm's senior partner, and with good reason. He was seven years older than Wellcome, and had established the business on his own, not only inviting Wellcome to join him, but lending his younger friend most of the money he needed to establish himself in London. Burroughs may have expected Wellcome to remain in London, where trade was already established, and keep an eye on the books, leaving him to power the business forward elsewhere. Wellcome, however, was not about to pass up the leadership opportunities his new status afforded him.

Although they shared an energy and determination to succeed, the two men came from very different backgrounds. While Burroughs enjoyed significant private capital—he was the son of a United States Congressman—and all the self-assurance that brought, Wellcome's father was an itinerant Adventist minister who had no money. Wellcome grew up, in the newly created state of Minnesota, in poverty, and only ever had his own resources to rely on. This gave him a dogged earnestness. 'I have never accomplished anything without severe efforts,' he explained to his mother as he embarked on his new life in London, 'and it is only such things as are not worth an effort that fall into the hands as bits of luck.' One of Wellcome's favourite sayings was 'God helps those who help themselves.'[2] Perhaps he, like his contemporary William Lever—the founder of Lever Brothers soap manufacturing empire, who was only two years Wellcome's senior and, like Wellcome, became an avid collector of art, furniture, and ethnographic artefacts—was a follower of Sam Smiles's doctrine of self-help, which became so popular in mid-Victorian Britain. The opening line of Smiles's book, *Self-Help*, was 'Heaven helps those who help themselves.'[3] But as Wellcome dutifully rose to the challenges of his business, Burroughs may have felt unduly restrained by his partner's meticulousness. Wellcome, for his part, was repeatedly frustrated by Burroughs's impulsive, and often reckless, decision-making, and his reluctance to consult before acting according to his inclinations.[4]

In December 1894, the fraught negotiations over the firm's future were failing and had been completely suspended when tragedy struck. Burroughs was suffering from bronchitis, and he retreated to Monte Carlo and a warmer climate for the new year. But his condition worsened. He developed pleurisy and then pneumonia, and in February 1895, he died, leaving the difficulties in the partnership unresolved. Wellcome's public response to his partner's death was muted. A number of his friends recognized that it might alleviate his anxiety about the future of the business. Instead, it thrust him into a new battle with Burroughs's widow, Olive, who was now determined to retain her late husband's interest in the firm. Wellcome found himself in much the same situation as before, defending his rights against constant and often insulting challenges from the Burroughs' lawyers: 'Perpetual vigilance, the utmost caution and every nerve of power has been required on my part to thwart the tricks which had been attempted', he told his mother.[5] It was not until July 1898, after years of financial worry, litigation, and hostile correspondence, that Wellcome successfully bought Olive Burroughs's interests in the firm and became the sole proprietor of Burroughs Wellcome and Company.

The dissolution of his friendship with Burroughs left Wellcome embittered. He became tense and resolute. He was now less trusting of others, and he hardened himself to the inevitable gossip that surrounded his professional difficulties. 'Please remember that I don't want the facts of my troubles discussed among our friends', he wrote to his mother before Burroughs died. 'I want no sympathy from outsiders—I don't believe in the sympathy of the outside world they are not essential to my happiness, and [I] only care for general results.'[6] Again, with echoes of Smilesian self-sufficiency, Wellcome relied first and foremost on himself. It was a characteristic that, years later, towards the end of his life, would shape his struggles to take control of the enormous museum collection he had created.

However tragic the circumstances of his independence from Burroughs, it did give Wellcome both managerial and financial freedom. Within a year of

Burroughs's death, Wellcome reported that he had 'extensively re-organised the various departments to great advantage and...already materially improved and increased the business'.[7] Profits continued to rise, and Wellcome turned his attention to other areas of development. He was now more interested in scientific research. He saw the long-term commercial potential of investing in dedicated research facilities, where new drugs could be scientifically engineered, tested, and synthesized. In 1894, the 'experimental laboratory' on the top floor of the Snow Hill headquarters had been replaced by the Wellcome Physiological Research Laboratories for the production of a diphtheria antitoxin. The laboratories must have received Burroughs's approval, but the project was driven forward by Wellcome.[8] Then, two years later, in the wake of Burroughs's death, the Physiological Laboratories were joined by the Wellcome Chemical Laboratories. Wellcome's research plans grew rapidly, and his attentions turned abroad. In 1902, after two previous visits to the Sudanese capital, Khartoum, he instituted the Wellcome Tropical Laboratories there, and in 1905 he established a novel floating laboratory housed in a specially designed boat on the Nile.[9] In little more than a decade, Wellcome had founded a cluster of innovative research institutions in England and in Sudan.

Under Wellcome's leadership, Burroughs Wellcome became the first pharmaceuticals company in Great Britain to prioritize privately funded, investigative research. Wellcome knew that these ventures would not be profitable straight away, but he also recognized the prestige the firm would accrue from engineering new drugs for market.[10] The new laboratories signalled a change in Wellcome's professional outlook. The business was flourishing, he was now a wealthy man, and gradually he came to see himself as patron of ground breaking research (Figure 4). Pioneering new techniques in the laboratory would attract the attention of the academic community as well as the trade, and Wellcome had begun to contemplate a more scholarly audience for his work. Although the commercial benefits of his research programme were difficult to ignore, Wellcome always emphasized the intellectual potential of his laboratories and went to great efforts to present them as academic institutions.[11] He secured a number of impressive scientists to work for him over the years, which often meant overcoming the academic community's prejudice against the pharmaceuticals industry. His staff produced innovative therapies in the decades leading up to the First World War—including serum antitoxins and vaccines for diphtheria, typhoid, rheumatic fever, dysentery, tetanus, cholera, and meningococcus;

Figure 4. Henry Solomon Wellcome, photograph by Lafayette Ltd., *c.*1900.

anti-venoms; numerous varieties of tuberculin; obstetric drugs; and a range of veterinary products—and also made enormous contributions to medical research, notably pioneering work on adrenaline, histamine, and malaria. By the onset of the Second World War, seventeen Burroughs Wellcome researchers had become Fellows of the Royal Society, and one had received a Nobel Prize for Physiology and Medicine.[12]

Wellcome's hard-fought professional security also allowed him to dabble in intellectual ventures of his own for the first time. He began to develop his interest in the history of human health, which had so far been marshalled for Burroughs Wellcome publicity purposes, and to think of publishing on the subject. And his research interests were intertwined with his passion for collecting. Artefacts—initially in the form of books for his library—accrued in tandem with his increasingly ambitious enquiries into the history and anthropology of medicine. For Wellcome, collecting things became an integral part of the research process, and, not insignificantly, promised a relatively smooth path towards acceptance in the academic community. In the closing decades of the century, piecing together a private collection of books, archaeological artefacts, natural history specimens, or ethnographic curiosities could win an amateur enthusiast scholarly respect, for these kinds of objects provided the empirical foundations upon which broader historical and scientific theories were built.

Wellcome's first formal foray into history began in the mid-1890s, when he became interested in the use of animal products in medicine. His interest may well have been stimulated by developments in the Burroughs Wellcome business at the time. The new diphtheria antitoxin produced in his Physiological Laboratories was raised in horses. In early 1896 a new subdepartment making thyroid and animal products was formed, and six months later eight 'animal remedies' were sent to the *Chemist and Druggist* for appraisal.[13] The company started producing 'thyroid tabloids', using thyroid preparations from pigs, and medicines derived from 'extract of the supra-renal glands', or adrenaline. The commercial value of animal-derived pharmaceutical preparations was clear to Wellcome, and in mid-1896 he applied to register his Laboratories with the Home Office for permission to experiment on animals and test animal substances.[14] Meanwhile, he devoted what little spare time he had to researching the broader history of animal products used for medical purposes.

He began to plan a book on the subject. Cleverly, if a little unrealistically, he conceptualized a sweeping overview of human ingenuity presented through the lens of a single medical resource—animal substances—which seemed to unite all cultures across history. Every society had turned to animals to cure their ills at some time or other, whether through symbolic or physiological means. Wellcome wanted to understand their reasoning. And it is in this respect that his intellectual motivations were particularly democratic for his time. He advocated an intellectual respect for all medical treatments, however unsophisticated they might seem. He saw his chosen subject matter as something of a cultural leveller, since he wanted to ascertain 'the rational [*sic*] of treatment even amongst the most primitive races'. The suggestion that there was any rationale whatsoever at work in so-called 'primitive' medicine was unusual for the time. Members of non-industrialized societies were popularly assumed to be illogical, juvenile, and dim-witted. Their apparent technological simplicity was automatically equated with mental naivety. 'Primitive' people, it was supposed, were more often than not led in their actions by habit and superstition rather than intelligence or reason. Wellcome had a different theory about man's medical past:

Some authorities have in a very off-hand manner declared that they [primitive people] came to use them [animal products in medicine] first as a part of their magic without rhyme or reason, and that there was no real efficacy in any of the primitive methods. I, for one, have long believed, and there may be grounds for so believing, that in most instances the adoption of remedies was due to the discovery that certain substances produced certain effects under certain conditions and that it was a matter of crude scientific or unscientific method in the study of the properties of these substances which led peoples to adopt their remedies.[15]

Wellcome understood, or at least suspected, that logic and superstition were impervious to cultural boundaries. Many of his contemporaries would have been content to find evidence that fitted their existing picture of the world (had they embarked on a research project of such ambitious proportions in the first place). Many would not have bothered to search for any indication of a reasoning mind behind 'primitive' traditions that they were content to believe were superstitious. What is more, many would have overlooked the numerous examples of specious medical practice in British and American society. But while Wellcome did not expect to find a rational mind at work behind every medical prescription he came across—there could be 'no doubt [that] many substances have been adopted purely from their imaginary and supposed association with animal life'—he also knew that superstition was not limited to non-Western peoples. He offered the example of a 'medical man in the Southern States' who, following in the old tradition of Western herbalists, had advocated the use of the Slipper Orchid to treat all sexual complaints simply because 'he found the male and female plants possessed physical features resembling the male and female sexual organs'.

Wellcome even intended to subject his findings to scientific scrutiny in the hopes of settling the method-versus-magic question once and for all. Whenever possible, he would collect samples of the various historical prescriptions he was investigating and test their attributes. 'I propose to go very thoroughly into the chemistry of the substances employed to ascertain what the actual physiological properties would have been', he wrote to one of his associates. As if confirming his own position within the vast historical compendium he was planning, as a man driven by science rather than supposition, Wellcome proposed that magic itself could be empirically tested. With the help of a series of chemical experiments, perhaps, he would know whether his theory of 'primitive' intelligence was actually true.

Wellcome's open-minded attitude to his subject matter was reflected in the grandiose scale of his research programme. Wellcome would never be content to focus on the medical practices of one or two cultural groups; he was searching for an altogether more ambitious story charting the long sweep of human history. As he researched, his vision for this history project developed. He became interested in all phases of medical culture, from the remedies concocted by the ancient Greeks, to the intricacies of contemporary Hindu medical practice. He set himself the massive task of chronicling the 'use of animal substances in medicine, dating from the last century back to the birth of the world'.[16] He envisaged an encyclopaedic anthology of references gathered from libraries, museums, and eyewitness accounts, which he would distil into a single illustrated volume.

In this, Wellcome's personal predispositions reflected the confidence of the age in which he lived. The late nineteenth century was a golden era for grand historical narratives. Wellcome took up his studies at a moment when the allure of a universal vision of the world was intoxicating the academic community. As telegraph cables, railway tracks, steam-powered ocean liners, and photographic plates rendered the world inexorably smaller, so theories about that world became more all-encompassing. Suddenly it seemed as though anything and everything might be within a single man's grasp. Pictures of countries that had previously fuelled fanciful travellers' tales now circulated as weekly magazine supplements; strange and wonderful artefacts from distant lands could be inspected in every provincial museum; moreover, a rapidly growing minority could witness this shrinking world for itself by joining a package holiday tour through Continental Europe, or even along the Nile or the Amazon.

Back in the metropolis, it was easy to feel as though the whole world could be collected up and spread out before anyone who had the time, inclination, and money to set themselves the challenge. Universities did not yet monopolize scholarly life as they tend to today. Scholarship was an honourable and relatively accessible pastime, pursued by many a rural vicar, army officer, and town doctor, and it often involved gathering together a small collection of specimens and curiosities to serve as investigative fodder and proof of academic character. The collections of the Pitt Rivers Museum, at the University of Oxford, are a case in point. Despite its academic reputation, the Pitt Rivers Museum's collections were not, as one might expect, created by a small number of well-known collectors, but by donations from thousands of modest contributors, the majority of whom gave less than ten objects each. A wide range of people gave objects to the Museum, including farmers, artists, sailors, and even a handful of miners, suggesting that the academic community remained open to 'ordinary folk' who expressed their interests through their private collections, however humble.[17] Wellcome was not being audacious in assuming that he, a businessman with no formal training in the subject, might write a book about the history of medicine. Nor was his desire to chart the broad historical sweep of his subject particularly extraordinary in itself, especially as he took a pragmatic approach to achieving his goal and decided to employ specialized researchers to carry out much of the groundwork for him.

After about a year spent looking into the history of medicinal animal products for himself, Wellcome realized that he would never be able to write his book alone: 'pressure of duties has rendered it impossible for me to make as rapid progress as I should have liked.'[18] He worried that other people might be working on similar material and publish before him. So he decided to hire a researcher. In late 1895 he came to an agreement with Dr William Brown, 'a very able medical gentleman in London', to begin working on the proposed book, but it was not until the summer of the following year that the project really took off. As Wellcome's interest in the subject grew, so did his aspirations for what he might contribute to the debate. If he was going to produce a book, it would have to be the most exhaustive review of the topic yet written, and the most fully illustrated, and the most thoroughly researched. Nothing less would suffice. He recruited two additional researchers to help produce 'a very full and complete volume which may run to 500 or 600 pages': the first was Dr Friedrich Hoffmann, a prominent German pharmacist who had spent much of his life in America but had recently moved to Leipzig, and the second was Charles John Samuel Thompson, who had studied pharmacy at Liverpool University College and was busy making a career for himself as a writer.[19]

Hoffman, in Germany, and Thompson, in Britain, set to work searching out old books and manuscripts, scouring libraries for information and copying interesting early illustrations for their new employer. Wellcome was quite happy to hire others to help him in his increasingly mammoth task. Indeed, he encouraged Thompson and Hoffmann to contribute their own ideas to the research. He did not want them to feel circumscribed by his thoughts on the matter. He told Hoffmann, 'I should like from your own fertile mind any and all suggestions you can give in the direction which may improve the usefulness of this book.' Wellcome's receptiveness to his employees' intellectual contributions was typical. Brown, Hoffmann, and Thompson were, after all, chosen on account of their particular expertise in the field. Wellcome always thrived on the creative participation of his staff. Indeed, he frequently demanded it. But he requested 'absolute secrecy' in return, so that potential competitors would not 'anticipate' the work or 'spoil' his plans for a landmark publication. This arrangement, of employing able researchers but insisting on their discretion, set a precedent for Wellcome's later museum collecting, and Charles Thompson was to become Wellcome's longest serving collecting agent.

Thompson's work was not merely investigative; he also began planning chapters for the book. By November 1896, he had 'mapped out chapters on the animal materia medica of the Romans, Arabians, Hindoos, and Persians'.[20] The work took Thompson to libraries all over the British Isles, from London to Aberdeen and over to Dublin, and he reported to Wellcome that he was finding 'something fresh on the subject in every library I visit'.[21] In May 1897 he informed Wellcome that he 'should like (when you think proper) to write a chapter summarizing the various theories I have brought forward, and put them in concrete form'.[22] The following month, Thompson completed the work he had agreed to undertake on Wellcome's behalf, and the resulting manuscript was sent to London to await Wellcome's editorial attentions.

There can be little doubt that the Animal Substances book, as it became known to those working on it, was responsible for enlarging Wellcome's private collection, and in particular his library. Indeed, it may well have been because there were always more old manuscripts and books to be found on the subject that Wellcome's long-awaited treatise on animal products in medicine was endlessly delayed. The projected book morphed into a kind of literary collection of its own, and the process of hunting down relevant material gradually began to arrest the drive towards synthesis and publication.

Soon after Charles Thompson finished his research for Wellcome, he came across an old vellum-bound handwritten manuscript inscribed, 'The Lady Ayscough Booke Anno Domini 1692' (Figure 5). He wondered whether Wellcome might be interested in buying it for his library. It was filled with 'Receits of phisick and chirurgery'; that is, medicinal recipes for complaints

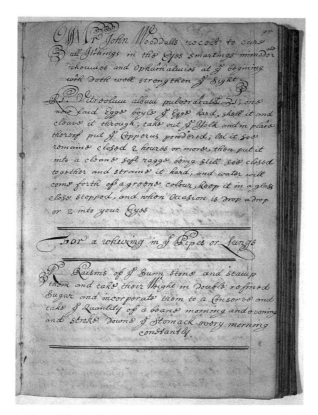

Figure 5. A page from 'The Lady Ayscough Booke Anno Domini 1692', Thompson's first recorded purchase for Wellcome's collection. WMS 1026.

such as 'a wheezing in the pipes', 'the wormes or wind in a child', 'the bitte of a mad dog', or simply, 'to comfort the braine'.[23] Wellcome did want the manuscript for his collection and he arranged for Thompson to buy it. The Ayscough recipes were followed by a copy of Pomet's *History of Drugs* printed in 1747, which Thompson also picked up on Wellcome's behalf.[24] By late 1898, Thompson was spending a considerable amount of time attending sales, bargaining with dealers, and visiting provincial shops, in the hopes of finding rare items for Wellcome's library. He knew how to navigate the rare book market, and, relatively quickly, he had transformed himself from historical researcher to consultant collector.

The results were impressive. On 24 March 1899, Thompson confirmed that he had 'forwarded altogether since Feb 5th, seven sacks, 1 basket and 3 parcels of books'. This meant that several hundred books had been purchased in less than seven weeks, since one of the sacks had held seventy-four volumes and the basket contained a further sixty-six.[25] Buying books for Wellcome was becoming a full-time job for Thompson, and Wellcome was about to reach an agreement with him that would transform his collection forever.

In December 1899, Thompson signed an exclusive contract with Burroughs Wellcome and Company. It was to prove a long-standing agreement. He became Wellcome's first collecting agent. Eventually he became curator of Wellcome's Museum, and his closest collecting collaborator. The two men worked together for more than twenty-five years, building up Wellcome's collection of artefacts, books, and pictures, and Thompson was the perfect man for the job (Figure 6). He was knowledgeable and enthusiastic, self-assured and tough. He drove a hard bargain with dealers (a talent Wellcome always respected, not least because it was his money that Thompson was bargaining with) and he had a clear sense of an object's market value. He

Figure 6. Portrait of Charles John Samuel Thompson, date unknown.

knew all the tricks of the trade, and enjoyed outwitting auctioneers and rival collectors while hunting for the perfect acquisition. He also proved to be a confident manager, and took charge of a burgeoning museum staff during the early 1900s with aplomb. But all this was still in the future. The contract Thompson signed in the closing weeks of the nineteenth century was purposefully vague when it came to designating a job title. 'We hardly think it necessary to state either in the agreement or the accompanying letter, the designation of the position you will occupy', wrote Wellcome's secretary. 'We may say that the last idea is that you shall be known as "Librarian".'[26]

'Librarian' was the most apt description for Thompson. After many months of travelling around Britain buying books and manuscripts for Wellcome, he had spent a considerable amount of time organizing the renovation of Wellcome's 'book room' at the company's headquarters in Snow Hill in the summer of 1899.[27] But Wellcome did not want to cast his new assistant solely as a librarian. Thompson was informed that his duties 'will be very varied in connection with literary and other work', and that he would be answerable to a number of different departments.[28] Wellcome sometimes referred to him as 'a responsible member of my technical and literary staff', sometimes as 'a worker in archaeological research', but Thompson was basically an historical consultant.[29] He looked after Wellcome's library and set about expanding it with frequent acquisitions, and he advised Wellcome and the company management on points of historical and literary contention, particularly with reference to the firm's advertisements.

More often than not, it was Thompson who ensured the historical accuracy of the images chosen to decorate Burroughs Wellcome advertising literature. He bought reference books and historical manuscripts, and scoured those Wellcome acquired, to come up with suitable themes for promoting the firm's products. He ensured that the mythical characters and ancient deities chosen for designs were accurately represented. He drafted drawings and text and advised on layouts for posters, pamphlets, guides, and product labels. His efforts were even required for legal disputes, as was the case when a Burroughs Wellcome application to register the word Oannes as a trademark—the name of a Babylonian god who took the form of a fish— was refused on the grounds of prior registration. During the course of the negotiations, Thompson provided references to prove that Oannes was not the same as Dagon, a Semitic god sometimes supposed to be a fish-god whose name had already been registered by the Glasgow Fishcuring Company.[30] More usually, however, Thompson was kept busy organizing the latest additions to the library, sourcing material for company publications, and writing promotional copy.

Thompson's relationship with Wellcome worked well. The company's book room was gradually filling up with volumes intended for commercial research. Thompson's job description, although flexible, had few academic pretensions. He was employed to assist in business decisions. He was no longer a freelance researcher, and was answerable to the firm's management. This meant that Wellcome was completely in control, and although he had outsourced some of his collecting interests to Thompson, they were clearly demarcated. Wellcome understood good advertising. He knew how to promote his company above all its competitors. He knew how to make products look good and work efficiently and sell well. He knew more about this than Thompson. He was in charge, as his manifold scribblings, sometimes irate and sometimes complimentary, all over the reports his staff wrote make perfectly clear.

But when it came to trading in old printed books, and even learning about medical history, Thompson may well have been more knowledgeable than Wellcome. He had published books on the history of alchemy and pharmacy, and encyclopaedic compendiums for pharmacists and nurses, before embarking on his work for Wellcome. He was a professional writer and researcher, unlike Wellcome, who had pursued his interest in the history of science as a hobby. What is more, Thompson had no qualms about expressing his opinion. One of his very earliest letters to Wellcome's secretary on the subject of purchasing books shows his strength of character, and indicates the nature of his relationship with Wellcome. Wellcome had put together a list of books he was thinking of buying, and had asked for Thompson's opinion. He got it, in no uncertain terms:

In reply to yours of 15th inst. I have examined the list of books you enclosed—the whole lot are of little or no value, and practically useless, with the exception of one, viz: Paris' Pharmacologia [1833], which being the 9th edition is only worth about 2/6 or 3/- if in good condition. I would advise Mr Wellcome not to buy any of the others at any price.[31]

Thompson had a confidence that he was not afraid to show, and Wellcome respected that. Wellcome quickly began to rely on Thompson to review auction catalogues, attend sales, and negotiate with tradesmen and dealers. The years Thompson spent at Burroughs Wellcome before the advent of the Wellcome Historical Medical Museum established a good dynamic to their relationship. Wellcome was a demanding employer. He was always looking to improve on existing achievements. He required accuracy, efficiency, creativity, and enthusiasm from his staff, and this is what Thompson offered.

Wellcome's talents as a businessman were beyond dispute, but Thompson may have looked back on this time and detected the earliest signs of Wellcome's troubles as an aspiring academic. The control Wellcome exercised, and with such mastery, over the firm's commercial affairs contrasted sharply with his hesitation when it came to intellectual projects. Thompson had shown, in the course of his Animal Substances work, many of the qualities that made him an excellent researcher and academic, and his role as librarian would gradually expand and mature to match his talents. Meanwhile, Wellcome began to display characteristics that threatened to undermine his desire for scholarly recognition. His insistence on secrecy, and his meticulous perfectionism, sat uneasily with the scope of his plans for the Animal Substances book, and may have contributed to the coming delays. For the time being, their different strengths—Thompson's confidence and Wellcome's ambition, Thompson's energy and Wellcome's resources—made them a formidable team, but in their differences there also lurked the seeds of discontent that would erode their relationship in later years.

As it was, Thompson's contributions to the Animal Substances book never saw the light of day. Preparation of the manuscript was endlessly postponed. Employing a group of people to undertake the research proved to be logistically complicated. Thompson's and Hoffmann's contributions were sent back to Wellcome's original researcher, William Brown, who revised them, but stalled for many months. Thompson then revised the revisions. All the while, Wellcome, with Thompson's able assistance, was finding more books and manuscripts of interest: the history of animal products used in medicine was hardly a modest subject. This, perhaps, was the real problem. Wellcome's intentions for the book were so grandiose that he had little hope of ever achieving them, at least, not to the standard he desired. He wanted a book that was encyclopaedic and richly illustrated. He wanted it to be absolutely accurate and exhaustive. What he really hoped for was to have the last word on the subject. But his expectations did not suit this kind of historical work, since it was necessarily open-ended and explorative. The history of animal products used in medicine could never be finished.

To his credit, Wellcome had recognized that he could not author the book alone. He had embraced the opportunity to employ other scholars to work for him, and he enjoyed their contributions. He liked the idea of sponsoring ground-breaking research, and, just as importantly, he had a genuine desire to learn from others. And yet, this desire to learn began to impede his drive towards expressing what he already knew. His receptiveness to his subject matter was an admirable quality, but it was one that would haunt his later achievements as a collector also: the more people he employed to hunt things out for him, the more there was to find. The hardest challenge for Wellcome was preventing the process of discovery from hampering the job of chiselling out a narrative from all that he and his colleagues had discovered. In 1905, Wellcome explained his motivations as a researcher to an acquaintance: 'In studying the history of the Art and Science of Healing, I have endeavoured to approach the subject with an open mind, but I am at every turn impressed by the fact that, as in the development of all the arts and sciences, there has been a struggle for light.'[32]

As Thompson and his colleagues at the Museum would eventually appreciate, Wellcome's own 'struggle for light' was only just beginning. During the summer of 1901, however, Wellcome's attentions were focused elsewhere. In his late forties, and against all expectations, he became a married man.

CHAPTER FOUR

THE IDEAL OF MY HEART

On 25 June 1901 Henry Wellcome married Syrie Barnardo, daughter of Dr Thomas Barnardo, the great Victorian philanthropist and founder of the Barnardo homes for disadvantaged children. News of the marriage delighted Wellcome's friends, but most expressed their surprise at his decision to marry after so many years alone. Wellcome was two months shy of his 48th birthday when he wed; his new wife was just two weeks short of her 22nd. They had known each other for four years, during which time Wellcome had become friends with Syrie's father, but nonetheless, their courtship was short and their marriage rushed. Many of Wellcome's friends had never met his future wife when they found themselves writing congratulatory letters at the news of their engagement. Only a few days later the same friends were reading announcements of the Wellcomes' small, family wedding at St. Mark's Church, Surbiton, in their morning papers.

But Wellcome's marriage to Syrie—known to family and friends as Queenie—lasted only nine years, ending in April 1910 as abruptly and decisively as it began. It was a relationship that coincided with the massive surge in his ambitions as a museum collector during the opening years of the twentieth century, and his sheer purchasing power permeated their lives together. Two years after they were married, Wellcome decided to arrange a public exhibition on medical history, and his collecting gathered pace as a consequence. Much of Syrie's time, she later claimed, was spent 'sacrificing' herself to her husband's collection, following him around the world in his endless search for books and curios. The marriage might, then, have opened a window for us, looking back one hundred years later, on Wellcome's private motivations as a collector. No one else witnessed Wellcome's daily hunt for museum treasures as Syrie did. But Wellcome was so injured by the break-down of their marriage (for he believed his wife to have been unfaithful) that he later destroyed almost all the documents relating to their lives together. Only a few tantalizing scraps of evidence remain, and most of these are formal papers relating to their divorce, leaving an historical void that has, ironically, condemned their marriage to just the kind of speculation that Wellcome was trying to prevent.

Wellcome's marriage to Syrie will always be intriguing, not least because amongst the few letters that do survive, Wellcome's collecting, and the couple's consumer habits more generally, emerge as dominant themes. They forged their life together in the early 1900s, when Wellcome's wealth was greater than ever before and he allowed himself more free time to travel and shop. Buying things, and the emotional consequences of buying things, appear to have played an important part in their relationship. This impression may have been exaggerated by the historical record, since the extant corres-pondence dates to after the couple's separation when Syrie was trying to secure her financial future—perhaps, in happier times, Wellcome's collecting had been less aggravating to her—but her letters give a rare, if fragmentary, insight into the personal implications of Wellcome's growing obsession for collecting. Still, the subtleties of their marriage are now virtually impossible to judge. What drew together two such disparate characters, remote in age and in interests, in the first place? And for how long did their fragile happiness last?

Many of those who heard the news of Wellcome's engagement to a woman they had never met expressed a sense of startled anticipation on his behalf. Wellcome's friends found themselves congratulating a man whose commit-ment to his work throughout youth and middle age had convinced them that he would never marry. One friend admitted his 'liveliest surprise', since he 'had almost ceased to believe in the possibility of your ever entering into the Benedict state'. Another 'mentally ejaculated "caught at last"', on reading his morning newspaper, and concluded that Miss Barnardo 'must possess excep-tional attractions to have induced a hardened bachelor to become repentant'.[1] Marriage, many thought, might restore some balance into Wellcome's life, after twenty years of unforgiving business obligations and the damaging effects of his troubles with Silas and Olive Burroughs. Wellcome's greatest friend, Mounteney Jephson, who served as best man at his wedding, wrote,

I don't know anyone who needs a wife more than you do, for your work has been made by you into a sort of moloch and you have sacrificed too little to the graces of life. Miss Barnardo will I am sure change all that, or at any rate modify it a good deal! A woman with tact and who really cares for you will improve you most enormously.[2]

Jephson had not met Syrie when he wrote this letter, but those who had, found her charming and high-spirited (Figure 7). One of Wellcome's friends,

Figure 7. Portrait of Syrie Wellcome, *c.*1901.

who had been introduced to her at Henley that summer, reported on his principal recollections of the auspicious occasion: 'I well remember, if I may say so, the splendid agility with which she sprang from a sinking canoe through the window of the barge.'[3] Such impressive displays of self-sufficiency must have appealed to Wellcome's own sense of adventure. Syrie had, quite remarkably for a young woman at the time, followed him to North Africa in early 1901 before any understanding had been reached between them. Wellcome had spent some weeks surveying the needs of the Sudanese population and planning his new research laboratory in Khartoum. Syrie's later arrival in Egypt, amidst a party of English ladies enjoying a cruise along the Nile, was unannounced and must have taken him by surprise. If so, it did not take him long to recover his composure. By the time the couple set sail for home their intentions were plain: Wellcome wrote to Syrie's father from Florence requesting his daughter's hand in marriage.[4] But perhaps even he had not fully appreciated the dynamism of his future wife; or maybe he imagined that marriage would chasten her a little.

Accompanying the happy couple on their journey home from Cairo in the summer of 1901 were no less than forty-four trunks and cases filled with belongings, shipped under the care of the travel agents Thomas Cook and Sons. Amongst the usual paraphernalia that accompanied an Edwardian traveller was Wellcome's latest hoard of African curiosities. Old guns, spears, pottery, textiles, and ornaments were shipped back to England: a tangible testament to Wellcome's fascination with the cultures he had encountered on his most recent travels.[5] Indeed, it was fitting that Egypt should serve as a backdrop for Wellcome's romance with Syrie, for he was rapidly falling in love with North Africa, and the ancient civilizations of Egypt and Sudan in particular.

Wellcome had followed recent events in Sudan with great interest. The death of General Charles Gordon during the siege at Khartoum in 1885, and Herbert Kitchener's vengeful campaign at Omdurman thirteen years later, had mesmerized the British public. In the wake of Kitchener's victory, Wellcome contributed 100 guineas to the founding of the Gordon Memorial College in Khartoum, 'to contribute, as soon as the Institution is ready for them, a complete medical equipment and stock for the Dispensary'.[6] In 1900, at Kitchener's personal invitation, he visited the region for the first time to help assess the medical and sanitary needs of the population on behalf of the government ('as well as to observe their ethnological characteristics').[7] Witnessing the ravages of malnutrition, malaria, and cholera, and the lack of sanitation in Khartoum, he planned new Tropical Research Laboratories to provide medical treatment and long-term research into the diseases that afflicted the local population. When Syrie joined him during his second visit to the region a year later he had been working on the Laboratories, which opened at the Gordon Memorial College in 1902.

The Khartoum laboratories provided the clearest expression of Wellcome's belief that scientific research could and should be a powerful humanitarian tool. All his private laboratories, including those in London, had commercial and academic objectives, but they also satisfied Wellcome's philanthropic conscience. He came to see his work, and particularly his contributions to Sudanese health care, as a personal investment in improving the human condition, and with good reason. The work undertaken at Wellcome's Tropical Laboratory, under its vigorous first Director, Andrew Balfour, was to help reduce the death rate in Khartoum from sixty per thousand to seven, making it one of the healthiest cities in Africa.[8] Surveys by the Laboratory's 'mosquito brigade', its sanitary inspections, water treatment programmes, and improvements in sewage and refuse collection transformed the city.[9] Wellcome later reflected that it had been his privilege to 'attempt the solution of certain problems which affected the welfare of the tribes of the Sudan', as one contribution towards the far greater challenge of 'reclaiming and making habitable the unhealthy and forbidding areas of the earth'.[10]

With the Tropical Research Laboratories successfully established, Wellcome would return to Egypt and Sudan again and again during his life. In 1905, he took up the idea of designing and building a floating laboratory to travel the Nile bringing researchers and their equipment closer to the subjects of their study in the field. 'The Southern Sudan is a country seamed by waterways,' Balfour pointed out, 'on the banks of which are clustered native villages wherein all manner of rare and interesting pathological conditions are to be found.'[11] When the purpose-built boat was launched in 1907 it became the first of its kind in the world, aiding investigations into tropical parasitology, epidemiology, and pathology.

Wellcome's Sudanese interests were not limited to the study of tropical disease. The Khartoum Laboratories housed an 'Economic and General Museum', nurtured by Balfour, which displayed indigenous remedies alongside medical specimens, and various items of ethnographic interest. Wellcome had encouraged Balfour to collect native iron work and leather work, for a section on 'Arts and Crafts'. Wellcome explained that he was particularly interested in 'examples of ancient and modern leather work both as regards the quality of the tanning and the quaint and artistic character of the tooling of the leather', and metal work that illustrated 'beautiful examples of chiselling and inlaying with brass and copper, and sometimes exquisite shapings' often found on local saddles, bridles, locks, and keys.[12]

Meanwhile, Wellcome had used his personal collection, including his books, works of art, and some of his weapons, to furnish the Burroughs Wellcome business premises in England, and, by 1901, his recent acquisitions from Africa had been put on display. Egyptian tents and couches (*angeribs*) graced the rooms of the manufacturing premises at Dartford, while ancient Egyptian charms, dolls, decorated tablets, and weaponry could be found in display cases lining the walls of the company's communal areas and corridors. The walls of the assembly room at the Wellcome Club and Institute, for employees, were hung with spears, shields, and hunting trophies (Figure 8). Staff were regularly reminded to take care of such treasures during routine

INTERIOR OF GYMNASIUM AND ASSEMBLY ROOM

Figure 8. The gymnasium and assembly room at the Wellcome Club and Institute for Burroughs Wellcome employees, in the early 1900s. Wellcome's collection of arms and hunting trophies decorate the walls.

cleaning, or asked to move them out of the direct summer sunlight to prevent them fading.[13] More souvenirs—although some of them were bought through London dealers—decorated the spaces of Wellcome's home at the time, where he kept various ivory carvings, an 'African stool' and an 'African pillow', poisoned arrows from the upper Aruwimi River, and a small china bust of Lord Kitchener.[14]

Soon after his first visit to Egypt and Sudan, just as research was grinding to a standstill on his ambitious Animal Substances book, Wellcome began to ponder the significance of his North African cache. His intellectual curiosity had been sparked by his recent travels. During his first visit to Sudan he had 'made some discoveries of neolithic objects', but 'the limited time then at my disposal rendered it impossible for me to do more than make hasty and superficial observations'.[15] He saw an opportunity to contribute to a thriving area of scholarship, for northern Europe's intellectual obsession with the history of the Nile was by now well established, and his collection might prove to be his way in.[16] He introduced himself to a number of experts on the subject who could give him historical information, and he even offered some of them gifts from his collection as a gesture of goodwill. In the first instance, the gifts he chose were from amongst a group of human skulls he had collected from Sudan. Somewhere within the 44 packing cases Wellcome and Syrie had shipped home in 1901 lay a collection of skulls he had 'picked up' during a visit to the battlefield at Omdurman, site of Kitchener's brutal victory over Muhammad Ahmed Al Mahdi's Sudanese army in 1898.[17]

If picking human remains from the scene of battle seems repugnant behaviour today, it was rarely questioned at the time. Collections of skulls and skeletons were welcomed by the specimen-hungry scientific community at home, regardless of the circumstances in which they had been acquired, because they were accepted as valuable contributions to a great—and, as we now know, entirely fallacious—exercise in racial classification then underway in every anatomy department in the country.[18] Wellcome hoped the 'dervish' skulls he had found, which he proudly explained had been 'picked up near where Emir [Jacoub], the Khalifa's brother, and his staff fell', would contribute to the convoluted scientific jigsaw puzzle that aimed to pin different racial 'types' onto an evolutionary ladder. Accordingly, he presented skulls to St. Bartholomew's Hospital; to Oxford, Cambridge, and Edinburgh Universities; to the Smithsonian Institution and London's Natural History Museum; and to the Royal College of Surgeons. He also gave skulls as gifts to his great friend and doctor, Alfred Chune Fletcher, and to his new father-in-law, Thomas Barnardo.[19]

The skulls were sent as donations, with no appeal for information in return; perhaps they were intended as an opening contribution to the current academic debates from a fledgling participant. But soon Wellcome was penning letters to leading Egyptologists, including Flinders Petrie, Gaston Maspero, Heinrich Schafer, and Victor Loret, with more open requests for advice:

I am very deeply interested in the origin and development of the sciences in ancient Egypt, especially in connection with Astrology, Alchemy, Medicine and Surgery, and should esteem it a great favour if you would kindly inform me of any sculptures, carvings, paintings, or papyri having reference to these subjects which there may be in the Museums or in other collections within your knowledge. I shall also be grateful to you if you can let me have any information about the early physicians of Egypt, and if you can tell me of any portraits of them. I will, of course, bear any expenses incurred in procuring the above mentioned information.[20]

Petrie, in response, offered to show Wellcome round his own collection of artefacts relating to early Egyptian medicine; other correspondents sent him references to books and the names of people who might be able to help in his quest. Wellcome started to build up a collection of literary citations and scholarly acquaintances to match his expanding collection of Egyptian souvenirs and curios. He had begun to use his collection as a platform from which he could announce his budding academic ambitions, and his commitment to collecting served as proof of his credentials in this new social sphere.

What Wellcome's lively, twenty-two-year-old wife thought of his growing intellectual aspirations is unclear. She certainly witnessed their effect on his bank balance from the first days of their married life. Shortly after their wedding, the Wellcomes set off on a long tour of Europe, which lasted eight months and stretched into the summer of 1902. Their route was marked out by the packing cases of acquisitions sent back to London from every destination they visited: eight cases from Geneva, four cases from Zurich, four cases from Vienna, six cases from Berlin, three from Budapest. Wellcome's staff set up a system for classifying, recording, and storing the mass of material as it accumulated. Each object was numbered, listed, then forwarded to the relevant Burroughs Wellcome department: things that Wellcome had bought as design prototypes were sent to the management; books and prints intended for reference or research were sent to Thompson in the 'Book

Department'; Wellcome's private purchases of 'curios' were organized for storage. A system of categorization was put in place, and material was divided into,

Silver, Cutlery, Plate and Metal Caskets
Bronze, Brass, Copper, Medallions etc.
Boxes—Snuff, Work, Inlaid, etc.
Pictures, Frames, Miniatures, Silhouettes etc.
Glass, China and Porcelain
Ivories, Pearl, Tortoiseshell, Horn, Enamel carvings etc.
Wood Carvings
Miscellaneous[21]

Wellcome and his wife relentlessly indulged their penchant for fine domestic accoutrements: silver dining services and china tea sets, small ornaments and sculptures, desk chairs, tables, mirrors and picture frames, all arrived at Snow Hill by the crate-load. Wellcome also found time to send old books on medicine and alchemy, old medicine chests and pharmaceutical mortars, and the occasional parcel marked 'Antique curios to be carefully stored unopened.'[22]

Years later, as the marriage crumbled, Syrie bitterly claimed to have martyred herself to her husband's collecting habits: 'the greater part of our time has been spent, as he well knows, in places I detested collecting curios.'[23] But the lists of acquisitions compiled by staff at Snow Hill suggest that, during their early travels at least, Wellcome spent considerable amounts of his money on luxury items that Syrie could enjoy as much as her husband: later in life she forged a successful career for herself as an interior designer. Indeed, there is little to suggest that the Wellcomes were not happy together during the early years of their marriage. Perhaps they both gradually came to realize that their differences were great, but they were no greater than the disparities shouldered by other steadfast marriages before and since. They had a son, named Henry Mounteney, in 1903, who was born the day after their second wedding anniversary. They travelled extensively and socialized intensively. No one, apparently, suspected that either was unhappy.

But sadly, their expressions of grief after the marriage failed are among the few surviving testaments to their contentment as a couple. In one letter, written directly to 'Dear Hal' in August 1910, Syrie wrote, 'you must know how hard its going to be—how hard it must be for a woman without the husband she has been accustomed to look up to and lean on and depend on and you know how I did depend on you how it seemed as if I <u>never</u> could do without you!'[24] Wellcome too suffered both physical and mental distress during their separation. Soon afterwards he caught 'a severe chill', and had to undergo surgery for a recurrent ulcer problem that plagued him for most of his life. He spent many weeks that summer laid up in a nursing home, 'unfit to read or write or to do anything', and then recuperating in Harrogate. He saw virtually no one, preferring to manage his sorrow alone. The few surviving letters he wrote to close friends only give an inkling of his grief. 'I cannot forget that my wife and I lived together on affectionate terms for nine years—that I adored her as the ideal of my heart—and that she is the mother of my child. I want nothing unkind said about her.' He had not, he believed, acted hastily—'the course I have pursued has been well and anxiously considered with an aching heart'—but that did nothing to ease his pain—'I am sure you will realize my distress about it all it seems as if the light of my life was put out—our happy home is broken up'; 'it hurts me to think of it and it hurts me still more to write of it'.[25] Meanwhile, a mutual friend informed him that his wife retained 'a really affectionate regard for you and feels a very genuine sympathy for you in your illness. She said to me one day "I only wish I could go up and read to him".'[26]

Both Queenie and Hal were so upset by the failure of their marriage that for a time it seemed—and still seems today on reading the little remaining correspondence—unthinkable that they should not be reunited. The catastrophe had taken place in Quito, Ecuador, in April 1910. Little more is known about it than is known about their hasty courtship in Sudan nine years earlier. On both occasions, Wellcome had been advising foreign governments on public health issues. He was now a recognized authority on tropical medicine and sanitation thanks to the success of his Tropical Research Laboratories in Khartoum. In Ecuador, he was inspecting the dreadful health and sanitary conditions in the Panama Canal zone. He and Syrie had spent the autumn and winter in California, enjoying a somewhat milder climate on account of Wellcome's health. The Panama Canal project was under fire from Congress and receiving heavy criticism in the American press as government expenditure, and the death toll from disease, escalated apparently unchecked. In the New Year, the American Secretary of War, J. M. Dickinson, asked Wellcome to survey the situation. Accordingly, itineraries were amended and the Wellcomes set off for South America.[27]

They stayed in Quito with Jordan Stabler, who worked with the American Legation to Ecuador. No one now knows what course of events sparked

Wellcome's fury during their stay, or how his anguish was conveyed, but he accused his wife of having an affair with another of Stabler's guests, Archer Harman, an American railroad builder and financier who was seven years Wellcome's junior. Syrie vehemently denied the accusation, then and ever afterwards. No direct evidence to sustain or disprove her innocence survives. The marriage had become troubled. Wellcome's traditional views may have caused tensions. He had once explained to Burroughs that 'A man must marry a woman who loves him in response to his own love for her. A woman who can sympathize with him in his social life, in his business cares, and can fill his home with sunshine.'[28] Syrie, who was so much younger and so spirited, may have seen things differently. Later writers have offered anecdotal evidence to suggest that Wellcome had sexually mistreated his wife in the past, but Syrie never claimed that she had been abused or offered any such grounds for divorce. On the contrary, she continued to assert her innocence, and it was she who had hoped for a reconciliation when she left Ecuador alone to join friends in New York. But Wellcome never spoke to his wife again.[29]

The most arresting aspect of the separation is not its swiftness, but Wellcome's utterly uncompromising response. He never allowed himself to doubt that the marriage was dead, despite appeals from friends to reconsider. Dorothy Stanley, who had remained a close friend since the death of her husband, Henry, in 1904, beseeched Wellcome on Syrie's behalf:

Oh dear Mr Wellcome <u>do</u> forgive her any folly or imprudence. She is so alone and needs your love and protection. Then, for your boy's sake do not separate from his mother, it will be bad for him; <u>they are both children and need infinite indulgence</u>; we <u>all</u> need indulgence and forgiveness let us then give it freely to one another . . . Queenie will forgive you for thinking she had done you a wrong she had not done, you only have to ask her to. The public know you have been ill, that is all, there need be no scandal, no talk.[30]

Lady Stanley had touched upon a matter that concerned Wellcome intensely, and one that he was not unfamiliar with thanks to his disagreements with Burroughs: public scandal. It was, of course, Dorothy Stanley's knowledge of the potential publicity that led her to intrude on her friend's privacy: 'Don't abandon your little Queenie; what will become of her!!' But it may have been the very same fear of gossip that set Wellcome ever more steadfastly on his chosen course. He did not try to patch together a reunion with his wife. His pride prohibited him, despite the obvious consequences. In an unmistakable echo of his reaction to the Burroughs situation, he pressed ahead with the necessary legal steps and refused to speak of the matter to anyone, not even his closest friends, who received short notification that 'grave trouble had arisen' and a request never to broach the subject with Wellcome again.[31]

We know so little about the nature of the marriage or the actual circumstances of its collapse that, in fairness, it is impossible to judge Wellcome. Having decided that the relationship was irredeemable, he was acutely conscious of the need to avoid any publicity, for the sake of the family, but also so that they might be allowed to reach a 'friendly' settlement without intrusion.[32] 'From the first I have not allowed myself to discuss the trouble with even my closest friends—I feel that this course is best for all concerned. If I am in consequence misunderstood by any I must stand it.'[33] This last sentence was crossed out by Wellcome as he drafted the letter to his friends. More than once he edited away his most unguarded expressions of distress while preparing his correspondence in the months following the separation. Today, these deletions, and the agonies of composition they betray, reveal as much about Wellcome's state of mind as the words themselves.

It is from this painful time that Syrie's criticisms of her husband's collection survive. They suggest that she had long found it difficult to position herself with regard to Wellcome's growing passion for collecting. Towards the end of 1903 he had begun to plan a public exhibition on the history of 'Medicine, Chemistry, Pharmacy and the Allied Sciences',[34] and he spent more and more time and money buying things for this purpose. The couple travelled often, and 'life abroad became one constant round of visits to bazaars, old pharmacies, bookshops, dealers in antiquities, and owners of private collections'.[35] It did not help that Wellcome had developed a love for touring Europe by motor car, which, in the early 1900s, was hardly the most comfortable way to travel. Poor roads, fragile mechanics, and suspicious border officials meant that Syrie had to put up with frequent delays and discomforts as Wellcome's passenger. More than once they arrived at their hotel drenched from a rainstorm or 'with the radiator boiling like a kettle'.[36]

Syrie alone was privy to the daily deliberations that marked Wellcome's private journey as a collector, but her own contributions to his project could hardly be on equal terms. As Wellcome's wife, Syrie was expected to join her husband on his collecting excursions—they took her, after all, around Europe and America—but she eventually accompanied him in body rather than in spirit. She could be a companion, and perhaps a sometime advisor, but never an accomplice in the grand historical narrative Wellcome was attempting to acquire. If she found herself little more than a witness to Wellcome's consumer excesses as the dust from their hasty marriage settled, she could be forgiven for beginning to wonder whether she was becoming something of a bystander within the marriage also, since so much of his time was spent pursuing collectables. Two suitors increasingly vied for Wellcome's attentions, and gradually Syrie felt her needs to be sidelined in favour of her husband's love for antiquities.

Her comments in 1910 were made alongside pleas for fair treatment according to the terms of the separation. One letter, written to Wellcome's friend Alfred Chune Fletcher (Wellcome refused to let Syrie contact him directly) in August, lurched from anger—'in spite of this, and my honestly sacrificing myself in a way I <u>hated</u> both to please him and to gather curios for <u>ourselves</u> I am treated in this way!'—to self-pity—'I am the mother of his child and as he well knows I've given him the best years of my life, my youth <u>and health</u> and the future is <u>blank</u> for me, and that should surely weigh with him in his treatment of me now.' She repeatedly set the money Wellcome spent on books and artefacts against the money he should give to support his wife and child. The first, Syrie's letter implied, was an aimless, materialistic indulgence (the majority of Wellcome's 'curios', as Syrie was quick to point out, were locked up in storage anyway); the second was a moral obligation and common decency demanded it. 'Does he then want me and his son to live in boarding houses and fifth rate hotels whilst <u>he</u> is staying where he pleases and spending on curios and otherwise what he pleases.'[37]

Syrie's angry references to her husband's collecting suggest that, at times, she felt her marriage was being crowded out by his obsession for shopping. 'Does he realize he is offering his wife and child about a third or certainly not more than half what <u>he</u> spends on curios—and with all his <u>store</u> of things grudges me what I would wish to take . . . to make a home.' That she had forgone her own interests for the sake of his, Syrie reasoned, and spent so much of her time supporting her husband's ceaseless craving for material belongings, meant it was only fair that he should now surrender those comparatively few items she now required. She was not so much concerned with the 'books, curios properly speaking', that they had bought, as with the household furniture, linen, and plate that they had chosen together on their travels: 'they are, or seem to me to be, mine as well as his, if hard work in securing them and giving up my wishes in order to get them means anything.' At one time, Syrie may have believed she could redirect her husband's acquisitiveness towards a more domestic goal, and for a while she probably succeeded in satisfying her own interests in interior design, and stimulating his, as they shopped their way around Europe. But Wellcome's fascination with things went far beyond home-making or aesthetic gratification. Indeed, relatively few of his possessions ever made it into any kind of lived environment at all, as Syrie pointed out. And so Wellcome's intellectual interests sparked and spread, while their domestic happiness as a couple seems to have gradually burnt itself out.

Syrie was not in a strong position. Her husband's money had, of course, paid for most of her possessions. She portrayed herself as a martyr to the excesses of Wellcome's consumer habits as well as rightful owner of the results. There was little else she could do. Just as she had sometimes felt powerless to intercede in any meaningful way in Wellcome's collecting work while she was his wife, her obvious frustration betrayed the realization that she was in an even weaker position now that, to all intents and purposes, she was no longer his wife.

Regardless of her feelings in the matter, Syrie had spent ten years, the whole of her short adult life, married to an extremely wealthy man, socializing with the elite of English and American society (however middle-aged and dull they might have seemed to her on occasion), and enjoying a luxurious lifestyle filled with fine things. Now she found herself, 'turned out with nothing to make life beautiful and liveable even though happiness has gone'. Syrie certainly enjoyed beautiful things as much as the next person, but her words were driven by fear. With the dissolution of the marriage she had lost her material and social security. The terms of the separation agreement would change everything. She felt the vulnerability of a woman suddenly dependent on a man who had rejected her. She continued to complain about her financial situation sporadically over the years, although Wellcome had given her an annual allowance of £2,400 in addition to financing the furnishing of her apartments.[38] Nonetheless, his emotional resolve must have scared Syrie. He never spoke to her again after Quito. He did what he had to do for her, legally and financially, but he punished her in other ways.

Not only was Wellcome silent, he neglected to give back many of Syrie's belongings. Syrie's personal treasures were treated in the same way as so many of Wellcome's were, packed up and stored away, and they proved just as difficult to recover. She wrote repeatedly, asking him to return things that were precious to her. Among them, a Chippendale cake table that had belonged to her mother, and a silver Queen Anne sugar basin that had belonged to her grandmother; various bowls, tea services, tables, fans, coats, mirrors; 'two silver Portuguese trays, the small ones, with pierced edges, long shape, that you gave me at one time for my dressing table, but that you never got out for me'; and, perhaps most touchingly, a silver box with cupid inlaid, listed as 'given me in Switzerland by Hal', along with an unset turquoise and a string of pearls, 'given me in Mexico by Hal'.[39] Syrie's requests, whether through neglect or spite, were not attended to for at least three years. Her possessions were withheld. Or perhaps they were lost amongst the rising ocean of things Wellcome owned. Or perhaps he and his staff were too busy buying other objects to attend to her requests for some of her own. In a final affront to their happiness as a family, even Syrie's most intimate belongings were shut away with all Wellcome's museum specimens.

One of the most arresting of all Syrie's remarks was a throwaway line in a long, emotional letter written to their intermediary, Fletcher, over the course of two days in August 1910. While detailing the extent of her hatred for her husband's collecting excursions, she added, 'and if I remonstrated he always replied—but it's to collecting things, they are as much for you as for me!'[40] While Syrie raged at Wellcome's failure to comprehend her lack of interest, Wellcome can be seen reaching out to his wife in the only way he knew how; and the chasm that the collection had opened between them becomes palpable. If Wellcome reconceptualized his collecting habit as an act of love for Syrie, it was never going to be enough. And his submissions must have sounded hollow, for she knew that he would still be pursuing his curios whether she was accompanying him or not. Whatever the truth of Syrie's extramarital intimacies, Wellcome may have pushed the boundaries of fidelity to breaking point in his relentless quest for things.

But if Wellcome could not share his interest in medical history with Syrie, he could share it with plenty of other people, not least with those people who worked *for* him as well as with him. Just as he had fifteen years earlier, after the breakdown of his friendship with Burroughs, Wellcome sought solace in his work. As the terms of the separation were negotiated, he tried to express this to his friends, although the words did not flow easily:

I shall try to drown my sorrow [illegible phrase, crossed out] by applying myself [illegible phrase, crossed out] in my life work—work is a great comforter. With God's help I hope to rise above and my life work is one that contributes to the welfare of others as well as myself and this thought helps to brighten ones life.[41]

In 1910, Wellcome returned to North Africa, where, essentially, his marriage began, to embark on a new passion. He began to act on his interest in the prehistory of Sudan. He returned to Khartoum, chartered a *dahabeah*, and went up the Blue Nile searching for evidence of ancient settlements. He found a likely site in the hills at Jebel Moya, in the middle Nile basin, and, with permission from the Sudan Government, employed a dozen locals to help him start excavating there.[42] The Jebel Moya excavations were to run for four seasons.

The Jebel Moya digs were conceived, from the start, as a philanthropic enterprise, designed to provide work for the local population. Because of this, the workforce escalated from a small team working alongside Wellcome with makeshift tools, to 500 men and boys by the end of the first season, and 4,000 during the fourth and final excavation season in 1914. Wellcome made it a rule that every applicant must be found some work to do. Besides those actually digging for archaeological finds, men were employed to build work-shops, transport water, take away rubbish, and run the sifting machines that sorted hundreds of tons of excavated soil; and to feed, guard, and police their peers. There was even a group of basket-menders and mat-makers. Wellcome set up financial and practical incentives to persuade his burgeoning Sudanese workforce to give up alcohol and save their earnings. He instituted the Wellcome Order of the Peacock, an honour ceremonially awarded to any employee who had managed to stay dry for two months. He established a savings bank, ensured his employees were well fed, organized training in engineering and carpentry skills, and introduced them to suitably 'civilized' games like football and hockey.[43] 'Our mission', he wrote to a friend, 'is to try and improve the condition of the natives, and to teach them the benefits of our civilization, and the advantages of truth, honesty, right and justice, and by our own lives exemplify the above precepts.'[44]

In Sudan, the Jebel Moya digs were as much an exercise in charity as in research, but back at home, Wellcome hoped his findings would prove intellectually ground-breaking. He believed he might even be exploring 'the veritable birthplace of human civilisation itself'.[45] He secured a special licence from the Sudan Government to excavate in the region of the Blue and White Niles, which he retained until his death, and he intended to excavate a large area around Jebel Moya, but the First World War halted his work in Sudan. Although his scholarly expectations eventually proved to be unfounded, for the site was actually a late Neolithic settlement, the massive enterprise produced a wealth of archaeological material. Wellcome shipped back tons of ancient stones, bones, and pottery fragments excavated from Jebel Moya over the years. Energized by his steadfast belief in the significance of the site, he insisted that every scrap of evidence be retained, however unpromising it seemed. Each object might one day 'help to form links in the broken chain of evidence of the Great Past'.[46] Not everyone shared his faith in the value of the material they unearthed: 'Every fragment of pottery, brick and stone had to be kept', one of his assistants later remembered. 'We were obliged to make a special compound and pile in it classified and labelled heaps of this useless rubbish.'[47]

And so, on the eve of the First World War, Wellcome's love affair with North Africa found him, quite literally, shovelling up Sudanese soil and shipping it back to England in the name of science. Over the next twenty-five years, Wellcome devoted more and more time and money to his museum collection, which was still embryonic in his eyes.

For a second time, Wellcome shrank back from a painful, failed relationship and turned to a realm of social alliances he controlled completely. In a professional environment, whether in London or in Sudan, everyone knew their responsibilities and everyone was there, at least in part, because they shared Wellcome's aspirations. At work there were no feelings of rejection to contend with, no emotional struggles that threatened to undermine his rationale as a collector. No one openly questioned the nobility of Wellcome's eternal hunt for collectables, even if it was sometimes their pay cheque that ensured they held their tongue. In this public milieu, acquaintances admired Wellcome's financial commitment to his intellectual endeavours. He could share his enthusiasms with his employees and with his paid collecting agents, and his money ensured that he was less vulnerable to their conceits.

It is no accident that few women penetrated the network of dealers, shop keepers, auctioneers, academics, medical professionals, and museum curators that lay behind collections like Wellcome's. Women may have become a powerful consumer force in the furnishing industry—Syrie herself became an internationally recognized interior designer; in fact, she was the first English-woman to pursue interior decoration as a career[48]—but antique collecting 'remained predominantly a male preserve'. The politician and writer George W. E. Russell had observed, in 1906, that a 'tendency to collect, manifested in early manhood, is a heavy blow and deep discouragement to the operations of the matrimonial market'.[49] Syrie, through no fault of her own, was largely excluded from the male world of buying, selling, and bartering antiquities during her marriage to Wellcome. If her sin had been her reluctance to indulge his obsession for museum specimens, one of his mistakes was to have expected a woman like Syrie to defer to a pastime she felt unable to collaborate in. So, one passion dissipated while another took flight. Just a few years after Syrie and Wellcome married, Wellcome had begun to collect his way towards a public goal, rather than for personal satisfaction alone. He started to plan a great exhibition, and with this plan the most enduring love affair of all came to flourish.

II. TACTICS

The fate of the Wellcomes' marriage cannot have rested solely on Wellcome's passion for collecting, but as his free time and his income grew, his hobby became a major operation. The early 1900s saw the inception of a great collecting enterprise, with Wellcome at its head: he hired staff, he established the hierarchies and protocols upon which they worked, and his team set about acquiring artefacts through every avenue open to them. The chapters in this section introduce the mechanisms upon which Wellcome's collection expanded and continued to grow for three decades.

As Wellcome's interest in objects brought more people into play, he receded from the frontlines of his collecting project. He entered the upper management of his own private collection, and spent his time monitoring all the people who bought things on his behalf. His presence in the historical record is clearest in the profusion of hurriedly written instructions that litter the far more detailed reports composed by his employees. This documentation was at its fullest when Wellcome was travelling abroad and his staff sent him weekly progress reports. And yet, Wellcome had little to say about the details. He often added only a few comments: 'very good', 'be sure and get it', 'this is very valuable', or 'follow up closely'. So, it is the experiences of his collecting agents that now take centre stage.

This is partly a consequence of bias in the archive. Wellcome met with his staff every day when he was in London, and he continued to collect objects himself, but these events were not documented. And if he was content to observe the progress his staff made from afar, it was not due to indifference on Wellcome's part, but because he trusted his deputy, C. J. S. Thompson, implicitly to fulfil his require-ments. Nonetheless, Wellcome's plans were routinely refracted through the work of his staff, and it is obliquely, through the successes and failures of his working relationships, that Wellcome emerges as a collector for us today. The acquisition systems he put in place, and his efforts to maintain those systems over the years, reveal his preferences, his aspirations, and his insecurities as a collector most clearly.

CHAPTER FIVE

AN HISTORICAL EXHIBITION OF RARE AND CURIOUS OBJECTS

In 1903, Wellcome and his closest colleagues discussed an idea that was to change the course of his collection forever. It was the idea of an exhibition. Wellcome was fifty years old, and Burroughs Wellcome and Company was established as a leading pharmaceuticals firm with the profits to match.[1] He was increasingly freed from the daily decision-making that the business had demanded of him in the early years. He spent more time travelling with his wife. His thoughts had already turned towards more altruistic projects, like researching history books and supporting charitable ventures abroad, and a lifetime of collecting meant that he now possessed many hundreds of rare manuscripts and artefacts, which were scattered throughout his home and decorated the hallways of his business premises. He owned so many things that a considerable number of his prized pieces were already confined to storage. An exhibition would allow him to bring these dislocated treasures together for the first time, and display them to a wider audience.

The idea was not for a public exhibition, exactly, but for something more ambitious. He wanted to organize a specialist 'historical medical' exhibition, aimed at a professional audience: 'The exhibition will be strictly professional and scientific in character, and will not be open to the general public.'[2] Wellcome was not interested in pleasing the crowds, although it would have been easy for him to do so with all the curiosities he owned. The exhibition he planned would be scholarly in tone. He wanted to impress members of the academic elite whom he most admired: among them, no doubt, the scholars he had approached for information about the history of Egyptian medicine, like Petrie, Maspero, and Loret. This show would be aimed at doctors, scientists, and academics, and it would provide them with the richest, most comprehensive exploration into the history of science that they had ever seen. The story of human health would be laid out before Wellcome's guests through objects that had been carefully extracted from the oldest archaeological sites, transported to London from the furthest tropical shores, and donated by the most famous scientific families in Western history. Wellcome strove for excellence in everything he did, and the historical medical exhibition he now dreamed of would be no different, not least because the firm's reputation had to be considered. It was surely no coincidence that many of the scientists Wellcome turned to for help with his forthcoming exhibition could be found on Burroughs Wellcome client lists.[3]

The 'Scientific Exhibition' was initially proposed as a promotional stunt for Burroughs Wellcome and Company. The firm's twenty-fifth anniversary would fall in 1905, and it seemed a good opportunity to launch a celebratory show.[4] Given the privileged audience Wellcome had in mind, and under the banner of Burroughs Wellcome, the exhibition's success would affect his social and his commercial status. He wanted publicity for the firm, but no deadline, however appropriate the upcoming anniversary might be, should be allowed to impede the quality of the exhibition. Disparaging reviews in the press, or criticisms overheard in the smoking rooms of London's gentlemen's clubs, would not only be embarrassing but potentially damaging to his professional reputation. And so the opening date for the exhibition was repeatedly postponed. An initial booking with the Portman Rooms—a 'magnificent suite of rooms decorated in the Italian Renaissance Style and lighted throughout by electricity'—for mid-January 1904 was cancelled, then plans to open the exhibition in early 1905 were abandoned, as were enquiries regarding suitable premises for the following September.[5] Soon it was clear that the show would never be ready in time to celebrate the firm's first quarter-century. But none of Wellcome's colleagues can have suspected that it would be nearly *ten years* before the exhibition finally opened its doors to the critical eyes of London's scientific establishment.

In effect, whether he admitted it to himself or not, Wellcome saw the exhibition, not as an opportunity to show people what he had achieved as a collector, but as an opportunity to achieve much more. The exhibition did not send him to unpacking and cataloguing his recent purchases, but propelled him into an even more far-reaching hunt for new acquisitions. He began to devote more staff, more time, and more money to buying things. The years of preparation were effectively years of intensive research. In 1903, Wellcome knew he had a great amount to learn about the history of human health. Gathering objects, as many as he could, was his way of finding out about the past. The more he could get, the more he would understand. 'I anticipate that the Exhibition will reveal many facts,' he wrote, 'and will elucidate many obscure points in connection with the origins of various medicines, and in respect to the history of disease.'[6] For him, planning the exhibition was to be a revelatory experience rather than merely a logistical one. For the exhibition to achieve the high academic standards he coveted, for it to be as complete and accurate as possible, he was going to need a larger collection to draw upon. Soon, Wellcome's managerial skills were set to work on his latest, and greatest, research project.

He began to write to friends and acquaintances, asking them for historical information or interesting artefacts which they might lend him: 'I think you may be interested to learn that I am organising an historical exhibition to be held in London in a few months' time, and enclosed I send you memo giving full particulars.'[7] But before long, this personal approach to canvassing support was superseded by a more efficient form of publicity. Special circulars were printed by the firm and distributed to prominent historians and medics, announcing an, 'Historical Exhibition of Rare and Curious Objects relating to Medicine, Chemistry, Pharmacy and the Allied Sciences to be held in London shortly. Organised by, and under the Direction of, Henry S. Wellcome.' The exhibition, it went on, was being organized '[w]ith the object of stimulating the study of the great past'. As the phrase suggests, it was to be something of a collaborative project: the circular was essentially an appeal for help.[8]

Of course, Wellcome wanted artefacts. 'Should you possess any objects of historical medical interest, I trust I may count upon your kind assistance by lending them, so that the Exhibition may be thoroughly representative. I should also highly esteem your kindness if you would inform me of any similar objects in the possession of others.' But he was also interested in research leads. He wanted people to send him information. The circular asked for references to early medicine, which might be found in old books and manuscripts, and noted that 'items of curious medical lore may often be gathered from peasants and others living in country districts'. Perhaps Wellcome was hoping that, in a rush of empathetic enthusiasm for the cause, recipients of his pamphlet—some of whom were stationed abroad—would

venture out into their local neighbourhoods and undertake a little anthropological interviewing on his behalf. The circular pointed out that missionaries
were in a good position to gather useful information about local customs.[9]

Wellcome was quick to assure potential patrons that their contributions to
the exhibition would be fully acknowledged and any objects they decided to
donate would be treated with the utmost care. His requests for gifts and loans
may have been written in the knowledge that a bigger exhibition would bring
him more prestige, but Wellcome's intellectual curiosity was not merely a
disguise for his covetousness. His desire to learn from others was a genuine
one. He had formulated a series of specific questions that particularly interested him at this stage in the proceedings: 'Why were certain substances used
in the treatment of disease? Was their adoption the result of study and
practical observation, or was it more usually the result of accident? Were the
alleged virtues purely imaginary and due to some superstitious suggestion?'[10]

The queries resonate with his earlier investigations into the use of animal
products in medical history for the Animal Substances book. Then, Wellcome
sought to 'ascertain as far as possible the rational [*sic*] of treatment even amongst
the most primitive races, that is to say, why did they use these various substances
for given maladies'.[11] Now he broadened his enquiries, but the same underlying
question motivated him. He was interested in detecting a scientific impulse deep
in the human past and, therefore, deep in the human psyche. He wanted to
ascertain whether medical traditions that seemed merely superstitious—
shamanistic visions, spirit possessions, animal-shaped remedies—were actually
developed according to an as yet undetected logic. This was why, for example,
he wrote to a curator at the India Museum in Calcutta, in January 1904,
requesting specimens of local 'plants, or parts of plants resembling the human
form which are employed for medical purposes'.[12] Perhaps, when tested, they
might reveal a chemical function beyond their aesthetic appeal.

Wellcome's curiosity, however, could hardly be said to be limited to the
anthropology of medical prescriptions. Any offer of information regarding
the history of science received in reply an earnest request for more. When Sir
Thomas Lauder Brunton, an eminent pharmacologist who was one of the
earliest supporters of Wellcome's project, sent him an old book on alchemy
in January 1904, Wellcome was quick to thank him, adding, 'I shall value any
suggestions and ideas you may find time to offer me in connection with this
Exhibition—I am anxious to make it very complete and comprehensive.'[13]
And no wonder Wellcome was so keen to enlist expert advice from others, for
the parameters of his proposed exhibition were virtually encyclopaedic.

The circular Wellcome had printed included a 'syllabus' divided into sixteen categories, including surgery, chemistry, pharmacy, anatomy, pathology, nursing, quackery, alchemy, physiology, anthropology, criminology, the 'adulteration and falsification of drugs', and the history of photography. To illustrate these themes, Wellcome intended to collect paintings, engravings, photographs, models, sculptures, manuscripts, books, periodicals and pamphlets, letters, prescriptions, diplomas, medical instruments and apparatus, archaeological finds, hospital equipment, shop fittings, advertisements, specimens of drugs, remedies and foods, plant samples, microscopic preparations, charms and amulets, ceremonial paraphernalia, costumes, medals, coins, and furniture. (One can only spare a thought for Syrie.) Hardly anything, it seemed, would warrant refusal. 'Even though the items be but small,' Wellcome assured any donor who might have reason to doubt the significance of his or her contribution, 'they may form important connecting links in the chain of historical evidence... Every little helps, and as I am desirous of making the Historical Medical Exhibition as complete as possible, I shall be grateful for any communication you may be able to make.'[14]

Wellcome was determined to make his exhibition accurate. In fact, completeness and accuracy went hand in hand, for the more material Wellcome could gather together, the more likely he was to be able to provide a precise portrayal of humanity's medical past, with nothing omitted or needlessly misconstrued. The best way to ensure completeness was to maximize the opportunities available for acquiring objects. This was why the printed circulars and syllabuses were so efficient, because they could be posted off to anyone and everyone who might be interested in the project with very little effort.

Wellcome also began to hire more staff to buy things for him. And, because of this, his collection entered a new phase in its development. From now on, Wellcome's own collecting interests would be distilled through the work of people in his pay. He began delegating his personal aspirations as a collector, utilizing the agency of others to achieve his aims. He became a collector who navigated the space between collecting as a private hobby and collecting as an institutional undertaking. With the promise of a celebrated exhibition on the horizon, Wellcome turned his personal collecting interests into a professional concern.

The company's librarian and researcher, Charles Thompson, assumed a place at the head of what eventually became Wellcome's Museum department. By the turn of the century, Thompson was overseeing a considerable influx of valuable literary material to the Burroughs Wellcome Library, but he now began to spend more of his time collecting historical artefacts. Thompson was soon organizing the delivery of numerous cases of new museum acquisitions to Burroughs Wellcome's headquarters every month. Most had been sent from London's auction rooms, and each was filled with old microscopes, pharmacy jars, surgical instruments, and other medical memorabilia, all of which took their place alongside the endless stream of books Thompson channelled in.

Wellcome employed a second collecting agent in December 1903, an Italian medic named Louis Sambon (Figure 9). Born in Milan, Sambon came from a family of archaeologists and classical scholars.[15] He was a rather flamboyant and unreliable figure, who developed a knotty relationship with Wellcome and Thompson, but he was well connected and therefore good at seeking out antiquities in Europe. He was a lecturer at the London School of Tropical Medicine and a collector in his own right, having organized a successful historical exhibition on behalf of the Italian Government for the International Congress of Medicine held in Rome in 1894. Sambon was initially employed for six months, on the understanding that he would 'devote [himself] to such matters in connection with the forthcoming historical, medical etc. exhibition as I may indicate'. His research for Wellcome would take him to 'the principal centres in Holland, Belgium, France, Switzerland and Italy' searching for insights into medical history in libraries and museums, and acquiring objects when possible.[16] Thompson also began to travel abroad in 1904, visiting France, Italy, Sicily, and Holland, and bringing back cases of objects from each of his destinations.[17]

With two experienced men regularly combing the Continent for medical treasures, Wellcome's collecting capacity increased significantly in a matter of months. Plans for an exhibition had given his collecting work new momentum, and the rate of acquisition soared. His collecting remit expanded dramatically, and even more of his money was finding its way into the hands of London's antiquities traders. Thompson was soon sending a small group of Burroughs Wellcome staff to bid at London salesrooms, as well as contacting traders, private collectors, and institutions, like hospitals and surgical instrument manufacturers, to ask for any interesting old relics they might have.[18]

In this new atmosphere of professionalism, Wellcome's staff began to keep more systematic records of his purchases. The objects Wellcome had bought and sent back to the firm's headquarters had been catalogued, using a system

DR. LOUIS WESTENRA SAMBON.

Figure 9. Photograph of Louis Westenra Sambon, date unknown.

of typed lists pasted into a notebook, since 1901. From 1905, Thompson's purchases were also recorded, using a similar method. Loose typed checklists were stuck into a thick, leather-bound ledger as each batch of objects was unpacked and stored for future use. And so, for the first time, the pace of acquisition emerges in the historical record. The system was primarily designed to help pinpoint objects in storage—Wellcome had leased a storage facility at Crystal Palace to house his objects until a location could be settled for the exhibition. The earliest ledger begins by recording the contents of storage case number 101, and finishes, hundreds of pages and about two and a half years later, with case number 287. The contents of the first, case 101, were typical:

An autograph of Astley Cooper; a balance and weights in an oak case; a chicken skin vase; a Chinese book and a small Chinese medicine case; two cauls; a Delft pottery drug jar; a drum made from two human skulls; three blue and white china feeding-cups; a pink and white china feeding bottle; a medicine-chest with brass handles; manuscripts and note-books of Dr. McCormick; a microscope in a case; a microscope of turned wood; two pewter measures; two blue and white china posset-cups; a white posset-cup dating to 1671; a blue and white china Persian spoon; a blue and white china pap-cup; a poisoned dart in red bag; a pilgrim bottle; a pair of spectacles in a brass case; another pair of large round spectacles; some wooden scales; a skeleton warrior; a broken, painted thermometer.[19]

No more information about the nature or provenance of this motley group of objects is given, but the breadth of Wellcome's interest is instantly apparent: Dutch ceramics were packed next to Chinese medical equipment; a microscope shared space with a skull drum, apparently of unknown origin; and a seventeenth-century drinking cup was stashed away alongside memorabilia relating to one of the early nineteenth century's most famous surgeons and anatomists, Astley Cooper. Many of the Crystal Palace boxes contained two or three pages worth of listed objects each. And these were just the items that came to rest in Crystal Palace. Other containers were redirected to the company's Snow Hill headquarters, the Dartford manufacturing site, the Wellcomes' home in Kent, or to Shoolbred's department store on Tottenham Court Road where Wellcome had rented warehouse facilities since the 1890s.[20]

The earliest Crystal Palace cases were filled according to object type, so it may be that these cases contained objects Wellcome already owned, which had been organized into themed groups for storage. Case 128 held a large number of bronze deities, many of Asian origin; amongst them a bronze god on horseback, a bronze elephant god on throne, a bronze god with eight arms, a bronze figure of Krishna on throne, and a brass god sitting with floral background. Case 129 contained quite a few spoons: four carved 'African' spoons, a spoon and a fork carved in one piece, a curious double spoon, eight carved wooden spoons, two 'Ashantee' water-ladles, a spoon from Vancouver Island, a spoon with handle carved in the image of a god, and a toast-master's horn punch ladle. Some cases were packed with paintings and prints, others contained wooden jugs and water vessels, one was devoted to old green glass bottles and retorts, another was filled with fifty-six different kinds of gourd.

Most of the objects in this ledger were bought in London's auction rooms. Later cases were filled as material was acquired, so that a number of successive cases might store items purchased from a single auction. The first sale recorded in the ledger (earlier auctions were not listed) was held at Sotheby's on 14 November 1906. Cases 138 to 143 inclusive were filled with objects from this sale—pottery vases, apothecary's vials, glazed cases, Roman vases, Delft pottery jars, and spirit bottles, as well as two cases filled with Peruvian ornaments and idols. But very large objects required a case of their own. Case 134 contained only an inlaid table 'with chemical design', case 135 held a statue of Grace Darling, and case 136 was required for Grace's pedestal (the story of this heroic rescue at sea qualified for an exhibition set to explore humanity's struggles for survival in the broadest historical terms). Case 137 contained only a 'swinging sign' that had probably once swung above the door to a pharmacy and had been given to Wellcome by a Dr Sutton Page.

One gets an overwhelming impression of the relentless rate of the collection's growth while leafing through fat leather logbooks like this one. Page after page, month by month, hundreds of objects were entering Wellcome's storage premises. The collection was multiplying as never before. Within a few years, Thompson was overseeing a bustling department, staffed with buyers, researchers, and collectors, all devoted to the business of museum-making. The clearest picture of this transformation comes at the beginning of 1907, from Thompson's earliest surviving reports to Wellcome.[21]

Wellcome had long received regular reports from his senior staff in other departments. Now that collecting was becoming a business in itself, Thompson began writing standardized reports every week when Wellcome was away. In fact, reports on the state of the collection followed Wellcome round the world for the rest of his life. Today they fill many archive boxes at the Wellcome Library.[22] The sheer number of reports is testament to Wellcome's intense concern for the development of his collection, now that he assumed a more directorial role in its creation. Having out-sourced much of the work of choosing, buying, researching, and organizing his objects, and frequently having to travel for work, he needed to feel involved with the minutiae of daily decisions back in London. Thompson's reports were finely detailed.

They listed exactly which items had been bought, considered, or rejected each week. They chronicled negotiations with dealers, meetings with fellow collectors and academics, events at the salesrooms, and the achievements of the staff. In addition, auction catalogues were sent to Wellcome for upcoming sales that might be of interest, and specific lots marked with guide prices and upper limits for his approval.

Wellcome responded with quick, scrawling flourishes in his own hand. He annotated each of Thompson's reports, scribbling notes where necessary, underlining passages of text that needed further attention, or simply crossing items in the margin to show that he approved of the general progress being made. He returned the sales catalogues with additional notes, or, if time pressed, he would despatch a telegram halfway round the world to confirm a particular purchase. Thompson's reports were typed down one side of the page, leaving a wide left-hand margin in anticipation of Wellcome's handwritten feedback. Later, successive items were numbered so that Wellcome could refer to them efficiently in ongoing communications.

The detailed attention Wellcome gave every single purchase or point of interest is remarkable. Despite the manifold demands on his time, he acknowledged almost every acquisition made in his absence, and Thompson's reports were particularly full, running to many pages and often listing between twenty and thirty individually described purchases along with the daily business of the Museum. These acknowledgements were not simply an automatic response on Wellcome's part, because the reports are also littered with more measured, comprehensive notes when he found a situation that required his judgement, or when an acquisition or development particularly excited him. The distorting effect of the historical record means that we now have a fuller picture of Wellcome's involvement with collection during the periods he was absent from London, but he was equally attentive in person, meeting his staff every day to discuss acquisitions and forthcoming sales.[23] Wellcome may have decided to delegate much of the work that went into creating his exhibition—later, his Museum—but he always considered it to be a personal undertaking. He worked hard to remind his staff that they were collecting things for him, on his behalf, and according to his approval. The reports reflect his determination to control the growth of what was quickly becoming, by his own design, a team venture.

When Thompson's reports begin, in January 1907, they immediately open a window onto a bustling world of activity. By this time, the days of Thompson's commercial advertising research were all but gone; he was now managing a project of vastly different proportions. The collection, together with the various people who worked on it, occupied several different sites across London. Thompson's time was spent coordinating efforts at each location: organizing cataloguing and storage at one, supervising researchers who worked at another, checking deliveries to a third. He managed a small team of buyers and freelance agents, whose efforts to acquire rare objects at low prices were constantly monitored, and he visited numerous dealers and shops to make purchases of his own. He toured London's salesrooms regularly to look through the latest pickings on the market, annotating sales catalogues for Wellcome, and kept an eye on the advertising columns of the daily papers and journals for private sales. He was making useful contacts too, and occasionally lunched with anthropologists, medics, or scientists who might be persuaded to make a donation or else could advise on research questions.

Alongside his own efforts to expand the collection, Thompson managed the enormous shipments of objects Wellcome sent to London during the course of his travels. Burroughs Wellcome men met deliveries at the docks, taking care to tip the customs officials before seeing each consignment was carefully packed into carts or vans and taken away without damage or additional cost. The influx of material was unremitting. Wellcome, to take one example, sent twenty-seven packing cases and twelve crates of goods during his visit to Lisbon in March 1907. A few weeks later, a further twenty-eight cases were met at the docks and driven away by Burroughs Wellcome men. Towards the end of May, Thompson received word that the next batch of cases Wellcome had sent, this time from Vitoria and Valladolid, via Seville, needed forwarding to London.[24] Every time Wellcome went away, a profusion of objects arrived back in London in his absence.

But most of Thompson's energies were focused on opening channels for objects to flow into Wellcome's collection for the exhibition. A quick survey of some of his earliest reports is enough to prove that he had a knack for rooting out interesting objects from little-known sources:

I have sent [Symmonds, one of Wellcome's collecting agents] down to Kingston to-day to see if he can pick anything up from the surgery of old Dr Cross, who, I hear, died about a fortnight ago. The doctor lived in the same house in which his great-grandfather carried on a practice in the middle of the eighteenth century, and he should have some very old instruments and books... I came across an old Italian in Soho last week, who had a roomful of old books. I picked out ten (medical) which include two early herbals and one very good anatomy. I paid him twenty-five shillings for the lot . . . I came across a man this week who makes long journeys throughout the country, buying up antique things in the villages and small market towns. I have made arrangements with him, and given him a list of objects likely to be of use to us, and he promises to buy such things for us if they are very cheap . . . Coming up Shaftesbury Avenue the other afternoon I noticed in a picture dealer's near Oxford Street a remarkably fine painting of a Moorish alchemist in an old laboratory. This picture is a most striking one . . . [Symmonds] went to Rochester market one day, and brought back several articles. He has also visited Uxbridge, Hitching, St. Albans and several other markets, at each of which he has been able to gather something . . . I called yesterday by appointment to see the Vicar of St. Sepulchre's who, you may remember, wrote to you concerning an ancient lead cistern which he wished to dispose of. The cistern was removed from the interior of the house about four years ago, and now stands in the yard. It is a very good one . . . I bought this week a very interesting amulet necklace that had belonged to an old Jewess in the East End of London . . .[25]

Such encounters permeated Thompson's daily routine, and made him extremely valuable to Wellcome in his quest for the ever-elusive 'complete' collection. Thompson's enthusiasm and resourcefulness assured Wellcome that he was gathering together historical evidence from the most unlikely places, and exhausting possibilities that other collectors might not have considered.

One of Thompson's earliest coups came in December 1908. While walking down Oxford Street, he happened to notice that 'the historic pharmacy of John Bell and Co., in Oxford Street, was closing and being dismantled'.[26] John Bell had been a founding member of the Pharmaceutical Society in the early 1840s, and the shop was 'a little bit of old London which had been overlooked in the sweeping changes which had taken place all around it',[27] all of which made it 'of more than ordinary interest' to Thompson and Wellcome. Thompson's ever watchful gaze fell on twelve old cylindrical carboys kept in the shop window, and he later succeeded in buying them for three shillings each. 'I am having a label affixed to each giving the history of the pharmacy and where they came from, and will have them properly stored.'[28] The acquisition encouraged him to enquire about other fixtures and fittings from the shop that might be destined for the scrapyard.

Then Thompson's thoughts turned to more monumental spoils. 'I think it would be well worth trying to get the old shop front of John Bell's pharmacy', he informed Wellcome. 'I was looking at it yesterday, and it could be taken to

Figure 10. John Bell's pharmacy reconstructed in the Wellcome Historical Medical Museum, Wigmore Street, London, c.1928.

pieces with very little trouble, and re-erected.' The suggestion hardly raised an eyebrow: 'Right . . . Good', scribbled Wellcome in reply.[29] And this is just what Thompson did. The entire pharmacy of John Bell and Company could later be seen, reconstructed with its original fittings, by visitors to the Wellcome Historical Medical Museum (Figure 10). And it would not be the last historic shop Wellcome bought outright and reassembled for the benefit of his visitors. By 1913, he was able to piece together a whole street of interiors—hospital rooms, drug shops, apothecary's workrooms—in the basement of his London exhibition hall. When Wellcome said that he wanted his collection to be as complete as possible he was not making idle declarations. John Bell's pharmacy was just the beginning.

With Thompson and Louis Sambon ferreting away at home and abroad, and a small group of support staff regularly being sent on collecting errands, Wellcome could feel satisfied that he was doing everything he could to ensure a ground-breaking exhibition. The date for the firm's twenty-fifth anniversary came and went: time was not an issue for him; neither was money. He had set out to buy up 'the history of medicine and the allied sciences', and he was determined to live up to his promise, 'preferring to do the thing with all thoroughness and completeness rather than hastening the time'.[30] He believed that his collection, if comprehensive enough, would teach him—and his audience—everything they needed to know about the history of human health. He would be the one to reveal this history to others; he would own it on everyone else's behalf. If all Wellcome had to do was to maximize his opportunities for buying things he could surely do it. He had the resources and the determination. And he had the managerial skills, for acquiring humanity's medical past was becoming a full-scale operation.

CHAPTER SIX

EXCUSE ME MR TREVE

On 26 January 1899, Thompson attended a sale at the prestigious auction rooms of Sotheby's in Covent Garden. It was one of the first auction sales he attended as Wellcome's agent. He was armed with a list of early medical manuscripts to bid for, and the price limits that Wellcome had agreed for each lot. His visit was a success and he managed to buy nearly everything Wellcome wanted. The only item he missed was a fifteenth-century manuscript, which was bought by the son of a well-known book dealer whom Thompson recognized at the sale. In a calculated act of revenge, once bidding had exceeded the £5 Thompson was willing to spend on the manuscript he continued to bid, driving the price upwards, merely for the satisfaction of knowing that Mr Quaritch would have to pay more for his prize. Thompson's presence at the sale had caused a stir among London's established book dealers, particularly as he had successfully outbid them a number of times during the sale, 'much to their annoyance'. As he was a relatively new player on the London auction circuit, no one recognized Thompson, but the considerable amount of money he was spending was enough to convince Sotheby's regular clientele that they needed to find out who he was.

Thompson was amused to watch the reaction to his presence at Sotheby's, particularly as he was acting under the false name of Treve.

I noted several little conferrals taking place between Leighton, Pickering and Chadwick. At length Leighton came round to me and said, 'Excuse me Mr Treve but do you know if Mr Wilton is in town?' 'I do not,' I replied. 'Oh!' he remarked, and returned somewhat disconcerted. He had evidently been put up to draw me. Another man asked me if I was connected with the firm of Treve and Co, publishers of Milan.

Thompson explained that he was not with Treve and Co, and took the opportunity to elaborate his deception still further by explaining that his name was spelt differently because it 'hailed from the South of England'.[1]

Thompson was clearly familiar with the conventions of the auction business. Within a few years he was devoting much of his time—and the largest measure of Wellcome's money—to buying lots at salesrooms, and directing a small team of agents to do the same. When Wellcome was in London, he took charge of this project himself, scrutinizing catalogues, viewing objects in advance of sales, and directing his staff personally. 'There were daily conferences when he was in England at which he personally decided the limits for bidding...Occasionally he attended sales himself.'[2] But as Wellcome was often abroad, Thompson assumed the pivotal role much of the time. Acquisitions at auction became the lifeblood of the Wellcome collection, and successfully navigating the sales demanded subtle strategizing. The ritualized etiquette of the sale room and the furious pace of the bidding meant all sorts of underhand tactics could be played out undetected by ordinary bystanders. And since many of the same dealers and collectors were on the sales circuit, rivalries and allegiances could unfold over the course of months, or even years.

Treve became a favoured name for Thompson in his efforts to disguise his professional allegiances, but his deceit cannot have lasted long. Thompson was making his presence felt amongst a close-knit group of established London dealers, and, in January 1899, they already suspected that he worked for 'Mr Wilton': 'Hal Wilton' was the name Wellcome had used at the sale of the William Morris library at Sotheby's a few weeks earlier.[3] Thompson and Wellcome had both bought lots at the Morris sale, and Quaritch and Co were intrigued by their new rivals on the salesroom floor. Quaritch's father, the German dealer Bernard Quaritch, had reigned over Sotheby's and the London book trade for fifty years. His presence had added 'zest and sparkle to the auction room', and ensured press interest at major sales, particularly during the closing decades of the nineteenth century as book collecting increased in popularity.[4] Now his son was taking over the business as heirloom sales of all kinds were becoming more frequent, fuelling the proliferation of collectors. In 1882, the Settled Land Act allowed the sale of property held in trusteeship for the first time: art, antiquities, and books that had previously been hidden away in aristocratic homes came onto the open market in greater numbers than ever before.[5] Prices increased, and collectors and dealers thronged to the salesrooms.

Although the number of public museums grew enormously during the nineteenth century,[6] the auction houses had long provided a forum for

connoisseurs to study the latest offerings on the market, and for idle specta-
tors to marvel at rare artefacts.[7] As the century progressed, the salesrooms
filtered a profusion of exotic specimens brought home by surveyors, builders,
government officials, military men, missionaries, and medics stationed overseas. The rooms of J. C. Stevens on King Street auctioned off rare birds,
insects and orchids, scientific relics, ancient mummies, Benin bronzes,
Japanese art, silks, fossils, and even lions, elephants, and giraffes during the
mid-nineteenth century. In the early 1900s, Stevens established itself as a
leading force in the trade for ethnographic specimens: 'the rooms became the
recognised clearing house of the spoils of war . . . there is practically nothing
extant that has not been brought to the hammer here, and it has been well
said that attendance in itself is a liberal education.' Wellcome was amongst
the ranks of museum collectors—including representatives from the British
Museum and other national institutions—who patronized Henry Stevens'
sales. Indeed, 'the rooms at King Street themselves are a museum, as well as
the galleries on either side, crowded as they are with the quaint, the beautiful,
and the useful'.[8]

Sotheby's presided over a rather more 'decorous' atmosphere, according to
Wellcome's friend and sometime rival at auction, William Osler,[9] but all the
auction rooms were dominated by professional dealers (Figure 11). In 1899,
old Bernard Quaritch died, at the age of 80, and was succeeded by his son,
Bernard Alfred Quaritch, who took his place at the centre of a powerful
group of book dealers, alongside the Maggs brothers, Francis Edwards,
Thomas Chatto, James Tregaskis, and Bertram Dobell. They sometimes
colluded to keep prices low, bribing other contenders when necessary or
else deliberately bidding high to 'preserve their ascendancy', and sharing the
spoils. There was 'an almost Masonic character to an arrangement by which
knowledgeable professionals, co-operating like members of a modern-day
guild, wield[ed] their trade expertise as one force against scattered, if individually more affluent, opposition'.[10]

Most private collectors, whether they were interested in art, antiquities, or
books, chose to collaborate with dealers rather than compete with them. The
Glaswegian collector, William Burrell, who, like Wellcome, began to collect
seriously during the 1890s, developed close working relationships with a
number of art and furniture dealers, among them Alexander Reid and John
Hurt, who both regularly bought things on his behalf. Burrell was not one to
surrender to pressure from a dealer; he was a canny, strong-minded collector,
who frequently sought a second opinion before buying and was not afraid to

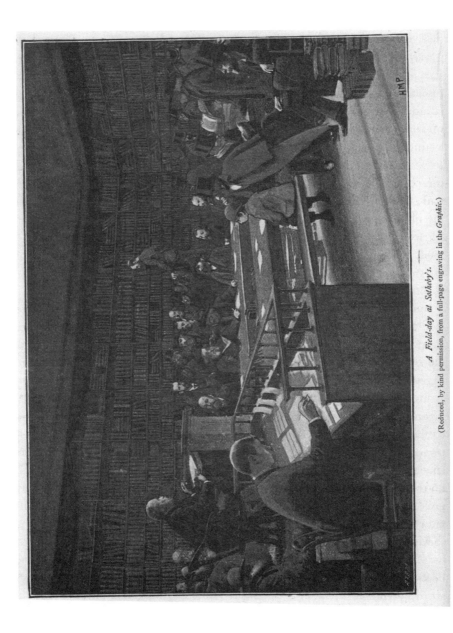

Figure 11. Engraving of a book sale at Sotheby's, *c.*1895, first published in *The Graphic*. Bernard Quaritch, with bald head and beard,

A Field-day at Sotheby's.

(Reduced, by kind permission, from a full-page engraving in the *Graphic*.)

return an object and demand his money back. Burrell only revealed his identity to a dealer once he had convinced himself of the quality of their work, but he felt a greater affinity for the commercial side of the antiquities trade than the academic world, and usually commissioned dealers to represent him at sales.[11] This strategy was not unusual, and it made sense, not least because it neutralized a potential rival at sales, but Wellcome chose not to commission dealers in the auction rooms. Dealers regularly sent Wellcome material privately, on approval, but he preferred to pit his tactical skills against them at sales.

Wellcome and Thompson adopted pseudonyms in an effort to disguise their interests from auctioneers and dealers alike: Wellcome often went by the name Wilkins or Wilton, while Thompson worked under Treve, or Epworth, his elder brother's name.[12] Meanwhile, Thompson managed a team of Burroughs Wellcome factotums—acting variously as delivery men, workmen, personal attendants, and caretakers—who bid for Wellcome in the salesrooms during the early twentieth century. They earned a few pounds a week, but ten times that amount regularly passed through their hands when they bought Wellcome antiquities. Two of Wellcome's longest serving men were Harry Stow and Henry Bourne, both of whom worked for Wellcome from the early 1900s through to their deaths in the late 1930s.[13] It was these men, and their colleagues, who packed and unloaded, and recorded and cleaned Wellcome's curiosities, week in and week out.

Using agents meant that Wellcome could buy more at more sales while protecting his anonymity. By the end of the first decade of the 1900s, members of his staff were attending several sales and negotiating numerous private transactions every week. But whenever possible, representatives were chosen who would not be recognized in the room. Wellcome was very firm on this point, warning Thompson to 'take every precaution that neither you nor the Museum shall be known as seeking for or bidding for the objects they are offering for sale. If the objects are desirable you can probably arrange for somebody to bid who wouldn't be recognized by them as associated with us.'[14] Staff were given strict instructions to disguise their identities during the negotiations for artefacts, whether they were collecting in London or further afield. Wellcome reiterated again and again in his correspondence the importance of ensuring 'the utmost discretion and secrecy' at all times. He insisted on the use of false names, advising his collectors to be scrupulously vague when questions were asked of them and warning them to be always 'on your guard'.[15]

Wellcome employed similar tactics himself. When arranging to meet a friend in London for 'a round amongst the book stalls', he added: 'If you are not too proud, may I suggest that it will be better not to wear fine raiment. I usually put on very plain clothes for such expeditions. A top hat usually excites the cupidity of the dealer, and the higher the hat the higher the price.'[16] But Wellcome's appetite undermined his stealth. Before long, everyone recognized Bourne and Stow and their co-workers, these modestly dressed but surprisingly moneyed bidders, as Wellcome's representatives. There was a patent contradiction in Wellcome's approach to collecting in this respect. He invested considerable effort in publicizing his collecting interests amongst the scientific fraternity. He despatched printed circulars giving full particulars of his aims as a collector, and requesting objects, information, and the names of people who might be interested in helping him. Meanwhile, he became obsessed with trying to hide his activities from his competitors in the trade. Not surprisingly, many of those who supported his Museum—including William Osler—occasionally found themselves competing against him at auction.[17] The worlds of commerce and scholarship came together in the salesrooms, and no creditable dealer would remain ignorant of Wellcome's interests for long. Indeed, by 1899, the book dealers were already on his trail.[18]

Nonetheless, Wellcome engineered elaborate deceptions, and some were more successful than others. In the early years Thompson wrote letters from his home address in Hampstead to disguise his affiliation with Burroughs Wellcome. Later, Wellcome leased office space in central London and Thompson began conducting business from there in the name of Epworth and Company, supposedly a rare book dealer. Barring brief visits from Burroughs Wellcome employees to pick up the latest delivery of books for the library, Epworth's Newman Street rooms remained empty most of the time. And yet the 'company' maintained such an extensive stock, buying books from all the established dealers, that its practices began to raise suspicions. One famous dealer based in Munich, Maurice Ettinghausen, sent 'case after case' to Epworth, but was 'puzzled that a firm not in the Booksellers' Directory should need such quantities of manuscripts, for which they paid considerable sums in the course of some years'. He eventually decided to investigate for himself and tracked the elusive Epworth down to Newman Street where he was perplexed to find no signs of life: 'I looked through the letter box and saw nothing but bare walls.' It was only years later, when a book that had been sent to Epworth on approval was rejected and returned to Munich wrapped in Burroughs Wellcome and Company paper, that Ettinghausen realized Epworth's true identity.[19]

Auction houses were less forgiving environments. Some of the tricks of the trade were occupational hazards. When a Brixton dealer, named Oldman, recognized one of Wellcome's men, Brookes, at Stevens, he 'suddenly started running Brookes up upon every lot on which he saw him bidding', pushing prices up and making Brookes pay more. On hearing this news, Thompson decided to 'let Oldman in pretty extensively in that last sale. I do not know whether Brookes has spoken to him or told him anything, but I shall keep Brookes out of Stevens's altogether now for some time, and so try to put Oldman off the scent.'[20] But it was the auctioneers who often had the upper hand. They would hike their prices if they knew that either an established dealer, or an acquisitive collector like Wellcome—or, even better, both— were represented at their sale. Wellcome's disguises, although strictly ob- served to the end, were usually inadequate. A common trick was to create group lots. Knowing Wellcome's interest in medical artefacts, auctioneers would put a few choice items in a lot with worthless bric-a-brac, hoping to tempt him into taking everything off their hands. On one occasion, at Stevens' rooms, Thompson noticed that,

there was again a small batch of ten lots, specially catalogued as 'An Unique Collection of Savage Medicinal Charms and Fetishes,' all to be sold together, that were got up obviously as a catch. There was nothing of special interest among them, so I only put small limits on each separate lot. When they came up, Stevens [the auctioneer] started them himself at £20, but there was no bidding and he refused to divide them up, so they were withdrawn.[21]

Thompson hoped that if he waited long enough, Henry Stevens would abandon his scheme and divide the lots: 'They will, doubtless, be put up again to be sold separately', he speculated. Auctioneers withdrew lots, while their clients might refuse to bid. As a result, some objects came up for sale again and again, playing their part in an ongoing strategic battle between auctioneer and patron, one trying to elevate prices, the other trying to keep them down.

Thompson was a skilled tactician, and his confident temperament was ideally suited to the hard-nosed tricks and back-room diplomacy that per- vaded the auction business. He probably spent more time strategizing before each sale than actually bidding from the floor. Sometimes, he could circum- vent the sale altogether by making an offer privately beforehand, while on other occasions the auctioneer gave him an option on a lot but he chose to take his chances in open competition instead. In January 1907, Wellcome and Thompson had their eyes on a relic that they simply described as a 'Mexican head with the grey hair'.[22] The Mexican head had been put up for sale before at Stevens' and Wellcome had agreed to offer up to £50 this time in order to secure it. Henry Stevens knew that Wellcome was interested and tried to clinch a deal in private, but Thompson refused to play his games:

I had not been in the room long before old Stevens pounced down upon me, and asked me if I was going to make any bid for the head. He said that the owners had considerably lowered their reserve, but if I would make an offer before the sale they would like to consider it. I told him that the highest I would give would be twenty pounds and the best thing he could do would be to put it up for competition.[23]

Thompson's strategy worked. Stevens was forced to put the head up for sale on the rostrum. Thompson sent Harry Stow to bid, but went along himself to keep an eye on proceedings.

There was a crowded room when it was offered, and Stevens delivered quite a little address and in his most impressive manner related how a genuine offer of one hundred and twenty pounds had been made for that very head at the last sale. It had been his greatest regret ever since that owing to the high reserve of one hundred and fifty guineas which had been placed upon it by the owners he had been unable to accept that offer. He trusted it would be repeated.

The bidding starting at twenty guineas, and he trotted it up to forty. An old man who I am told is a doctor in the West End bid forty-five guineas, which I believe was the first genuine bid. Then the bidding stopped, and just at the last moment, Stowe [sic], who had held back very well, made one bid only, bringing it up to fifty guineas, and after a long wait Stevens knocked it down to him.[24]

The owner's tactics had backfired, and Stow had secured the relic for a bargain price. He was even 'accosted by two well-dressed men' as he left the sale and told that if he sent the head to the Smithsonian Institution they would pay him £200 for it, almost four times the selling price. The Smithsonian's representatives had waited for the uncertainty of the bidding to finish before making their offer privately, but Wellcome would never have taken their money, and the Mexican head was destined for his storage warehouses instead.

Harry Stow was one of Wellcome's most reliable men and often his first choice for auction sales. Choosing the right man for the right sale was an important matter. Sometimes mistakes were made, and, in the fast and furious atmosphere of a sale, the results could be disastrous. Once, when Thompson arrived at Hodgson's—a well-known room for rare books on Chancery Lane—to watch one of his men, Llewellyn, in action, he was appalled to see him bidding on the wrong lot. Thompson could do nothing as Llewellyn confidently began bidding for an early Hebrew Bible that Wellcome did not want: 'I did all I could to attract his attention by signs, but he did not take the remotest notice, but went on bidding.' The mistake proved expensive: Llewellyn eventually bought the book for £54 and Thompson was incensed.

I could not conceive how he had made this serious blunder, but of course could not speak to him in the room...I had to wait until the following morning for an explanation. When I charged him with making this foolish blunder, he only replied that he could not say how it happened, but had mistaken lot 478 for lot 479 upon which I had put the large limit, and he had not found it out until afterwards. This was, as I told him, sheer stupidity, for my limit was plainly and clearly placed against lot 479, and no mark or limit was placed against lot 478 in his catalogue. I went for him very strongly over the matter, and made him realise the seriousness of his error. For the present I have suspended him from all sales...It is most annoying, and I feel as if I could not trust him again.[25]

Poor Llewellyn had to get in touch with the man he had outbid and try to persuade him to buy the book after all, for the full £54. After a great deal of negotiating the man agreed, and before long Llewellyn was back on the front lines of Wellcome's auction sales offensive, but errors of judgement or a sudden loss of nerve could have costly consequences.

Fifty pounds was a lot of money—half the amount men like Llewellyn earned in a year[26]—but Wellcome rarely spent so much on a single item. While he was quite capable of spending tens, even hundreds, of pounds on an artefact of particular historical importance, the vast majority of Wellcome's acquisitions cost a few pounds or less. He was thrilled when he could pick up a book or a relic for a couple of shillings. This set him apart from many of his peers. Some of America's collectors, men like John D. Rockefeller Jnr, Henry Clay Frick, and John Pierpont Morgan, spent thousands on the works of art that filled their homes. These men followed in a collecting tradition quite distinct from that which guided Wellcome. They patronized the fine arts market, where astonishingly high prices reflected the cultural status of the artist as well as each artwork's unique identity.

Wellcome, in complete contrast to collectors like Morgan and Frick, for whom high prices confirmed the singularity of their acquisitions, revelled in securing objects at relatively low cost. He was happiest when Thompson could report, as he often did, that acquisitions had come in well below the expected price. A typical haul from an auction included a small 'African' wooden figure for 12s, an 'African medicine stick' for 9s, a carved seated figure from the Congo for £2 10s, another figure decorated with boar's teeth for £2 2s, a parcel of books for 18s, five engravings—including one of a village doctor—for £1 6s, and a watercolour picture of an alchemist for £1 12s.[27] While Wellcome may well have spent as much on his collection as his more selective countrymen did on their famous works of art, he was interested in an artefact's history, function, and subject matter before its artistic merits. Wellcome was neither searching for aesthetic beauty nor seeking critical recognition when he collected. He was chasing something far more elusive and just as expensive: he craved ownership over an encyclopaedic vision of the past.

Wellcome wanted to chronicle everyday practices from around the world. He was interested in commonplace artefacts as well as rarer items, and he wanted one, and often more than one, of everything. This is what made him an attractive target for auctioneers and dealers, particularly those hoping to get rid of inferior goods. He spent huge amounts of money, but he spent it on huge numbers of objects. The figures speak for themselves. With the Historical Medical Exhibition approaching, Wellcome's spending escalated. By 1907, when Thompson began writing regular reports and his purchases were entered into a system of accounting ledgers, Wellcome rarely spent less than £100 a month in the auction rooms, and it was not uncommon for his expenditure to rise above £500 a month. In October 1907 alone he spent more than £1,400 in the salesrooms, buying nearly 600 different lots; the following month he spent more than £700 on around 450 lots. During the second half of 1907, a total of £3,560 was spent in the salesrooms on 1,800 lots.

And this was just the beginning. By the late 1920s, when all around him people were losing their jobs and their fortunes as the world economy collapsed, Wellcome was spending tens of thousands of pounds every year on auction sales: he spent around £25,000 in 1928 (7,549 lots); £17,600 in 1929 (5,545 lots); £35,600 in 1930 (10,483 lots); and similar amounts over the years that followed. During the last six months of 1932 alone, he spent £20,000 on sales, buying around 7,000 auction lots. On the basis of these figures, extracted from Wellcome's accounting ledgers, the average cost of a lot—which often comprised a selection of different objects, prints or books—remained remarkably constant, at between two and three pounds, but cumulatively he was investing millions in his collection.[28] No wonder if

London's auctioneers rubbed their hands with glee at the sight of one of Henry Wellcome's agents combing the salesroom floor before a sale began.

Inevitably, the result of this acquisition strategy was many thousands of very similar objects. Wellcome presided over a steady accumulation of hundreds of spatulas and spectacles, spears and swords, pharmacy vases and prehistoric flints. Each week, Thompson reported the purchase of another ancient bronze mortar or another fine oil painting called 'The Surgeon' or another 'excellent haul' of surgical instruments: Wellcome already owned 'several thousand' of the latter by early 1909.[29]

Paging through the account books and reading Thompson's reports, it is hard to avoid the conclusion that Wellcome's wealth exposed in him an astonishing lack of self-discipline. Perhaps he was someone who simply failed to curb his greed, and, worse, his greed happened to be hopelessly misdirected towards things that were often worthless. Wellcome knew that many believed it was the auctioneers and dealers who controlled his transactions, selling him mixed lots of questionable value. Later in life, he gave dubious excuses for his avarice:

If he was criticised for paying far too much for things, as he often did, he would argue that his many bargains balanced the account, and add 'if I badly need an object normally worth £5 and I need it far more than I need £10 in money it becomes worth my while to pay £10 for it'.[30]

Wellcome had put in place an acquisition system that proved hard for him to rein in, particularly as he had few financial incentives to do so, but his eagerness to secure everything available to him stemmed, at least in part, from his academic aspirations. His acquisition policy was not haphazard. He was scrupulously attentive to his own spending patterns, however extravagant they became. Every lot in every sale catalogue of interest was marked up with agreed limits and, later, prices achieved, regular meetings were held to discuss priorities and strategy, and Wellcome himself approved the vast majority of his purchases in advance.

Wellcome perceived his work as a contribution to a specific academic collecting tradition, and his buying habits can be better understood in this context. His own natural inclination was to use objects for inspiration and instruction, which is why he regularly collected things during his research into product design and advertising for Burroughs Wellcome. His investigations into the history of animal products used in medicine provided his first venture into scholarship, and the project was fashioned as a collecting

exercise, undertaken by researchers whose relationships with Wellcome set
the precedent for his later endeavours as a collector. He admired, and often
visited, the great educational museums of the late nineteenth century, with
the South Kensington Museum (forerunner to the Victoria and Albert
Museum and the Science Museum) foremost among them. He had spent
time studying the collections at the British Museum.[31] But as Wellcome later
explained, 'The nearest counterparts of my projected museum are the Pitt
Rivers Museum at Oxford, and the Horniman Museum at Forest Hill.'[32] In
these ethnographic museums a 'science of mankind' was laid out for the
visitor's edification. Wellcome particularly admired the comparative approach to collecting that had been popularized by General Augustus Henry
Lane Fox Pitt Rivers, whose anthropological collection had formed the
foundation for the Oxford museum.

General Pitt Rivers and his contemporaries worked to make anthropological collecting a scientific pursuit. Pitt Rivers' approach was a reaction
against earlier collections of curiosities designed to inspire wonder at the
world. Cabinets of curiosities provided the kind of kaleidoscope of accumulated oddities—a cherry stone carved with 80 faces, a mug of magical clay, a
horn shed by a mysterious sea monster, a cup that proved impossible to drink
from—that escaped the rational strictures of science. Now, in the later
decades of the nineteenth century, Pitt Rivers firmly advocated the collection
of common, everyday objects. If collecting was to be a scientific exercise, then
large groups of similar items must be gathered together and compared, so that
their relationships to each other could be verified. Collecting became an
exercise in classification, and objects (along with their makers) were assigned
a position in relation to their nearest counterparts. Was the design of a spear
from the Solomon Islands more similar to one from Papua New Guinea, or
Fiji, or Tonga? What about boomerangs, or baskets, or boats? Pitt Rivers
concluded that, 'without the connecting links which unite one form with
another, an ethnographical collection can be regarded in no other light than a
mere toy-shop of curiosities, and is totally unworthy of science'.[33]

What is more, this 'science of man' was inherently historical and progressive. Writers like Herbert Spencer, Edward Tylor, and John Lubbock had
adopted Darwin's theory of natural selection and endowed it with social
significance: biological *and* cultural variation were governed by natural laws;
diversity accrued over time, and, in a twist on Darwin's own writings, change
was deemed to be inherently progressive. 'The principles of variation and
natural selection have established a bond of union between the physical and

culture sciences which can never be broken', Pitt Rivers wrote. 'History is but another term for evolution . . . [and] our position with regard to culture has always been one which has forced on our comprehension the reality of progress.'[34] History, perceived as the purposeful march of time, offered a framework for charting human diversity. All cultural traditions could be fitted into a single 'evolutionary' scheme, which was, in reality, a hierarchical ladder stretching 'downwards' and 'backwards' from Victorian society to encompass people who relied on supposedly simpler technologies to survive.[35] Museums were to be the laboratories where this science of human history took shape.

Wellcome's own collection, although created decades after these ideas gained popularity, is best understood within this late Victorian philosophical milieu.[36] He had planned his Historical Medical Exhibition, in 1903, 'with the object of stimulating the study of the great past'.[37] Since then, he had collected to 'connect the links in the chain of human experience and living things which stretch back from the present time into the most remote ages of the past'.[38] He had read books by Tylor and Lubbock that described an all-inclusive science of man, unfolding from prehistoric times to the present in a great arc of progress.[39] Science validated the detail in Wellcome's collection, while history gave him his universal scope.

Wellcome had embarked on an eternal search for the 'complete' collection. It became important to gather together as many varied objects of the same general type as possible, to ensure that the resulting picture of the world was thorough. If everyday objects were a kind of historical data, then collections were giant data sets, and missing objects meant missing data, which could very well lead to faulty conclusions regarding the human past. Only when all the relevant objects were arranged under one roof would a clear vision of human history be possible. In short, applying scientific collecting methods to cultural spheres gave some credence to Wellcome's extravagant consumer habits. Years later, he explained,

I consider that so far as is practicable in dealing with the subject of ethnology, all ethnographical material should be gathered together. The more you can complete the various series of ethnographical objects, the more effectually the collections will visualise and demonstrate the characteristic features; thus you would be able to trace the evolution from A to Z in the development of any particular branch . . . The more you can get the material for demonstration concentrated and in consecutive order, the better.[40]

There is, however, an important, although subtle, difference between Wellcome's collection and other collections that strove to marshal cultural diversity for the sake of science. Wellcome brought to his collection an unusual, and, ultimately, rather debilitating, open-mindedness. Pitt Rivers had used his collection to demonstrate his theory that societies with simple material forms, like spears and blow-guns, were ancestral to societies with more complicated technologies, like cross-bows and rifles. Pitt Rivers's confidence as a narrator of the human condition imbued every aspect of his collection, which he used to illustrate his many lectures and papers on the subject. His general hypothesis was applied to a variety of different case studies. All Australian weapons, Pitt Rivers argued, could be 'traced back' to the use of a 'simple stick', and he arranged his collection of Australian weapons to demonstrate his point;[41] figurative art predated abstract designs, or so his assortment of New Ireland paddles seemed to prove;[42] simple canoes made from hollowing out tree trunks eventually gave rise to vessels made from separate planks sewn together;[43] and all this, Pitt Rivers claimed, was clear from the objects he had acquired.

Wellcome, in contrast, was almost completely silent on such theoretical matters. He certainly saw his collection as an exploration of cultural diversity that was inherently progressive, but he was less sure about the details of the historical progression. In all his years of collecting, he only published two short academic papers relating to it, one describing an Egyptian bas-relief that appeared to show a cabinet of gynaecological instruments, and the other detailing his experiences excavating in Sudan.[44] He was a man who 'preferred experiment to theory',[45] and, because of this, his approach to collecting was peculiarly democratic, in that each and every object he bought, however similar to all the others, however plain or cheap or commonplace, had something to contribute to the story he was striving to tell, quite simply because he did not yet know how to tell it. There would be—there had to be—a place for everything. Each new artefact had the potential to revise his accumulative vision of the past.

Wellcome was far more focused on completeness than on using his collection as a platform for championing his own contributions to the story of the human past, as Pitt Rivers had. He did not want to be hasty or misrepresent the great vision he was crafting for the sake of short-term recognition. Working out what it all meant could wait; the most important thing was having enough data to make working it out possible in the first place.

And so, Wellcome sent his men to the salesrooms to haul back all the medical antiquities they could find. He devised careful strategies for disguising their activities—false names, empty offices, and a studied indifference when asked—so that he might get as much material as possible for his money. And, as a result, the day-to-day rhythm of collecting became a strategic game, as Wellcome, Thompson, and their men worked to outwit the dealers and auctioneers who became the gatekeepers to Wellcome's encyclopaedic intellectual jigsaw puzzle. In practice, all the lofty theories about classification and social evolution and historical accuracy simply became a job. 'He would often suggest that his extensive purchases gave work to many people and was of more practical benefit that indiscriminate charity.'[46] Wellcome had transformed his collecting interests into a professional organization, and navigating the next string of sales was something that Wellcome's staff did to earn their money. It was part of their working routine. It was a job in which they could succeed or fail, and where success was measured in museum acquisitions. Regardless of whether it was a 'justifiable luxury', as one contemporary described it,[47] buying things became a way of life. Wellcome's staff earned their living, while Wellcome set about trying to earn, or rather buy, a place within the academic community.

The community Wellcome actually joined, at least until his Historical Medical Museum opened in 1913, was that of the antiquities trade itself. And it proved to be a community that suited him far better than the academic community he aspired to. The auctions provided a set of intense social relationships that centred on a common need to determine the value and ownership of the various objects that were put up for sale. No one who attended an auction knew what price an artefact would raise, but the ambiguity of the scenario was shared by all the participants, and it could only be resolved through a kind of 'professional togetherness'. Wellcome, Thompson, and their fellow bidders, had to compete *and* cooperate with each other, and any individual triumph came, not only from a constant monitoring of rivals, but from a respect for the power of the community as a whole. In short, the stronger the sense of an auction community, the stronger the sense of individual entitlement it generated.[48]

The auction circuit was populated by people not very different from Wellcome, and, anyway, during a sale, all grandiose motivations were forgotten in the heat of competition. Wellcome may have poured more money into the British antiquities market than any other patron of the salesrooms, but it was a world in which he belonged, where his tastes and habits made sense. His competitors at auction were collectors just like him, whether they collected things for business or for pleasure. The museum curators, traders, amateur enthusiasts, and professional academics who patronized London's salesrooms may have competed against each other most of the time, but they did so only because they shared a desire to collect, and this common desire made all their conspiracies against each other seem perfectly rational. It was their respect for each other, and for the job in hand, that made their occasional rivalries so intoxicating. For the more serious the collector was, the more elaborate the auction games he had to play. Collecting at auction was a form of gentlemanly sport, underpinned, as all good gentlemanly sports were, by perfectly earnest objectives, whether they be an appreciation for great works of art, a penchant for the curious, or an interest in recent scholarly debates.

Wellcome, despite his careful attempts to protect his anonymity, quickly became an important player in this dynamic world of competitive consumerism. His agents became familiar figures; his personal preferences were catered for and taken advantage of; his motivations went unquestioned. And no wonder, when one considers the financial consequences of his activities. Wellcome's spending habits no doubt kept many an auctioneer's family in domestic comfort. He had bought his way into a respectable position in the antiquities market. Whether he could successfully transform that same purchasing power into academic prestige remained to be seen.

CHAPTER SEVEN

FELLOW FEELING
AS A COLLECTOR

Daniel Davidson wanted his mortar back. It was an early English example, dated 1560; a heavy, straight-sided, flower-pot-shaped metal container, with relief decoration and an inscription around the rim that gave the name Philip Palmer. To the untrained eye it was a modest object. The metal pot had been used to crush and mix medicines hundreds of years ago, but it was one of the most unusual mortars that Davidson, who was himself a pharmacist, had ever acquired. And now Wellcome had it and he was refusing to return it. Sending the mortar to Wellcome in the first place had been a mistake, but Davidson had not appreciated the nature of the organization he was dealing with when he had packed up his prized collection of mortars in three large barrels filled with wood wool and despatched them to London as agreed.[1]

Davidson had first approached Wellcome seven years earlier, in 1904, as a fellow collector and connoisseur. He owned a chemist shop in the seaside town of Cromer. Along with pharmacists throughout the British Isles, he had received a circular announcing Wellcome's Historical Medical Exhibition, and, with an eye to his own reputation as much as Wellcome's, had offered some of his collection of pharmaceutical mortars on loan for the exhibition. But five years later hard times struck and Davidson was forced to contemplate selling instead: 'I have spent more than I can well afford on this hobby and with sons growing up I should be glad of the money.' Wellcome and Thompson jumped at the opportunity to buy the collection—Thompson judged the mortars to be 'an interesting lot'—and they set their considerable powers of negotiation to work on the unsuspecting chemist.[2]

Pestles and mortars were becoming collectors' items despite their functionality. Even the plainest types began appearing in sales catalogues with greater frequency during the opening years of the twentieth century, and the pharmaceutical revolution that Burroughs Wellcome and Company had participated in was partly responsible. The very same compressed medicines that had funded Wellcome's ambitions as a collector had rendered the pestle and mortar outdated. Pharmacists no longer mixed their prescriptions by hand. Instead, they discussed new orders of pills and solutions with visiting drug company representatives and received their deliveries direct from manufacturers. Wellcome's company was leading the medical innovations that opened up a place for pestles and mortars in museum display cases.[3]

Wellcome both pushed and pulled mortars into the history books. His business may have helped to propel them into medical history, but his collecting staff bought them in such great numbers that they must have increased the resale value of the humble mortar considerably. A quick count reveals more than eighty occasions when Thompson mentioned buying pestles and mortars in his reports, and more than 700 mortars were displayed when the Historical Medical Museum opened in 1913.[4] Most had been bought at auction, although a number were acquired direct from pharmacists, doctors, and their families. But, as Davidson himself modestly admitted, the eighty early English mortars he offered for sale were 'without doubt the finest collection in Great Britain either in public museums or in the hands of private collectors'.[5] The most valuable was one of the oldest known English mortars, an elegant bronze specimen, cast in 1308 by Brother William de Towthorpe for the Infirmary of Saint Mary's Abbey in York, and still 'in beautiful preservation'. The collection had, as Davidson frequently reminded Wellcome, been shown at the St. Louis World Fair in 1904. But Thompson, who mediated the situation with Davidson, was not easily impressed: 'I have found Davidson rather a flamboyant style of individual, who had a great deal to say concerning the time and money he had expended in gathering the mortars together. After being exhibited at St. Louis, he seems to think he has only got to ask a price and he is quite certain to get it.'[6]

Davidson had stated £250 to be his lowest price. Wellcome countered by offering £120. Davidson baulked. He had spent sixteen years building up his collection, he argued, and it had cost him far more than £120 to put together. However, he lowered the price to £200 on the condition that he could keep one mortar 'as a souvenir'. Wellcome increased his offer to £150 and agreed that he would be 'quite willing to hand you over one of their number as a souvenir but the selection should be left to my approval'. Davidson could not bring himself to accept £150 and promptly withdrew his mortars altogether: 'I can honestly tell you that I should not have been willing to accept £200 but for the sentiment of keeping the collection of so many years intact.'[7]

But a year later, ongoing financial difficulties forced Davidson reluctantly back to the negotiating table. 'I have had some reverses and must in consequence realize the mortars and shall be glad if you will take them at £150.' The only consolation now was the one mortar he intended to keep for himself. The Philip Palmer mortar was one of the more valuable in the collection, but Davidson proposed to retain it 'by reason of sentiment'. He was ready to pack up the other seventy-nine mortars—despite being 'possessed by a similar feeling to that experienced in delaying to go to a dentist i.e. an extreme reluctance to part with something which one has become much attached'— when he received a letter explaining that Wellcome's cheque for £150 was dependent on receipt of all eighty mortars. Davidson had not intended to send his Philip Palmer mortar, but Wellcome, who had yet to see the collection himself, claimed his right to decide exactly which mortar should be returned to Davidson. Once the collection, in its entirety, had been examined, the chosen mortar would be sent back: 'I see no reason why you should not have the mortar you describe returned to you . . . I shall do my best to meet you in the matter.'[8]

Davidson dutifully wrapped up his mortars, despatched them to London, and never saw the Philip Palmer mortar again. Thompson, who received the collection, quickly confirmed that it was one of the most valuable in the collection—'I do not think it is fair that he should have this returned to him'—and sent Davidson one of the more common specimens instead. Davidson was distressed, and wrote to Wellcome twice to complain, but to no avail. Thompson supposed that, 'Probably after some months have elapsed, he will not feel so sore with respect to this special mortar.'[9]

Davidson's early letters had been self-assured; almost pompous. He had considered himself Wellcome's equal, as a fellow collector generously offering his valuable antiquities on loan. A few years later, as he accepted a low price for his collection and failed to retain the one mortar he felt most strongly about, his letters became submissive. 'I venture to make one more request [for the Palmer mortar] appealing both to your generosity and fellow feeling as a collector. I wish to say however that if you do not consider the collection is worth what you paid for it without your retaining this particular mortar I should not wish it to be returned, much as I desire it.'[10] Davidson did not know what kind of collector Wellcome had become. He had assumed he was corresponding, gentleman to gentleman, with a collector like himself; an amateur who engaged his interest in medical history in his free time according to his means. In fact, Thompson was now running Wellcome's collection like a well-oiled acquisition machine.

Davidson had thought he was corresponding directly with 'Mr Wellcome', but most of the letters he received had been written by Thompson, on Wellcome's behalf and in his name. Davidson was actually negotiating with a different man entirely. Some of Thompson's drafts were marked 'Mr Wellcome's paper' at the top, reminding his secretary to maintain the deceit. Thompson, who went to Cromer to inspect the collection as a 'representative' of Wellcome's, did not reveal how crucial he was to the ongoing negotiations, so Davidson merely showed him the mortars without trying to pin him down to a price.[11] Thompson was not the only one to inspect Davidson's collection under false pretences. In October 1910, Mr Macvie Hill, the Burroughs Wellcome and Company representative responsible for sales in Norfolk, was asked to check on the collection during a business trip to Davidson's pharmacy. 'We do not wish to ask Mr Davidson any questions in regard to these mortars,' his instructions read, 'but merely to let us know if you saw the collection about and also if Mr Davidson is at home.' Macvie Hill filed a positive report in response: 'No mention of mortars was made during my interview with Mr Davidson. I have however inspected his collection at various times and satisfied myself that they were there on Friday last.'[12]

Davidson was being duped and he was being watched. The deceptions that characterized trade in the auction rooms also had their place in private negotiations for antiquities. Thompson kept Wellcome fully informed, but for much of the time, particularly during the final months of the negotiations, Wellcome was not even in the country. Thompson managed the entire project:

I wrote to him in your name stating that as you had not seen them you would prefer that the whole of the eighty mortars were sent on, as it was only fair to you that you should see them before any selection was made, and that you thought the selection should be left to you, as you originally stipulated.

It was Thompson who refused to return the Palmer mortar and chose another instead, and Thompson who fended off Davidson's protests in Wellcome's name. Meanwhile, Wellcome's contributions from abroad amounted to a couple of approving comments written in the margins of progress reports: 'Very good'; 'You did quite right.'[13]

Thompson often negotiated private sales with fellow collectors on Wellcome's behalf. It could take great patience and perseverance to persuade a collector to part with his or her valuable possessions for a good price. Negotiations sometimes stretched out for months, or even years. But there were various benefits to this diplomatic approach to acquisition, even though it took time. Cutting out the dealer meant that collections could be acquired more cheaply, and buying a group of objects *en masse* was far more efficient than pursuing items individually. The advantage of a private collection was that someone else had done all the hard work of tracking the objects down and gathering them together. Private collections, particularly the more specialized ones, were often of a very high quality; they contained little of the dross that surfaced from mixed lots at auction. And Thompson frequently benefited from a collector's financial distress: many he met, like Davidson, had been forced to consider selling their collections because of straightened circumstances. He was also quick to take advantage of their *naïveté* when it came to the antiquities market: Thompson was adept at persuading people that their possessions were worth far less than they had first imagined.

Much of the business was transacted by letter, and Thompson's meetings with other collectors were reported to Wellcome while he was away. What emerges from this paper trail is a sense of the wider collecting community that Wellcome and Thompson had begun to operate within. People of all backgrounds found themselves selling objects to Wellcome over the years: pub landlords, army majors, doctors' daughters, sailors' sons, businessmen, and widows. Private collections were dragged from dusty attics and laid out on dining room tables for Thompson and his staff to assess. Many of the people who sold artefacts to Wellcome made no mark on the intellectual history of the late nineteenth and early twentieth century. They were members of ordinary, middle class families who had acquired or inherited small collections of objects during the course of their unremarkable lives. Men like Daniel Davidson might well have slipped from the historical record entirely had it not been for their communications with Henry Wellcome about objects.

Although Wellcome had arranged his private collection in his home in 1881 to emphasize his gentlemanly credentials, collecting as a hobby was by no means limited to the wealthy elite. Children's magazines encouraged their readers to explore hedgerows and parks for natural history specimens, since it was a healthy, cheap, and educational form of amusement. Even young Londoners could indulge their scientific interests not far from home: in 1882 the *Boys Own Paper* suggested Chingford, Finchley, Hampstead, Highgate, and along the banks of the Thames from Putney east to Northfleet and Gravesend as good 'hunting-grounds' for budding entomologists. Those children who followed the magazine's advice would never regret 'the day when they passed from the ranks of mere collectors into those of entomologists in the true sense of the word, and learned to study for themselves some of the manifold wonders of the world we live in'.[14] Many did so, and natural history collecting was popular amongst adults for all the same reasons. It promised outdoor exercise and intellectual rigour at very little cost. Local ramblers clubs and natural history societies organized expeditions, and the 'arsenal of collecting equipment' that accompanied amateur geologists, botanists, and zoologists into the field was cheap to buy, as were the various pocket manuals on sale in the shops.[15]

Meanwhile, household guides encouraged people to incorporate a few 'curiosities' into their homes. Robert Edis, in his *Decoration and Furniture of Town Houses*, explained that he had 'an arrangement of cupboards and shelves which I have designed for guns, fishing rods, swords and china, cigars tobacco, and pipes in my own library' which was made for him by 'an ordinary builder'.[16] And while, 'it was generally expected that well-to-do travellers would return from trips abroad with their luggage swollen by new treasures',[17] even those who could only afford to take the train to Bournemouth or Brighton might pick up an unusual shell or stone to display alongside the family silver. Since the nineteen-acre spread at the Great Exhibition in 1851, temporary exhibitions of 'arts and industries' had become increasingly popular in all regions of the country: thousands visited their local shows, and millions were thrilled by the exotic curiosities and technological wonders at the larger international exhibitions.[18] Meanwhile, those who patronized the burgeoning ranks of Britain's museums—100 had been founded during the first 70 years of the century[19]—were urged to 'Make a private collection of *something*. Remember that a collection of postage stamps has many uses.'[20]

The first few years of the twentieth century saw the publication of new magazines, like *The Connoisseur* and the *Burlington Magazine*, entirely devoted to collectors' interests, and many of the general weeklies offered their readers regular features on collecting. *The Queen* published its articles as a book, called *The Collector*. The first two volumes appeared in 1905, and the third in 1907, and they were, 'intended primarily for an interchange of ideas amongst those with small collections'.[21] Meanwhile, *The Bazaar, Exchange and Mart*—a weekly 'journal through which to buy, sell, or exchange anything; to get a place, to obtain a servant etc.'—had been putting collectors in touch with each other since the late 1860s. Thompson regularly advertised his requirements here, and received useful offers in response; while the 'country papers', as Thompson called them, also advertised collectables for sale.[22]

Wellcome, although more wealthy than most, was a member of this collecting community; he competed within it and took advantage of it whenever he could. His collection became a vast collection of collections, absorbing the time and energy countless others had devoted to gathering unusual artefacts. It was usually Thompson who met these modest collectors, and his work took him across the country and into a whole range of homes and workplaces. He mentioned in one report, 'an old lady at Littlehampton', whose father had been a doctor and who still had some of the medical antiquities he had owned, including a seventeenth-century book on astrology, a set of old sight-testing glasses, and some early-nineteenth-century diplomas. Thompson offered her a few pounds for her father's things: 'She agreed to accept this but had to obtain permission from her brother before forwarding them.'[23] Years later he went to Bristol to visit 'a little low-class public house down near the quays among the worst slums' in the city, to buy a large 'juju' figure—a wooden carving believed to have supernatural powers—from the Congo. In a room above the bar he was amazed to find 'a most extraordinary collection of ethnological items from various parts of Africa, laid out like a museum. Weapons and other objects were in beautiful condition and laid out on benches, and I was simply amazed to find such a collection there.' It emerged that the pub's proprietor, Mr Iles, had travelled a great deal in the Congo and Nigeria collecting for himself, and had also inherited a valuable collection of weapons bought by his father from the sailors docking in Bristol over the years. Thompson bought the Congolese figure and a number of other objects from Mr Iles, including some Indian, Chinese, and Afghan guns, for what he thought were 'absurdly low prices'.[24]

Thompson most often dealt with medics and their families. Georges Marie Felizet was a typical example of a doctor who had spent his spare time collecting scientific relics. In 1909, when Felizet died, Thompson travelled to Paris to inspect his collection. Felizet had been an expert in children's surgery; Thompson remembered him as 'a very nice fellow, [who] offered to come over to London to give us the benefit of his experience when we were arranging the Exhibition'. Now Madame Felizet was considering selling her husband's collection. He had left behind, at the family's country house, an assortment of medical paraphernalia: pewter bowls and basins, surgical equipment, an 'ancient trepanning instrument', scales, dissecting knives, books, a tobacconist's sign, a stained glass window depicting old surgical instruments. Madame Felizet brought all her husband's things to Paris for Thompson to see. He found them, 'far more numerous and interesting than I expected and they were well worth going for' but seeing that she was 'quite willing to take any reasonable sum', he offered her only 243 francs for the lot, admitting to Wellcome that this 'was about as little as I could offer. At a dealer's price these things are really worth about three times that amount.' Madame Felizet accepted his offer and Thompson shipped his acquisitions back to London.[25]

Collecting may have been a common hobby, but some of the enthusiasts Thompson met were rather eccentric. Soon after the deal was settled with Davidson, Thompson began talks with another collector, 'very curious character, a type of cunning Dane', who spoke in broken English.[26] Mikael Pedersen was an engineer and inventor who had made his fortune designing a new kind of centrifuge for churning milk, and had gone on to create the Dursley-Pedersen bicycle in the 1890s, an elongated but elegant contraption, with a suspended woven seat, that was lighter and more stable than existing bicycle models. Pedersen lived in the country town of Dursley, in Gloucestershire, 'in a large old-fashioned Georgian mansion in the main street', which he had furnished with an array of interesting objects he had gathered together during the course of his life:

I came into a large room full of carved furniture with a huge crystal chandelier hanging from the ceiling, and with swords and other weaponry covering all the walls. There were musical instruments all over the place, and all kinds of strange things, machines, and models of inventions hidden behind all the furniture. Then this remarkable, wily Dane entered the room, a tall dark man with a mop of hair and full beard.[27]

Wellcome, who, like Thompson, had a tendency to litter his prose with pejorative adjectives when discussing foreigners, thought Pedersen 'very crafty' and insisted he would need 'careful handling'.[28] Words like 'cunning', 'crafty', and 'wily' revealed an innate ethnocentrism, added to the drama of negotiations, and, no doubt, increased the satisfaction that came from outwitting these supposedly shrewd dealers. Pedersen, for one, was not as crafty as he seemed.

Thompson had arrived to look at one particular group of Pedersen's belongings: a collection of memorabilia relating to Edward Jenner. Wellcome had first seen the collection in 1896, at an exhibition in Cardiff to mark the centenary of Jenner's discovery of the smallpox vaccine. He had tried to buy it then, from the owner, Frederick Mockler, but was refused.[29] Mockler, a bank manager, later fell on hard times and sold the collection to his friend Pedersen for £450 to alleviate his 'immediate pressing necessities'. Pedersen had little interest in the Jenner material himself, but he knew that, sold to the right person, it could raise him a lot of money. He had even added a few choice pieces to the collection in the hopes of increasing its value.[30]

The collection included many of Jenner's belongings—his surgical instruments, a snuff box, some medals, a medicine chest, his visiting books, diplomas and letters, and paintings, even the armchair in which he had died (Figure 12)—and Pedersen was asking £1,000 for the lot.[31] He was reluctant to reduce his price, so Thompson, who visited Pedersen in January 1911, persuaded him to divide the collection and take a smaller price for a

Figure 12. The Mockler collection of Jennerianna, including Edward Jenner's armchair. This photograph probably shows the room in Pedersen's house, 'which he uses as a kind of museum', where he laid the collection out for Thompson to examine.

portion of the things. It was a clever move, because Thompson promptly took control of the negotiations, deciding exactly which objects he would take and which he would leave behind, and recommending a revised price as a result.

[T]o facilitate matters we went through the catalogue and I ticked off all the items that I thought most desirable for us. These included the whole of the portraits and oil paintings, original drawings, miniatures on ivory and all the objects of interest and relics connected with Jenner, all his diplomas and certificates, and the whole of his autograph letters.[32]

Thompson retained everything of value and interest. He left out only printed books, which could be bought elsewhere, the minute books of the Jennerian Society, a single manuscript written by Jenner, and an auctioneer's inventory. For the sake of these insignificant sacrifices Thompson managed to reduce the price by half, to £500. It was a good result, especially as Thompson intended to negotiate for the remaining items separately at a later date. 'I think, therefore,' he wrote to Wellcome, 'you will see that we have got the best of the bargain.'[33] Pedersen realized that he had been conned. When Thompson and Bourne arrived in Dursley in March to take away their purchases, the Dane was regretting his decision.

Pedersen seemed very reluctant to part with them when I got there, and I think had it not been that I had his contract for sale, and his receipt for the deposit paid, he would have tried to back out. But in the end he behaved very fairly, and handed me over all the objects and documents separately, and allowed us to do the packing at his house.[34]

Thompson valued the remaining Jenner items at £60, but Pedersen said he would accept nothing less than £500 for the rest of the collection. So Thompson left him clinging hopelessly to his original asking price, as the core of the collection was transported back to London for Wellcome to inspect.

Thompson was a brilliant negotiator. He was cool and confident. He enjoyed auction sales, strategizing and competing for the latest prizes on the market, but he also relished the opportunity to play mind games with the private collectors and agents he dealt with personally. He rarely flinched. He took his time and stuck to his price, however incredulous his counterparts were at the paucity of his opening offer, and however much they threatened to find a buyer elsewhere. 'I have found,' he wrote to a colleague, 'although they go away, they generally come back, and you get the object in the end.'[35] He was a master of his art, and knew how to force a price down. By the 1910s,

Wellcome was spending considerable sums on private collections, but Thompson did not seem to be at all worried by the large amounts of money he dealt with. And even when Wellcome anxiously encouraged him to offer more, for fear of losing a valuable addition to the collection, Thompson held his ground, and rarely failed to meet his objectives.

One of Thompson's greatest triumphs came in 1910, when he seized the opportunity to buy a famous collection that had interested Wellcome for years. The Oppenheimer Collection of Italian antiquities had been assembled in the early 1890s by Louis Sambon, the Italian medic and lecturer at the London School of Tropical Medicine who later came to work for Wellcome as a collector. It had been exhibited at the British Medical Association's annual meeting in 1895, and then at the International Medical Congress the following year, and attracted considerable attention.[36] It included hundreds of rare Roman surgical instruments and miscellaneous curiosities, but chief among its attractions was a group of ancient terracotta votive offerings, many hundreds of them, that Sambon had collected from Roman and Etruscan temples and tombs. Sambon had been the first to realize that the little models represented parts of the body, and not pieces of fruit, as had previously been assumed. He claimed that they were not, as other archaeologists had argued, household ornaments or statuettes used in funeral rites, but offerings made to the gods for relief from disease and deformities.[37] These objects were rare, and Sambon later said that he had never found such high-quality examples again.[38]

When Sambon started to work for Wellcome, he was asked to meet with Oppenheimer and find out what he proposed to do with his collection, but nothing came of this approach.[39] Six years later, in 1910, a representative from Oppenheimer, Son and Company, named Mr Pearmund, contacted Thompson to see whether he was interested in buying. The ensuing negotiations were coloured with as much intrigue as any auction sale. Oppenheimer had apparently targeted Wellcome for the sale. It was surely no coincidence that Pearmund had previously worked in the advertising department at Burroughs Wellcome and Company, but he professed not to know who Thompson was, and told him in conversation that Oppenheimer's would never consent to the collection being sold to the firm of Burroughs Wellcome. Pearmund was, he claimed, hoping to reach a private agreement with Thompson, but Thompson could see right through the pretence: 'The mystery that they made of it was so clumsy as to be absolutely ludicrous.' For one thing, there was no way Thompson could have afforded the collection for himself, even if he had wanted it. Pearmund was quick to report that Cambridge University had offered £2,000 for it a few years earlier, but now the asking price was £1,000.[40]

Thompson engaged all his negotiating skills to secure the Oppenheimer collection. He managed to dissuade Pearmund from employing an independent expert to value the collection, and he fabricated an impending trip out of London to disguise his impatience to see it. Meanwhile, he met with Sambon, who told him the whole history of the collection, gave him a full catalogue of the objects it had originally comprised when Oppenheimer bought it, and briefed him as to its value. On arrival at Oppenheimer's, Thompson was taken to 'a large room where they had the collection of terra cotta votive offerings stored in large chests, and the bronze and other objects in the glass cases I should judge in which they were exhibited seventeen years ago, covered thickly with dust'. The collection had hardly been touched since its exhibition at the International Congress of Medicine, and only a handful of unimportant items were missing. Thompson disguised his interest carefully, remarking that 'a very large proportion of the terra cottas were simply plaster casts that could be got for a few shillings without any difficulty in Italy'.

Thompson knew the Oppenheimer collection was worth considerably more than £500, and the asking price was twice that amount. Still, his own 'liberal' offer came in at just £350. In a calculated attempt to close the deal quickly, he added that he, 'could not allow this offer to remain open for long as I should probably be leaving London and if anything was to come of it they must come to a definite conclusion'. His prevarication worked: a counter offer of £500 was quickly dropped to £400, and a deal was finally struck at £375. Thompson had pulled off a major coup. The collection numbered more than 1,200 objects of considerable value. Perhaps the staff at Oppenheimer's recognized in Wellcome their best hope for a sale. The collection had been gathering dust for years and they wanted rid of it; Thompson thought they might be in financial straits:

It is a very curious thing that after all these years of stalking this collection, it should come about this way, and I should judge from all appearances that the firm in question are wanting money, and although I betrayed no anxiety to obtain it, I think the urgent card was the best to play in the matter, and do not think we should have got it for less.

Thanks to Thompson's ruthlessness, by 1910, Wellcome was regularly acquiring other people's private collections. With Thompson and his men attending auction sales, touring European towns, and visiting collectors in their homes, Wellcome had become the director of his own collecting organization, and it was an organization run with businesslike efficiency, with profits counted in artefacts, pictures, and books, rather than pounds, shillings, and pence. Unbeknownst to fellow collectors like Daniel Davidson, Wellcome did little more than guide this activity, often with a few encouraging annotations to Thompson's weekly reports. Nevertheless, Wellcome continued to think of his work as a personal project. He saw himself as a private collector, one among many, but one who had decided to employ other people to achieve his aims. And in some ways, Wellcome's collection retained its personal character.

It is interesting that despite Thompson's growing staff and influence, over the years Wellcome's collection remained closely associated with his home life. Of course, his artefacts and books furnished his private lodgings, but once the collection was housed in its own premises in London Wellcome lent items of furniture for special events there,[41] so that the style of the Museum reflected his personal taste. In later years, the Museum's reception areas sported Queen Anne settees and armchairs, an Elizabethan-style oak dining table, Persian and Turkish rugs, elbow chairs in mahogany or walnut, a Florentine velvet and damask wall hanging, and an old English mahogany suite of settee and chairs in the gothic style. A miscellany of furniture filled the rooms and hallways, charting Wellcome's personal taste, his travels, and his years as a patron of the London salesrooms.[42] Many of his 'private' things—chairs, tables, china and silver, pictures and books—were stored for years alongside his museum acquisitions, and it was hard to draw any clear line between them. Objects were occasionally moved from his house to his museum or back again. But perhaps the plainest indication of a lasting link between his home and his museum is found in the special status granted to some of his employees.

Wellcome's domestic life and his professional life overlapped in numerous ways, and since it was his museum staff who dealt with his belongings and maintained many of his London premises for storage purposes, they were called upon most frequently to answer his personal needs. Harry Stow, who devoted so much of his life to the collection, was remembered as Wellcome's 'right-hand man when he was in London', buying his shirts, shaving brushes, and shoes, as well as bringing him the latest auction catalogues and updating him on recent sales. Henry Bourne also ran errands for Wellcome, although his duties were often confined to the office, sorting and distributing the mail.[43] Both men, and later their manager, Harry Port, who became head of the Museum stores, regularly worked in Wellcome's home, which, from 1920, was at 6 Gloucester Gate, in Regent's Park. They dealt with routine maintenance at the house: patching a leaky roof, sorting out the electrical fittings, or fixing a faulty kitchen range that had interrupted the hot water supply. Vans drove between Gloucester Gate, the Museum, and the stores, transferring objects, paperwork, and people, and answering Wellcome's daily needs when necessary.[44]

In later years, Wellcome's Museum staff even took responsibility for the care of his beloved pet cats. In the 1930s, Peter Johnston-Saint, who became the most senior of Wellcome's collecting staff, gave detailed instructions for the care of the cats while Wellcome was abroad. Apparently they were London's luckiest felines: Saint noted that they were accustomed to eating cooked beef, ox and lamb liver and kidney, boiled hake and cod, salmon and sardines, cooked vegetables 'with a little gravy', and, occasionally, a little raw beef 'if it is finely cut up'. They were not, however, allowed to eat small lamb or chicken bones, pork, pork liver or kidney, and they 'must not be given potatoes'. Furthermore, their food 'MUST NOT be purchased from a "cats meat" butcher; but is to be purchased from good reliable shops'.[45] When Zipper the kitten died from feline influenza on 16 August 1935, it fell to Saint to break the news to Wellcome. A postmortem was conducted to confirm the cause of Zipper's death, and Wellcome's Physiological Research Laboratories provided a vaccine which was immediately administered to the other cats at Gloucester Gate. Saint reassured Wellcome that 'the floors, cat bedding, and baskets which were used by the kitten are being disinfected,' and he thoughtfully sent, along with a full report by Wellcome's housekeeper, two press cuttings that described the recent outbreak of cat influenza across the country.[46]

By the 1930s, Wellcome's home had become an administrative addendum to his Museum. His collection had begun at home—in 1894 he had written to his mother of his desire to find 'suitable apartments' where he could have his 'books and things about me'[47]—but towards the end of his life he seemed to eschew domesticity and entrust his home and its contents to his Museum employees, preferring to live in hotels. His 'books and things' had long outgrown his living quarters, but despite the scale of the institution he had created, key members of his collecting staff, like Stow and Thompson and Saint, always acted as Wellcome's personal assistants. His collection permeated, and bound together, his public persona and his private aspirations. But it could be an uneasy union. How private could his collection be when it was created by a diverse group of employees? As Wellcome relied increasingly on other people to collect things for him in the early 1900s, he had to find ways to assert his authority over his staff. He felt he needed to remind them exactly whose goals they were working towards—to show that he, too, like Davidson and Pedersen, was a private collector first and foremost—but his approach to this problem caused tensions, most noticeably amongst the specialist collecting agents he employed to travel and collect for him abroad.

CHAPTER EIGHT

THE WHOLE OF INDIA SHOULD BE RANSACKED

Wellcome had begun his career, in the 1870s, as a travelling representative in the pharmaceuticals trade. He explored the American continent, from Canada to Peru, picking up artefacts of interest and souvenirs along the way, and travel became part of his identity. In the summer of 1879 he had spent some weeks researching the production of cinchona bark in central Ecuador, trekking into the mountainous forests on mules (Figure 13), and, when the terrain became too dangerous, on foot, accompanied by local *cascarilleros* (bark hunters) and a convoy of carriers. The sheer cliff faces and narrow trails through the vegetation made for slow progress, and the chasms below were littered with the skeletons of *cascarilleros* who had stumbled under the weight of the 150-pound bark bales on their backs.[1] Wellcome's own journey was not without incident. While travelling on horseback along the Guayllabamba River in northern Ecuador, apparently alone, he was injured in a landslide. He was already suffering from malaria, but he managed to reach a nearby village where he 'collapsed', and the villagers spent a week nursing him back to strength.[2]

After years as an itinerant, Wellcome found it difficult to adjust to a more sedentary lifestyle when he first moved to London. He explained to his mother that 'having travelled so much it is irksome to remain in one place'.[3] He identified with other adventurers, both socially and professionally. He made friends with famous explorers, like Henry Stanley and May French Sheldon, and Burroughs Wellcome quickly cornered the market in tropical medicines and first aid equipment. The firm's products were

Figure 13. Henry Wellcome, on the left, and J. Bazi, his guide and interpreter, during his journey through Central America in 1879.

endorsed by both Stanley and Sheldon, and were promoted as invaluable additions to any expedition abroad. But while Wellcome mingled with, provided for, and profited from those who frequented the outer edges of the navigable world, he had comparatively little time for his own travels while he established the business in London.

Wellcome's first two decades in London were punctuated by an occasional short holiday to mainland Europe and a handful of longer visits to the United States, at least one of which, in 1886, was advised on account of his deteriorating health due to overwork.[4] But by the end of the century Wellcome's travel schedule had begun to dominate his life again. A caricature in *The Chemist and Druggist* in 1900 depicted him as an exotic bird, rarely sighted in London, because it 'prefers the warmer climate of the Canaries. In fact, if it stays in England late on into the year, a beautiful ruffle appears around its neck.'[5] Wellcome had taken to wintering in Madeira, on account of his health, and that year saw the first of his many expeditions to Egypt and Sudan. During the early 1900s, Wellcome distanced himself from the day-to-day running of

Burroughs Wellcome and Company and began to indulge in his love for travel, a pleasure enhanced by the advent of the motor car.[6]

Wellcome enjoyed touring by car (Figure 14). He had explored Europe by automobile many times before Henry Ford's Model-T production line made cars a familiar sight after the First World War. In the early years, he had 'a very fine Daimler motorcar' adapted to his personal requirements. It was fitted with a special gear 'for crossing small rivers out in the wilds, where bridges were non existent'.[7] A special wooden platform, a 'motor car conveyor', and box was designed to secure it on the decks for sailing to the Continent; barges and cranes helped manoeuvre it to shore; on occasion a team of men had to push the boxed car, weighing 3.5 tons, the final distance to the customs house 'baggage department' for inspection. Cars were an unusual sight at the docks, and organizing the paperwork, permits, and payments could take hours, although Wellcome found that handing out cigarettes to the officials could speed up the process.[8]

Early motor enthusiasts were often thwarted by mechanical problems. They spent as many hours scratching their heads over a failed engine as they did manoeuvring their horseless carriages across the open countryside. The art critic Sir Martin Conway remembered a collecting trip he had taken through the south of France in 1903 when 'motor-cars were not the safe and sound means of locomotion they are now supposed to be'. Conway's excursion was regularly postponed by burst tyres, engine problems, and, on one occasion, a collision with a cow, which did not bother the cow in the slightest, but from which the car never quite recovered.[9] Wellcome's diary for one of his motor tours in Portugal and Spain in 1908 is a catalogue of transportation challenges. In towns, the car struggled over the 'polished' stone paving and steep, cobbled streets, but on rural roads the holes and bumps made Wellcome 'tremble for the springs'. The experience for the passengers—usually Syrie, sometimes accompanied by friends, her maid, or an interpreter—was hardly relaxing. 'The road was bad, I have no words to express its badness', Wellcome wrote of their drive from Lisbon to Leiria in May 1908.

Holes a foot deep or more, ridges a foot high, yard after yard, mile after mile. To make matters worse the road was too slippery to avoid them. So on we went up stairs, down stairs, slithering in the greasiest of grease, dropping one wheel into a hole while the other climbed a ridge and then dropped off side ways into another hole. Bumping all the time, braking to ease the bumps, deceived by holes filled up with earth which no more supported the car than water would—Such was our progress,

Figure 14. Henry Wellcome, wearing a flat cap, with friends, during a motor tour of Kent, outside the Swan Hotel, Appledore, in 1906.

2nd speed most of the time, 1st sometimes, 3rd occasionally, top very rarely. I don't think I shall ever meet a worse road, speed was out of the question, it was all I could do to get the car safely along the road.

Big bumps threatened to tip the car altogether. Pigs, bullock carts, mules, and donkeys along the way slowed progress; maps were often inaccurate and misleading; the car became a target for village boys throwing stones; and avoiding dogs could be 'very treacherous work'.

Every day before setting out Wellcome had to wash his car, check the engine, and replace and grease any problem parts (usually with a crowd of admiring locals standing around to watch). In wet weather he fitted non-skid tyres, but nonetheless the car had a tendency to slide across the flooded, muddy roads. During one particularly wet spell they spun round full circle on a bridge; the next day, they ended up in a wall. Luckily nothing was damaged, but a team of villagers and their oxen had to be commandeered to pull the motor out of the mud in the driving rain. If it rained hard there was nothing for it but to seek shelter under the nearest bridge or tree and wait it out under an umbrella. The Wellcomes knew what it felt like to arrive at their hotel soaked to the skin. But sunny weather brought its own problems because the car's radiator would over-heat and had to be regularly refilled.[10]

At each stop, Wellcome fired cables to London requesting more tools, spare parts, additional tyres, and inner tubes. His diary only records a few weeks during a journey in 1908, but an employee remembered that at least one of the Wellcomes' motor tours ended in complete mechanical failure. 'Unfortunately, the aluminium crankcase cracked badly under the strain and spoilt the tour [through Spain and Portugal], and [the Daimler] had to be towed for many miles. The car was eventually taken back by the makers.'[11] In later years, Wellcome became a devotee of Reno cars, even though they became 'hopelessly out of date and caused a good deal of derision from taxi and bus drivers in London, especially when they would suddenly stop in the middle of a stream of traffic and have to be started up by the handle'. He continued to have his cars customized, and they were 'fitted up inside with all sorts of gadgets' so that he could work while being driven from place to place.[12]

From 1907 onwards, Wellcome was often abroad, motoring through Europe, visiting friends and colleagues in America, or exploring North Africa. Initially, he maintained a massive, and meticulous, correspondence with his staff. In five months during the winter of 1907–8, he wrote 502 letters, not including cables and private correspondence.[13] Meanwhile, his leisure time was spent searching the shops, museums, and book stalls, and sending crates of purchases, lined with wool and wood chips, back to Thompson in London. The thought of finding interesting objects at cheap prices in out-of-the-way places inspired much of Wellcome's travel. Collecting tours to the Continent were a relatively common occupation for the wealthy at the time. A friend who travelled with the Glaswegian collector William Burrell in the early 1900s remembered: 'When we arrived at our hotel the first thing that Willie Burrell did was to ask the hotel porter to make up a list with the names and addresses of every antique shop in the town. When this was completed we ordered a cab and went round all the dealers.'[14]

Wellcome's goals were similar to Burrell's—both men were on the lookout for good value antiquities—but his tactics were slightly different. He tried to keep his identity a secret from the locals and often visited less salubrious establishments while shopping. He told Thompson,

Pawn shops Blacksmith shops and rag and bone dealers are amongst the most likely to yield results. The roughest places are often the best—but they require patience... I find it best to always make a rapid survey of a town and incite the people to hunt out things and always give an earlier date for departure than I intend or they will put off until the last minute and be too late.[15]

He trawled bookshops, junk shops, and antique shops, and found 'a number of curio shops in private houses [but] a good guide is necessary to root them out'.[16] Touring in a motor car bestowed the collecting venture with a new sense of spontaneity, and brought distant villages out of isolation. While motoring, Wellcome could be the master of his own consumer fantasies writ large across the European countryside. Little wonder if his young wife and travelling companion, Syrie, found her husband's tenacity wearisome at times.

Wellcome's collecting assistants were also touring around Europe by this time, looking for bargains on his behalf, although Charles Thompson and Louis Sambon usually travelled by train. Thompson had begun regular trips to Paris in 1904, and during the years that followed he occasionally travelled to Switzerland, Holland, Italy, Spain, and Portugal looking for old books and medical paraphernalia. It was in the same year that Wellcome reached an agreement with Louis Sambon, who agreed to collect historical information and artefacts for Wellcome on the Continent. But if Wellcome was willing to subcontract his collecting work, the terms on which he did so were strict. Many of his collectors found it difficult to meet his demands. Friedrich

Hoffmann, who had been hired to research Wellcome's 'Animal Substances' book in the 1890s, was the first to find his regulations stultifying.

From his home in Berlin, Hoffmann had agreed to investigate the history of animal products used in Germany, but his professional relationship with Wellcome did not run smoothly and Hoffmann's difficulties presaged those of later collecting agents. Wellcome offered Hoffmann payment in exchange for monthly progress reports, but Hoffmann felt it was unreasonable to expect open-ended research to accrue consistently each month. 'One does not work according to measure and time', he told Frederick Power, a mutual friend. 'Mr Wellcome does not approach the matter in the right manner.' Hoffmann wanted a block payment, up front, which would give him the flexibility to fulfil Wellcome's requirements over a longer period, and allow him to employ assistants should he need to. He felt that Power, who was a scholar rather than a businessman, would understand his point of view.

You can better explain to him [Wellcome], after his return, the impossibility of complying with his requirements as to prices and statement of time for historical work. The material, and especially the amount of literary matter to be examined, is also very considerable, so that the total amount of time for the work cannot be determined in advance. If Mr Wellcome wishes to engage collaborators here he must have confidence, and for the purpose of assuring these collaborators as also for the covering of unavoidable expenses of travelling etc. he must place at our disposition a minimum or maximum sum at one of the Banks here (Leipzig) or otherwise at our disposition.[17]

Wellcome had approached Hoffmann's research project as he might a new business venture. He wanted quantifiable results, ideally lists of references, a steady accumulation of relevant facts, and regular updates on interesting manuscripts, illustrations, and books consulted. When this information was received, Hoffmann would be given his month's payment. Hoffmann maintained that historical work did not unfold so predictably each week: 'such work which, for the most part extends late into the night, cannot be measured according to time and number of pages.'[18]

Hoffmann concluded that Wellcome did not trust him enough to give him payment in advance. Establishing a monthly exchange of information for money allowed Wellcome to control a research project he had contracted out. As with all the other aspects of his pharmaceuticals business, he monitored progress meticulously, checking every addition and alteration as it was made. Facts and figures were rewarded appropriately, but money was not forthcoming in advance. Salaries, and good professional relations, were offered in return for regular progress reports from his staff.

Hoffmann's grievances regarding report writing and payment schedules in the late 1890s can be seen as a clash of intellectual cultures, between the scholar who believed that historical research should be truly collaborative and qualitatively judged, and the businessman who required accountability and quantitative results. Hoffmann expected to steer his research independently before consulting with his patron, but Wellcome saw his staff as facilitators, and believed that he could accrue historical information a little like merchandise: ideas could be gathered together, forwarded on, and transferred unambiguously between colleagues, at a reasonable price.

Hoffmann was the first in a long line of researchers and collectors who were expected to write Wellcome regular statements detailing their achievements. Years later, when the rhythm of report writing had long permeated all the Museum's procedures, Wellcome reiterated their importance to Thompson. His comments here concerned the work of Paira Mall, a medic, linguist, and expert on Asian culture and history, who began working for Wellcome in 1910:

It will be desirable for you to require from him very explicit reports, giving a list of the objects and their character, and he should send those to you at frequent intervals, and his report also should give you a good clear idea of what ground he is covering, indicating the places and the character of them . . . it is very essential that you should keep him well in hand, and see that he is not wasting time, but is putting fullest energy into the work and is carrying out our requirements efficiently.[19]

Paira Mall had been working for Wellcome for eight years when this letter was penned. Neither he nor Thompson needed a reminder of Wellcome's requirements when it came to writing reports. But as Wellcome's collecting staff spread themselves out around the globe, he became quite dependent on their regular feedback. When information was not supplied, or staff reports were vague, he quickly became frustrated. His patience was most sorely tested in the late 1920s by a series of reports from Thompson's successor, Louis Malcolm. Malcolm hesitated to give his opinions and his descriptions of objects were thin. Wellcome's irritation became overt, and each of Malcolm's reports was sent back with scribbled complaints: 'most of the catalogues have arrived very late and without expressions of advice or explanations', 'your statement one room crammed conveys no helpful information', 'I can only guess about this item—the subject matter being so vaguely described', 'you have not described nor given me any comprehensive detailed information'.[20]

As Malcolm's report writing continued to disappoint, Wellcome became dissatisfied with the style of paper and envelopes that he used:

It is much better to fold your letter sheets threefold and post them in 'legal size' envelopes. Very often I receive several thin sheets, with or without a few other items, in one of your very large heavy envelopes—badly crumpled—sometimes doubled up, and when photographs and prints are enclosed they are badly damaged . . . If you have a large number of sheets of correspondence and reports they may be sent in the large brown envelopes such as you have been using.[21]

By this stage in life—Wellcome was in his mid-seventies when he wrote this, and it was more than thirty years since Thompson and Hoffmann had despatched their first research reports—Wellcome had become so reliant on his weekly updates that the size of the envelopes, the weight of the paper, and battered edges of the enclosures he received had become a matter for concern. Ever the perfectionist, years of routine had shaped Wellcome's relationships with successive generations of staff. When the system began to fail, his dependence on it became plain.

When Paira Mall began collecting for Wellcome in India in 1911, his obligations were framed in terms of a business investment. Thompson informed him that Wellcome was considering an extension to the agreed route, but,

He desires me to point out to you that of course the expense of the journey is very great, and he naturally expects an adequate return for the outlay. I am sorry to say that so far he is disappointed with the result, and if a better return is not likely to follow later on, he might find it necessary to recall you.[22]

The 'return' from a collecting agent was somewhat easier to measure than the return from a literary researcher. Objects were tangible goods that could simply be counted up and listed off. Even when they were not actually buying objects, Wellcome's collectors were taking photographs, making sketches, and noting down all the items they came across in the course of their travels. Their enquiries usually resulted in an acquisition of some sort that could be passed on; an object or photograph that represented their latest research discoveries. Fifteen years earlier, Wellcome had probably expected Hoffmann to operate in a similar way, more as a collector or fact-finder than an academic historian.

Thompson took to report writing with aplomb. He was efficient and purposeful. His letters were unfailingly thorough and filled with triumphant anecdotes. Nonetheless, Wellcome's emphasis on quantifiable results could cause problems for his collectors. Other staff members found report writing arduous. Louis Sambon did not particularly enjoy reporting home and avoided it whenever possible. Like Hoffmann, he felt the pressure of having to detail results when, in reality, foraging for treasures involved its fair share of frustrations. Collecting, photographing, and sketching could be just as unpredictable as literary research, as Sambon explained, in typically entertaining style, in a letter about his travels through France:

You cannot imagine what time one loses. The Museums are often closed. They are always closed the very day you want to see them. The officials are never there, the authorities, in small towns, are not to be found. Sometimes, on your third or fourth call, you may be lucky, Ms. le Directeur is in his office, but he has someone with him, probably a lady. You are asked to take a seat and you may have to wait an hour or more. Time is of little importance in the South of France. At last you are face to face with the very man you want, but he knows nothing, can do nothing or will do nothing. That is bad enough, but there is worse. Monsieur le Directeur may be a most amiable person, he is charmed with your visit, he has nothing special to do, he has had his dinner, wine and coffee and is quite happy and in a talkative mood. So he pins you there and you may find it almost impossible to get away. He will insist on showing you things you do not want to see, and telling you things about which you do not care. But it would be too long and tedious to tell you of all our tribulations. You need only know that we have succeeded to some extent, and that if the harvest is not greater it is not from want of goodwill and energy.[23]

Library opening hours were frequently prohibitive. In Florence, Sambon found 'real treasures', but the librarian who guarded them insisted on supervising him while he worked: 'He says he must be present himself, but he comes to the library at 10.30 or 11 a. m. and leaves at 12, and during that short time he has a number of people to attend to.'[24] In these circumstances, work was unavoidably slow. On another occasion, at the Bibliothèque de l'Arsenal in Paris, Sambon's research 'was retarded by excessive politeness on the part of the Director'.[25] More mundane activities could prove just as disabling while travelling abroad: 'We partook of an abominable and most expensive luncheon at the Station of Geneva and were literally poisoned by some mushrooms which were served with the meat. I was obliged to spend the 18th in bed, and the night preceding mostly out of bed.'[26]

Paira Mall, who became one of Wellcome's most successful collecting agents and spent ten years combing the Indian subcontinent for manuscripts and artefacts (Figure 15), experienced similar setbacks during his travels, and

Figure 15. Photograph of Paira Mall, date unknown.

the risks to his health were exacerbated by the tropical climate. He endured at least four bouts of malaria over the years, and, in 1911, was prevented from visiting the Mubarak Mandi palaces, in the foothills of the Himalayas, because of an outbreak of the plague.[27] But most of Mall's grievances, like

Sambon's, were with traders and officials. The Kashmiri Pandits who brought him manuscripts for sale, 'ask sometimes enormous prices, and to beat them down to one third or half the price asked takes up about three or four hours a day'.[28] While in Uttar Pradesh, he complained,

Before getting access into a library I have to waste three or four days in visiting the officials, who seem to be quite unconcerned and nothing in the world will make them to hurry up. Mss are lying somewhere in dark cells which have not been opened and viewed for the last 10 or 15 years. Sometimes the illiterate keeper of these precious mss is away and no one knows where the keys are.[29]

Collecting was never going to be as straightforward in practice as Wellcome might have hoped. Thompson was constantly relaying Wellcome's insistence that 'nothing should be overlooked, and no part of the country skipped' in the hunt for antiquities. Mall should 'excavate every possible detail of information connected with the antiquity of the medical art'. He must 'leave no stone unturned' and should not come home until 'India is completely ransacked as far as we possibly can for literature and other objects of interest connected with ancient medicine, and all the great centres of learning, visited and ransacked'.[30] Mall, who was himself of 'Hindoo extraction', although he had been brought up by 'an English lady' and sent to a missionary training college in London, replied, politely, that, 'Mr Wellcome is quite right in thinking that first of all the whole of India should be ransacked',[31] but the relentless demands for results from London must have grated at times when Mall's progress was slowed through no fault of his own, by transport problems, or the intense summer heat, or the onset of sickness.

At least Mall seemed happy to write regular reports: Sambon's temperament was not suited to record-keeping. The Italian was knowledgeable, humorous, and extremely well connected, but also flighty and offhand. As the years went by he tended to scribble a hurried postcard rather than typing out a full letter. Although he had a knack for unearthing treasures in unlikely places, in later years he seldom kept Wellcome or Thompson up to date with his movements around the Continent, often failing to leave forwarding addresses and slipping out of contact for days or weeks at a time.[32]

Sambon's increasing reluctance to keep in touch may have been partly a statement of defiance. The constant obligation to account for himself began to constrain him, particularly as Sambon's relationship with Wellcome was complicated by his varied responsibilities. He only worked for Wellcome part-time, while maintaining a lectureship at the London School of Tropical Medicine during term, and pursuing an ambitious research programme of his own into the cause of pellagra, a disease common amongst populations reliant on maize crops. In the early twentieth century, pellagra was the 'greatest disease scourge of Southern Europe and Egypt and other tropical and sub-tropical countries'.[33] It is now thought to be caused by a diet deficient in niacin, or vitamin B3, but at the time its cause was unconfirmed and Sambon was keenly pursuing the theory that it was conveyed by a protozoon, which he hoped to identify.

During the early 1910s, Sambon's pellagra research began to undermine his commitment to Wellcome's collection. Wellcome supported Sambon's scientific work to a certain extent, providing equipment and some funds, and he was flexible over the timing of Sambon's field trips, but Sambon's reluctance to issue proper reports on his collecting work wore Wellcome's patience thin. An internal memo in 1912 noted that Wellcome was withdrawing financial support:

Mr W felt that he had more than done his share towards the expenses of this Pellagra work and he was also keenly disappointed in Dr Sambon's disregard for our instructions to report to us regularly respecting his work and movements—he never let us have an address to which we could write him the whole time he was away.[34]

Wellcome had given £700 to the pellagra project, but had received only three or four weeks' work on his collection from Sambon during the previous eight months.[35]

According to Thompson, Sambon took advantage of Wellcome's good faith, and spent most of his time pursuing personal glory through his pellagra work: it was here that his real interests lay, and Wellcome's collection suffered as a result. Thompson noted in 1911,

From a long observation of Dr. Sambon's manner of work, I may point out that his chief drawback is a lack of staying power, and no method whatever, and there is the greatest difficulty in keeping him concentrated on any one branch of work, even for a few days. It is in these points that failure is to be expected in carrying the investigation to a successful result.[36]

But Sambon's talents as a scholar and his connections in Europe made him too valuable to dismiss. He promised to devote more of his time to the collection, to stick to the agreed timetables for research work, and to write weekly reports on his progress, but the promises proved empty. Sambon's colourful turns of phrase—'You must really forgive me. My life has been a veritable inferno.'—began to sound increasingly hollow.[37]

Sambon, meanwhile, felt that Wellcome had been less than supportive of his pellagra research. Wellcome, he claimed, denied him 'latitude of action' as a medical scientist.[38] More than once, in 1905 and again in 1909, Sambon threatened to terminate his agreement with Wellcome because he had been denied permission to pursue his own scientific interests: 'really, I could not accept the conditions under which you expected me to work for you, and I felt the need of keeping more in touch with my own branch of research and with those engaged in the same kind of work.'[39] Sambon thought he could investigate pellagra *and* collect material for the exhibition during his European travels, conveniently leaving Wellcome to foot the bill. If he had shown a little more commitment to the exhibition work, he might have succeeded in this plan. But Sambon saw no reason why Wellcome should not become the primary sponsor of his pellagra work. Wellcome was not so inclined. He had employed Sambon to collect objects and information for his historical medical exhibition, and this was the role he expected him to fulfil.

For all his eccentricities, Sambon's grumblings were not entirely without foundation. Wellcome was suspicious of individual research agendas. None of his employees was allowed to conduct research that might encroach on Wellcome's own academic aspirations, which were unusually expansive. Because his interests were so broad, and his standards so exacting, topics that his staff became interested in were often 'reserved' by him for future projects that never materialized. Sambon managed to maintain some autonomy as an academic because he was employed on a part-time, temporary basis, but he was still denied any opportunity to profit from the work he undertook for Wellcome. When he wanted to deliver a paper on the history of plague at the British Medical Association, Wellcome reminded him of his parameters, writing,

I believe you are aware that this is a subject which I hope to investigate very exhaustively later on, and, naturally, I should not like that work forestalled. If your paper only contains matter which, as you state, you have published previously in the 'Times,' I have no objection to your reading it. Further, with reference to your suggestion that the work be carried out under my auspices, if you think it will be any benefit to you, you will have my permission to do so, but I cannot see my way to consent to any additions being made to your paper from material in my possession, as that I am reserving for future work, and as I have stated, a very exhaustive research on the matter.[40]

This was typical of Wellcome. He fiercely guarded his rights to the intellectual value of everything in his collection, and since the academic scope of the collection was so broad, there was little he could not register a claim to if he chose.

From the 1910s, Wellcome's Museum employees signed confidentiality agreements with the Burroughs Wellcome company management. His staff not only promised to hand over anything they acquired that might be of interest to him while in his employment, they also renounced their rights to communicate their research to others without written permission, and such permission was rarely forthcoming. Their activities were classified:

All work done, discoveries made, researches undertaken and information procured by you, or others, either during working hours or at any other time, either upon our premises or elsewhere in connection with or relating to any thing in which you or others have been or are engaged for us or in which we are interested, are to be considered as strictly confidential and as our sole property, and shall not at any time be communicated in any way to others than ourselves or our authorised representatives without our written permission.[41]

Clauses like this were standard issue for the pharmaceuticals company: innovation was a central plank in the Burroughs Wellcome business strategy and work at their manufacturing site was conducted in great secrecy. Sometimes members of the same team did not even know of their colleagues' responsibilities; orders for machines were sent through special channels to disguise the firm's interests, and identification marks were chiselled off on arrival. Staff were left in no doubt that confidentiality agreements would be strictly enforced. When the firm's chief engineer, who had designed a new tablet machine for Burroughs Wellcome, resigned in 1901 he was promptly visited at his home. A management memo ordered his supervisor to: 'Threaten strong punishment in any country in the world if he breaks the [confidentiality] agreement. Demand all his papers, go fearlessly to his house. Do quickly. Do not allow him bluff or evasion. You can bluff and frighten if troublesome.'[42] Luckily, the engineer was not at all troublesome and had no intention of using his designs elsewhere, but the message was unmistakable: Burroughs Wellcome would not hesitate to defend their contractual privileges.

Wellcome extended similar terms to his collecting agents. Museum collecting shared certain similarities with the pharmaceuticals industry when it came to competitive tactics. To find unusual artefacts, and then secure them at a low price, it was important to conceal your interests, your contacts, and your identity from potential competitors and salesmen. Wellcome's staff were privy to information of enormous value to others in the antiquities trade. They knew his sources, his hunting grounds, his financial priorities, and his requirements. Wellcome had to ensure that his staff were advancing his own interests as they hunted for collectables and not anyone else's, not even their own.

Wellcome's collecting staff were not allowed to buy for themselves, privately, 'any books, pictures, engravings, drawings, manuscripts, antiquities or objects of archaeological, ethnological, anthropological, anatomical, botanical, historical, medical, surgical, chemical or pharmaceutical interest, or anything relating to natural history, or anything relating to any work in which you or others are engaged for us'. No personal flights of fancy were allowed, no modest private collection to display on the mantelpiece at home. 'The purpose of this clause is to leave no doubt that members of our staff are not to enter into competition with our libraries, museums, laboratories, bureaus etc. in the acquisition of things by purchase or otherwise.'[43]

The question of whether museum staff should be allowed to collect in fields relating to their work is a perennial issue. Today, the Museums Association issues guidelines that advise curators to declare their private collecting interests, and 'refuse . . . to engage in private collecting in competition with the museum or to use a connection with the museum to promote private collecting'.[44] It may not have been unreasonable for Wellcome to expect his agents to forfeit their own collecting interests while they worked for him, but their intellectual fulfilment was harder to negotiate. He tried to make his collecting staff into extensions of himself: officially, everything they did and knew belonged to him. Wellcome's intransigence proved destabilizing in this respect, particularly when his staff had academic careers in their own right.

The Burroughs Wellcome contracts formalized a long-standing position, one that Wellcome had felt impelled to clarify in the late 1890s during the Animal Substances project. When William Brown, the first researcher to work on the history of animal products for Wellcome, described himself in passing as the 'author' of his work, Wellcome was swift to correct him:

While I presume the description of yourself as Author was an inadvertence on your part, yet to avoid any possible misconception or misunderstanding as to the nature of the position you occupy in respect to this work, I must point out that no question of

Authorship arises in any way whatsoever, inasmuch as the work has been carried out for me under my direction and at my expense, and consequently there should be no misunderstanding about the matter, as everything connected with it is my property. Awaiting your acknowledgement of this, I remain, yours sincerely, Henry S. Wellcome.[45]

Wellcome's approach was common in the commercial sector, where employees have always been expected to contribute research and writing without individual accreditation. Wellcome had bought Brown's authorship. He saw no reason why his money should not secure for him, as well as thousands of historical papers and objects, his employees' intellectual contributions. Just as the chief engineer at Burroughs Wellcome had relinquished the rights to his tablet-making machine, so Brown's work had also become Wellcome's property. Wellcome was a businessman in an academic world. He paid men and women to do his historical research in much the same way he might have paid them to design the firm's first aid kits. But he asked a lot from the researchers and collecting agents he employed when they stood to gain so little from their intellectual investment in his projects.

For Wellcome, it was not simply that collecting was a form of intellectual inquiry; intellectual inquisitiveness was a form of collecting. Artefacts could be stockpiled and reserved, and so could academic projects and people's ideas. Perhaps it was not so much that his appetite for knowledge required a businesslike approach to acquisition, but more that his businesslike approach to research permitted him to employ other people to do the work for him, in the expectation that he had secured their ingenuity as well as their collecting skills. Collecting may give knowledge the gloss of ownership, the feeling of possession and control, but collecting artefacts is not the same as collecting ideas. Wellcome saw his collectors as fact-finders, who could gather information on his behalf and hand it over to him in return for their salary, but good fact-finders have ideas of their own.

Wellcome's faith in his financial clout betrayed his academic insecurities. He did not have the self-assurance, as a historian at least, to encourage the intellectual interests of his staff.[46] Instead, he tried hard to contain them. No wonder a slightly eccentric but talented academic like Sambon, or an established and well-respected researcher like Hoffmann, found his demands unreasonably restrictive. 'With regard to my method of work,' Sambon wrote in September 1909, 'I must ask you to be some what indulgent. Every original worker has methods of his own. His brain does not work in the same way as that of others. If you desire to obtain good results you must allow a certain amount of freedom. I must feel that I have your entire confidence.'[47] It was an echo of Hoffmann's appeal more than a decade earlier: 'If Mr Wellcome wishes to engage collaborators here he must have confidence.'[48]

Wellcome was at his most confident, and his most content, when he could track a steady accumulation of artefacts into his storehouses. Owning things, and stacking them away for safe keeping, brought him a kind of reassurance. After all, if his staff were kept busy enough buying things they would have little time to ponder the significance of what they acquired. Wellcome sought to keep his collectors at this work, feeding his academic aspirations and dampening any they might be tempted to pursue at his expense.

Not surprisingly, Wellcome's relationships with his collectors often ended badly. Sambon continued his work until the Historical Medical Exhibition finally opened in 1913, and he undertook a little research, collecting, and translation work after the war, but suspicions and disappointments infused his relationship with Wellcome and Thompson, and before long the arrangement petered out. Mall had been about to return to England in 1914 when Thompson wrote of 'the terrible war that has broken out in Europe' and 'upset everything'.[49] Mall did not come home until 1921. After ten years abroad, his health had suffered, and he had spent the last three years of his travels negotiating, unsuccessfully, for an increase in his salary. He had only received one pay rise, from £300 to £350, in 1913.[50] Back in London, Mall began cataloguing his collection, but his work was constantly interrupted by sickness and his damaged 'nerves'. He became embittered and felt that he 'should have been treated a little more generously after ten years labour in India in consequence of which there has been a complete breakdown in my health'.[51]

The last letter in Mall's correspondence file is written by Thompson, dated 10 October 1924. It concerns some 'pipes' Mall had bought at auction. Thompson informs Mall that he has arranged to 'take over' 'the pipes that you purchased at Stevens' sale', and adds that Mr Wellcome wanted to draw Mall's attention to the clause in his contract—helpfully copied out in full—that forbade the acquisition of any artefact for anyone other than Wellcome without his written consent.[52] After all Mall's contributions to the collection, the letter is a fitting commentary on Wellcome's management style. His refusal to see his collectors as anything other than assistants, when things were going well, or competitors, when difficulties arose, caused many of his relationships to fail. Mall was a doctor, who had served as chief medical adviser to the Maharajah of Kapurthala, and as an army surgeon in the Russo-Japanese War. And he was a scholar, who was fluent in German, French, Italian, Sanscrit, Persian, Hindustani, Punjabi, and Arabic. He could be forgiven for thinking of himself as something more than a fact-finder.

CHAPTER NINE

AN IMPOSSIBLE MAN
TO DEAL WITH

Soon after his arrival in India, Paira Mall warned that it would become increasingly difficult to find good value manuscripts there: 'Americans and Germans', he said, 'have ransacked the whole place, and paid exorbitant prices.' Although Wellcome was unconcerned by Mall's warning in 1911, and simply advised him 'not to lose his head',[1] over the course of the next twenty years the perceived threat from wealthy American collectors would justify much of Wellcome's own greed. He became a British citizen in 1910, and he increasingly saw it as his task to secure antiquities before they could be 'carried away to America from whence they will never be returned'.[2] Thompson had regularly detected 'American buyers' lurking in the background during his transactions, and by the late 1920s Wellcome's senior collecting staff had become obsessed with the presence of 'the Americans', whose new money, it was implied, tarnished their discernment as collectors. Wellcome's own American roots and self-made fortune seem to have been counterbalanced by his social and economic investment in Europe. Most importantly, however, the objects he acquired were destined to remain in London, so he could present himself as a champion of European history, acting on Europe's behalf. In this regard the collecting world was split in two by the Atlantic Ocean, and Wellcome congratulated himself that his money was buttressing Old World glory.

Wellcome's quest for one collection in particular—an astonishing assemblage of artefacts created by an Italian opera singer named Evangelista Gorga—encapsulated his concern for the American threat and his corresponding perception of himself as a guardian of Europe's heritage. Evangelista Gorga turned out to be 'an impossible man to deal with',[3] but the quality of his collection more than justified a little perseverance.

Gorga lived in Rome. At the height of his career, in 1896, he had been chosen by Puccini to create the part of Rodolfo in the first production of *La Bohème* at the Regal Theatre in Turin. But it was as a collector that his ambition and appetite found their true force. He began collecting things— musical memorabilia and instruments, archaeological finds, and medical antiquities—in the late 1880s, and, in 1899, at the age of 34, he gave up his singing career to devote himself entirely to his collection. Like Wellcome, Gorga was a collector of stupendous proportions. At one time, he rented ten apartments in Rome simply to warehouse his artefacts, which filled room after room from floor to ceiling. When one of Wellcome's staff visited Gorga's collection in the late 1920s, he was amazed at what he found. 'Here is a veritable museum of medical history in itself, the like of which I had never dreamed existed outside the [Wellcome] Historical Medical Museum. Gorga has enough medical and pharmaceutical material to fill the whole of our basement and a lot more. I was astounded and astonished.'[4]

Wellcome found himself inescapably drawn to a collection that paralleled his own in both size and substance without, according to his staff, duplicating it significantly. The Gorga collection was widely admired by collectors and historians of medicine alike, and Wellcome's competitive instincts were piqued. He badly wanted to acquire it. By securing Gorga's artefacts Wellcome would encompass within his own collection—and thus surpass—one of the greatest rival accumulations of historical material known in Europe. And, since so many of Gorga's things were ancient Italian antiquities that excited interest from other American collectors, Wellcome was determined to secure them for London. He stalked the Gorga collection for years. Luckily for him, financial difficulties compelled Gorga to consider selling his collection from time to time, but it pained him intensely to have to do so, and he imposed unreasonable conditions whenever the idea of a sale was broached. Negotiations between the Italian collector and Wellcome's staff were difficult and protracted, eventually involving at least four of Wellcome's agents and lasting for more than twenty years. They began a year before Wellcome's Historical Medical Exhibition—later Museum—opened in the summer of 1913. Although partially resolved in 1924, when Wellcome acquired a large portion of Gorga's collection, Gorga continued to collect, and Wellcome's staff acquired more of his antiquities, piecemeal, during the early 1930s.

Louis Sambon had been the first to mention Gorga's work, while travelling through Italy in February 1912. He wrote to Wellcome: 'In Rome there is an antiquarian Signor Gorga who has a splendid collection of medical antiquities he will not sell.'[5] Sambon went on to mention, rather hopefully, that Gorga had promised to loan part of his collection for Wellcome's forthcoming Historical Medical Exhibition. A fortnight later Wellcome offered to buy Gorga's Roman antiquities, but his proposal was turned down.[6] The first, brief, and fruitless interaction between the two men was over, and communication between them ceased temporarily. It was not until late 1914 that Wellcome heard Gorga had decided to sell his collection to meet some debts. He saw his opportunity, and arranged for Thompson to take up the negotiations with Gorga in earnest on his behalf.[7]

Gorga drove a hard bargain. He had been amassing objects for thirty years, and he informed Thompson that his collection was worth £12,000. But Thompson hoped to reach an understanding on the amount of £4,000.[8] Gorga's opening offer indicates, not only what he thought his collection was worth, but what he thought Wellcome might be persuaded to pay. A cat and mouse game began, as Gorga tried to take advantage of Wellcome's huge wealth, and Wellcome preyed on Gorga's impending financial downfall. Neither man was willing to admit his weaknesses to the other.

Negotiations were opened by letter, but Thompson refused to make a firm offer for the collection without seeing it. Arrangements for a proper viewing were difficult. By the end of 1914, Europe was experiencing the tightening grip of war. Travel to Rome was already almost impossible and it became clear that Thompson would not be able to view the collection there. Gorga, meanwhile, refused to bring any of his objects to Milan, as suggested in October 1914, or Paris, as Thompson proposed in March 1915. The Italian was concerned that a few select pieces would not do justice to the richness of his collection as a whole. He wrote, rather loftily, to Thompson,

From the proposition you make in your letter of Oct 30th I gather that you have not a conception of the grandness of the matter. It is a museum which cannot be easily transported wherever one likes . . . therefore kindly make the sacrifice and come up to Rome and you will be pleased of having done so.[9]

He was adamant. His objects had to be seen in person, all together, in Rome. And perhaps he was right: when Thompson did finally see the Gorga collection, after the War, he would be stunned by its sheer size and scope.

Negotiations now seemed to be stalling for a second time. Gorga managed to deposit some of his artefacts with money-lenders, which alleviated his immediate financial crisis. Although he was still interested in selling to Wellcome, his prices became even more inflated and he refused to consider splitting his collection up to sell only a part. Despite this, Thompson's interest did not waver. Against all the odds, he managed to arrange for one of his assistants to see the collection in Rome in 1915. Arthur Amoruso, who had joined Wellcome's staff in 1910, had been stationed in Naples with the army, and for this reason he was able to reach Rome while his colleagues could not. In off-duty moments, Amoruso did a little local research and prospecting for Wellcome and Thompson. Temporarily, he became their man on the ground in Italy.[10]

In December 1915 and again the following February, Amoruso visited Gorga in Rome and dutifully reported to Thompson on all that he saw. There were, Amoruso wrote, 'no end of objects' in the collection. The young Italian serviceman was taken through twenty rooms, each stacked with boxes and trays of artefacts. He wrote of a corridor filled with Renaissance bas-reliefs, statuettes and ornaments, and Roman artefacts. There were a number of modern church votive oil paintings, showing sick and wounded patients being healed. He saw two rooms packed with weights and measures, Roman daggers, spear heads, pharmacy vases, a whole range of spoons of different ages, pottery, intaglios, amphorae, glass phials; even Gorga, Amoruso found, 'was not well acquainted with all he has'.[11]

Signor Gorga would not let Amoruso take any notes, and he evaded any direct questions regarding price: 'He was almost irritating in that respect.' 'Unfortunately, besides his own particular vices, he has also those of most collectors who wish to sell their precious wares. As a consequence his conception of prices is fabulous and he not seldom exaggerates the importance and age of objects.' Even so, Amoruso could not fail to be impressed. He wrote to Thompson describing what he could remember of the collection, and reporting on Gorga's distinctly cool attitude towards a potential sale, but his time was limited. In February 1916, his regiment was despatched to the mountainous Trentino front, and his dealings with Gorga were brought to a close.[12]

It was not until February 1919 that Thompson was able to visit Rome himself. Peace had come to Europe only three months earlier, and travelling east from Paris Thompson found a scene of 'absolute desolation' for miles. The devastation of the towns he visited 'baffled description'. Villages lay in ruins; huge shell craters pocked the ground every few yards, and muddy trenches cut open the countryside. In some settlements not a single house or building remained standing and the streets were obliterated. There were few vehicles and no lights were visible at night. 'One has to see these places to realise what <u>utter destruction</u> means', he wrote to Wellcome. He found Rome much altered since the war, more so than London or Paris. Most of the hotels were closed, while others had been taken over for government offices, making the few rooms available extremely expensive. There was no meat, milk, or butter to be had anywhere, although there was still plenty of wine and fruit. But for Thompson's purposes, the devastation had its advantages: 'in Rome we are hearing of collection after collection to be sold, and we are evidently here at the right moment.'[13]

Thompson hoped that Gorga might also be vulnerable to the strictures that came with surviving the War: maybe he would finally be ready to sell his great collection. Gorga lived in an apartment in a fashionable part of new Rome, across the Tiber, and Thompson set off early on a Thursday morning to call on him, as arranged. But things did not go to plan.

He came in in his dressing gown—a wily and cunning-looking type of Italian. He looked surprised at seeing us, and asked if we had not received the telegram he sent to Paris, asking me to put off my visit as he was ill. I told him I had received no telegram from him, and had come to Rome to see his collections which he had asked me so often to do.

Gorga announced that it was impossible for him to show Thompson the collection that day, and they arranged to meet the following Sunday instead. 'He is a most curious and eccentric man, and [he is] evidently going to be most difficult to deal with', Thompson concluded. But the collection spoke for itself. Thompson spent three days examining it. For hours he went through 'room after room stacked with Greco-Roman antiquities'. He saw hundreds of votive offerings and ancient surgical instruments, paintings and statuettes, reliquaries with papal documents attached, mortars and pestles, baths, taps and sanitary equipment, drug jars, old books and manuscripts, pharmacy cabinets, laboratory apparatus, medicine chests and boxes, bottles and phials, pharmaceutical presses, scales, lamps, and even a large surgical bed from St. Spirito. After one day Thompson had seen enough to conclude that 'this is the largest collection of medical antiquities we have come across, and up to now [we] have only seen a third of it . . . You will judge from this, we are up against a big thing, and I shall do my utmost to get the lot.'[14]

Gorga's starting price was one million lire, around £32,000. Thompson thought this 'preposterous' and countered with 40,000 lire, an offer that was immediately rejected 'with scorn'. Unable to agree, the two men met with Gorga's money-lender, a ship-owner named Moroli who had lent Gorga 600,000 lire on his collection and now wanted some of his money repaid. By way of a compromise, Gorga agreed to set a value for each room of objects separately, and to allow Thompson to eliminate certain non-medical items. Eventually, Gorga brought his price down to 500,000 lire, but Thompson would only go up to 60,000. He informed Gorga that he was leaving Rome the next morning, in the hope that this threat would spur the Italian into a more favourable decision. Sure enough, he was called upon to continue last minute negotiations that evening, but they were futile. He wrote to Wellcome from his hotel afterwards:

I have just returned from Gorga's without result. He first said I could eliminate certain non-medical objects, and directly I commenced, he said he wouldn't. He is an impossible man to deal with. His wife implored him to sell the things and relieve them of their difficulties, but he refused. In the end he went back to his original price of 500,000 lire, and said he wouldn't sell a thing for less. As it is only a waste of time to delay with him longer, I have decided to leave it for the present . . . He is hoping against hope that someone will come along and give him the million lire he requires. We leave here at 7am in the morning.[15]

Gorga was struggling to reconcile his emotional investment in his collection with the monetary value of his possessions. The same challenge faced every collector forced to sell against their wishes. Daniel Davidson, the chemist who sold his mortars to Wellcome in 1910, had been compelled, with great reluctance, to drop his price from £250 to £150. Wellcome and Thompson drove a hard bargain, but it happened all the time that collectors struggled to reduce their relationship with their belongings to financial terms. Davidson had only succumbed 'for the sentiment of keeping the collection of so many years intact', and believed he would have got a higher price had he been willing to split his mortars up.[16]

Gorga, in the end, would make a similar justification for selling to Wellcome: that it was better to maintain the coherence of his collection than raise a higher price by splitting it. Of course, we will never know whether either man could have made more money in different circumstances. Every agreement was a gamble in this respect, but collections like Gorga's, and Davidson's, and Wellcome's, were about more than money. These objects had shaped their owners' lives, influencing their interactions with other people and the places they visited. Acquiring things demanded research, strategy, and, perhaps, personal sacrifices. And collecting was an enduring occupation: Gorga's collection could not fail to become part of his identity. It was the material for which he was known. It had secured him a place within an elite, international community of collecting specialists. It was part of his life, furnishing his experiences and articulating his memories.[17] The only way Gorga could bring himself to place a market value on his objects was to inflate that value. The time and effort he had invested in selecting his objects and creating a coherent set, with its own internal logic, certainly added value, but Wellcome wanted the best price, and that meant disregarding Gorga's personal investment and valuing his artefacts on their individual merits. Gorga's collection would always be worth more to Gorga than to anyone else: the battle over price was a psychological battle for him first and foremost.

As it was, nothing more happened for two years. In December 1921 the Italian wrote to Wellcome unexpectedly: he was in trouble over his taxes, he said, and he raised the possibility of a sale again. The collection, he insisted, now included a number of 'important additions' that would interest Wellcome. According to Thompson, Gorga was 'evidently in a panic and has got to raise money'. Thompson fancied his chances this time, and noted that the exchange rate was currently very favourable for a sale in Italy. Wellcome was also cautiously optimistic:

It is a very remarkable collection and I hope we may be able to get it at a moderate figure but it will all depend on his antics and if he still opens his mouth too wide. You must be careful to see that he has not sold any of the good things and not substituted copies or fakes.

But he cautioned, 'It is a very difficult time to expend large sums and I must consider this question very carefully and understand well what we are to get for our money if we decide to make an offer.'[18]

And so, the following March, Thompson found himself in Rome again, inspecting the Gorga collection for a second time. Two years earlier, Gorga's medical objects alone had occupied five large rooms, now they were packed into eight rooms, as well as filling all the corridors in between. Gorga demanded £20,000 as an opening offer. On hearing this, Thompson told him that they would not even consider such an amount, adding that Wellcome was not really interested in buying the collection now anyway, and he promptly left for Naples, leaving Gorga to consider his options. Privately, however, Thompson was as eager as ever. He wrote to Wellcome: 'The advantage of it to us would be that it does not duplicate to any extent anything we have got, and he has not collected in the departments in which we are the strongest.'[19]

Wellcome's fascination with Gorga's collection may also have been partly rooted in his competitive spirit. The Gorga collection would elevate Wellcome's Museum by association as well as in substance. Few had the means to consider purchasing such a wealth of material; most private collectors could only marvel at the famous Gorga collection from afar. If Wellcome could acquire it, it would be a famous coup. Buying the Gorga collection would secure his reputation as the foremost collector of scientific relics in the world.

As their manoeuvrings gathered pace during 1923, Thompson and Wellcome became increasingly concerned that they might lose the Gorga collection to a rival collector. Louis Sambon had warned of this possibility in January 1922 when he wrote, 'you cannot afford to let so large and valuable a collection fall into other hands. It might any day form the nucleus of a rival museum.'[20] American collectors posed the biggest threat to Wellcome's bid: Gorga had told Sambon he was entertaining an offer from an American for purchase of his collection. Although the unnamed American had given an undertaking that he would buy the material and a catalogue was being produced, Gorga claimed he would still prefer to see his collection in London.[21] Wellcome knew of two men who were thought to be courting Gorga at the time, Dr Crummer and Dr Streeter, and he tracked their movements carefully.

Leroy Crummer and Edward Streeter were both successful American medics who increasingly devoted their lives to scholarship and collecting. Both had spent time in Europe during the course of their careers. Streeter had served in France during the war. He was particularly interested in the history of weights and scales, and he built up a collection of more than 3,000 artefacts during the 1920s and 1930s that included Assyrian, Egyptian, Islamic, Greek, Roman, and European measuring devices. He must have been enticed to Rome by word that Gorga's collection included two rooms stacked with nothing but weights and measures. Leroy Crummer, meanwhile, was primarily interested in books and manuscripts—of which Gorga had many. Crummer married Myrtle Kelly in 1922, who was also an enthusiastic bibliophile, and together they set about creating an important library dealing with the history of medicine.[22]

Wellcome was acquainted with the Crummers. They had visited his Historical Medical Museum in 1922, writing afterwards, 'We have never had such a delightful visit anywhere nor received such inspiration as we did at the Museum, and it drove us to the quest for similar objects wherever we visited.' And Thompson maintained an occasional correspondence with Dr Crummer regarding his collecting interests.[23] Wellcome had supplied them with various social introductions for a collecting trip they had taken to Holland. He met them by chance while in Washington, DC, in April 1923 and heard about their travels. But underneath the pleasantries lurked their rivalry as collectors. The Crummers seemed to enjoy telling Wellcome that they had bought, 'a very remarkable microscope' from a Dutch dealer, which should have been kept on reserve for him. Wellcome immediately wrote to Thompson asking his advice when it came to preventing 'such mischances' in the future. Thompson was able to reassure him that the microscope in question was 'of quite a common type' and that he had, in fact, already rejected it before the Crummers met with the dealer because there was a similar one already in Wellcome's collection. Crummer, Thompson added pompously, would no doubt have paid too much for the object. But Italy was much on Wellcome's mind when it came to his American acquaintances. 'We must also consider what can be done about a round up in Italy before they (Crummers) get there as they are going with plenty of money and a big thirst.' And Thompson confirmed in reply that both Crummer and Streeter were interested in the Gorga collection.[24]

Thompson, meanwhile, became concerned about a third American medic with an eye for European antiquities: Dr Harvey Cushing. Cushing was a leading neurosurgeon from the east coast who was busy gathering together an impressive medical library and a collection of portraits and engravings.[25] With Cushing's arrival on the scene, the complex web of collecting rivalries and friendships surrounding Gorga's collection extended further.

Thompson had heard of Cushing's interests by chance, through Edward Streeter, with whom he also maintained a friendly, if sporadic correspondence.[26] Thompson had met Streeter in London where they discussed the Crummers. In the course of their conversation, Streeter showed Thompson a letter he had received from Cushing, who, 'regretted to find that [the Crummers] had been bitten with the mania for making a collection of medical antiquities'.[27] The Crummers had told Cushing of the valuable old pharmacy equipment that could be found in Italy. But Thompson was interested in Cushing's own ambitions as a collector. Cushing had asked

Streeter to acquire objects in Venice on his behalf, for he also had a 'fine collection' that he hoped to make into a museum for Yale University.[28] Cushing's collecting interests increased the pressure on Wellcome, particularly when it came to the Gorga collection. 'There is no doubt', Thompson concluded, 'that Streeter will tell Cushing about Gorga's collection, which he has not seen.'[29] In the face of mounting interest in Gorga's antiquities from across the Atlantic, Thompson suggested a visit to Rome at the end of August 1923 to 'see if by any means we can get Gorga to part with the portion of his collection that we really want, secure it, have it packed and sealed and sent to Milan' before it was too late.[30]

Thompson and Wellcome were determined to reach Italy and the Gorga collection before the Americans. In June, Thompson informed Wellcome that he had received a letter from Crummer, 'in which he says that he and his wife "will arrive in London about the first of October"—I expect on their way to Italy. If we were able to get away the last week in August it will give us over a month in advance of them.' Wellcome, however, corrected him. He must have spoken to the Crummers in America, because he knew that they were actually travelling to Italy first, and then to London. He scribbled in reply: 'No. On his way from Italy. He takes the steamer to Naples from New York.'[31] There is no record of what happened in Rome that summer. Perhaps the Crummers and their friends found Gorga's conditions prohibitive when it came to negotiating a sale, because, at last, in the opening weeks of 1924, Thompson successfully bought a large portion of Gorga's relics.

Thompson had promised Gorga that the part of the collection Wellcome bought would always be known as 'The Gorga Collection', and 'to save his face' in bringing down the price Gorga had agreed to give some of the objects to Wellcome as a 'gift'. It was less humiliating for him to appear to give away his life's work than to sell it for money. But in reality, Gorga was unable to evade his financiers any longer. This, of course, could be the only reason for his submission. Thompson suspected that Signor Moroli had threatened to sell the collection outright to the highest bidder before the end of the year, regardless of Gorga's wishes in the matter. So, in expectation of an agreement with Wellcome, arrangements were made to catalogue the objects for sale. And, in the late autumn of 1923, Thompson made a firm offer of £8,000. Initially, Gorga held out for £10,000: Thompson wrote that he was 'very much grieved at our evident system of procrastination and strongly angered at the idea of our lack of confidence in him'.[32] In January, however, Gorga gave up his fight. Thompson speculated that his most recent loan must have fallen through, and suspected that Moroli had threatened to seize Gorga's property unless he sold the collection.[33]

Wellcome had finally secured his prize for £8,000. Thompson and Sambon travelled to Rome in February 1924 to take possession of the collection. Thompson was given keys to the Gorga premises during their stay. A complete list was made of every object as it was packed up into a series of wooden cases, each sealed with wire and a lead seal, to be transported to the Burroughs Wellcome depot in Milan and await shipping to England.[34]

The Gorga negotiations had survived a threat from American buyers, and Wellcome was now increasingly aware of competing collectors from his homeland. American purchasing power had been long established in the fine art market. Art dealers like Joseph Duveen and Jacques Seligman made their fortunes selling European antiquities to American millionaires—among them Henry Frick, Andrew Mellon, William Randolph Hearst, and John Pierpont Morgan—and they presided over the transfer of hundreds of thousands of pounds worth of art to America during the 1910s and 1920s. The exodus prompted the art historian Robert Witt to call for a review of the British export tariffs:

In America there is a vast empty continent to be filled, and with the steadfast conviction that what time has done for Europe, money can do for America, and that, moreover, it is well worth doing, the Americans have come crowding into our auction rooms, after first prudently removing their own twenty per cent import duty which stood in their way.[35]

No review was forthcoming, and so American collectors continued to succumb to 'the combined pressure of taxation and temptation'. Wellcome, too, bemoaned the depletion of British heritage, when he spoke to the Museums and Galleries Commission in 1928:

I wish something could be done in regard to rare ethnographic materials, also in regard to British works of art, manuscripts and other precious historical things, to prevent them from being taken abroad. So many of the historical treasures of England are going abroad every year...it is a very grave matter, and we ought not to go to sleep over it. The country is now being drained of many of its choicest historical records.[36]

By this time, growing numbers were collecting historical medical artefacts. The exhibits at the Wellcome Historical Medical Museum, which opened in 1913, had 'aroused throughout Europe and America intense interest in the

subject of medical museums and particularly in the history of medicine',
according to Wellcome. American medical institutions were raising large
amounts of money, he wrote, 'to ransack Europe and other parts of the
world to make collections and to establish museums on the same lines as the
WHMM, or to surpass it'.[37]

The image of these Americans, hungry to acquire Europe's heritage, instilled Wellcome's mission with a new sense of urgency. He now regularly
advised his staff to 'work these [European] fields thoroughly before the
Americans catch the idea and sweep up the land'.[38] Any encounter with an
American collector, whether a connoisseur or a holiday cruise tourist, was
reported by Wellcome's staff. American interest was pushing up auction prices
in London, and some sales catalogues began listing reserve prices in dollars.[39]
Wellcome's two most senior staff in the late 1920s, Louis Malcolm and Peter
Johnston-Saint, both received offers of work from 'the Americans'.[40] In the
spring of 1928 Harry Stow was finding 'material ordered in advance by
Americans all over London, even in smaller out-of-the-way shops'.[41]

Meanwhile, the rest of the Gorga collection played on Wellcome's mind
and haunted the activities of his staff. The artefacts that Gorga had refused to
sell to Wellcome in 1924 came to represent the ancient cultural—and material—wealth of Europe, the very history that Wellcome wanted to protect
from eager American hands. Gorga was still buying antiquities and Wellcome's principal collecting agent in Europe at the time, Peter Johnston-Saint,
heard his name mentioned all over Italy:

> It is a curious thing that almost every shop I have been into enquiring for the material
> which we are looking for has mentioned the name of Gorga as being a great collector
> of this sort of material and also possessing a very fine collection—not only of medical
> items but musical instruments, terracotta, etc.[42]

Saint found that many of the antique shops he visited had a standing order
arrangement with Gorga, so that suitable material was kept to one side for the
Italian collector. Luckily for Wellcome, Gorga was an unreliable client:[43]
'Most of the shops in Rome keep things aside for us. Gorga had a similar
arrangement but he was such a bad player and kept them waiting so long that
they no longer keep to the arrangement and we get the material that was put
aside for him in the past.'[44]

In 1930 and 1931, Gorga's financial troubles returned and he was forced to
place some of his objects in antique shops throughout Rome and beyond.
Johnston-Saint found that Gorga was keeping his prices prohibitively high in

these shops, but the material Saint brought back from Rome in March 1931 was dominated by objects from the Gorga collection that were, by then, more reasonably priced. Saint quickly learned to recognize the little blue labels attached to Gorga's objects in shop displays. One shopkeeper told Saint that all his things were from Gorga, and Saint noticed that 'practically every object had his little numbered label on'.[45] Soon, Saint knew exactly which objects had come from the Gorga collection without having to ask. And he was sure he could acquire these objects more cheaply now than if he had been dealing with Gorga directly.

Gorga's collection was permeating the Italian antiquities market, and Saint began to use it as a gauge for evaluating other objects he came across in Europe, elaborating his reports with comments like 'I do not remember seeing anything like these in the Gorga collection',[46] and, 'better than anything I have seen in the Gorga collection'.[47] Gorga's collection symbolized the richness of the Italian antiquities market, and its vulnerability to the whims of the highest bidder. Many of the objects were Italian and Roman in origin. Louis Sambon had written that Gorga's museum included rare historical treasures, unearthed during 'the great days when the Tiber was being embanked': it included artefacts that would never be found again.[48] But Gorga's financial vulnerability ensured that his collection was barely protected from the fierce consumer market that had helped to create it. He constantly struggled to keep his property from seeping back into the hands of his hungry rivals. Thus, the Gorga collection stood for the power, the potential rewards, and the ruthless cruelty of the collecting game. Success was sweet, but it was hard fought and easily squandered; it demanded determination, money, tactical skill, restraint, and a good deal of luck.

In his acquisition of such a large proportion of the Gorga collection, Wellcome had outdone his American rivals and defeated Gorga himself. The Italian's reluctance to sell had only added to Wellcome's eventual triumph. Gorga had courted offers from other prospective buyers over the years, but he knew that Wellcome was the only one who could seriously consider spending the amount of money he demanded. Their battle had confirmed Wellcome's ascendancy as a collector. While no one could accuse him of financial recklessness, after so many years spent waiting for a good price, neither could anyone else compete with his purchasing power or the savvy of his staff.

Crummer, Streeter, and Cushing were in awe of Wellcome's Museum. Cushing claimed that he never visited the Museum 'without making a vow that I will come [back] to London and spend a month in trying to get acquainted with some of your amazing collections'.[49] He repeatedly asked for a catalogue of Wellcome's great collection of books, but it was never produced. Streeter, meanwhile, was effusive in his praise, wishing he had more time to study Wellcome's 'marvellous museum', and writing from America, 'I long to see the Museum and all your new acquisitions.'[50] When Streeter sent off-prints from his latest paper for Wellcome's library, he added, 'there is nothing within our gift that we would not gladly do for one who has done so much in gathering that great collection'.[51]

Wellcome had secured so much of Europe's medical heritage by the time his main rivals got in on the act that their efforts paled in comparison. He had been the first major collector to focus his attentions on the history of human health, and the breadth of his vision, coupled with his financial resources, dwarfed the work of his contemporaries. This did little to assuage his fears regarding American competition, but he increasingly used those fears to justify his own voracious appetite as a collector. His Museum had been established in London, and for this reason alone he could fashion himself as a generous custodian of Europe's past, protecting it from the grasp of America's culture-hungry elite. Others were not so sure. In the eyes of some of his London peers, Wellcome's own American roots left his allegiances open to question. But this, too, may have played to his advantage. There were rumours that leading historians of medicine in England, including Sir Humphry Rolleston and Sir Arthur Keith, were afraid of 'treading on Wellcome's toes' in case he suddenly decided to uproot and transfer his 'marvellous museum' back to the other side of the Atlantic in retaliation.[52] As it was, they need not have worried. The Wellcome Historical Medical Museum remained in London throughout the nineteen years it was open, from 1913 and 1932.

III. OUTCOMES

With more than a decade of focused collecting behind him, the time came for Wellcome to share his achievements with his peers. His long-awaited Historical Medical Exhibition—which became a permanent Museum almost immediately—opened in 1913, and the richness of Wellcome's collection impressed those who visited. The Museum was a critical success, but it embodied some of the unresolved ambiguities at the heart of Wellcome's collecting mission. Was it a serious, scholarly institution, or an entertaining, promotional stunt? Was it designed to stimulate new research, or to present a conclusive commentary on the history of science? Wellcome did not provide a consistent response to these questions. When it came to providing a research resource, his actions tended to undermine his declarations on the subject.

Successive generations of staff at the Wellcome Historical Medical Museum presided over a unique collection, unsurpassed in its range and quality, but they failed to reach a consensus when it came to deciding what to do with all the things Wellcome had acquired. Wellcome was, on the one hand, reticent to develop his plans, preferring to focus his time and money on the antiquities market. Although he wanted to join the scholarly community, he resisted dialogue, even with his own employees. On the other hand, he was determined to harness the talents of the people who worked for him for his own purposes. They, not surprisingly, had their own agendas, and their own ideas, but instead of building on the inspiration provided by the collection, Wellcome found it hard to trust the people he relied upon as a collector. He was unable to share his collection with others, even though *he enlisted them in the creative process. The result was a project that lacked a cohesive vision and a staff who struggled to live up to Wellcome's high standards. Despite, or perhaps because of, his talent for marketing and advertising, Wellcome found it difficult to convert his success as an acquirer of things into success as the director of a museum.*

CHAPTER TEN

THE FINEST HISTORICAL MEDICAL MUSEUM IN THE WORLD

The Wellcome Historical Medical Exhibition—later Museum—opened in the summer of 1913. Wellcome, who had already postponed the opening for eight years, later said that he had not meant to open his Exhibition for a further ten years, but various 'eminent medical men insisted' that he make his collections 'the centre' of the historical section of the International Medical Congress that year.[1] Wellcome's claim that he had been persuaded to exhibit only by his peers was not entirely true: Thompson had suggested synchronizing the Exhibition with the Congress, and had been lobbying the organizers for their support since early 1910.[2] Wellcome liked to think his collection had been propelled into the limelight, against his better instincts, by the medical establishment, because it was the medical establishment that he wanted to impress with his efforts as a collector. The International Medical Congress was held every four years and had not visited London since 1881. In 1913 it attracted around 5,000 delegates from twenty-eight countries, 'the most remarkable gathering of the world's doctors that has ever assembled'.[3] It was the perfect backdrop for the opening of Wellcome's Exhibition, because it brought an international audience to his doorstep.

The Exhibition's opening ceremony was held on 24 June 1913 and invitations were extended to scientists throughout the country. It marked the culmination of ten years of dedicated collecting, and three years of preparations for the displays. A suitable venue had been found in central London in

1910, and Thompson and his staff had moved in early the following year to begin unpacking, classifying, arranging, and labelling Wellcome's collection for exhibition. The opening ceremony was a formal affair, chaired by Sir Norman Moore, consultant physician and emeritus lecturer in medicine at St. Bartholomew's Hospital. Other speakers included Sir Thomas Barlow, President of the Royal College of Physicians; Sir Rickman Godlee, President of the Royal College of Surgeons; and Sir Francis Champneys, President of the Royal Society of Medicine. Wellcome took the opportunity to announce that his Exhibition was to remain open as a permanent Museum, although his collection was far from finished. He said that he regarded his Museum 'as at its very beginning, though the collection and organisation have occupied many years', and he planned to establish a Bureau of Scientific Research, to which the Museum 'might well form a fitting and permanent adjunct'.[4] The speeches were given in the Museum's main hall, and later Wellcome played host and mingled as people examined his collection. As his guests wandered from room to room, they found laid out before them an outstanding array of material; as one journalist wrote later, here were 'stores of knowledge culled from every age and every clime'.[5]

The exhibits in the first room, the Hall of Primitive Medicine, did not comprise the orderly rows of surgical instruments and laboratory apparatus one might expect in a museum of medical history. The Hall of Primitive Medicine was filled with dancing masks, 'fetish figures', arrangements of ancient skulls and human remains, weaponry and witch-doctors' costumes (Figure 16). Objects here had been brought from the Pacific islands, the American plains, the Amazonian jungles, and the African savannah. The walls of this room were hung with pictures, diagrams, and maps illustrating tropical diseases; their names alone conjured up a world of heat, risk, and adventure: yellow fever, sleeping sickness, filariasis, leishmaniasis, malaria, schistosomiasis, ankylostomiasis. The Hall of Primitive Medicine, as its name suggested, showed a world that biomedical science was only just beginning to penetrate.[6] The medical equipment here was spiritual and artistic as well as practical. Wellcome had collected feather, skin, and textile costumes, brightly painted shields and tattoo designs, wooden carvings, drums, pipes, and flutes. Many things had been bought at the auction rooms of J. C. Stevens, some had been shipped back from Wellcome's excavations in Sudan, and a few had been acquired through friends and associates. They introduced a rich and distinctly 'other' world—and one far more culturally varied than that of biomedical science—but it was, nevertheless, concentrated in a single

Figure 16. The Hall of Primitive Medicine at the Wellcome Historical Medical Museum, Wigmore Street.

opening room at the Historical Medical Museum. Cultures as disparate from each other as they were from those of northwest Europe were massed together and given the depreciative designation 'primitive'. But this room, at least, presented the visitor with the notion—however poorly analysed—that there *were* different cultural attitudes to health, and that they too belonged in a museum for scientific history.

From the jostling exoticism of the Hall of Primitive Medicine, visitors passed through a small annexe which housed an exhibition on the science of parasitology and the history of the microscope. The microscope, which magnifies and objectifies the causes of disease, is one of the most resonant symbols of the development of biomedical research: this display space was in complete contrast with what had gone before. So too was the main room of the Museum, the Hall of Statuary, a large, airy room with a high ceiling and balustraded gallery (Figure 17). It was in this room that Wellcome's guests gathered to attend the Museum's opening ceremony. Here, select statues, elevated on simple plinths, were interspersed with the occasional palm tree in a pot. The statues were of healing deities from China, India, Ancient Egypt,

Figure 17. The Hall of Statuary at the Wellcome Historical Medical Museum, Wigmore Street.

Ancient Greece, and the Roman Empire. These were the great civilizations into which the roots of Western science and medicine could be directly traced. These exhibits, unlike those in the Hall of Primitive Medicine, were widely spaced to allow for considered admiration. Whereas the material found in Ecuador and New Guinea excited curiosity and wonder, that of India, China, and the Mediterranean demanded awe and respect.

The gallery overlooking the Hall of Statuary housed surgical instruments, optical appliances, and a collection of charms and talismans. There were two further main rooms on the ground floor: the Gallery of Pictures, where the walls were thick with portraits of the great men of science, memorialized within their heavy gilt frames; and the Gallery of Ancient Manuscripts, Books, Diplomas and Engravings, where visitors could see some of the papers and manuals used by these famous medics. Visitors had moved from the startling anonymity of the Hall of Primitive Medicine, through the measured spaces in the Hall of Statuary, before finding themselves face to face with the select few individuals who were praised for transforming medicine into a modern, scientific enterprise.

The exhibits continued below. Stairs at the back of the building led down to the basement where there was a large area depicting the history of hygiene, nursing, and orthopaedics, and housing a range of pharmaceutical apparatus—flasks, pestles and mortars, weights and scales, and the like. There were also displays showing gruesome instruments of torture, dating back to the Middle Ages, from Asian, African, and European countries, and an exhibition exploring the development of photography and the X-ray photograph. The main attraction in the basement, however, was a series of open-fronted rooms, reconstructed to represent practitioner's rooms from the past. There was a sixteenth-century hospital, a barber-surgeon's shop and a lying-in room, a seventeenth-century Italian pharmacy, a London apothecary's shop, and an eighteenth-century London chemist's shop. There was also a Turkish drug shop (Figure 18) and a Roman surgery. Costumed mannequins greeted the visitor from within these assembled rooms: a barber-surgeon attended his client, while an alchemist held the contents of his glass flask up to the light.

Many of the journalists who wrote about the Wellcome Historical Medical Museum drew attention to the delights of this final section. It was as if, having diligently studied the rather dry and academic exhibits upstairs, visitors were rewarded with a more exciting museum experience as they were taken 'back in time' through the weird and wonderful history of scientific study. As one journalist explained in 1914, there were various scenes on show, 'some of which are entertaining, others chiefly ghastly'.[7] Another, writing on the mostly unchanged displays 14 years later, echoed this sentiment:

The lay mind will probably find its greatest delight, however, in the street of chemists' shops, each one representative of the alchemist's art in ancient times. Mysterious, gloomy, and dark, with strange animals and fishes hanging from the roof and casting fantastic and eerie shadows on the old stone walls, the alchemist's laboratory of the sixteenth century is a fearsome haunt.[8]

These 'learned side-shows', as the *Manchester Guardian* described them, appealed to the lay mind as well as to the professional scientist. One newspaper ran a story about Wellcome's Museum under the headline 'Alchemist's Den Below London Street',[9] another gleefully exclaimed, 'Shops you never see—unless you take in the Wellcome Museum where they are

Figure 18. Reconstruction of a seventeenth-century Turkish drug shop at the Wellcome Historical Medical Museum, Wigmore Street.

kept in ancient glory';[10] and, in later editions of the Museum's handbook similar evocative descriptions of the basement displays could be found. Indeed, the description of the 'mysterious' alchemist's laboratory quoted above was lifted directly from the Museum's handbook, although the words 'fearsome haunt' had replaced the claim that the alchemist's workshop offered 'a glimpse of the surroundings of the worker in Science some four centuries ago'.[11]

Thompson had drafted the text for the handbook,[12] and he may have instigated some of the more entertaining displays at the Museum. In May 1913, he had advertised for eight nurses to work as attendants at the Exhibition, and had planned to dress them in character: 'I had an idea, if it could be carried out, of having each nurse dressed differently in a historical nurse's costume, dating from the 15th, 16th, 17th down to the end of the 19th century.' Wellcome thought the suggestion was 'excellent', but decided that there was too little time before the opening and the idea would have to be left for future consideration. Plain uniforms were issued instead.[13] In public, however, Wellcome presented his Museum as a serious research institution. 'In organising this museum,' he said at the Opening Ceremony, 'my purpose has not been simply to bring together a lot of "curios" for amusement. This collection is intended to be useful to students and useful to all those engaged in research.'[14] He may have intended his Museum to be chiefly educational, but neither he, nor anyone else, could deny that he knew how to put on a good show.

Years later, Wellcome argued that museums should be 'attractive, but not fantastic'. 'There are two kinds of museums;' he explained, 'one is simply for entertainment, a place where people go to see curious and attractive things, freaks and objects of that sort; and the other museum which is designed for intellectual and scientific study.'[15] His own Museum, he insisted, belonged in the latter category. But Wellcome had a talent for entertainment, as his work on the Burroughs Wellcome trade fairs had shown. He had displayed Henry Stanley's medicine chest, battered from its travels through central Africa, knowing it would attract the attention of passing clients, and he had ordered the installation of a tank filled with live cod so that people would talk of his firm's products as they browsed the exhibits. Wellcome knew how to use artefacts for promotion, and how to create a spectacle. He appreciated that objects could amuse as well as inform; in fact, the effectiveness of their latter role often depended on the success of the former. So it was that the more macabre exhibits at the Historical Medical Museum stirred journalists into descriptive reveries. They did not linger long over the tiers of microscopes and oil paintings of Edward Jenner, but they were happy to relate their impressions of the shrunken heads, mummified moles, trepanned skulls, and witches' glass balls. A correspondent for the London *Nation* found Wellcome's Museum to be 'a haunt of delightful horrors'.[16] While the *Amateur Photographer* concluded that this was 'a museum which has more curious things per cubic foot than any other museum in London'.[17]

Complimentary reviews of the Museum were common in the press and in scholarly journals throughout the nineteen years it was open. It was frequently presented as a hidden gem, virtually unknown but no less remarkable for that fact. One Dutch publication urged that 'Everyone who visits London should pay a visit to the Wellcome Historical Medical Museum...Its contents can be valued only in millions and it includes not a single ugly or unaesthetic thing.'[18] *Pearson's Weekly* termed it 'the world's strangest museum'.[19] H. M. Walbrook, meanwhile, informed readers of *The Bazaar*,

I have lately been permitted to spend two afternoons in it [the Wellcome Historical Medical Museum], and no man possessing a spark of imagination could come away unmoved from such an experience...even as I write I feel that the more things I mention the more I have to leave out...in the Wellcome Museum, as in Euclid, the whole is greater than the part.[20]

And a correspondent for the *Evening Standard* quipped, 'That hour among the sinister marvels of the Wellcome Museum—the finest historical medical museum in the world—was more fascinating than a dozen "thrilling" novels.'[21]

The Museum was full of curiosities, and it is little wonder that journalists found them noteworthy, because the broad scope of Wellcome's collection was what made it distinctive. Other museums that dealt with the history of medicine, including the Museum of the Royal College of Surgeons and the Hunterian Museum in Glasgow, had some archaeological, ethnographic, and zoological exhibits, but none had set out expressly to illustrate 'the healing art' in all its cultural guises. Perhaps because he was not a doctor himself, Wellcome was interested in chronicling the limits of the medical discipline. He could take an outsider's view. And, while he shared with the founders of other medical teaching collections the desire to push forward the boundaries of scientific knowledge, he was also hoping to survey the cultural limits of medical practice. 'In the course of my long researches into the history of medicine', he explained at the Opening Ceremony, 'I have come to the conclusion that we can gain a great deal of useful information from primitive peoples in the art of healing, and particularly in surgery. In my own personal experiences amongst primitive races I have sometimes found traces of the origin of what are usually regarded as entirely modern discoveries.'[22]

Again, there were echoes of Wellcome's early work on the history of animal substances in medicine, when he sought to give scientific credit to 'primitive' medical practices. Wellcome seemed to approach medicine, not as a profession to be buoyed up, so much as a cultural phenomenon to be taken apart and pieced back together again. Scientific learning, he suggested, should be outward-looking and explorative. All humanity shared a concern for health and well being. Indeed, some form of medical knowledge was crucial for survival, however 'primitive' a culture might be. Why not, then, learn from each other? Wellcome promoted medicine, not simply as a means for healing the sick, but as a lens for viewing, and learning from, the human world in all its diversity. 'Medicine has a history which has touched every phase of life and art, and is, to a large extent, bound up with the records of humanity', later editions of the guidebook to the Wellcome Historical Medical Museum pointed out.[23]

Wellcome's attempt to celebrate the wealth of cultural attitudes to health, and show that even the simplest solutions to human ailments could be inspirational, was of limited success. He stated that the Museum's exhibits were educational, but the press saw many of them as little more than entertainment. And they could hardly be blamed when the Hall of Primitive Medicine overflowed with unfamiliar objects, poorly labelled and poorly understood, while the surgical instruments and gilt-framed portraits were laid out in orderly rows and individually identified. 'Our views of progress', Wellcome wrote later, 'are often exaggerated, owing to our ignorance of the past',[24] and by 'the past' he meant both present-day 'primitive' cultures and truly ancient societies, but he had little grasp of the significance of the foreign objects his staff had bought at auction or while travelling. Only one artefact in the Hall of Primitive Medicine was individually identified in the 1913 guide-book—the 'Maori talisman of Life and Death', 'The Manuka of Whaka-tane'—and the other references were vague: 'African witch-doctors, weapons and other implements used by them', and 'The Witch-doctor and his Hut', which referred to a reconstructed dwelling apparently of no specific proven-ance (it was later identified as from New Guinea).[25] Wellcome's idea that science could learn from other cultures, and that his Museum would provide the necessary data, was undermined by his failure to communicate—or likely even understand—the meaning of the so-called 'primitive' material he put on display.

Wellcome may have believed that the unique juxtaposition of objects from all over the world would humble his visitors into treating the traditions of 'primitive' cultures more respectfully. In fact, most journalists, and, one can assume, most visitors, to the Museum came away with a heightened sense of pride in Western medical practice, and little understanding of the significance of ancient or foreign customs. Wellcome claimed that inspiration could be found through the study of 'exotic' and prehistoric cultural traditions, but his own taste for the curious could not be completely denied and, in any case, his argument was made from a safe, scientific distance. In truth, these exhibits reaffirmed the popularly perceived hierarchy between biomedical research and other medical customs. Wellcome and his staff had, after all, endeavoured 'to arrange the Museum on a rational basis'.[26]

The prevailing rationale at the Wellcome Historical Medical Museum was that of 'cultural evolution', which, during the late nineteenth century, had come to dominate in scientific museums throughout the world. The typological approach, advocated by Pitt Rivers, was adopted in many museums because it emphasized the structural and historical links between objects that had previously been thought of as 'mere' curiosities.[27] In Wellcome's Museum, artefacts were grouped typologically, that is, according to form and function: dental forceps from various periods and places were arranged together in a group, as were lancets, surgical knives, toothbrushes, and stethoscopes, so that their different designs could be mapped through time. Evolution was interpreted as a progressive system of development, linking the simplest artefacts—and, by extension, the simplest, most primitive, human minds—to more complicated technologies through a continuous chain of gradual modifications and improvements. It followed that natural phenomena came below, and before, man-made artefacts. So, in the Historical Medical Museum, the displays of weaponry began with animal tusks and ended with repeat firing muskets.[28]

Objects became markers of a particular developmental 'stage' in history, and scholars searched for continuous series of objects to complete their theories of history. Visitors to Wellcome's Museum had to enter through the Hall of Primitive Medicine, before moving on to rooms that explored scientific responses to disease, and this arrangement emphasized the notion that the history of medicine and the allied sciences 'began' in the realm of magic and superstition, and that this realm was far removed from contemporary, civilized life. Wellcome meant to

[t]race from the awakening dawn through the principal stages of evolution the varying forms of primitive life up to the full development of mankind through all periods . . . I have for many years been collecting for the purpose of demonstrating by means of objects that will illustrate the actuality of every notable step in the evolution and progress from the first germ of life up to the fully developed man of today.[29]

When 'primitive' things were found in 'civilized' communities, like the amulets still used by many Londoners that were displayed in the Museum, they were theorized as 'survivals' from an earlier stage in evolutionary development.[30] This meant that the chronology implicit in the Museum's displays was a cultural chronology, based on each artefact's form and function, that did not have to conform to details of geography and date. Ancient things and modern things, British things and foreign things, were all perceived according to their place within the hierarchy of cultural evolution.

The Wellcome Historical Medical Museum reassured those who visited—simply because they were in a position to visit at all—that they were more 'civilized' than many of those who had made and used the objects they were viewing. The *Westminster Gazette* summed up this response in 1913:

Visitors to the new Historical Medical Museum, opened yesterday at 54a, Wigmore Street, W., probably experienced two sensations—one of horror at the barbarous methods in this and other lands of the medical practitioners at the period represented, and the other of satisfaction that in civilised countries—and especially our own—the healing art has by study and research become an exact science. In the exhibition itself not the slightest attempt is evidenced to create unpleasant sensations or to stir morbid sentiment. Inevitably, however, the intelligent observer contrasts the rough and ready and often cruel attentions of the surgeons of past generations with the trained specialist of to-day.[31]

The London *Evening News* remarked in 1929 that Wellcome's exhibits 'set us sympathetically wondering how the poor invalids of a century or so back managed to survive'.[32] Wellcome's determination to explore practices from all over the world and from all time periods was original and groundbreaking, because many would not have considered that a shaman's rattle or a Neolithic hand-axe had a place in the history of medicine at all, but it was not radical enough to undermine the ethnocentric mindset of the English professional classes.

Most of those who visited Wellcome's Museum must have assumed that if they could not perceive the rationale behind the objects they viewed then there was none. Non-scientific approaches to health were the opposite of rational approaches; they were superstitious or magical. And historical attempts at scientific methods represented little more than the 'dark days' of the past. Wellcome, pondering the ancient trepanned skulls he had acquired and other evidence that suggested early surgery had not been completely disastrous in every case, asked whether Western science could learn from the past, but his own society always provided the standard by which all other cultural practices could be judged as successful or misguided, logical or irrational. Mostly, they were found to be, if not misguided, then clumsy and crude. The prevalence of human discomfort was one of the strongest messages to be found in the Wellcome Historical Medical Museum, and it left visitors reaching for the security of their own traditions: 'The collection appeals eloquently to us for a renewal of our vows of dogged devotion to the best interests of our patients, be the latter rich or poor.'[33]

The Historical Medical Museum was created by a pharmacist, for scientists. Wellcome was very clear that his Museum had not been intended for the public. During the Congress, admission was restricted to members of the medical profession. From 1914, members of the public were only admitted in organized groups or with a letter of introduction from a doctor, while women had to be accompanied by a medical man.[34] Meanwhile, letters of invitation were sent to medical training institutions, hospitals, and government departments, and circular letters and posters were sent out to universities encouraging formal visits from groups of students who could be guided round the exhibits by their teachers. Thompson received enquiries from the Missionary Leaves Association, the Institute of Hygiene, the Matron's Council of Great Britain and Ireland, the Midwives Institute, and members of the Red Cross, as well as from archaeological societies, ramblers clubs, library associations, photographic clubs, and historical societies who wanted to arrange a visit. The regulations were strict. An individual without medical qualifications was told to provide a letter of recommendation from a doctor in order to visit.[35]

The majority of those who visited the Museum were doctors, nurses, pharmacists, dentists, and medical students, but the Wigmore Street galleries also opened their doors to civil servants, teachers, anthropologists, architects, bankers, printers, and military men over the years. Visitors hailed from places like China, Denmark, India, Syria, Uganda, Trinidad, Italy, and the Isle of Man. A few craftsmen even made the effort to visit: according to the visitors' book an upholsterer from Hallam Street paid a call, and a potter from Surrey also gained admittance. In fact, quite a few artists and the occasional sculptor came to the Museum, as did, on one occasion, a playwright accompanied by a stage designer. But the most intriguing of all the entries in the Historical Medical Museum visitors' book is dated 17 August 1926. On this day, M. Haynes, a parlour maid, and P. Panlir, a house maid, both from Coombe End, came to peruse Wellcome's pictures and relics. Their unrefined handwriting is conspicuous among the confident rows of middle-class names and addresses. What led these two women to travel to Wigmore Street and present their credentials at the Museum door? Few in their position seem to have had the inclination, or the determination, to do so.[36]

Although Wellcome did not exclude the public entirely, he distrusted them. In 1928 he told the Museums and Galleries Commission that,

For an instructional research museum there must be some restrictions and the question of admission of the general public requires careful consideration. A great many people visit museums simply as stragglers. It is necessary to take precautions to safeguard the exhibits. Many objects are liable to be taken unless under lock and key, especially valuable things.[37]

His qualms about security could be answered by admission restrictions, but he still believed that museums should have guides on hand to show visitors around, and labels and notices to direct them, 'because many people who visit museums become confused and miss the most important objects'.[38] In the mid-1920s, when the Museum guidebook was being revised, he suggested, 'the use of comprehensive plans of the Museum rooms with small arrows indicating the best route the visitors should follow if they desire to survey the entire collection in the proper sequence', although not everyone agreed that this was necessary.[39] Wellcome felt that he and his staff knew which objects were 'the most important' for his visitors, and he was not entirely happy about leaving them to find out for themselves.

As it was, Wellcome's Museum was not visited by many people at all. He could take heart that he had managed to establish 'a spot which conceals its delights from the vulgar'.[40] Indeed, before the First World War, the Museum received only a few hundred visitors a year. By the late 1920s, annual visitor figures had risen to between 3,000 and 4,000, but many small provincial museums could expect ten times that number, and, by the outbreak of the First World War, the British Museum was welcoming close to one million people through its doors annually.[41] The Museum's relative obscurity was compounded by the fact that it was located at the heart of London's medical district, on Wigmore Street, around the corner from Harley Street, and surrounded by hospitals and the university. Thompson and Wellcome had considered various sites for their Exhibition since 1905, including the Prince's Hotel in St. James's, the Cavendish Rooms in Mortimer Street, the Portland Rooms in Portman Square, and, in early 1910, the disused Orange Street Baths behind the National Gallery.[42] Most were in the medical district, but the Wigmore Street premises also happened to be next door to the Burroughs Wellcome and Company showroom.

It is unclear whether Wellcome thought the Museum's proximity to the company's showroom was a good thing or not. When it came to the relationship between the Museum and the business, his views were ambiguous, if not downright contradictory. As Wellcome's collection developed, he began publicly to deny any formal link between the Museum and the firm, but the earliest circulars had announced that the Historical Medical Exhibition was being held 'in commemoration of the elapse of a quarter century since the foundation of the firm of Burroughs Wellcome & Co'.[43] Thompson was a Burroughs Wellcome employee, whose collecting work during the 1890s and 1900s had been primarily for the company's advertising department. And during the 1900s and 1910s, the series of illustrated pamphlets Thompson drafted that were inspired by Wellcome's collection—on diverse subjects like anaesthetics, missionary history, dentistry, and journalism— were bound together with the latest Burroughs Wellcome product lists and information about the firm, and circulated to clients at conferences to promote the company's business.

All members of staff, throughout the Museum's existence, signed contracts with the General Manager at Burroughs Wellcome and were placed on the company's payroll, which obfuscated Wellcome's later claims that the Museum was separate from the business.[44] The collection may have begun as a personal hobby, but it is unclear whether the funds for his later acquisitions were drawn from his personal account or directly from the firm's profits. From 1919, annual Library and Museum expenditure was recorded in the company's accounts, suggesting that money was diverted before it reached Wellcome's pocket. And a note in these accounts for 1925 records a payment to Wellcome of £30,000 to purchase his private collection of 'curios, relics, armour, furniture, etc. and all other chattels belonging to Mr Wellcome'.[45] Particularly expensive purchases—including the £8,000 offered to Evangelista Gorga for his collection in 1923—were agreed in advance with the General Manager.[46] By this time, Wellcome's collections appear to have been officially funded, at least in part, by Burroughs Wellcome, but the company had always provided support for Wellcome's collecting efforts behind the scenes.

Thompson regularly used the Burroughs Wellcome printing department, bookbinding and cabinet-making staff, and transportation and storage facilities for Museum purposes.[47] Staff salaries, insurance arrangements, rents on properties, and, occasionally, disciplinary problems amongst the staff were dealt with by the firm's management. In practical terms, the Wellcome Historical Medical Museum was a department of Burroughs Wellcome and Company.

Thompson was constantly corresponding with his colleagues at the firm's head office, and at the Wellcome Club and Institute and the manufacturing site at Dartford. In the early 1900s, he liaised on the furnishings for the employees' Club and Institute, delivering 'an American bowling or skittle alley' Wellcome had bought, and buying pianos for the club rooms and books for the library.[48] A good number of objects from Wellcome's collection were displayed at the Club: his weapons and pictures decorated the walls, there were display cases filled with smaller objects, and full-size ships' anchors and figure heads adorned the grounds. Exhibition cases in the Snow Hill general office displayed 'historical medical cases' and decorative pharmacy vases from the collection. Thompson provided specimens of fruits and roots for the Materia Medica Museum at Dartford, and sent samples from the Museum collection—arrow poisons, plant extracts, and the like—to the firm for identification. Dr Hooper Jowett, the manager at Dartford, sometimes supplied exhibits, of chemicals and early product prototypes, like wound pads and tampons, to be displayed in the Historical Medical Museum.[49]

Museum display cases were made at Dartford; medicine chests, books, and manuscripts from the collection were repaired by the staff there; Museum publications were printed by the firm; and objects from the Museum were stored at various company sites. Burroughs Wellcome drug representatives, who were posted around the world in ever greater numbers during the opening years of the twentieth century, were regularly called upon to buy objects or meet with people who might help the Museum.[50] Burroughs Wellcome medicine cases and medical supplies were sent to missionaries, academics, and officials who had promised to acquire things for Wellcome, sometimes in lieu of payment for artefacts.[51] Meanwhile, the Museum's collecting agents, including Paira Mall, sent local remedies back to headquarters in case they could be produced for sale.[52] Company client lists were used for distributing Museum circulars. And, in return, the firm's clients were invited to visit the Museum, where they would be shown around by Wellcome or his staff, and their own personal research requests were sometimes answered.[53]

Wellcome admitted, in private, that the Museum was a great marketing tool. Evening receptions were regularly held there: a carefully chosen group of medics would enjoy dinner, cigars and speeches in the adjoining Welbeck Palace Hotel before moving next door to peruse Wellcome's collection at the Museum. An employee remembered Wellcome's businesslike attitude to these events:

These receptions cost approximately £250 a time, and Sir Henry said that as the front page for advertising in a leading daily newspaper cost £1,000 he could therefore afford to give four receptions for the price of one advertisement and his receptions reached the real people who would recommend or give to the public the products he made.[54]

But Wellcome and his staff feared that too transparent an association with the business would undermine their scholarly credentials.

In 1903, Wellcome had reassured interested parties that his Historical Medical Exhibition was to be 'free from any shoppy elements, and to be [...] thoroughly scientific and instructive'.[55] Twenty years later he was making the same argument: 'I need scarcely say that this Museum is not, and will not under any circumstances, be associated with my business or with any other business. It is purely a private interest of mine.'[56] But his favourite phrase, that the Museum had been created 'on strictly ethical lines' and had nothing to do with his drugs company, had to be repeated often, because no one seemed to appreciate the distinction. Thompson and his successor, Louis Malcolm, were often called upon to clarify the situation when people referred to the 'Burroughs and Wellcome Museum'. Thompson warned against adding the words 'Wellcome Foundation Ltd.' on the Museum's doors, for it 'will not for several reasons be looked upon with favour by the leading medical men who come to the Museum, as it so closely identifies it with the business next door'.[57] Malcolm had been told that 'the vast majority of doctors regarded the W.H.M.M. as part of the Firm' and pointed out that 'nearly every day visitors are being corrected on this point'.[58] It did not help that the firm's showroom next door left visitors with the impression that the Museum was an entertaining annexe provided by the company.

Wellcome insisted that his Museum was an academic venture. But to some extent his belief in the scientific value of his collections undermined the supposed 'purity' of his research agenda, since, for him, scientific success had been profitable. When he stated, at the Museum's opening in 1913, that he believed, 'the study of the roots and foundations of things greatly assists research, and facilitates discovery and invention',[59] his own success at Burroughs Wellcome and Company lent weight to his words. After all, if the Museum's collections were going to inspire any scientific innovations, Burroughs Wellcome would be the first to lay claim to them. The specimens and samples that Thompson and his collecting agents sent to Dartford for identification show some effort to put this collaborative philosophy into action, and yet Wellcome worked increasingly hard to hide the logical interplay between his commercial interests and his intellectual curiosity.

The Museum could not have existed without the firm. It was sustained by the business financially and administratively. And, for Wellcome personally, collecting and commercial success had always gone hand in hand. He used historical artefacts as prototypes in product design and advertising, and for communication, both with his staff and with his clients. Collecting penetrated so many aspects of his professional life, and yet he tried to eradicate all reference to Burroughs Wellcome and Company from his Museum and its dealings. The cover-up job was made harder, and more necessary, by the fact that the same people Wellcome sought to impress intellectually were useful to him commercially. If research scientists could recognize the academic value of his collections, they could also spend money on his products in the course of their researches.

Perhaps Wellcome felt the entrepreneurial spirit that had secured his fortune somehow sullied his academic pretensions. His research laboratories—the Wellcome Physiological Research Laboratories and the Wellcome Chemical Research Laboratories—had faced prejudice from the medical establishment and the government because they were perceived to be commercial outfits rather than academic institutions. Wellcome's application to register his laboratories with the Home Office for animal experimentation was refused in 1896, and then delayed, until, in 1901, Wellcome could convince 'the Home Office and much of the medical profession that research on "commercial" premises was not necessarily tainted or substandard'.[60] The medical Royal Colleges were suspicious of supposedly commercial laboratories; the Pharmaceutical Society refused to elect the director of Wellcome's chemical laboratories to a Fellowship and refused to publish papers by Wellcome's staff in their journal, classifying them as advertisements. The *British Medical Journal* also declared that papers bearing the name 'Wellcome' would be considered as advertisements, and only agreed to publish them if no address was given. As a result, every paper published by Wellcome's scientific staff was printed with a separate cover giving the laboratory's address.[61]

The laboratories were indisputably part of the Burroughs Wellcome empire. They were funded by the drugs company, and product development and quality control were central to their remit, but Wellcome tried to maintain the fiction that these interests were independent, and went to great lengths to prove that his products were based on 'high-minded scientific principles'. He imposed strict rules governing correspondence: all letters to or about the laboratories had to be signed on Wellcome's personal behalf rather than by Burroughs Wellcome staff. Letters from laboratory staff had to be forwarded up the organizational hierarchy before being sent on to Burroughs Wellcome head office. And advertisements promoting products developed in the laboratories referred to Burroughs Wellcome only as their 'distributing agents'.[62]

Similar tensions characterized Wellcome's attitude to his Historical Medical Museum: it provided the perfect promotional platform for the firm, but its scientific integrity would be compromised by too close an association with commerce. Many felt, when Wellcome was knighted in 1932, that the honour had been long overdue. The research laboratories he had founded in England and in Sudan, the Historical Medical Museum, and the Museum of Medical Science (formerly the Museum of Tropical Medicine and Hygiene, which had been founded in 1914 as a teaching collection) had all been in existence for twenty years or more. Wellcome had been under consideration for many years. In January 1926 a friend told him that he had been omitted from the New Year's honours list because 'commercialisation had suddenly cropped up', and the charge was made with specific reference to his Historical Medical Museum. There was concern that 'Mr W had handed over the Historical Museum to Burroughs Wellcome and Co.', the implication being that there were business motives behind his philanthropy. Wellcome—who had overseen the formation of the Wellcome Foundation Ltd. in 1924, to include all his business and research institutions, including his museums—sent his lawyer to clarify the situation. The laboratories and the museums were still independent entities, free from commercial interests. 'The allegation about turning my Museum over to B. W. & Co., or to commercialising it in any way is absolutely false, and without a figment of foundation', Wellcome wrote. 'The statement is a malicious invention.'[63]

There may have been a deeper insecurity at work here too. As a child, Wellcome had been advised by his uncle to train as a doctor. He chose, instead, a career path that suited his talents as a designer, his vision as a salesman, and his desire for wealth.[64] He became a businessman, not a scientist. And he successfully served the medical community that he might have joined on different terms. Wellcome's research laboratories and his museum collections were an attempt to reassert himself within the scientific community as an academic equal. In this arena, he downplayed his proven abilities as an entrepreneur, because they were a reminder that commercial success, not intellectual merit alone, had secured his status.

Wellcome's first biographer, A. W. J. Haggis, believed that Wellcome sought academic prestige but he 'knew his own limitations', and because he was not qualified to work in the medical sciences, 'only the history of medicine, of which he possessed a wide general knowledge, provided an opening'.[65] Haggis thought that personal quest for recognition lay behind Wellcome's philanthropic projects, which served as a substitute, in this context, for his lack of scientific training.

As his business success became more and more established, his cultural contacts widened and gradually aroused in him the desire to achieve distinction in the world of Science. His preoccupation with business affairs and his own lack of academic training rendered it practically impossible for him to gain renown by personal scientific achievement. Doubtless he was conscious of the fact that whilst honorary rewards might enable him to become a 'distinguished guest' of the scientific world, as a great 'Patron of Science' posterity might associate his name in perpetuity with scientific research and discovery.[66]

In fact, Wellcome's wealth gave his philanthropic objectives far more reach. He could do more good for humanity as a wealthy benefactor than as a solitary worker in science; but his position as a patron of research, rather than a researcher himself, appears to have left him uncomfortable. Wellcome's triumph as a businessman seemed to haunt him.

The ambiguity of the collection's relationship with the firm was inherent in the displays at the Wigmore Street Museum, which were designed to entertain and impress as much as to inform. The public may not have been entirely welcome, but the newspapers declared, 'A tour of inspection is more fascinating than a visit to a good play. The exhibition might be described as a pageant.'[67] Wellcome, who remained unconvinced that visitors could fully appreciate the importance of museum exhibits without guidance, hoped the exhibits would prove his academic credentials. But there was a fine line between providing his visitors with a scholarly resource, and demonstrating his ability to provide them with a scholarly resource. The visually arresting yet poorly identified ethnographic collections, the dramatic reconstructions in the Museum's basement, and the relics that offered a tantalizing glimpse into the lives of famous explorers and scientists: these may all have had educative potential, but it lay buried beneath their more superficial charms. Perhaps this was one reason Wellcome proclaimed his Historical Medical Museum to be a research institution so often and so loudly.

CHAPTER ELEVEN

WHEN THE WHOLE IS COMPLETE, IT WILL BE AN EXACT FACSIMILE OF THE ORIGINAL

When the Hope heirlooms were offered for sale by Christie's in 1917, *The Times* reported that 'No such sale has been held in this country for several generations, and it is not likely that another collection of equal importance will be offered to the public in the time of anyone living.'[1] The Hope collection, first assembled by Thomas Hope at the turn of the nineteenth century and now to be sold by his descendant, Lord Francis Hope, the 8th Duke of Newcastle-under-Lyme, was one of the best known private collections of antiquities in the country. It was particularly admired for its exquisite Greek statues and vases; never before had so many ancient sculptures been offered in a single sale. Thompson and Wellcome were interested in two of the Hope statues. Both were more than six feet high and depicted Greek gods of medicine and healing: one was a statue of Hygeia with a snake coiled round her left shoulder, described as 'surpassing merit', which had been found at Ostia in 1797; the other, a figure of Aesculapius, with a serpent twined round his staff, had been found in Hadrian's villa at Tivoli. The statues were exceptional and bound to raise enormous prices. Realizing this, Wellcome gave Thompson permission to bid up to £700 for each.[2]

Playing to the drama of the occasion, after considerable publicity, Christie's sold the Hope statues, on 24 July 1917, in the entrance hall of their rooms; the auctioneer directed proceedings from a gallery above the main door. Thompson described 'the great day' to Wellcome: 'There was a tremendous gathering; the balconies and stair-cases were packed to suffocation, and people were standing out into the street, the figures having been so well advertised and illustrated in the daily papers.'[3]

Thompson went to the sale himself to bid on the statues. One of his main competitors turned out to be the wealthy American department store owner, Gordon Selfridge, who had positioned himself near to the auctioneer. Neither Thompson nor Selfridge placed any bids until the statue of Hygeia came up. The bidding started at 500 guineas and escalated quickly. Thompson's £700 limit proved grossly inadequate; Selfridge was outbid on the statue at £1,650, and it was finally sold to a dealer, Spink, who was acting on behalf of Sir Alfred Mond, for 4,000 guineas. In view of this, Thompson decided to concentrate his efforts, and his budget, on the statue of Aesculapius, which was put up next.

My man did not bid until it [the Aesculapius statue] reached 1,000 when Selfridge came to the front of the gallery and took up the bidding. He out-bid us at 1,400, the limit I had put upon it, and it was going to be knocked down to him at that when I saw he meant to concentrate his efforts upon getting it if he went to 2,000, so I thought I would make him pay a bit more. He could not see me from where he was standing up in the gallery, and I ran him up to 1,700 guineas, and then felt I had better let go as it was evident he meant to go on. It was knocked down to him for that amount.[4]

The thought of spending 1,700 guineas on a marble statue by mistake caused Wellcome to scribble a cautionary, 'Watch this', in the margins of Thompson's report. The Hope sale was one of the very few occasions when Wellcome patronized the mainstream art market and bid for an extremely valuable piece. He demurred at the suggestion of spending so much money on a single item, but Gordon Selfridge went on to spend £3,517 on three statues at the Hope sale—he bought the statue of Zeus, the Apollo and Hyacinthus, as well as the Aesculapius—which were installed in his palatial residence, Highcliffe Castle, in Hampshire. Perhaps he intended them to grace 'the biggest castle in the world', which he planned for Hengistbury Head, opposite the Isle of Wight, but never built.[5]

Selfridge and Wellcome were not the only affluent collectors represented at the Hope sale. Many of the statues were bought by wealthy industrialist art collectors: Sir Alfred Mond, Viscount Cowdray, and William Hesketh Lever all bought Hope statues on 24 July 1917. Lord Cowdray, who had oil interests in Mexico, bought the most expensive piece on the day, the Hope Athena, for £7,140; Lever bought the largest number of statues, fifteen in all, for his Lady Lever Art Gallery in Port Sunlight, which was under construction at the time.[6] Perhaps the most extravagant private collector of all, William Randolph Hearst, bought three of the Hope statues, including the Athena, and the Hygieia that Thompson had bid for, during the 1930s, albeit for much reduced prices, for his castle estate at San Simeon in California.[7] Wellcome rarely competed with these men, and his motivations as a collector were different.

Hearst, although deemed by the artistic establishment to be 'an accumulator rather than a collector',[8] bought to indulge his aesthetic taste and did not care to strike a bargain. Like those other great American art collectors of the day, Andrew Mellon, J. P. Morgan, and Henry Frick, Hearst was advised by the leading dealer Joseph Duveen, and he bought from the American Art Association, the Anderson galleries, and, indeed, 'every major dealer and gallery in Europe and New York City'.[9] Hearst's interests were eclectic, but he had no educational remit and he bought purely for his own enjoyment. He spent, on average, $1,000,000 each year on art and antiquities, and would happily part with tens of thousands of dollars rather than lose a single item that he had set his heart on. Indeed, he became known amongst dealers as 'the world's premier push-over', because, for Hearst, price was a secondary consideration. He would frequently agree a limit with his representative at a sale, but then start bidding himself once the limit had been reached because he could not bear the thought of losing. Hearst was greatly influenced by the charismatic Duveen, and, although he had a good understanding of the market for things like armour, tapestries, and antiques, it was Duveen who benefited most from Hearst's tendency to pay twice the real value for works of art.[10]

Lever did not share Hearst's self-confidence, or his budget, but he, too, worked closely with art dealers. In particular, he relied on the advice of Scottish art connoisseur James Orrock, along with the leading dealer in Wedgewood, Frederick Rathbone, and, later, he took advice on prices from F. W. Fox. Lever was a social reformer who believed art should elevate and improve, but he collected furniture, paintings, and decorative pieces as an aspiring—if uncertain—historian of art.[11] Lever's earliest acquisitions, like Wellcome's, can be linked to his professional interest in advertising design, but the two men's priorities differed: while Wellcome was busy studying pencil tins and calligraphy samples, Lever was buying contemporary paintings by William Powell Frith and John Henry F. Bacon at the Royal

Academy to be reproduced as Lever Brothers soap advertisements.[12] Neither Lever nor Hearst was solely motivated to collect masterpieces, but they both saw themselves as art collectors, and regularly spent thousands on individual works. Wellcome, in contrast, remained 'a picture collector who was not interested in collecting art'.[13] He had bid for the Hope statues, not on aesthetic grounds, but as an historian.

Wellcome's collection was shaped by its subject matter. He was interested in the Hope statues as premier representations of the Greek god and goddess of medicine. Although he acquired many things of great merit and rarity, they were, in theory, bought for their historical, rather than their artistic, value. The desire to document ran through Wellcome's collection of paintings. Pictures were hung together because of their shared theme. Wellcome's was an iconographic collection, designed to provide study material relating to specific subjects. He collected pictures that showed doctors examining their patients, alchemists toiling over their furnaces, astrologers studying the stars, and saints healing the sick. He collected pictures that other pharmacists had displayed on their premises, and the shop signs they had hung above their doors. He gathered together portraits of famous scientists. He bought anatomical pictures because they demonstrated medical knowledge at the time they were made; he bought pictures of workshops and laboratories because of the scientific equipment they depicted, and pictures of operating theatres because of the surgical techniques they recorded.[14]

The emphasis on the image's content, rather than its execution, spurred Wellcome and Thompson to buy many very similar pictures because of slight variations in perspective or substance. Others may have sought unique works of art on the art market, but Wellcome did not prioritize originality. Unlike Selfridge, Hearst, or Lever, Wellcome was constantly balancing his interest in any single item against his desire for an extensive comparative collection. In this respect, the more bargains he could find, the better. He bought numerous seventeenth-century Dutch genre paintings, many of which depicted alchemists, apothecaries, doctors, and dentists at work. The Flemish artist David Teniers the Younger produced more than 350 compositions of alchemists, and his work was copied extensively.[15] Thompson bought pictures by Teniers in the London salesrooms quite cheaply, as well as paintings that were 'after Teniers'. He often listed his recent acquisitions in his reports to Wellcome: 'picture on panel called "The Dentist" by Teniers', 'oil painting of "An Alchemist" after Tenier', 'two small oil paintings, "The Alchemist" and "The Chiropodist" by Teniers', 'picture "The Barber-Surgeon" by

Teniers', 'old oil painting of the Dutch School, on panel, of a surgical operation (good)'. Thompson would pick up more than one in a single sale, or three or four in a week. Wellcome's collection of compositions by Teniers soon numbered in the hundreds.

Wellcome was attracted to genre paintings because of their representational style and everyday subject matter. Teniers and his followers had been inspired by the same scenes that now fascinated Wellcome. Taken as a group, Wellcome's collection of genre paintings created a kind of meta-picture of European daily life that paid particular attention to the work of doctors, barber-surgeons, dentists, scholars, and chemists. The genre paintings became one element in Wellcome's exhaustive, multilevel reference collection, where any medical topic could be studied through the relevant literary references, artistic representations, and physical remains. Words, images, and objects would be married together in the pursuit of knowledge, all providing different perspectives on the same historical story. In this context, a painting was not to be isolated, or revered on account of its technical, or even aesthetic, merits. On the contrary, Wellcome was 'generally indifferent to the aesthetic quality and condition of the pictures, books and manuscripts' he bought.[16] A painting had a job to do; it was historical evidence; it was there on account of its content not its quality alone.

This was all very well, but many paintings were as much flights of fancy as historical documents. The Dutch genre paintings are a case in point. They did not depict specific people or events or places; they presented generalized scenes, lifted as much from the artist's imagination as from the real world. They were painted to entertain the middle classes rather than to teach them. Their characteristic composition was fashionable, conventional, and sprang from a desire for good storytelling. Medical scenes gave genre artists an enticing array of paraphernalia to play with. Alchemy in particular offered the perfect subject matter for exploring different qualities of light—blazing furnaces, eerie shadows, high windows, dark corners, a child's curious gaze— and all the chemist's accoutrements—vases, hammers, crucibles, books, globes, skulls—ensured an image full of interest and technical challenges. The same elements were repeated again and again, so that each picture was a palimpsest of all the others that had gone before; reworking some elements, copying others, making room for more, arranging them afresh to form a new composition.[17]

It was in Wellcome's picture collection that the tension between entertainment and education was hardest to unpick. He aimed to document the past, but he wanted the vision he created to be inspiring. Although he did not patronize the fine art market, he commissioned a number of illustrators whose work satisfied both these requirements. Louis Sambon had been accompanied on his early travels for Wellcome by the Italian illustrator Aleardo Terzi, who made sketches and watercolours of interesting objects they encountered along the way.[18] During the earliest years of the century when taking a photograph often caused more problems than it solved, a competent artist could be just as efficient, more reliable, and could produce very realistic results. Illustrators like Terzi also provided large-scale exhibition pictures of tiny engravings and manuscript miniatures that only one person could study. There were many good reasons for employing illustrators in a research museum, since they worked to record evidence and make it more accessible, but they also *recreated* the past for Wellcome's purposes. The artist Ernest Board, best known today for his mural *Latimer preaching before Edward VI* in the Houses of Parliament, painted a series of scenes for Wellcome memorializing great events and famous characters in the history of Western science. Board painted Edward Jenner inoculating the eight-year-old James Phipps against cowpox in 1796; and Ambroise Paré securing a ligature before performing an amputation on the battlefield at Bramvilliers in 1552. He painted Anton van Leeuwenhoek studying single-celled organisms under his microscope; and the anatomist Mondino de Liuzzi making his first dissection in the anatomy theatre at Bologna in 1318. Working in oil on canvas, Board celebrated these moments for posterity.

Thompson kept an eye on Board's progress as he painted, providing him with research information. In the summer of 1910, Board embarked on a painting of the first operation under ether, showing the Scottish surgeon Robert Liston using the chemical during an operation in December 1846 (Figure 19). In preparation for this painting, Thompson, 'after considerable trouble', gathered together portraits of all the surgeons who had been present at the operation, and arranged, through the University College Medical School, to borrow the original table on which the operation had taken place. A drawing of the original apparatus and an engraving of the operating theatre at University College, which had since been demolished, were also obtained.[19] Thompson's research proved worthwhile. In December he told Wellcome that Board had been, 'most successful and happy in his treatment of the subject. The figures are well-grouped and the portraits are excellent, and, beyond a few trifling alterations, I think it is the best thing he has done for us.'[20]

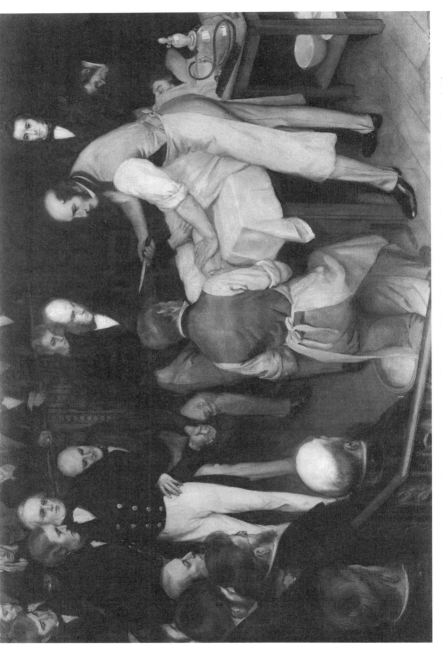

Figure 19. Robert Liston using ether during an operation at University College London in 1846. Oil painting by Ernest Board. The painting was

Thompson was not beyond giving Board advice on composition. While Board was tackling a 'Greek subject'—possibly his painting of patients in the temple of Aesculapius at Epidaurus—Thompson gave him such intense guidance that 'he has practically painted the greater part of the old study out'. Thompson was, however, reassured by the alterations and believed that Board would 'now make a better thing of it'.[21] Thompson kept a close eye on all the illustrators who worked for him, and it is reasonable to assume that Wellcome took an interest in their work when he was in London. The pictures produced for the Museum were collaborative ventures to a certain extent. Thompson provided historical information, but his guidance also ensured a striking overall effect. Twenty-three of Board's oil paintings were hung in the Museum's Hall of Statuary when it opened in 1913, constituting an impressive roll call of famous moments in the history of Western science. Board dramatized a catalogue of experiments and discoveries, and in so doing he transformed the unpredictability of history into a series of ingenious breakthroughs. He immortalized the 'great men' of science on Wellcome's behalf.

Another illustrator who worked for Wellcome, Richard Tennant Cooper, produced imaginative works that sought to convey the emotional power of disease, and the fears that sickness and surgical intervention could provoke. While Board celebrated the power of scientific thinking, Cooper indulged in the horror of the diseases that inspired it. And horror could be just as visually arresting as ingenuity, if not more so. In February 1909, Thompson had spotted 'a very extraordinary picture' by Cooper in the French publication *La Chronique Médicale*. It was called *L'Ether* and was 'supposed to represent the sensations of a man under the influence of ether during an operation for appendicitis'.[22] Thompson wrote to Cooper, who lived in Paris, to enquire about the painting, and later visited him while on his collecting tours in France.[23] By the end of the year they had come to an agreement, and Cooper was commissioned to complete a series of pictures 'illustrating the various great diseases that had afflicted humanity'.[24] Thompson wrote in January 1910:

Cooper is a man of peculiar temperament, who apparently takes things very ser-iously, and once we get him interested in the subject, he has distinctly original ideas and a characteristic method of treatment. I believe his pictures will be worth money later on. I think his charge to us is very moderate, and he now seems to be thoroughly enthusiastic on the subject.

Wellcome was keen: 'Keep him steadily on one after another continuously and enthuse him. Get everything and as many subjects possible from him.'[25]

Cooper's allegorical paintings were sinister and fantastical, and often featured angels or ghosts or figurative representations of death. His portrayal of *Diphtheria* depicted a child unaware that an ethereal skeleton was hovering above her bed, about to tighten its grip around her throat as she slept. In *Chloroform*, a swarm of small, grey demons, brandishing surgical instruments, crawled over an unconscious man on the operating table. And, in his painting of the *Plague*, Cooper had 'succeeded in elaborating a very weird idea', according to Thompson:

The scene represented is an ancient, tumble-down, dirty, narrow street, taken from a sketch he made in Spain. In the foreground on the rough stones are lying several victims of the epidemic, and some dogs are seen slinking away . . . Rushing down the street in mad terror, is the figure of a woman, clasping the body of a child, the figure being pursued by a huge hand, which apparently comes down from the sky, between the roofs of the houses. At the street corner, a lamp burns beneath the shrine of the Virgin, and the whole picture is conceived in a harmony of moonlight blues, weird and ghostly.[26]

Thompson, who seemed to have been impressed with Cooper despite himself, felt the picture would benefit from the addition of some rats, 'scuttling from under one of the doors', and Cooper obliged, completing the picture to Thompson's satisfaction.

Thompson entered into the drama of Cooper's work, and Wellcome commissioned ten watercolours by him, but these pictures were not primarily educational. Both Cooper and Board, in their different ways, worked to evoke an emotional response from their audience. Interestingly, Cooper's paintings were not hung in the Hall of Statuary, but in the Gallery of Ancient Manuscripts, the last room visitors walked through before descending the stairs to the basement and the reconstructed rooms below. Cooper's work was imaginative rather than documentary, and it added to the entertaining panorama on view at the Historical Medical Museum. There can be little doubt that Wellcome and Thompson sought to create a visual spectacle for their guests. The galleries were filled with an array of objects from different times and places, and pictures in different styles. Wellcome's Museum bombarded the senses and conjured up the past. In fact, much of what was on display was little more than an illusion, because at the Wellcome Historical Medical Museum the real and the fake existed side by side.

1. Skull mask from Bhutan, 1850–1920. SM, A193924.

2. Sinhalese dancing mask with cobras from Sri Lanka, date unknown. SM, A101694.

3. German gas mask from the First World War with container and Christmas card. SM, A51114.

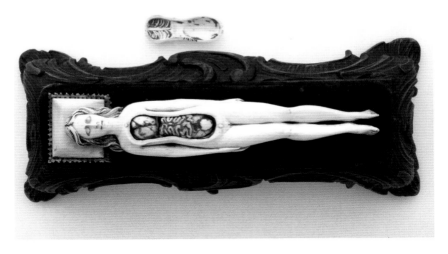

4. Ivory anatomical model of a pregnant female. Possibly German, seventeenth century. SM, A127699.

5. Artificial lower leg with laced leather thigh socket, made by W. R. Grossmith, 1861–1920. SM, A603149.

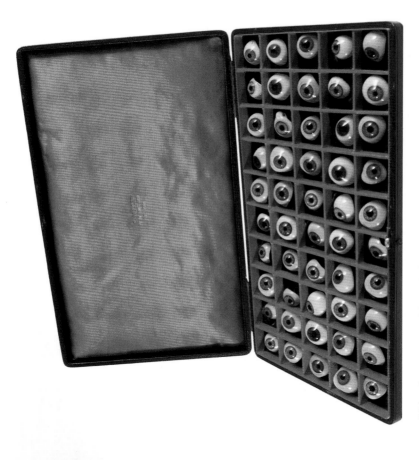

6. A case of fifty glass eyes, possibly made by E. Muller, Liverpool, *c.* 1900. SM, A660037.

7. Illustration from a copy of Kiśordās's vernacular translation and commentary of the Sanskrit Bhagvadgītā, India, 1820–40. WL, Panjabi MS 255.

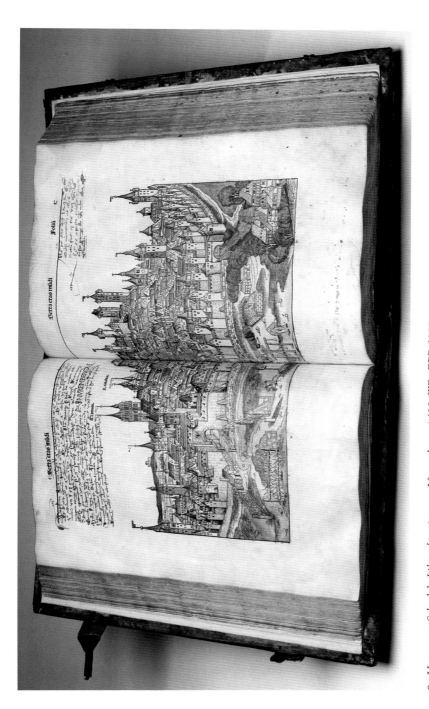

8. Hartmann Schedel, *Liber chronicarum*, Nuremberg, 1493. WL, EPB 5822.

9. Ceramic pharmacy jars used by Carmelite nuns to store the medicinal herbs theriaca and bugloss, France, 1725–75. SM, A85787, A633656.

10. Glass infant's feeding bottle in shape of bird with three legs, eighteenth century. SM, A85612.

11. A funerary reliquary for the bones of the deceased, designed to protect ancestors from evil forces and to help the living communicate with their ancestors for good health and success in hunting. Upper Ogowe, Gabon, 1870–1920. SM, A657377.

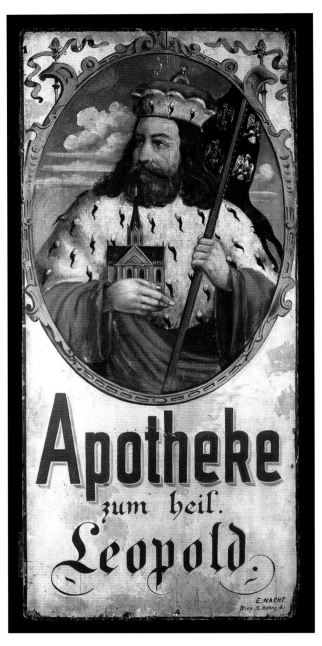

12. Shop sign for St Leopold's pharmacy, Vienna. Oil painting by E. Nacht. WL, 44797i.

13. A savant in his cabinet, surrounded by chemical and other apparatus, examining a flask. Oil painting by Mattheus van Helmont, 1670s. WL, 45123i.

14. An unconscious man being attacked by demons armed with surgical instruments, symbolising the effects of chloroform on the human body. Watercolour by R. Cooper, c. 1912. WL, 24004i.

15. A gold memento mori pendant, a decaying corpse inside a coffin, eighteenth century.
SM, A641823.

16. Whalebone walking stick with ivory skull pommel and green glass eyes, once owned by Charles Darwin, 1839–81. SM, A4962.

17. Napoleon Bonaparte's toothbrush, with a silver gilt handle and horsehair bristles, 1790–1820. SM, A600139.

18. Moccasins said to have been worn by Florence Nightingale when she worked at Scutari, 1850–1856. SM, A96087.

In his hunt for completeness, Wellcome created a show that relied on faithful copies. While efforts were made to authenticate personal relics, like Jenner's armchair or Darwin's walking stick, in other parts of the Museum replicas were abundant. Many of the statues that graced the Hall of Statuary were made of plaster. In 1911, Wellcome had set up his own temporary plaster casting workshop, in a basement room, where deities of medicine were produced by an expert sculptor, working from studies of statues in London's museums.[27] He also bought casts, which illustrated all the epochs in scientific history: he owned a cast taken from a statue of Andreas Vesalius, 'founder' of modern human anatomy in the sixteenth century; and a cast of a statue of William Harvey, who first described the circulation of the blood in the seventeenth century; and one of Herman Boerhaave, the early eighteenth-century Dutch physician; and another of Joseph Lister, nineteenth-century pioneer of sterile surgical procedures. Plaster casts could be found in virtually every section of Wellcome's Museum. He had casts of ancient coins and votive offerings, casts taken from human bones, limbs, brains, and faces showing anatomical features and pathological conditions, casts of old plaques and tablets, casts of wooden carvings, casts of stone tools, and amulets, and surgical instruments.

Great care was taken to make each replica as indistinguishable from the original as possible. When objects were received on temporary loan, Wellcome's staff would set about to make copies for the collection. William Britchford, one of the Museum's carpenters, remembered,

Whenever we borrowed a bronze surgical instrument he [Wellcome] would ask us to make a replica of it before we returned it. We usually did this in wood, and would then paint it with thin glue and dip it into a barrel of verdigris. Providing it was not knocked about it would last quite a long time in the showcase.

But Wellcome worried that repeated dusting would rub the fake patina off with time. He wanted the bronze effect to be produced chemically so it would be permanent. Britchford dutifully asked the company's chemists for advice, but they had no experience with metal work or paint effects. So he set to experimenting.

I did find the answer. It was necessary to clean the brass objects, then rub them with acetic acid and hang them over a bath of ammonia for a couple of days. They were then allowed to dry in the open air, after which they were plunged into a bath of hot linseed oil. When Sir Henry saw the finished articles he was very pleased, and said 'You see, lots of these things can be overcome if you really try.'[28]

Thompson also devoted some of his time to perfecting replica artefacts. In 1909 he had found a 'remarkable vellum scroll' in the Royal Library in Stockholm, dating to 1245. The scroll measured eighteen feet and depicted more than fifty medical operations and anatomical diagrams along its length. Thompson took photographs, and on his return, had them enlarged to the size of the original and mounted on canvas in four sections. He then spent some time experimenting with stains to imitate the aged look of the old vellum. Eventually he 'hit upon a stain composed of coffee and saffron, which proved most successful in giving it an ancient appearance'. ('Excellent', Wellcome noted in response.) Then, he found a young watercolour artist who was paid £8 to colour the whole length of the scroll and illuminate the letters, so that 'when the whole is complete, it will be an exact facsimile of the original'.[29]

Unless a visitor paid particular attention to the notes provided in the Museum's guidebook, where many casts, at least, were identified, the replicas would intermingle, virtually imperceptibly, with all the original artefacts Wellcome owned. In practice, however, historical accuracy had its limits. Damaged artefacts were routinely repaired by Wellcome's staff, a job which allowed for a degree of artistic creativity. One of the joiners, H. C. Barlow, reported working on a pair of damaged wooden figures:

I had to carve in wood two new complete arms on the female. I have also made her holding a stick or staff. It was difficult to tell how the arms should be placed, but I think my idea is not very far out. I should like you to examine these two sets of figures when I send them back.[30]

There were even rumours that the ingenuity of the staff occasionally turned them a profit at Wellcome's expense. Alfred Wilkes—'the redoubtable Wilkes'—had joined the staff in 1912, to clean and restore Wellcome's paintings.

The legend was that he used to purchase old family portraits at second-hand junk-shops, paint in retorts and appropriate inscriptions, e.g. 'Dr. X aetate X' and then put them up for Dr. W. to buy at Stevens' Auction Rooms! Lacaille [an archaeologist who joined the Museum in 1928] used to walk around the gallery and remark 'An early Wilkes', 'a middle-period Wilkes', etc.[31]

This story plays on the illusionary aspect of Wellcome's collection. Wellcome had to count in a few fakes and replicas in his quest for a comprehensive— and inspiring—vision of the past, but, in the end, it may be that he only fooled himself. Perhaps, as the years rolled by and his acquisitions continued to pile up in storage warehouses, others recognized that his perfect, complete museum was little more than a mirage, and his buying habits left him vulnerable to ridicule. By the 1930s, his determination to finish a project that could, by definition, never be finished, seemed misguided. But, during the nineteen years that the Wigmore Street Museum was open, before the patina had worn off the fake bronze instruments in the showcases, Wellcome could be forgiven for believing in the fantasy he had begun to create there. Given that his success as a businessman rested, in part, on his skills in advertising and promotion, and on his ability to create a spectacle, perhaps he revelled in the more evocative displays at Wigmore Street despite his desire for academic recognition. The manikins parading as plague doctors, hooded and masked, and the figure dressed as a Native American shaman, and the reconstructed drug shops manned by waxwork models (Figures 20 and 21), all

Figure 20. Reconstruction of a seventeenth-century London apothecary's shop in the Wellcome Historical Medical Museum, Wigmore Street.

Figure 21. Reconstruction of a barber surgeon's shop in the Wellcome Historical Medical Museum, Wigmore Street.

brought to mind one of London's most popular tourist attractions, Madame Tussaud's, which was just around the corner on Marylebone Road. Indeed, Wellcome had known the Tussauds well since the 1890s.

Wellcome was on friendly terms with three members of the Tussaud family: Victor, Marie Tussaud's grandson, and his nephew, John Theodore, who both worked for the business on Marylebone Road, and John's brother, Louis, who established his own touring exhibition and later founded the Tussaud's waxworks in Blackpool.[32] When Louis, who, like his brother, was a skilled modeller, had been unable to find studio space to prepare for a show at the Victorian Era Exhibition at Earl's Court in 1897, he had asked Wellcome if he could spare 'a small space for sittings at your private house' twice a week.[33] Meanwhile, John Tussaud willingly arranged tours for Wellcome and his friends at the Marylebone Road waxworks,[34] and Victor, knowing Wellcome's interest in medical relics, had on one occasion presented him with a walking stick 'late in common use by Napoleon at St. Helena'.[35] Wellcome's own assessment of the Tussaud shows does not survive, but he happily sent his friends and family there when they visited him in London, and he was in touch with both John and Louis.

Today, Tussaud's stands at one extreme on the continuum between commercial spectacle and educational institution, but Marie Tussaud had always referred to her exhibition as a museum—in Wellcome's day it contained genuine historical artefacts as well as models—and it was perceived as a museum well into the twentieth century.[36] The distinction between entertainment and education was, in any case, harder to define at the time.[37] Waxworks were a relatively common sight in museums, and museums developed in parallel with, and competed with, other entertainments, like panopticons, lantern slide shows, and even zoos and the pageantry of the great world's fairs, all of which profited from conjuring reality for the public.[38] In this context, Wellcome's Museum was not unusual. Museums throughout Britain found different ways to balance the sensational and the educational in their displays.[39] Indeed, all museums are places of instruction and amusement, and Wellcome clearly appreciated the benefits of both.[40] What is more, the Wigmore Street galleries drew on a distinct museum tradition that blurred the lines between science and entertainment, because the Historical Medical Museum was full of anatomical models. On one level, these effigies—in wax, ivory, wood, clay and plaster—charted the history of medical teaching, but they, too, had been used to shock and profit from the public in the past.

Anatomical collections were central to medical training during the nineteenth century, and most medical schools boasted a museum where their students could observe and identify pathological conditions. Many medical museums began as collections of curiosities, since it was life's 'malformations, monstrosities and curiosities' that had most intrigued the people who donated the objects in the first place.[41] The ghoulish aspect of the medical endeavour had—and still has—great public appeal. Although, in professional terms, anatomical models were ideal substitutes for cadavers, since they protected the dead from exploitation and could be studied at leisure, they also catered to the popular appetite for sensationalism. A genre of public anatomy museums sprang up, in which models of sexual organs, venereal disease, skin eruptions, and bodily disfigurements were displayed to the paying public. These institutions claimed to be educational—lectures were given to warn visitors of the dangers of venereal disease, and to promote various quack remedies—but they were increasingly criticized by the medical establishment and, in the 1870s, the last one had been closed down under the Obscene Publications Act.[42]

Forty years later, Wellcome's Museum had its fair share of gory exhibits. There were plenty of pictures and models showing physical abnormalities, a whole section was dedicated to instruments of torture, and a large number of preserved human remains were on display. But, of course, unlike Madame Tussaud's or the anatomy museums of the past, the Wellcome Historical Medical Museum was not intended for the public. It opened its doors, primarily, to 'professionals, [who] by virtue of their education, social background and character, were deemed impervious to the influences that could corrupt the weaker-minded public'.[43] Wellcome explained to some enquirers when the Museum first opened that, 'on account of the nature of many of the exhibits, the Council [of the International Medical Congress] have felt it necessary to restrict admission to members of the profession'.[44] This reflected a broader trend at the time, as medical museums sought to refine their audiences and encourage certain codes of behaviour among visitors. Museums of anatomy and pathology were increasingly 'accessible only to those who knew how to react properly'. Curators were trying to reinforce the distinction between education and entertainment in museums, to differentiate these serious institutions from more frivolous shows and fairs.[45] Wellcome's insistence that his Museum was an elitist institution helped to neutralize its baser charms. He was interested in 'those genuinely concerned and interested in the subjects represented . . . who attend entirely for beneficial information', but, as the frequent press descriptions of 'delightful horrors' and 'ghastly' exhibits proved, visitors often came away from the Museum with a mix of emotions.[46]

Nonetheless, anatomical models were educational tools, and in Wellcome's Museum they represented the development of medical knowledge and prevalence of disease over the centuries. Both the anatomical exhibits and the plaster casts in the Hall of Statuary were important for research purposes. The English cast collecting tradition was associated with proper training in the principles of art and design. One of the best known private collections of plaster casts had been assembled by Sir John Soane during the early 1800s, and Soane used the architectural casts that filled his home in Lincoln's Inn

WHEN THE WHOLE IS COMPLETE

Fields—capitals, friezes, relief fragments, sculptures, and chimney pieces covered every available surface—to teach architectural principles to his students from the Royal Academy.[47] Soane believed that students could only learn to appreciate proportion and the effects of light and shade by copying three-dimensional specimens, and it was this same educational philosophy that sustained the burgeoning cast-making industry of later decades, and Wellcome's own collection. Casts were instruments of learning, and the museums that housed them were perceived to be institutions for public education.

Cast collecting, and manufacturing, had reached its heyday in the late nineteenth century. By the mid-1880s, Berlin's Neues Museum housed 2,000 casts, while the Museum of Fine Arts in Boston displayed 800 casts, which filled more than 14,000 square feet of floor space, and the ground floor of the north wing at the Metropolitan Museum in New York, which opened in 1894, was devoted to casts.[48] The most impressive English collection was at the South Kensington Museum, now the Victoria and Albert Museum, in London. The Architectural Courts there, dominated by the vast two-part cast of Trajan's Column, had been championed by the Museum's director, Henry Cole, and opened in 1873 as a comprehensive inventory of ornamental art in replica.[49] Like many other institutions, the South Kensington workshop issued a catalogue of its casts, which could be bought for 'the use of schools of art, for prizes, and for general purposes of public instruction'.[50] A whole industry, equipped with specialist reducing, pointing, and carving machines as well as legions of skilled craftsmen, fed the late-nineteenth-century interest in reproduction statuary.

To some extent then, Wellcome's casts exemplified his stated desire to document the past. Casts were working objects, produced primarily to teach and inform. So it is fitting that one of the most expensive works of art Wellcome ever bid for at auction, the Hope Aesculapius, eventually found a place in his collection in the form of a plaster cast, worth a fraction of the price but, in Wellcome's eyes, just as valuable as historical evidence.

After the Hope sale at Christie's in 1917, Wellcome prompted Thompson to 'get [a] plaster cast' of the Aesculapius statue from Gordon Selfridge. A good cast of the figure would be just as interesting to his museum visitors as the original, and would allow him to fill a gap in his collection. Organizing for a cast presented few difficulties. Thompson arranged to meet with Selfridge soon after the sale and found him only too 'delighted' to give permission for a mould to be taken from the Aesculapius figure at Wellcome's expense. Thompson had Selfridge's five-ton statue transported to the British Museum, which housed a casting studio in its basement, and the work was 'carried out with great care by two of their oldest and best men'.[51] Two plaster casts were made, one full length and the other of the head and shoulders. Thompson kept Wellcome up to date with progress, claiming in one report that 'we shall in all probability get a cast that will exceed in beauty the original'. Later, he added: 'The dignified expression of the face has come out stronger in the cast than even in the original, and it is the most beautiful head of Asklepios [sic] I have ever seen.'[52] Thompson's admiration would not have been out of place had he been watching a master artist at work, and, in many ways he was, because it took great skill and experience to make a fine cast, without blemish or weakness, without harm to the original and yet perfectly true in every detail.[53]

Wellcome and Thompson took care to ensure the casts and replicas they displayed were true to the originals. They wanted to present an accurate representation of the past, one good enough for serious study, and Wellcome's interest in a broad range of artistic media was extremely valuable. He aimed to assemble all the extant documents and materials that, together, constituted the history of human health. Then, all the evidence could be weighed up and patterns would emerge. A single patient could, after all, be studied in various contexts: as a participant in intellectual history, as a spiritual being, as an economic actor, as a demographic statistic, as a biological agent, or as a microbiological host.[54] All these spheres had to be considered together to fully understand the patient's historical significance. Thus devotional paintings were collected alongside botanical drawings, and political caricatures were as important as anatomical diagrams. Wellcome's collection would become a kind of meta-picture of its own. Like one of Teniers's alchemists emerging from his laboratory clutter, so Wellcome's image of humanity's medical past would surface from midst of all his books, paintings, and artefacts on the subject.

Wellcome's iconographic collection shared its philosophical roots with the typological collections popularized by General Pitt Rivers in archaeology and anthropology. For both, it was the relations between objects that were important rather than the singularity of any one artefact. In fact, the slightest variation between two records was important, for it was at this site of divergence that the work of comparison could begin. The collecting endeavour became focused on gap-filling, as each new addition promised to provide another link in the chain of history. The aim was for a continuous sequence, so that the past could be 'seen' in all its different guises. An object's uniqueness or authenticity now counted for less than its 'substitutability': things were valued for their ability to stand for a moment in time, or a particular event or tradition.[55]

The result was a vast, overlapping series of objects, in which it mattered little whether an individual object was an original or an accurate copy, or whether a painting conformed to the standards set by the art market, as long as it was historically significant. The value of the whole was greater than the sum of its parts. No acquisition was meant to be studied in isolation. It was more important that each subject should be represented exhaustively, from every angle. But if replicas and illustrations were educational props, they also conjured a vision of the past that, in the case of the Wellcome Historical Medical Museum, was designed to induce awe, respect, curiosity, and, occasionally, horror, in those who visited. Casts, models, photographs, and pictures could be ordered to illustrate the stories Wellcome wanted to tell his visitors. They provided entertainment as well as, and sometimes rather more than, an education. They were relatively cheap and could be acquired in large numbers. *En masse*, they did not symbolize a collector's luck or perseverance so much as his purchasing power. With sufficient funds, scientific history could be recreated—brought to life—for the benefit of Wellcome's guests, and in the process it could be understood, and marvelled at. Wellcome chose to present his eclectic panorama of the past to a limited number of people, but no amount of exclusivity could diminish the Museum's power to entertain.

CHAPTER TWELVE

THIS IS THE HISTORY
OF MEDICINE

Wellcome insisted that his Museum was for research, but very little research went on there. He spoke of his aim to create a museum 'as an institution for post-graduate study', with workrooms and laboratories and lecture halls,[1] but he never opened its doors to the researchers that could bring such a place to life. The Historical Medical Museum was nominally part of the Wellcome Bureau of Scientific Research, which had been established in 1914 as an umbrella organization for the Wellcome Research Laboratories and the Museum of Tropical Medicine and Hygiene. The latter was a specialized teaching collection established in London that year in the wake of Wellcome's successful research programme in Sudan.[2] The Museum of Tropical Medicine and Hygiene was part of the Bureau, both physically and administratively, and was used by army officers, missionaries, and educationalists preparing to work abroad. But the Wigmore Street museum remained independent and self-contained, and no formal teaching programme was developed there. Moreover, publishing was discouraged,[3] staff were not allowed to discuss Wellcome's historical collections with anyone outside the institution, and only a few papers were given at conferences. Thompson had drafted one or two booklets each year between 1905 and 1914, but they were designed primarily as promotional literature for the firm and were published anonymously under the Burroughs Wellcome name. After the First World War, these dried up.

At other institutions within the Wellcome Bureau of Scientific Research, in contrast to the Historical Medical Museum, scholarly output was brisk. Wellcome positively encouraged innovative research at his Physiological and

Chemical Research Laboratories, sending his staff the latest reports and scientific papers about new developments and competing products to inspire their work.[4] Between 1897 and 1921, scientists working at the Wellcome Research Laboratories published a total of 430 academic papers.[5] The atmosphere in the laboratories was open: staff were encouraged to participate in academic conferences, communicate with other scientists, and exchange information with them.[6]

The Historical Medical Museum had opened, to great fanfare, as the first research institution of its kind in the world. 'A museum illustrating the history of medicine has never before been attempted in England... Mr Wellcome's Museum will be the most important addition to the means of studying the History of Medicine', the chairman announced at the Opening Ceremony in 1913.[7] Sir Thomas Barlow, President of the Royal College of Physicians, speaking next, believed Wellcome would come to reflect with happiness on 'what instruction this museum has given to this generation and will give to generations to come'.[8] But few people were allowed to study Wellcome's collections. Chosen guests were invited to admire the exhibits, but actually working on them was another matter. Most of the collection, including almost the whole of the library, could not be displayed and remained closed to researchers. A handful of people were helped with specific queries, and the staff were given access to the library and some borrowing rights, but there was no space at Wigmore Street for studying—even the staff found it difficult to work in the congested rooms. Wellcome planned, in the long term, to find better premises, but the First World War intervened.

Gradually, Charles Thompson's team was dispersed during the War. Amoruso, the museum assistant who visited Gorga while serving in Italy, remained there after the War. Another assistant, G. R. Carline, joined the civil service in 1917 and then got a job at the Pitt Rivers Museum in Oxford. The librarian, T. W. Huck, and the secretary, F. G. Shirreff, were both killed on the Western Front. Thompson had taken time out to run a convalescent hospital in Harrow, where Sambon was a medical officer. The Museum remained open, and a small staff continued to register objects on display, but temporary appointments had to be made, and after the War Thompson could not regain the momentum generated a decade earlier. A monograph series, Research Studies in Medical History, was begun in 1922, but only three titles were published before 1925, and the fourth and final title not until 1932.[9]

Wellcome's obsession with new acquisitions did not help. The War had brought many antiquities on to the market and prices were attractive. The new assistant librarian, C. C. Barnard, wrote to Thompson, who had recently returned from his visit to Italy to meet Gorga, in 1919:

Ever since you left, Mr Wellcome has kept me busy attending sales, and I have had absolutely no time to get on with my librarian's work. Some weeks I have had to go to a sale every day, and when I am not actually at the sale there is all the viewing, looking up in our catalogue, and hunting up previous prices to be done...I am afraid, therefore, that you will not find much progress when you return.[10]

Barnard resigned in 1921, and was replaced only on a part-time basis. The Museum was open, and provided the venue for academic meetings and evening soirées, but the lack of space took its toll and most of the staff's work had to be focused on the stores while acquisitions piled up. As Wellcome systematically amassed rare historical documents and relics from all over the world, the wider scientific community began to take note, but their requests for information were answered in the vaguest terms and questions from visitors were evaded.[11] Wellcome created an atmosphere of intense secrecy that began to affect his relationships with his staff and his peers. The expectations set at the Opening Ceremony remained unfulfilled for a decade, and in the mid-1920s the situation reached its nadir.

Charles Thompson, who had run Wellcome's collection for two decades, left under a cloud of mutual distrust in 1925. Little more than a year later, Wellcome was to become the subject of a stinging attack by one of the country's leading historians of medicine, Dr Charles Singer, a lecturer at University College London. Together, these events exposed, in a startling light, Wellcome's uncompromising character. His response in the aftermath of Thompson's departure echoed that of earlier failed relationships, particularly his treatment of his wife, Syrie. Wellcome cut all ties and ceased all communication.[12] He was proud and resolute. He rarely questioned himself publicly and the disagreements with Thompson and Singer only set him ever more steadfastly on his chosen course. He dismissed their complaints, and remained defiant in his decision to limit access to his collections. Wellcome was convinced that the collection could, and would, be finished, and that he only needed a little more time to perfect it. It was a belief Singer scorned, and with good reason. Wellcome was simply unable to share his collection with anyone else until he deemed it presentable, but there was no hope of this while his acquisitive urges continued to run unchecked.

No one knew Wellcome's collection as Thompson did. Perhaps this was why his relationship with Wellcome ended bitterly. For decades Thompson had visited salesrooms, negotiated with private collectors, and travelled throughout Europe in the pursuit of relics. He had monitored every purchase his staff at the Museum had made. He had stored Wellcome's objects, and planned how they would be exhibited. He had written letters, and drafted leaflets and guidebooks. He had overseen the fitting of the Wigmore Street galleries, and the arrangement and labelling of the exhibits there. It was Thompson who had assumed a pivotal position at the centre of the Historical Medical Museum. The collection could only lay claim to a proportion of Wellcome's time, but Thompson had devoted his working life to its creation.

The terms of Thompson's agreement with Burroughs Wellcome left little scope for individual research. Publishing opportunities were few and far between. The booklets he prepared were printed by Burroughs Wellcome without attribution. When, in 1911, Thompson arranged for a report to be published in the *British Medical Journal* outlining his research into Henry Hill Hickman, 'the forgotten pioneer in anaesthetics', whose work Thompson had recently rediscovered, Wellcome responded cautiously. He was concerned about inciting competition in the antiquities market. Any news like this might push up prices:

The editorial is excellent but it is contrary to our policy to indicate the individuals who carried out these researches. It opens up many difficulties. Sambon and others might follow suit and Southerbys [*sic*], Stevens and others may get on to it and thus prejudice purchases. I have expressed intention of giving credit at right time re H.M.E.[13]

Thompson did publish a full article on Hickman in the *British Medical Journal* a few months later,[14] but it stands virtually alone amongst the anonymously authored booklets he drafted for the company during the opening twenty years of the century, as a scholarly publication he actually put his name to.

It had not always been so. Thompson was a successful author when he took full-time employment with Burroughs Wellcome. His bestselling *Chemist's Compendium for Pharmacists, Chemists, and Students* was first published by Whittaker in 1896 and went through several editions during the next thirty years. The 1890s also saw him publish a book on the history of alchemy, a book on poisons, a pharmaceutical guide for nurses, and a romantic novel, *Zorastro*, which he brought out under the pseudonym Creswick J. Thompson.[15]

But the Burroughs Wellcome contract was prohibitive, even when it came to Thompson's existing work, like the *Chemist's Compendium* and *Zorastro*. He could continue to receive royalties only, 'with the express condition that you are not to devote any time to these publications'. He was allowed to make revisions for later editions, but permission was granted on the understanding that such work would be, 'of a merely nominal character, and can usually be done in a couple of hours', and would not interfere with his work for the company. Neither could he write or publish in his own time: 'It is also expressly agreed that no outside work of any description whatsoever shall be undertaken without permission of our firm, first obtained.'[16] For a while, Wellcome turned a blind eye to the fact that the papers Thompson gave at various meetings of the Royal Society of Medicine were routinely published as part of the Society's *Proceedings*, but Thompson's literary output shrank between 1900 and 1925. He authored a few leaflets printed by the Museum— one on the 'rules of health' prescribed for Queen Isabella in the early fourteenth century, another on ophthalmological practices in Roman times, a third on ancient massage traditions—and a longer booklet on Holmleigh Military Hospital, where he had worked during the war.[17]

Thompson would have received little support had he managed to devote a few hours a week to research in his free time, but the wealth of historical material that passed through his hands every day—the ancient documents, the old books, the memorabilia and precious relics from the past—was unparalleled. And, in the early 1920s, in defiance of his contract and Wellcome's good faith, he began to spend his morning hours working on a new book of his own, in collaboration with his friend, D'Arcy Power, a consulting surgeon at St Bartholomew's Hospital. *Chronologia Medica: A Handlist of Persons, Periods and Events in the History of Medicine*, by D'Arcy Power and C. J. S. Thompson, was published by John Bale, Sons and Danielsson Ltd, in 1923. Whether borne of indifference or defiance, Thompson's decision to pursue this project had momentous consequences for his career.

Wellcome allowed the publication of *Chronologia Medica*, but asked Thompson to sign over his royalties to the Museum, in accordance with his contract. When, by November 1925, nothing had been done to this effect, the publishers were approached, but they refused to make the necessary adjustments to Thompson's royalties. In fact, no royalty payments had ever been made, and, the publishers argued, their agreement with Thompson was none of Burroughs Wellcome's business. No matter that the breach of contract was purely academic, later that month Wellcome entered Thompson's office in a rage, and, throwing the book down on the desk, coldly informed him that he could either resign or be asked to leave. Angry words were exchanged, and Thompson left the Museum there and then, for the last time. He was given six months salary and a pension, but his service to the Museum was never publicly acknowledged.[18]

This dramatic end to Thompson's long tenure at Burroughs Wellcome caused a frenzy of activity. Wellcome set his staff to compiling a dossier of Thompson's supposed crimes: they recovered some dubious accounting records, gathered evidence of books and manuscripts that appeared to be missing from the library, made lists of papers Thompson had published without proper permission, and collected the names of researchers he had allowed to study the collections against Wellcome's regulations. The results, however, did not amount to much, and Wellcome's lawyers eventually persuaded him that the case against Thompson was not worth the time and effort required to prove his guilt.

Thompson's departure was sudden, but his relationship with Wellcome had been strained for months. The exaggerated accusations over Thompson's royalties disguised deeper misgivings on both sides. Thompson's final reports, written in the summer of 1925, had been formal, muted, and left unsigned. His monthly updates to the company's management had consisted of little more than the phrase, 'Nothing of importance to report', for more than a year.[19] Thompson had used Museum resources, for typing and photography, while working on the *Chronologia Medica* manuscript with D'Arcy Power, despite the fact that his work on the book was in breach of contract.[20] He had allowed his peers to work in the library without authorization. He felt, no doubt, that he had paid his dues; he had proved himself an extremely able and loyal member of staff. His talents had been rewarded with institutional status—Wellcome had quickly become dependent on Thompson as an administrator and manager—but, after two decades running Wellcome's Museum, Thompson had been given little freedom to establish a reputation for himself within the scientific community. His research interests had been contained, when they might have flourished.

In addition to these long-standing issues, Thompson's commanding position at the head of the Museum had recently come under review. Wellcome had streamlined Thompson's responsibilities. Two new senior positions—Conservator and Chief Librarian—were created in August 1925. The Library had been cared for by a separate librarian since 1913, but for the past four years only on a part-time basis. The new, energetic Librarian, C. R. Hewitt, took up his post in September. Hewitt's appointment signalled a fresh commitment to the Library on Wellcome's part, with the promise of more staff and resources for his literary collections. Then, one month later, Louis William

Gordon Malcolm, a Cambridge anthropologist, started work as the Museum's 'Conservator' with responsibility for Wellcome's ethnographic collections. Thompson, at 63, would now concentrate his energies on the historical medical collections.[21] The Museum, whether Thompson liked it or not, was outgrowing his monocracy. From here on, he would have to share control and focus his interests.

Perhaps Wellcome's decision to reorganize his staff was little more than an acknowledgement that the collections had become too large for one person to manage. Or maybe he was concerned that the Museum had not fulfilled its promise as a 'scientific' institution.[22] Thompson had played his part in the more entertaining aspects of the Museum displays, under Wellcome's guidance, suggesting, for example, that the gallery attendants dress up in historic costumes. He had tried to introduce 'as many incidents and anecdotes as possible' into his writing for the firm, 'to make it interesting'.[23] His own books were aimed at a popular audience and had evocative titles, like *The Mystery and Romance of Alchemy and Pharmacy* (1897) and *Poison Romance and Poison Mysteries* (1899). Malcolm, meanwhile, had a more scholarly background. He had a master's degree in anthropology from the University of Cambridge, had written numerous papers in scientific journals, and had worked as curator of Archaeology and Ethnography at the Bristol City Museum.[24] 'In future', Wellcome wrote to him in 1926, 'the Museum is to be run on strictly scientific lines.'[25]

Thompson's growing complacency had also made Wellcome uneasy, and the fact that Malcolm inherited responsibility for all the collections after Thompson's departure suggests that the decision to reduce Thompson's remit had been personal rather than purely administrative. There are hints of a more fundamental dissatisfaction on Wellcome's part, and the suspicion that Thompson was getting too big for his boots: 'I have reason to believe', Wellcome wrote to Malcolm in 1926, '[Thompson] conveyed the impression that he was the all-in-all and that the Museum was his creation, and that everything was due to his initiative.'[26] Wellcome became convinced that Thompson had taken advantage of his position, allowing visitors to leave with the impression that the collection was his work, and Wellcome was a passive benefactor. Wellcome claimed that Thompson had kept him from meeting important visitors, preferring to deal with these people himself. In January 1930, for example, Dr Spielmann, author of *The Iconography of Andreas Vesalius*, which had been published by the Museum four years earlier, wrote to ask why he had never heard from, or met, Wellcome:

I understood at the time, and thenceforward, that you were travelling—that you were much pre-occupied with other matters—that you were not quite in good health—that you would rather be spared all correspondence—that you were not desirous of sending or receiving messages; and on one occasion when I visited the Museum and heard that you were there, I was told that you were engaged and would rather be spared an introduction, at least at that time.[27]

Wellcome scribbled 'C.T. This is amazing' on the letter and quickly replied to Spielmann explaining that Thompson had 'always made some excuse' when Wellcome asked him to arrange a meeting for them.

Thompson became honorary curator of the historical collections at the Royal College of Surgeons in 1927, and devoted more of his time to writing and attending conferences. While Wellcome never regretted ousting Thompson, he became concerned that his own reputation might suffer as a result of Thompson's continued success. It fell to Malcolm, who took charge of the collections, to smooth Wellcome's reputation within the medical establishment. When a meeting was planned with Sir Arthur Keith, curator of the Hunterian Museum at the Royal College of Surgeons and a good friend of Thompson's, Wellcome suggested, 'You might in a guarded way set Sir Arthur right,' when it came to Thompson's stories, 'otherwise he might inadvertently eulogize him on the basis of C.T.'s own estimation of his accomplishments.'[28] Malcolm was able to reassure Wellcome on this occasion that 'C.T. has not had the slightest influence here. Both Sir Humphry Rolleston and Sir Arthur Keith have expressed an extremely high regard for what you have done.'[29]

Good relations were also re-established with D'Arcy Power, Thompson's collaborator on the *Chronologia Medica* book. Malcolm wrote to Wellcome in May 1926, 'You will be interested to know that Sir D'Arcy Power has been here three times, and that he was impressed with the rearrangement of the collections.'[30] Wellcome, however, remained wary of Power for years. In December 1929, he wrote to Malcolm,

You have mentioned recently that there is a change in the bearing of D.A.P. toward the H.M.M. You should be extremely cautious, but cordial and friendly. There should be no renewing of the free run of the Museum as had occurred in the past—as he seems still to be closely associated with a certain man.[31]

Research at the Museum continued to be strictly controlled, particularly when 'a certain man' might be lurking behind the scenes.

Even as late as 1930, five years after Thompson's departure, Wellcome was anxious that the whole matter should be treated delicately. When, in January that year, Malcolm reported that a meeting of the Royal Society of Medicine was to be held at the end of the month in the Museum, Wellcome responded, 'I am glad to learn of this, but we must be very cautious although always cordial, yet must avoid mention of a certain individual and avoid his presence at the Museum under any circumstances.'[32] Thompson was an active member of the Society and there is no doubt to whom Wellcome was referring. Later that year the Museum celebrated the centenary of Henry Hill Hickman, the anaesthesiologist whose work Thompson had researched eighteen years earlier. But Thompson's contributions caused difficulties during the celebrations in April 1930, because Wellcome ordered that neither he nor his work could be mentioned during the proceedings.[33]

Thompson's departure signalled deeper problems for the Historical Medical Museum. Later, Malcolm would be told that 'the profession were somewhat apprehensive' as to the collection's future. It was not clear whether the Museum was part of the Burroughs Wellcome firm, and some people told Malcolm it was a shame more material had not been made 'available to people'.[34] In 1926, not long after Thompson left Wellcome, a handful of leading historians of medicine were given an opportunity to voice their concerns in public, at the Wellcome Historical Medical Museum itself. Within weeks of Thompson's departure the Museum had closed for six months of redecoration and refurbishment. Much of the work was aesthetic—the lighting was improved, new paintwork, cases and labels were installed, objects were cleaned, some rooms were renamed—but Malcolm also rearranged a number of the exhibits, bringing more objects out of storage and altering the sequence of the displays here and there. The changes were deemed important enough to warrant a formal 'Re-opening Ceremony' in the autumn of 1926, and leading medics again congregated in the Hall of Statuary to hear congratulatory speeches and admire the refit, although this time Wellcome was in America and unable to attend. Humphry Rolleston, Arthur Keith, and D'Arcy Power all spoke, but their admiring words were infused with criticisms of Wellcome's regime.

Sir Arthur Keith gave the main address. He had first met Wellcome at a tea party in 1912, and since then had tried to persuade him to give financial support to the Royal Anthropological Institute, but without success. He concluded that Wellcome was 'magnificently generous to public benefactions which bore his name but mean towards those which did not'.[35] He also disapproved of the publishing restrictions Wellcome imposed on his staff. Thompson had told Keith 'that he had been dismissed because he had published papers on the historical significance of certain things in the museum without first having obtained Sir Henry's permission. For doing a public service of such a kind I would have rewarded a curator, not dismissed him.'[36] So Keith accepted the invitation to speak at Wellcome's Re-opening Ceremony, but chose as his title, 'What should Museums do for us?'[37] His words were a directive as much as a tribute to Wellcome. He stated that a curator's first duty was to encourage scholarship amongst his staff and his public. 'Unless a museum is permeated with a spirit of enquiry it is dead', he said bluntly. Knowledge must not only be generated by museum staff, it must be expressed freely: papers must be written, meetings attended, students welcomed, and publications forthcoming; 'the literature which issues from a museum determines it status', he argued. The accoutrements of 'primitive' medicine were particularly susceptible to misinterpretation and must be carefully studied and contextualized. Keith's statements were made in general terms, and he also praised Wellcome for directing his wealth into the service of others, albeit 'in his own quiet but efficient way'.

D'Arcy Power was more direct in his speech. Perhaps there was a note of sarcasm in his voice when he opened by saying, 'I may claim perhaps to be the one who has profited most largely by Mr. Wellcome's liberality in throwing open the collection to every student of the history of medicine.'[38] The access Power had been given had been unprecedented and unofficial, and after the *Chronologia Medica* debacle, Wellcome insisted he would never enjoy a 'free run of the Museum' again.[39] Power continued by making a frank request:

There is still more than a lifetime's work to be done in arranging and describing the present collection, which is being added to daily. I hope, however that Mr. Wellcome will not wait until it is complete—for that will never be—but will continue the plan he has already begun of making parts of the Museum known to the world at large by individual publications bearing the stamp of the Wellcome Historical Museum.[40]

Keith and Power clearly had concerns about the Museum's role within the academic community. Would they have said the same if Wellcome himself had been in the room to hear them? Did Wellcome register their disquiet when he read over their speeches? A few months later Wellcome was subjected to a sustained attack from another eminent academic and friend of Thompson, Keith, Power, and Rolleston. This time the criticisms could not be so easily ignored.

Charles Singer was a doctor and a leading historian of medicine. He was a founding member of the History of Medicine Section of the Royal Society of Medicine, and had served as its president. He had written numerous papers on medieval and renaissance medicine and the history of anatomy, as well as a two-volume treatise on the history of science.[41] He held a lectureship at University College London, and he had given lectures at the Wellcome Museum in the past, getting to know Wellcome, Thompson, and other members of staff. But good relations soured in 1925. During a year when Thompson's bond with Wellcome was weakening, Thompson had given Singer permission to work in the library and reproduce some illustrations in the collections for publication. When Wellcome heard this, he not only rescinded the permission, but banned Singer from working in the library at all.[42]

In early 1927, Singer began publicly to criticize Wellcome and his protocols at the Historical Medical Museum. If Thompson had resented some of Wellcome's policies, Singer gave those resentments full voice. The opening round came, unexpectedly, at a meeting for members of the British Medical Association. Plans were afoot for the next gathering of the Association's History of Medicine Section, and a small group of organizers had met over dinner in February 1927 to arrange presentations and events. Singer was to give the opening address, and Wellcome's Museum was asked to provide some exhibits for his talk. But Singer wanted nothing to do with the Wellcome Historical Medical Museum. He argued that it was always closed or else he was refused admission, and 'he would rather not come near the place'. Discussion at the table moved on, but later, Singer spoke to one of Wellcome's staff:

He again said that he considered that there was too much secrecy about the place. He said that he had once discussed the matter with Mr. Wellcome, and that Mr. Wellcome had said that he did not wish anything to be worked on until it had been completed in every detail. Dr. Singer said that he considered that when a thing was completed it had no further need for scientific research, and that in this respect science was dead. He said that he was out for knowledge, and that what he wanted to get at were the unknown and incomplete objects in order that research could be made regarding them. He said that it was no good laying out a lot of instruments and having a sort of Madame Tussaud's show and saying, 'This is the History of Medicine'. He said that this might appeal to the lay mind, but not to the scientific research worker who is thirsting for scientific knowledge.[43]

Singer had identified the ambiguity at the heart of Wellcome's Museum: it was presented as a serious research institution, but a number of its exhibits were rather more evocative than informative. In the wake of this assault, Malcolm decided to meet with Singer privately for a further discussion, but he found the historian was still in a 'most abusive' frame of mind. Singer continued his offensive: the Museum claimed to be for study and research, but provided no research facilities. In reality it was simply private property. Did this not mean, Singer asked, that Wellcome was obtaining donations fraudulently, since his assurances that they would be 'freely available' were misleading? Singer's own enquiries had always been 'met with evasion'. By now Singer had really hit his stride: Wellcome's staff were under-qualified, their publication record was hopeless, the Museum was too frequently closed for one reason or another. And, he claimed, he was not alone in his opinions. Rolleston and Keith both agreed with him, but were afraid of 'treading on Wellcome's toes' for fear that he would take his Museum back to America.[44]

Singer's anger betrayed his arrogance. He was annoyed that Wellcome's library held the only manuscripts of interest to him and that he, despite his academic distinction, had been unable to study. He told Malcolm he 'was the only man competent to deal with this work, and his "seniority" gave him the authority to direct how it should be done'. He added that should Wellcome ask him to undertake research on the collections—for Singer would now have to be asked—he would expect a fee for his expertise.[45]

Egotism aside, Singer recognized the deeper philosophical principles that conditioned Wellcome. He understood that a quest for perfection was paralysing Wellcome, and believed that everyone else had to suffer for it. Wellcome, for his part, remained unmoved. He belligerently annotated Malcolm's report as he read it: 'He said that you told him *I told him* that the material would be made accessible *under circumstances and regulations* when it was complete. This meant, according to Dr. Singer, that it would be dead, because science was never dead, and would never be complete. *nonsense.*'[46]

But Singer had a point. Wellcome did want his Museum to be complete, and the notion of completeness, taken to its logical conclusion, undermined the principles of research. Neither science nor history could be finished. So what, Singer asked, was Wellcome waiting for?

Science could never be finished, but a collection of books and objects promised the ultimate exhibition, a grand opening and a triumphant moment of recognition. Wellcome had long-term plans for a new museum. The galleries in Wigmore Street were seen as a temporary measure and he intended to move to bigger premises when the opportunity arose.[47] His staff continued to buy new things, but only a fraction of the collection could be exhibited at Wigmore Street. There was no room for his library, or for the study rooms and lecture hall he intended to provide. Wellcome's plans for proper research facilities at the Museum were genuine, and he began to act on them a few years later. He believed that 'the modern research museum should be at once a repository and a laboratory'. The best kind of collection would be divided into two, providing an 'illustrative' collection for general education, exhibited in the normal manner, and a second, 'comparative series' of artefacts, with restricted access, specially for research purposes. Objects were to be handled and studied.[48] Wellcome truly envisaged opening up his Museum to researchers one day.

The problem was that he was in no rush. His main priority was still acquiring artefacts and books, and, while this was the case, he feared high-profile research work would compromise his tactics as a buyer by prejudicing dealers. Staff were not allowed to announce any new additions to the collections, or talk about where they had been obtained.[49] One of Well-come's clearest extant statements on this issue came in 1928, when he wrote in response to the draft text for a pamphlet on the history of Welsh medicine to accompany the British Medical Association's annual meeting in Cardiff that year. He found that he had to make various changes to the text,

especially to eliminate the various statements as to what we are intending to do in the way of researches for this historical volume, and giving information as to where we will seek for our material. Such announcement of intention and statements of sources from which we would draw information and material is entirely contrary to our very definite policy at all times. In principle our policy might be expressed in the words 'We will say what we are going to do after we have done it'. I see no good reason for informing our would-be rivals or anyone else in advance or at any time, when, where or how we obtain our materials.[50]

'Never tell anyone what you propose to do until you have done it' was one of Wellcome's favourite mantras.[51] He was distrustful of all publicity, unless it was conducted strictly on his own terms. He was reluctant to allow any photographs of the Museum to appear in the press, and insisted that all images had to have the appropriate copyright inscription 'being prominently imprinted on the negatives so that the words cannot be eliminated when the photo is processed for illustrations for our own and outside publications'.[52] His strict rules often meant that national publications, particularly news-papers, refused to publish illustrations of the Museum at all. Even if the

London editors had agreed to print them, images could still be cropped or altered by syndicated papers. Malcolm found Wellcome's approach difficult: 'I have been informed, on more than one occasion, that we could have had much greater publicity . . . if these restrictions had not been in force.'[53]

Wellcome was not particularly interested in publicity. Popular articles were generally 'not of the character wished for': Malcolm had turned down a request from *The Star* to take a photograph of Nelson's Medicine Chest with a man pointing to it, which would have undermined the serious nature of Wellcome's enterprise.[54] The visitors Wellcome was interested in heard about his Museum by word of mouth. He wanted well-educated visitors who knew someone who knew someone who had mentioned Mr Wellcome's wonderful museum; visitors who would happily produce a letter of introduction from an eminent scientist or medic. And he wanted his visitors to study the Museum's exhibits carefully, so they could appreciate the enormity of his achievements as a collector. Pictures in magazines were superficial and unnecessary:

pictures are much more beneficial to journals because of their attractiveness to their readers while to us the more we publish pictures of objects in the Museum we make them commonplace and many people are satisfied to look at the picture and save themselves the trouble of going to the Museum. I hold very strong and definite views on this point.[55]

As long as Wellcome had his eye firmly on the antiquities market he failed to focus his attention on the immense, and growing, task of organization desperately needed at the Museum. After Thompson's departure expenditure on new acquisitions sky-rocketed. Wellcome rarely spent less than £30,000 a year on his Museum and Library between 1926 and 1935, and in two of those years he spent more than £60,000.[56] In reality, it was a little difficult for his staff to attend to research requests when most of the collection was uncatalogued; and cataloguing work was virtually impossible when there were so many sales to attend to, as the assistant librarian, Barnard, had pointed out.[57] The Museum could not open its doors to the research community, whether Singer liked it or not. Wellcome's staff could barely keep up with the day-to-day tasks of buying, accessioning, cleaning, and stowing objects safely.

There was no sense of urgency from Wellcome. Malcolm immediately recognized the huge increase in staff time and resources required just to get the collection catalogued, never mind re-housed and accessible for research,[58] but Wellcome was unhurried. In response to Singer's accusations, he wrote,

It is unnecessary for us to have any controversy. None of these allegations require answer. It is quite satisfactory that he ignores the H.M.M. We do not need his assistance and after what he has said he should not be invited to the museum nor in any way encouraged to enter the museum. We shall continue our policy strictly in respect to the collections in the Museum and the Library.[59]

And finally, 'We are not worried we have plenty of time to carry out our plans.' It was typical Wellcome: defiant; self-assured. He was in his seventies, surrounded by stacks of unprocessed goods and a staff struggling to keep pace with his enthusiasm for buying things. But perhaps all the unpacked riches in his London warehouses gave him his confidence. Singer and his friends could grumble all they liked; one day the great show Wellcome was planning would silence them. Then they would be invited to study in his Museum. The invitation would come on his terms. He was not providing a service, he was giving them a gift—a gift so valuable they would be astonished—a gift for which they would be duly grateful, in time. And despite losing his closest colleague and adviser, despite frustrating prominent academics in the field, and despite entering his eighth decade, Wellcome still believed there was plenty of time for all this beneficence to unfold.

CHAPTER THIRTEEN

ALL TIED UP IN KNOTS

In his own way, Louis Malcolm tried to transform Wellcome's suspicious attitude to the wider academic community, but he struggled. He found it hard to follow in Thompson's footsteps. Thompson and Wellcome had shared a brutally efficient relationship for many years; both had delighted in the intrigue, drama, and ruthlessness of the collecting business. Malcolm never enjoyed such an effective relationship with his employer, and he found it difficult to acquaint himself with the sprawling collection that Thompson had spent so many years creating. He was more attracted to academic collaboration than to the frenetic pace set by the antiquities market. His time at the Museum was recurrently tense and stressful, and he did not thrive on pressure as Thompson had done. While his predecessor had worked exhaustively and gone out in a blaze of anger, Malcolm tried methodically to take command in his wake, but could never quite settle to his role as manager.

Malcolm arrived at the Wellcome Historical Medical Museum full of promise and enthusiasm (Figure 22). He had graduated from Christ's College, Cambridge, in 1921, with a master's degree, having submitted a four-volume ethnographic thesis on the Eghap people of central Cameroon, whom he had studied while stationed with the Nigeria Regiment of the West African Frontier Force during the War. Between 1920 and 1925 he published eighteen academic papers on Cameroonian and Nigerian culture. Then, armed with his Cambridge qualification, he embarked on a museological career as an assistant curator at the Bristol City Museum.[1] The opportunity offered to him by Wellcome in 1925, to take charge of his ethnographic collections, was too good to turn down. 'The material is

Figure 22. Photograph of Louis William Gordon Malcolm, date unknown.

amazing, and . . . I am a free agent absolutely, and my movements are my own affair. Naturally this makes me full of beans for the work ahead.'[2]

Malcolm described his new post as 'an important one in the scientific world', and talked of 'the vast resources behind the Wellcome Foundation'.[3] His first concern was to elevate the Museum's public profile, and counter the stagnation that had set in after the War and the disruption of Thompson's departure. In his early letters he often alluded to the Museum's potential to become the 'leading institution of its kind in the world', and his hopes for 'advancing the status of the Museum'.[4] He wrote to Wellcome in February 1926,

You may rest assured that I am determined to have your instructions carried out, and that this Museum will rank as one of the finest and most progressive scientific institutions in the country ... I am anxious that the W.H.M.M. should be a serious factor in the scientific life of London—and as a result, transcontinentally.[5]

Malcolm had hoped that his job would open up a place for him within the academic community and to some extent, it did. In 1927, he was appointed Honorary Lecturer at University College London, in the School of Medicine and Institute of Anatomy. He thought it might help to get 'definite classes attending here for specified courses and degrees'.[6] The following year he became Honorary Secretary of the Folk-Lore Society, and his eagerness to please Wellcome shone through in his reaction to the news. His appointment was 'of definite importance to us, because it will give me absolute control of the Society in various ways'. And he went on to claim, 'I shall be able to use my position as Secretary to the Society to influence societies and people all over the country.'[7] Working at the Wellcome Museum brought him into contact with societies, scholars, and students, and this, Malcolm believed, would prove fortuitous for Wellcome, for the Museum, and, not least, for his own career. Fraternizing with the academic elite would enhance the Museum's status and encourage people to make donations to the collections. 'A great interest is being taken in what we are doing,' Malcolm wrote, 'and each day we are receiving material either on loan or by presentation.'[8]

Malcolm's first task was rather pedestrian, but he revelled in it nonetheless. He organized the cleaning and refurbishment programme at the Wigmore Street galleries and the Museum's Re-opening Ceremony in the spring of 1926. His meticulous reports to Wellcome were filled with details of new lighting fixtures, the rearrangement of displays, heating improvements, and plans to re-paint. For Malcolm, who had to respond to Charles Singer's disparaging remarks early in 1927, these cosmetic improvements signalled a new era in the Museum's history. He planned to have research students in the Museum, and he identified objects that could be used for teaching; he made space for a workroom and 'laboratory'; he organized for labels in display cases to be reprinted more clearly, aiming for 'extreme accuracy and simplicity' throughout. He believed he was in charge of 'more than the germ of an institution which will rank higher even than a University, which will be more of the "post-graduate" standard'.[9] The Museum would be more outward-looking, more responsive to the intellectual debates of the day, and more relevant to the community it professed to serve.

Wellcome was flattered by Malcolm's verve in the months following Thompson's departure. While the disagreement with Thompson was threatening to drag Wellcome and his staff over and over the problems of the past, Malcolm, in his late thirties, was full of promises for the future. Wellcome's collecting project had been directed towards generating prestige within the scholarly community, and Malcolm, who represented a new generation of university-trained professional anthropologists, was clearly impressed with what he saw. The energy that he brought to the job gratified Wellcome. Wellcome commended Malcolm for his 'spirit' and wrote, rather clumsily, that he could 'look forward with confident anticipation that the continuation of such zealous cooperation and efficiency will ensure the full realization of my ambitions for much greater development in the future'.[10]

Wellcome had employed Malcolm as a specialized anthropologist. His decision to divide his Museum collection into three administrative sections—the library, the medical collections, and the ethnographic collections—had signalled a new phase in the Museum's development, and the emphasis on anthropology was affirmed when Malcolm took sole charge of the artefact collections. Wellcome was pushing his Museum in a different direction. Although the history of human health remained his intellectual focus, his medical collections were by now well established and he began to see his Museum as a centre for cultural learning in a broader sense.

Wellcome's interest in anthropology was long-standing. He had been intrigued by different cultures since his childhood in Minnesota, living nearby Native American communities.[11] During the 1880s, he had become a fervent supporter of the Anglican lay missionary William Duncan and Duncan's work with the Tsimshian people, and had even written a book about them, *The Story of Metlakahtla*, which had played an important part in securing US protection, in 1887, for the Tsimshian community Duncan led.[12] And, as a collector, Wellcome's earliest recorded acquisitions in London included Canadian bark canoes, Chinese and Japanese artworks, and rugs from India.[13] Thompson's purchases for Wellcome in the early 1900s had been varied: Persian spoons, poisoned darts from Columbia, Mexican masks, Bornean agricultural tools, Samoan hair combs and Nigerian necklaces, Tibetan lamps and Hindu statues had all been packed away into the first Crystal Palace storeroom.[14] These were artefacts that could be classified as medical only in the widest sense of the term. Most of them ensured social or spiritual well being, rather than specifically addressing a person's physical health. They betrayed the breadth of Wellcome's curiosity; and, by the late 1920s, it was a curiosity he no longer presented as purely medical.

In 1928 Wellcome was asked to contribute to the Royal Commission on National Museums and Galleries. The Commission had been set up the previous year to investigate funding priorities for national collections, in response to lobbying from the trustees of the British Museum, who complained of overcrowding and an inadequate budget.[15] One of the Commissioners' tasks was to make recommendations for the future accommodation of the British Museum's ethnographic collections, and Wellcome was among the experts called upon to answer their questions.

Given that the Commissioners were interested in ethnographic collections it is hardly surprising that Wellcome emphasized his interest in anthropology—he told how his interest in anthropology had been 'awakened' in childhood, whereas his focus on the history of medicine only began while he was a student—but his answers came at a time when he and Malcolm were trying to shift the emphasis of his Museum in a new direction. Wellcome told the Commissioners he believed medicine was one particular lens for viewing cultural diversity. 'It is my intention . . . to enlarge [the collection's] scope and develop a Research Museum which will deal with anthropological questions in a wide sense. If anthropology is the study of man, then medicine is a branch which must be considered together with other human sciences.'[16] He likened his Museum, not to the great scientific collections at South Kensington or the Hunterian Museum at the Royal College of Surgeons in Lincoln's Inn Fields, but to the Pitt Rivers Museum in Oxford and the Horniman at Forest Hill, which were two of the largest ethnographic collections in the country. He even played down the medical bias in his collecting, claiming that this section was 'only one feature of my historical museum'. He had concentrated on medicine first, but anthropology, 'takes us from the beginning and covers all', and he intended to develop other aspects of his Museum to illustrate this breadth, 'in due course' (Wellcome, it is worth noting, was 75 years old when he attended the Royal Commission meetings).[17]

The anthropological community had taken note of Malcolm's appointment at the Historical Medical Museum, and he began liaising with staff at

University College London, who were keen to use Wellcome's Museum as a teaching collection and felt there was 'a crying need for a modern Anthropological Library in London'. Malcolm hoped to establish a working relationship with Grafton Elliot Smith, the Reader in Social Anthropology and Professor of Anatomy at University College London, so that books and collections could be made available to his students. 'I think it is most essential that you should meet him when you return,' he wrote to Wellcome, who had been in America for many months, 'as he has some projects in hand which will dovetail with some of your own.'[18]

Malcolm also set about forging links with the Royal Anthropological Institute and the Folk-Lore Society. Both organizations held regular meetings and lectures, but neither had the resources to care for a large collection of artefacts. Malcolm saw the opportunity for more productive collaborations that would ensure a steady flow of eminent anthropologists through the doors at Wigmore Street to consult Wellcome's collections. In 1927 he reported that the Royal Anthropological Institute was forming a committee to locate all the country's museum collections, and was addressing the need for an anthropological museum to support its research projects. Malcolm was sure that the Wellcome Museum would fit the bill. 'The need for an Anthropological Museum was never more needed than at the present time, and there is no doubt that one developed on the lines we have discussed, will be the leading institution of its kind in the world.'[19]

Wellcome was cautious: 'Keep in touch and learn all their plans. When we develop our scheme I think we can win the cooperation of most of the best authorities on anthropology.'[20] But Malcolm was unfazed. Wellcome's Museum would become a key feature in the academic landscape of London, providing material resources for anthropologists from all over the country. It 'would not only be a research institution, but a training centre for students'.[21] Malcolm knew that Wellcome's over-riding priority was still increasing the size of the collection, so he framed his plans for collaboration as a way of securing more objects for the Museum. A formal affiliation meant that researchers associated with the Royal Anthropological Institute or the Folk-Lore Society would send their field collections directly to Wellcome. 'This all means that providing the Royal Anthropological Institute and Folk-Lore Society had a Museum affiliated to them, all the incoming material would come to it. This needs serious discussion and I am waiting until your return [from America].' Malcolm wanted Wellcome to meet with the secretary of the Royal Anthropological Institute to discuss the 'tremendous possibilities in this forthcoming scheme'. In the meantime, both Societies were planning to hold evening receptions at the Wellcome Historical Medical Museum, which Malcolm argued would be 'useful propaganda' for his plans.[22]

Malcolm was quick to reassure Wellcome that the Museum could retain its independence while representing this new 'practical side of anthropology': 'There is no question of usurping or affiliating to anybody.'[23] And Wellcome was initially enthusiastic, and cabled: 'Gladly cooperate anthropological institute folklore society receive all suitable materials merge permanently our extensive collections and facilitate research and educational study.'[24] But his interest waned. He did lend some objects for a temporary exhibition organized by the Folk-Lore Society, and a number of people gave collections to the Museum as a result.[25] Closer ties with both the Royal Anthropological Institute and the Folk-Lore Society certainly raised the Museum's profile: both groups held conversaziones at the Museum, and mentioned Wellcome's collection in their publications.[26] But no strong working relationship developed, and the Historical Medical Museum never became the anthropological research museum that Malcolm had envisaged.

Wellcome probably baulked when he saw the terms Malcolm had drafted for collaboration. Malcolm had proposed a 'joint advisory committee' and an 'agreed common policy' to unite the Historical Medical Museum and the Royal Anthropological Institute. The joint advisory committee would coordinate with British universities teaching anthropology and arrange for 'practical instruction to be given in the Museum'. And, Malcolm suggested, Fellows of the Royal Anthropological Institute would automatically become 'Fellows of the Wellcome Museum', and as such, they would have

the right of entry to the Museum at all times as its rules of opening allow, have a right to make use of the collections for purposes of research under such regulations as the Museum may lay down, may use the reference library and shall have prior right of admission to such lectures as the Museum may arrange.

Fellows could also coordinate their own courses of lectures in the Museum.[27]

It is hard to see Wellcome agreeing to such an open arrangement. Despite assurances that Wellcome's Museum would retain its independence, Malcolm's six-point plan was premature. Wellcome could hardly bare to let his own staff research his collections; he was not about to throw the doors open to hundreds of unvetted academics and unknown numbers of students. Malcolm was told that there was plenty of time for collaborative projects later, when Wellcome had been able to 'establish his museum finally'.[28]

Malcolm's association with Elliot Smith may also have cooled. Elliot Smith's theories regarding the worldwide diffusion of cultural traits originating in ancient Egypt were controversial and widely condemned, and he had fallen out with Flinders Petrie and Arthur Keith. His correspondence with Malcolm seems to have petered out after 1927.[29]

The atmosphere of intense secrecy that Wellcome had engineered permeated all Malcolm's dealings. As the Museum's profile increased—by the summer of 1927 the staff had noticed 'a very much larger number of visitors than we used to have'[30]—his rules became more frustrating. Information was withheld at every level in the chain of command. When Malcolm received an enquiry about Wellcome's archaeological work in Sudan from someone who was wondering about job opportunities, Wellcome replied, 'Be cautious and noncommittal. It is best for you to have no information as to my plans, views or movements or about anything concerning the Sudan, but listen and make note of everything that is said.'[31] When Malcolm was asked by visitors how they had assembled such a large collection relating to Joseph Lister, Wellcome reminded him, 'Our methods and sources must never be published as that would assist our rivals who would follow up and take advantage of any information.'[32] It was at this time that Wellcome's fears about American collectors reached their peak and added to his resolve. 'America especially is keen and hungry but they do not understand our methods and we must keep our system and policy strictly private and confidential.'[33] Meanwhile, Malcolm tried to persuade Wellcome to loosen his copyright restrictions so that more photos of the Museum could be published, but Wellcome was unmoved, claiming that photographs made the Museum seem 'commonplace' and actually dissuaded people from visiting.[34]

Malcolm was unable to effect any change in Wellcome's conspiratorial attitude, and, instead, became reconciled to it. In 1930, when he was asked by a researcher whether the Museum would consider publishing his book on Thomas Pettigrew, a surgeon and antiquarian who had died in 1865, Malcolm wrote to Wellcome rather resignedly, 'Although I knew Mr Dawson was working on this book, I have not mentioned the fact that many of Pettigrew's original letters are in the possession of this Museum on account of your rigid rule.'[35] Wellcome was happy for the Museum to host social events, exhibitions, and academic meetings, because they provided opportunities for him to show off his collection, and he schooled Malcolm in entertaining guests: 'Always make a point of the fact that this museum is the result of life-long research and collecting throughout the wide world. And that for want of adequate space only a small portion of the collections have been placed in the museum.'[36] Many lectures and receptions were held at the Museum during the late 1920s and early 1930s, but behind the scenes few serious research proposals were entertained.[37]

How could Malcolm forge useful partnerships with academic institutions when, in Wellcome's eyes, every friend who showed an interest in the Museum was a potential enemy in the hunt for antiquities? Wellcome and Malcolm were beginning to pull against each other. Malcolm's attempts to strengthen the Museum's academic status were hampered by Wellcome's paranoia when it came to publicity, while Wellcome's unceasing enthusiasm for securing new acquisitions was gradually frustrated by Malcolm's prudence as a collector. Malcolm was neither confident nor enthusiastic when it came to navigating the antiquities market. His reluctance to enter into the spirit of buying things annoyed Wellcome.

Malcolm's attitude to acquisitions was in complete contrast to Thompson's, and Wellcome had become used to leaving his collection in the care of a man who appreciated the hunt for a bargain. Thompson's weekly reports to Wellcome had been thoroughly entertaining. He had enjoyed his escapades in the salesrooms and his dealings with fellow collectors, and he described his collecting adventures with assurance and style. He knew that Wellcome loved to read about this work as though it were an adventure, in which scheming rivals were duped and Wellcome's staff returned home heroically, bargain prize in hand. Thompson dramatized the 'chronic restiveness' of collecting for Wellcome; he made the endless search for the next trophy into a story that confirmed their mastery over their rivals, and he could share with Wellcome the thrill of control that this brought.[38] Malcolm did not have Thompson's panache. His heart was not in it. His reports were long, dutiful and often mundane. He felt over-whelmed—'The material available in London alone seems to be endless'—and he was concerned by the cramped conditions in the stores.[39] Malcolm had been told in no uncertain terms that 'The main function of the Museum is to acquire material, and to record, register and number existing material on exhibition', but he was unable to assert himself in this role, either with dealers or with Wellcome.[40]

Malcolm constantly referred decisions to Wellcome, despite the fact that Wellcome encouraged him to make his own judgments. What really bothered Wellcome was his unwillingness to express any opinion of his own when discussing objects which had been offered for sale. Malcolm rarely added any consideration of the price, quality, or significance of potential acquisitions in his reports, but Wellcome thrived on other people's advice. He liked to say, 'I never give instructions I only suggest.'[41] He wrote to Malcolm,

You must never take my suggestions or criticisms as being made in a spirit of 'fault finding' for they are invariably intended to frankly indicate my ideas and policy and to assist you constructively. I want you always, with equal frankness, to criticize and point out whatever you may consider defective in my plans, methods or systems, etc. I prefer frank criticism to praise. Criticism is a most helpful aid to improvement and progress, while praise is likely to lull us into a state of 'letting well enough alone' which I know is not in accord with either your temperament or mine.[42]

He wanted Malcolm to act as a consultant, and steer the collection with conviction, as Thompson had. Wellcome was happiest when responding to the opinions of his staff. He would make improvements on their plans, question and over-rule decisions, or confirm a possible course of action, but he had too many other calls on his time to take the lead, and he was used to the Museum running along happily by itself. He insisted on hearing about all the new acquisitions, and the Museum's activities, but he could do little to shape events when he was abroad so often. From the start Wellcome made his requirements plain to Malcolm. He wrote in May 1927,

I would say that in all such cases [where material is offered for large amounts of money] it would be best for you to explicitly formulate your ideas and make your recommendations with tabulated estimates showing exactly or approximately what you deem to be necessary expenditures to carry out your views. You should give as full particulars as possible stating the nature and character of all items and the reasons and use to be made of the same.[43]

But Wellcome had to ask Malcolm repeatedly for more comprehensive descriptions, illustrations of material, and estimates of value. Malcolm was persistently unforthcoming, and his descriptions were vague. He simply passed on the basic facts—what the object was and the asking price—before politely enquiring whether Wellcome would like to buy it. Wellcome struggled to respond, and worried that Malcolm was letting opportunities slip by. He began to voice his criticisms: 'your statement one room crammed conveys no helpful information', 'you should always investigate first and then advise me', 'I can only guess about this item—the subject matter being so vaguely described', 'you send no helpful descriptive information after inspection', 'you should indicate your estimate of values as well as the price asked by the vendor', 'Please always state sizes and nature and character . . . when submitting offers of pictures.'[44]

Malcolm claimed that he did not have any more information.[45] When it came to buying books, he admitted, 'I often hesitate as to the procedure you would accept.'[46] Moreover, 'routine matters' made it 'nearly impossible to get about to search for material',[47] and, in the spring of 1928, he admitted attending his first sale at Knight, Frank and Rutley because he 'wished to ascertain what was going on at these sales'.[48]

Wellcome, who had always been wary of sending telegrams that did not use code words because they were expensive and might reveal his interests to competitors if intercepted, became so concerned about missing important acquisitions that he took to cabling lists of lot numbers and price limits for sales: 'Limit six pounds each twothirtyseven twofiftysix twoseventyfour twoninetynine threefourteen threefortyfive threefiftyeight...'.[49] By early 1928 expense and confidentiality had been forgotten and he wrote a detailed cable to Malcolm prior to a sale of Edward Jenner material at Sotheby's. He listed all the lots he was interested in and then gave instructions on strategy:

arrange privately with Sotheby bid for us under name Robert Jenner to limits half amount our limit send Webb or some efficient keen less known man to watch carefully and start bidding when Sothebys reach their limit our buyer must pick up sharply and continue bidding against any competing bids far as necessary to our limit and even to twentyfive percent beyond our limit if others bid that extent'.[50]

Telegrams like this had been unheard of in Thompson's day, but Malcolm's reticence compelled Wellcome to take action.

His frustrations peaked in December 1929—a full four years after Malcolm took charge of his collections—when he wrote a long and irritated letter. He began, 'You have evidently overlooked the instructions I gave you in regard to sending to me the foreign catalogues without translation or explanation of the essential features of books or manuscripts quoted in such catalogues, and the special need we have for them in our library.' And continued,

It would be very helpful to me, and would save me a great deal of time if you would be more explicit and informative in your letters and telegrams in which you ask for my authorization to purchase items for the Museum. I do not ask for very lengthy descriptions, but most of your messages could be simplified still briefly give me much more information in comprehensive wording.[51]

Wellcome then detailed the Museum's 'standing rules' for buying material at auction, and pointed out the important lots that had been missed recently. He asked Malcolm to find out who had bought these lots and for how much money. Wellcome was no longer content to leave his collection in the hands of his deputy. The comfortable days of Thompson's premiership were over. When Malcolm admitted that he had eight sales catalogues on his desk with recommendations from the Librarian, but was 'hesitating as to whether I am to buy books in such large numbers',[52] Wellcome was incredulous.

> I very definitely authorized you to act and act quickly in these matters, and therefore, I do not understand why you have hesitated unless the prices were unreasonable. Some books naturally have increased materially in value and the increased price may still be reasonable . . . I hope that I have made myself sufficiently clear in confirmation of my previous instructions on this point, so that you will no longer collect large numbers of catalogues which are useless unless acted upon quickly.[53]

Wellcome only accepted delays if individual prices were too high, but Malcolm was concerned by the sheer number of books being purchased. A month later he informed Wellcome that the General Manager of Burroughs Wellcome, George Pearson, had repeatedly voiced concerns about the Museum's expenditure, which had been 'extremely high' for the past two years. Spending on the Museum and Library had surged to £30,000 in 1928, and then to £65,000 in 1929. This far exceeded the totals reached in the early 1920s, which had hovered around £3,000 per annum (although the purchase from Gorga in 1924 had pushed the total for that year up to £12,700). Pearson's cautions left Malcolm even more eager to get Wellcome's permission to 'go ahead on the lines you have planned and to obtain material wherever possible'. But Pearson's disquiet did nothing to quell Wellcome's zeal. Only once would expenditure dip below £30,000 per annum again during Wellcome's life, and then to just £28,700.[54]

Malcolm was concerned by costs and distracted by administrative demands. He was reluctant to buy new things while his staff were struggling to catalogue the objects Wellcome already owned. Within six months of working at Wellcome's Museum, Malcolm had warned that it would take 'several years' before the collections he had inherited could be put in order and properly recorded.[55] It proved to be a serious underestimate. After a year, in 1926, as new acquisitions poured in to Wellcome's storehouses, he admitted that his staff were already struggling to keep up. In fact, they could hardly manage to sort through the objects that had been recently donated, never mind the things being delivered from the salesrooms, or the crates of artefacts already in storage.[56]

Malcolm tried to effect change. The storage facilities were inadequate: artefacts were kept in eight different buildings across London, including one in Stanmore in the north-west, one in Weybridge in the south-west, and one in Southwark in the south-east. Eventually, a large warehouse was found in Willesden, and material was transferred there in 1928.[57] Now Malcolm only had to deal with two storage sites, at Willesden and Stanmore, and, in the same year, new recruits were drafted in. D. Pender Davidson took charge of the paintings and prints, A. L. Dean took over from the secretary, Peter Johnston-Saint, so that he could focus on organizing acquisitions, and seven young archaeology and anthropology graduates, known as the 'Scientific Staff', were employed to help register the collections.[58] The scientific staff were given little scope for scientific work, as Joan Braunholtz remembered:

Soon after our arrival in Wigmore Street, we, the 'scientific' staff were supplied with stiff heavy khaki overalls of the kind worn by warehousemen and furniture removers, and dispatched to a disused factory or warehouse at Willesden . . . The factory was in a district unsurpassed for sordidness and desolation; it lay between a tannery and an anchovy essence factory, and there were appalling smells (especially on Fridays) . . . The premises where we had to work were practically unheated, and the winter of 1928–9 was a particularly cold one; all of us were more or less ill.[59]

The scientific staff spent most of their time at the Willesden warehouse, unpacking objects, cataloguing them, and repacking them again. Most remembered the Museum fondly (although Braunholtz later admitted that she 'had no particular interest in this subject, but was entranced by the thought of a job in central London and £200 a year'[60]), but the working conditions were not ideal.

The job certainly brought its rewards. Theodore Gaster recalled, 'the constant thrill of recovering some of the most precious antiquities from the Ancient Near East which Wellcome had purchased years ago and which no one had heard of since'.[61] But the heterogeneity of Wellcome's collection rendered their inexperienced efforts at cataloguing 'largely guess-work'.[62] Even when they were installed in Wigmore Street, recording the objects on display, conditions were cramped and 'far from pleasant'.[63] Malcolm, meanwhile, was aloof and it quickly became apparent that he could not tolerate being challenged.

One of the scientific staff, Montague Ashley-Montagu, a young graduate who later became a distinguished physical anthropologist at Princeton University, was asked to resign after six weeks in post for reasons of 'incompatibility'.[64] Ashley-Montagu's playful irreverence rubbed Malcolm the wrong way. On one occasion, while he was working on the objects from Wellcome's

Jebel Moya excavation in Sudan, he 'came up with the astounding discovery of an occiput which he claimed to be older than Neanderthal Man and which he duly registered as Cranium "Ashley Montaguanum" '. Malcolm took his claim seriously enough to call in academic experts especially to examine the find, but their verdict was 'that it belonged to a village idiot who had lived some fifty years ago!'[65] Malcolm was incensed. 'He is twenty-four years of age, with all the assurance of youth, and he claims to be the leading anthropologist of Great Britain, belittling the work both of Sir Arthur Keith and Professor Elliot Smith. He claims to be geologist, palaeontologist, physiologist, anatomist, phrenologist and a psychologist, all at the age of twenty-four.'[66] It cannot have helped Ashley-Montagu's prospects when, during his final showdown at the Museum, he took the opportunity to 'apprize Mr Malcolm, the conservator, of the feelings of the rest of the staff toward him—feelings generated by his demand that they clean the glass exhibition cases, which they properly felt was not what they had been appointed to do.'[67]

Malcolm was rather proud of his standards for cleanliness—'There is one thing I think every member of staff will tell you, and that is my stringent rule for absolute cleanliness. I never pass a fingermark or trace of dust on any of the glass'[68]—but Ashley-Montagu and his colleagues had seen through his bluster. They sensed that his interest in menial cleaning tasks disguised his unease managing bright, young academics. He was fastidious about time keeping and discipline, but, despite their commitment to the job, he was suspicious of time spent on research work rather than cataloguing.[69]

Malcolm was struggling to keep on top of administration. He often mentioned the amount of correspondence he had to deal with in his reports to Wellcome, writing, in March 1927, 'I may say that our correspondence is very large. In seven weeks we have despatched five hundred letters.'[70] Then, two months later: 'my time [is] taken up very often for six hours or more in the day attending to correspondence, seeing visitors, viewing sales, etc.', which meant that 'we have to go slowly with regard to certain things'.[71] In December, he noted that he had written 800 letters in the past two months, and there had been 'several days in which work in the Museum has not been possible owing to visitors, telephone calls, etc'.[72] In 1928 he claimed that there was four times as much work to do than in 1925, although he did not elaborate on his reasoning. He admitted that he no longer dealt with 'matters concerning the staff', leaving this to the secretary, A. L. Dean.[73] It was Dean who liaised with staff and dealt with any personnel issues, which would explain why they developed the impression that Malcolm 'did not seem to want us or to like us'.[74]

Braunholtz, who thought Malcolm had 'an enormous talent for bluff', remembered his discomfort when he feared others might perceive his weaknesses: ' "I know those fellows!" Malcolm would say knowingly, when confronted with some ethnographical problem and felt he was out of his depth. "I'm all tied up in knots", he would moan, clutching his head with both hands, giving the impression of one crushed by a vast load of complex responsibility.'[75]

Malcolm did gradually sink beneath the weight of his responsibilities, but, for all his limitations, he had been trying to swim against a rising tide that no single person proved capable of conquering. The buying systems that Thompson and Wellcome had put in place decades earlier were unrelenting. Every day, new objects arrived from all sources. It was this work, the work of acquiring things, that continued to satisfy Wellcome, while only adding to Malcolm's discomfort.

There are moments when the debilitating effects of such a well-oiled collecting machine are all too clear. On one occasion, Malcolm reported that 350 early printed books had been identified in the library, which 'would take one man a full year's work' to catalogue, but there was little hope for such a specialist job when the staff were occupied writing '10,000 author cards and 12,000 subject cards' in a year, in the vain hope of establishing the basic coordinates of library collection.[76] Meanwhile, 540 drug pots displayed in the Museum had been registered—more than many collectors could claim for their entire collection—but this was a minor achievement and merely provided 'an index of what is to be expected in other sections'.[77] In one report, Malcolm casually mentioned that they were expecting 'three truckloads of the building stones from the Lister Ward' in Glasgow. The stones were sent straight to one of Wellcome's storage buildings and disappeared from sight for years.[78]

Malcolm had planned to 'influence societies and people all over the country'[79] on behalf of Wellcome's Museum, but he influenced very few people during his tenure, at least not in the way that he had hoped. His efforts to elevate the Museum's profile simply added to his workload. He was unable to familiarize himself with Wellcome's possessions, which numbered hundreds of thousands when he arrived at the Museum. It did not help that Wellcome was so often away, but Malcolm was wary of him and unable to assert himself; all his attempts to please and impress only added to

Wellcome's frustrations. As the collection overwhelmed Malcolm, he proved to be a poor manager who found it difficult to communicate and could not win the confidence of his juniors. And, at the root of all his problems was Wellcome's unerring greed. Malcolm simply could not stem the tide of new acquisitions. It went against his own inclinations, but he was powerless to halt it. Thompson had built the collection up from small beginnings, buying hundreds of objects and books every week for decades, and all those who succeeded him would struggle with his legacy. Wellcome, meanwhile, still seemed intent on adding to the challenge rather than containing it.

CHAPTER FOURTEEN

WE NEED VERY COMPLETE COLLECTIONS OF ALL THEIR FABRICATIONS

Despite his difficulties, Malcolm's efforts to associate the Historical Medical Museum with the 'practical side of anthropology' did bring some successes.[1] During his tenure, Wellcome began to support anthropologists working in the field. Wellcome offered them money to fund their travels, and they, in return, gave him objects they collected during the course of their research. Sponsoring anthropologists had two potential rewards: it would bring Wellcome recognition as a patron of cutting-edge research, and it would satisfy his desire for new acquisitions.

British anthropology had largely been a museum-based profession since the late 1800s. Artefacts, along with linguistic data, physical measurements, and other information sent home by colonial officers, missionaries, explorers, and people stationed abroad, provided the intellectual currency upon which many early anthropological theories were based. The theorists themselves felt no compulsion to travel to the places they discussed (although some did). Much of their work was undertaken at home, collating observations from various sources to draw a broad picture of human diversity. This collaborative approach was thought to be effective because those collecting the data worked free from theoretical bias, while those analysing the data could judge its quality by comparison with other information they had to hand. Material culture was an ideal form of evidence because it offered a direct link between the 'armchair anthropologists' and the people who had actually made and used the objects they studied. Objects, it was thought, could not mislead in the way that information arising from poorly framed questions or badly translated responses could.[2] This system fuelled the grand visions—the 'science of man'—advocated by General Pitt Rivers, and admired by Wellcome. Museums were places where all this information could be arranged into a great picture of the human past, and where the 'natural laws' governing that past could be visually demonstrated.

By the 1920s this was changing. A new generation of professional anthropologists, who competed for the first University posts in the subject, saw the imprecision generated by many amateur observers who did not understand the significance of the customs they witnessed, who often relied on interpreters, and who were under no obligation to check their facts.[3] A brilliant Polish student from the London School of Economics named Bronislaw Malinowski, whose own research in the Trobriand Islands had been unexpectedly prolonged by the outbreak of the First World War, championed a different style of anthropological fieldwork. Anthropologists, he argued, should be regional specialists. They must live amongst their subjects for long periods of time; they must dispense with translators and learn the local language for themselves; and they must immerse themselves in all the daily tasks, like eating, working, and worshipping, that rendered their subjects' lives meaningful.[4] The nature of fieldwork was changing. Short, survey-style collecting trips were out and long-term residence was in.

Wellcome's contributions to the anthropological endeavour came in the midst of this disciplinary shift, and provided a bridge—at times a somewhat precarious bridge—between two methodological worlds. His philosophy was rooted in the late nineteenth century. He was intent on bringing together a broad picture of human diversity, along historical lines. He saw his artefacts as incontrovertible evidence: objects were the hard data upon which his panoramic project would flourish. His collectors had to be skilled and experienced, but their experience was valuable primarily because it ensured him the highest quality acquisitions. Collectors were still essentially facilitators. For Wellcome, the important intellectual work went on at home, in the Museum itself, when all the information his aides had collected could be assembled into a single story. 'The one thing most desirable', Wellcome had said in 1928, 'is to show from the beginning, the evolution and development throughout, the passing on from one stage of progress to another of particular objects. This is what invites interest and instructs.'[5] It was the links between the objects that was most important to him. The emphasis was on getting a broad range of material, rather than a specialized, heavily documented group of objects from a single place. In the late 1920s, collaborating with a number of anthropologists who were each regional specialists might provide satisfaction for everyone.

Wellcome established some productive relationships with anthropologists, particularly with Mervyn D. W. Jeffreys, whose work in Nigeria and Cameroon enriched Wellcome's collections for many years. Other collaborations were fruitful, but not always straightforward. The women anthropologists Wellcome supported, who felt indebted to his generosity as they tried to find a niche for themselves in a male-dominated sphere, were given less freedom to steer the course of their research. Winifred Blackman, an anthropologist who worked in Egypt, was one of these women. She was an experienced academic when she asked Wellcome for funds, but she struggled to gain his trust.

Winifred Blackman was one of the first anthropologists to reach a financial agreement with Wellcome. She asked him for a research grant in 1926, and she could present her credentials with some confidence. She was in her mid-fifties and had been affiliated with Oxford University for nearly fifteen years. She had already spent six successive seasons amongst the rural communities of Upper Egypt. She was fluent in Arabic and had gathered a wealth of information on local customs and beliefs. She was on the verge of publishing an account of her findings, *The Fellahin of Upper Egypt*, which was due out in early 1927 and became a standard work on the ethnography of the region.[6]

Blackman needed between £200 and £250 to supplement her British Association grant and allow her to return to Egypt and continue her research. Malcolm met with her, and examined some of the things she had brought back from the field, and he wrote enthusiastically to Wellcome, describing her impressive qualifications, and adding, 'Her material is . . . unique and of great value to the W.H.M.M. . . . She is most anxious to obtain your support, and I can recommend her request for your consideration.'[7] Blackman also wrote to Wellcome directly, stressing her well-established position as an anthropologist in Egypt, her intimate relationship with the local people, her knowledge of medical practices, and her ability to collect rare museum material for him.[8] But Wellcome was cautious. He was concerned about Blackman's allegiances to other institutions, particularly to the Pitt Rivers Museum in Oxford, where she had worked for many years.

You should inspect all she has got and promises to us. It is important to know what she has promised to Pitt Rivers Museum. It is very important that we get definite written statement as to all she promises to collect and do for us. I await cable report on these points before deciding. [Her work] appears to be of peculiar interest to H.M.M. but of little interest to other Museums.[9]

He decided to give her a grant, but only once Blackman had promised not to collect for anyone else (including herself). She agreed to transfer all her own collections to Wellcome's Museum. She also submitted a list of material she intended to buy for the Museum during her trip, which included charms, medicines, jewellery, pottery, and baskets used for medical purposes.[10]

Other collectors were not subject to these conditions,[11] but Blackman was in no position to argue. Money had been a constant worry to her, and Wellcome agreed to provide her with £250. In the past, she had been forced to rely on her family for financial support, and had spent much of her time applying for small grants that did not cover her expenses.[12] She was trying to establish herself as a professional academic, but despite her considerable expertise, as a woman, and without an undergraduate degree, she was at a disadvantage. University positions for anthropologists were few and far between. Blackman might have found, in Wellcome, a private patron who would become intellectually engaged with her work and give her long-term financial security. Wellcome, however, was concerned only with the objects she could acquire for him.

Blackman began collecting for Wellcome in March 1927. On her arrival in Egypt, she bought a couple of donkeys and set about 'riding to various villages, trying to get to know the people' who could help her in her quest for objects.[13] She bought local pottery, a drum, baskets, and models of agricultural and irrigation tools, amongst them a miniature water wheel that 'really *will* draw water'.[14] She arranged for a parturition chair to be specially made for the Museum—at Malcolm's request—in a nearby village. By July, she had gathered around 170 objects, and had packed them into travelling trunks ready for shipment to England. Pleased with her achievements, she wrote to Malcolm in June,

I wonder if it would be possible for you to let me know before I leave Egypt if Mr. Wellcome will help me again next season. I should be glad to be able to make all the arrangements here before I leave, and to be able to come out here quite by the beginning of November and stay out for 8 or 9 months.[15]

Holding onto this possibility, she stayed in Egypt for the next few months, while her funding ran dry and her confidence wavered, waiting in vain to hear whether Wellcome would support her again and save her the trip home. News from London was slow. It was only in the middle of October, four months later, that Malcolm told her she would have to send her collection back to London for inspection before a second grant could be awarded.[16]

As Blackman's anxieties and financial difficulties grew, she wrote to Malcolm constantly, beseeching him to let her know about a second grant. She stressed the unique position she was in as an anthropologist in the field who had taken the time to live amongst the people she studied:

It requires very intimate acquaintance with the people to get most of the things I have got. For instance, it took me weeks and weeks before I could get the air anklet worn by a child, it is a thing never parted with. The alabaster bowl and the rhinoceros horn are also priceless things. The latter I could only get with the assistance of my friend.[17]

Hoping to reassure Malcolm, her fraught letters actually had the opposite effect. In November, he told Wellcome that he was beginning to feel that her collection was 'not all we might have expected', even though he had yet to see it.[18]

When Malcolm did finally see the collection, he was disappointed. He summoned Blackman's brother, Aylward Manley Blackman, an Egyptologist at Oxford who had as yet had no formal role to play in Blackman's association with Wellcome, to discuss his reservations: 'I should like to have a chat with you with regard to the future attitude of this Museum to this type of collection from Egypt.'[19] There is no record of what was said during this meeting, but Malcolm explained to Wellcome afterwards that 'the chief value [of Blackman's objects] is in their authentication, and although they are not of outstanding value as specimens, they do illustrate to a certain extent the life of the Fellahin of Egypt'.[20] Perhaps he thought her objects were too general—with agricultural hoes, models of water wheels, domestic utensils and baskets—and not medical enough. Still, Blackman was given a second chance by virtue of her anthropological expertise rather than her initial contribution to the Museum's collections.

Wellcome, having seen a catalogue of the collection, some photographs, and Malcolm's comments, asked Malcolm to reiterate his conditions of exclusivity, and demand more particulars about each object and more photographs. Blackman was asked to submit a detailed list of her existing collection, which was stored at her home in Oxford, and which she had promised to donate to the Museum in accordance with the initial terms of her grant.[21] Blackman had been awaiting news of a second grant for more than six months—it had been 'very trying waiting in this uncertainty, not knowing if all my work is going to be knocked on the head or not. It worries me dreadfully.'[22]—and this cautious attitude irked her. She wrote rather point-edly that she could not produce an inventory of her own collection until she returned to England, but that she had every intention of standing by her word and giving Wellcome all her things when she got home.[23] Eventually, in March, her grant was renewed, although she was only given £200 this time, and she set about acquiring a second field collection for Wellcome.

Blackman's second collection, made during 1928, was more focused. It consisted of local charms and cures, with none of the domestic and agricul-tural artefacts she had bought before. 'I shall have some large specimens to bring back, but this very unique collection of charms and cures will not take up so much space as the larger objects last year, so perhaps two large trunks will be enough.' Financial limitations also impacted on her second Wellcome collection. 'I found that with the sum of money placed at my disposal it was impossible to go to the expense of travelling about. You do not know how difficult it is to manage with such a sum. I cannot run into expensive things.'[24] Her financial insecurity meant that she could not afford to stray far from Wellcome's requirements. If he and Malcolm wanted charms and cures, that is what they would get. Malcolm thought, 'her collection this time has exceeded by far anything she has previously bought'.[25]

Blackman continued to collect for Wellcome until 1933, focusing her attention on 'medical and magico-medical objects'.[26] Her 1929 collection, nearly 1,000 objects strong, included stones, skins, shells, and seeds used for their therapeutic or supernatural properties, and simple pieces of jewellery and beads used as amulets.[27] Blackman, in other words, was acquiring objects worth little beyond their medical and ethnographic significance. She ex-pressed an interest in buying more expensive objects, like musical instruments and local costumes, but her suggestions were either ignored or denied by her sponsors.[28] Since she could never be certain that they would renew her grant, she had to abide by their requests.

Blackman's experiences were similar to those of another female collector who worked for Wellcome at the time, Phyllis Kemp. Kemp set out on her first collecting expedition for Wellcome in September 1929. Although she only undertook two collecting tours, she, too, was discouraged from spending money on expensive artefacts for the Museum. Both women were working in regions characterized as 'folk' cultures: settled, peasant communities. Black-man was not researching the ancient civilizations of Egypt, nor the urban population of Cairo, but the farming communities that spread out south along the Nile. The fellahin followed a simple way of life, without complicated technology, that had, apparently, been little altered for centuries. Kemp, meanwhile, travelled through the rural villages of Romania, Bosnia, and Yugoslavia. Wellcome and Malcolm seemed to *expect* the objects that Blackman and Kemp collected to be plain and inexpensive, and Kemp's experiences support this.

Kemp, like Blackman, made some concerted efforts to buy valuable artefacts for Wellcome's Museum, but she was thwarted. She had joined the Museum as a researcher in February 1929 aged twenty-five. Malcolm saw that Kemp, who had worked as a school teacher in Belgrade, had 'an extraordinary knowledge of things relating to the Balkan States'.[29] She spoke German, Serbian, and other Slavic languages, and during the autumn of 1929 she was sent on a three-week collecting tour of Romania and Bosnia to buy things for Wellcome. At Wellcome's behest, following Malcolm's encouragement, Kemp then went to Yugoslavia for a three-month collecting trip in March 1930.[30]

Malcolm's instructions to Kemp were very specific. He wanted her to get objects used by 'common folk...not expensive rarities'.[31] He told her that she

must exercise rigid economy in every direction in obtaining the material required.... In particular you should do your best to obtain material used by the peasants for preventing and curing illnesses, including charms, amulets, talismans and prophylactics. These can all be obtained at an almost nominal cost in the country villages, and you should make full notes regarding their provenance.[32]

Malcolm made a point of telling Kemp that she would not be required to visit libraries or research in archives during her trip. He reminded her that her 'success in obtaining Museum material will considerably influence our decision in regard to future field work, so I urge you to concentrate on this, as it is for this purpose that the trip was approved'.[33]

But Kemp was confronted by some treasures on her travels. Soon after her arrival in Yugoslavia in the spring of 1930, she found a Serbian painting of the Madonna and Child, probably from the sixteenth century, that had been owned by an inn-keeping family for generations. A local expert told her that 'One very seldom comes across such a well preserved and beautiful specimen—the workmanship is exquisite.'[34] Clearly excited, she wrote to Malcolm in great detail about the painting, outlining its artistic influences and the history of its ownership. Although expensive, at £250–£300, she knew it was a bargain, and given that Wellcome was now spending £30,000 every year on his Museum and Library, her enquiry was hardly unrealistic. Other objects had also caught her eye: a number of rare books, a 'fine collection of coins', and some of the instruments used by popular surgeons in Belgrade.[35]

Malcolm's response to all these suggestions was firmly negative. He felt the objects mentioned were either too expensive or not of great interest.[36] Two weeks later, on 11 April, with similar enthusiasm, Kemp wrote of a five-metre-long, paper and silk amulet scroll in an engraved silver case, which dated to the early seventeenth century and was 'written over in minute and beautiful Arabic characters in various coloured inks, and as far as I could see, containing magical texts from the Koran and formulae for divination and charms against every possible misfortune'. Again, Malcolm curtailed her excitement, writing that it seemed to be expensive and the Museum already had a 'vast collection of Arabic charms from all parts of the world', and she should only buy it for half the price asked.[37] Later, Kemp began visiting aristocratic houses, and looked into buying a room and furniture complete, but it was only when she asked Malcolm about price and extra furnishings that he finally replied, 'No—thank you, we will not require this.'[38]

Kemp was disappointed, but she began to understand that Wellcome and Malcolm were not interested in her buying anything particularly valuable. Of the Madonna and Child painting, she agreed that 'its value is certainly rather from a purely artistic and technical point of view', and added, 'I will see later on whether I can get some of the books more cheaply and if not I will let the matter drop.'[39]

Kemp gave up mentioning expensive material. Instead, she bought small amulets, local cures and ointments from peasants at markets and on visits to local doctors. She bought some traditional costumes and a few manuscripts that were cheap and directly related to medicine and occult sciences. She wrote down the prescriptions used for specific illnesses and collected herbs and plant samples used for making remedies. She obtained a child's cradle and instruments used by surgeons and doctors, including pincers, knives, bloodletting equipment, razors, and tweezers. These were things that Malcolm had requested. The vast majority of them cost her less than £1, and the most she spent on one item was for an elaborate piece of clothing made of velvet with silver embroidery that cost £4 14s 6d. Kemp became concerned with economy and often said that she would only follow up objects if she could 'get them cheap'.[40] In May, when she learned that one of her informants had 'another important branch of business—sifting through rubbish heaps', she searched a couple of dumps with him but found nothing of interest.[41]

Malcolm and Wellcome wanted Kemp to document peasant life. They knew what they wanted before they sent their collectors into the field, and they were not prepared to adjust their expectations in the light of evidence that emerged later. Theirs was a partial view, and Kemp and Blackman found themselves unable to elaborate on it. Eastern European countries were popularly associated with folklore, superstition, and magic, and it was these traditions Kemp was to concentrate on, not expensive Christian or Islamic artworks. There was little she could do about this when she had been so plainly reminded that any future fieldwork depended on her ability to meet her employer's criteria. Her efforts to include more expensive items in her collection failed. Would Malcolm have been as quick to confine the work of a male colleague who had a similar level of local knowledge? Kemp had adopted a deferential attitude early on in her relationship with Malcolm. She had not made a museum collection before. In April she asked, 'Will you kindly let me know if possible by return whether or not in your opinion I am on the right track?' Malcolm's response was characteristically mindful: 'Yes but obtain the most common objects—for magic and medicine.'[42] A few weeks later, Kemp was still hesitant: 'If you are satisfied with what I am doing then it should be remembered that as I say I am still only feeling my way.'[43] Malcolm encouraged her, but he continued to worry that she might be 'tricked' over price.

Male collectors were hardly subject to the same concerns as Kemp and Blackman. Indeed, when it came to sponsoring one particular man, Major A. Stanley Clarke, who was planning a trip to Tanganyika in East Africa, Wellcome's unchecked enthusiasm for the project backfired. Clarke met with Malcolm in the summer of 1929, and asked for £200 to support his journey, in return for a museum collection. But Malcolm seemed unable to pass on much information about the 'explorer' to Wellcome. Clarke had 'spent most of his time in East Africa since the late War and he is well acquainted with the natives'; he had been introduced to Malcolm through a mutual acquaintance, but 'beyond this, I do not know much about him'.[44] Blackman had to provide references, show her collection, write proposals, and sign a contract before Wellcome agreed to support her, but his response to Clarke, who was equally unknown to him, was practically joyous:

Major Stanley Clark regions between Lake Tanganyika and Belgian Congo—this is one of the most interesting and unexplored regions of Central Africa and do not hesitate to add more to the Two Hundred Pounds if needed to secure ethnological collections from the natives... Full information as to the local natives themselves, their types, cults, habits, customs, etc., will be of intense interest and we need very complete collections of all their fabrications, etc., etc.[45]

Wellcome raised no questions about Clarke's background, experience or reputation. Instead, he requested a comprehensive ethnographic collection, documenting all aspects of local life, and immediately authorized a £300 grant.[46] Malcolm was more cautious and gave Clarke the requested £200, 'which will be quite sufficient under the circumstances'.[47] Clarke left for Africa at the end of August 1929, intending to stay for more than a year.

Despite the high hopes, Clarke's work proved unsatisfactory. His rate of acquisition was slow. By January, four months into his journey, Malcolm had only received one copper pot and a witch doctor's outfit from Broken Hill. Seventeen medicines from Kapiri Mposhi, which Clarke had sent in early December, were on their way. By April, three woven baskets and thirty-four more medicines had arrived in London, and Malcolm was awaiting a further sixty medicine samples. Then Clarke announced that he had begun duplicating his collection of remedies. 'This in case Doctor Wellcome should decide to retain my services, and if possible to avoid the confusion of duplication under different names in other countries.'[48] It seems that Clarke felt the need for a reference collection for his own use in the field, but it was surely a mistake to start retracing and repeating his work eight months into his field trip and to spend Wellcome's money on material he would never see.

Clarke lacked confidence and was not sure what to buy for the Museum even though Malcolm claimed to have briefed him fully before he left for Africa. In early December, Clarke wrote a list of items he could buy, but he felt that they 'would be costly to send home, and I do not think of very great interest to you'.[49] The list included baskets, spears, bows and arrows, drums, hoes, axes, pots, sticks for making fire, and a hollow log and post used for grinding. Malcolm wrote in reply that he wanted all these things, adding, 'we would like material illustrating the life, crafts and cults of the natives and the objects you enumerate would be just what we want'.[50] But Clarke continued to send nothing but batches of local remedies and drugs. While Blackman and Kemp had tried to broaden their collections and been prevented, Clarke seemed reluctant, even when explicitly encouraged, to expand his horizons at all.

Clarke's first statement of accounts, sent to London in late December, showed that he had spent more than £100 on travel, living expenses, and advance payments to mission houses for help with collecting, but he had so far spent only a few pounds on actual acquisitions.[51] In April, as he started to duplicate his existing collection of drugs, Clarke wrote:

There is only one more thing I want to ask you about, which is this. The further I go with this work, the slower will be the results-: I mean it is comparatively easy to collect say fifty medicines, and I can do it fairly quickly and travel on from district to district. But to do it thoroughly, after the first rush medicines will come in slowly. Personally I would rather do it thoroughly, but if you employ me it is for you to say what you want me to do.[52]

Wellcome was nothing if not a stickler for swift results, and Malcolm was now having second thoughts about Clarke's work. He had already warned Wellcome, 'I do not consider ... that the material he has sent is commensurate with the sum of £200 which has been allocated for his work ... I consider that his expenses are excessive in relation to the material acquired.'[53] A month later he reiterated his discontent:

Up to the present, Major Clarke has sent us four parcels of material. I do not consider that he has the collecting instinct and I cannot recommend, therefore the retention of his services on the terms he asks ... I do not think the sum total of his collecting is very good and justifies the money granted to him.[54]

The arrangement with Stanley Clarke was terminated in May 1930.[55] In January, Wellcome had told Malcolm to 'Continue to contribute liberally to his fund as he can secure for us many rare ethnological and other objects for the Museum in the regions to which he is going.'[56] But, with no rare ethnological objects on the horizon, Wellcome, too, voiced discontent on reading a list of Clarke's latest botanical specimens: 'Specimens without means of identification of plants yielding these remedies have little value.'[57] Clarke had failed to react decisively to Malcolm's request for a wider range of cultural artefacts. He persisted in buying medicines—the kind of remedies that Blackman and Kemp had been told to procure—even when he was encouraged to document other aspects of local life.

A far happier working relationship was struck with Mervyn Jeffreys. Jeffreys was an anthropologist and officer with the Nigerian Colonial Civil Service, who had no difficulties gathering the kind of 'material illustrating the life, crafts, and cults of the natives' that Malcolm had hoped Clarke would collect.[58] Malcolm and Jeffreys may have known each other through their work and interests in Nigeria, because they came to an agreement only a few

months after Malcolm's appointment as Conservator.[59] Jeffreys was offered
£100 as an initial payment for making a collection, but he insisted it was too
much—he was, after all, living in Nigeria at the time, so could collect at
leisure in his free time—and he suggested rolling payments of £20 instead.[60]
An informal relationship was established, where Jeffreys asked for more
money as he needed it. Malcolm showed none of the financial concerns
expressed to Kemp, and Wellcome was happy to let Jeffreys develop his
collection as he saw fit without insisting on the annual checks that Blackman
endured. All Malcolm wrote, as Jeffreys embarked on his first collection for
the Museum in 1926, was 'I think you know the sort of material which we are
anxious to obtain, and I can safely leave the selection in your hands.'[61]

And, unlike Clarke, Jeffreys did seem to know the sort of material Wellcome and Malcolm wanted. He continued to collect for the Museum for
more than ten years, sending his final consignments of objects in 1938
(seventy-three cases of material) and 1939 (twenty-four cases).[62] His relationship with Wellcome was one of the most successful of any independent
collector associated with the Museum. And the collections he made over
the years, documenting the lives of the Igbo and Ibibio in Nigeria and the
people of Bamenda in Cameroon, are amongst the most valuable of their
kind. He sent nearly 200 packing cases of objects back to London during the
thirteen years of his association with Wellcome.[63]

Jeffrey's good relations with the Museum probably owed something to the
fact that he was not particularly expensive. He received money sporadically;
spending less than £45 between 1926 and 1930, and thereafter either £50 or
£100 each year.[64] His collection developed in phases, and when he needed
money he would simply announce, 'I have started buying for you again', and
ask for funds.[65] Wellcome's staff did not always know when the next
instalment would arrive. In 1932 they received a cloakroom ticket for Pad-
dington Station in the mail, with a note from Jeffreys to say that 'a bundle of
paddles and spears' from Nigeria had been left there for them to pick up.[66]

As his collections grew, Jeffreys planned to spend time at the Museum
documenting his things and preparing publications, and, most unusually,
Wellcome did not seem to argue with his intention to publish.[67] Jeffreys
spent some time at the Museum storerooms in the early 1930s with one of
Wellcome's staff members, cataloguing objects and selecting some for photographing.[68] He even managed to use the Museum secretaries for his own
typing work,[69] and the Museum paid for his personal subscription to the
Royal Anthropological Institute and the Royal Africa Society.[70]

Despite this, Jeffreys did not feel indebted to Wellcome's generosity as other collectors had. In fact, he felt quite the reverse: he thought Wellcome was lucky to have secured his expertise on such good terms. Jeffreys was a government official and a professional anthropologist, and he did not need Wellcome's money. He collected for the Museum when he could find the time. Sometimes his letters came with lofty apologies: 'I am afraid the information I have given you is sketchy but I cannot spare more time. I have five murder cases to try, two slave dealing [*sic*], two raids to deal with, and a large number of assaults, and I am in a room full of stuff to pack and dispatch to you.'[71] He knew that the material he sent was precious and the Museum had acquired it cheap. In 1936, he wrote:

For ten years the Museum has had willingly, and joyfully placed at its disposal the services of a trained Anthropologist... the Museum, beyond paying for my subscription to the R.A.I. and to Africa, has paid nothing for the services rendered. I did not expect any, and I do not ask for any, remuneration. I like collecting the material: nevertheless the fact remains that the Museum is getting all this attention and skill free.[72]

It was hard to disagree. Malcolm judged 'that Mr. Jeffreys' material as a whole is one of the most complete collections which have ever come from West Africa, because he has not, as is so often the case, collected only rare specimens, but has dealt with the culture of the people as a whole'.[73] In 1939, an internal memo written by staff as they sorted through Jeffreys's objects noted that the collection was of 'definite scientific importance to all collectors interested in the nature and history of native material culture, since it covers nearly every aspect of native life: weapons of war and the chase; domestic implements; utensils; furniture; technology—e.g. basketry, pottery, weaving, carving, metal-work, tools; costume and ornaments; musical instruments; ritual and ceremonial accessories'.[74] Jeffreys also took around 3000 photographs that were transferred to Wellcome's Museum.[75]

Jeffreys enjoyed the financial security that Winifred Blackman never had, but Blackman's collections were important, and could have been more so had Wellcome given her the freedom to broaden her horizons. Egypt had excited the attentions of archaeologists, but not anthropologists, and Blackman remained the only person to have studied the rural communities of Egypt in any depth until after the Second World War.[76] But she had to scrape together funds year after year to pursue her academic research, never quite knowing where her next instalment would come from, and frequently becoming indebted to members of her family. She tried and failed to secure an academic post, but she had mixed feelings when it came to pursuing an academic career. In 1928, as she waited for news about her application for a Readership at University College London, she admitted, 'I could not in any case take it if it meant giving up my yearly visits here [to Egypt]. This is the work for which I have trained and prepared myself for years, and I could not give it up.'[77] Still, every season in Egypt was a struggle. She was dependent on Wellcome's good grace in a way that Jeffreys never was. Both Blackman and Kemp were constantly monitored. They were given little opportunity to challenge either Malcolm's or Wellcome's preconceived expectations for their collections, and efforts to do so were futile.

The restrictions they worked under were partly due to prejudice regarding the places they worked. Clarke and Jeffreys were encouraged to make wide-ranging collections to document the lives of little known 'primitive' peoples in the heart of Africa. In the popular imagination, Sub-Saharan Africa was shrouded in elemental mystique. The people who lived there were thought to be ancestral survivors, whose cultural traditions were somehow more ancient than other people's. The traditions of such 'noble savages' seemed at once both shockingly base and startlingly majestic, and was variously romanticized and sensationalized in the popular press.[78] The rural economies of Egypt and Eastern Europe held little of this exotic charm. Similar peasant traditions could be witnessed near at home, and, while these customs were interesting, and declining (the growing fascination with rural English traditions at the turn of the twentieth century was partly fuelled by fears they would soon disappear altogether[79]), it did not excite the urgent wonder of Sub-Saharan Africa. Kemp and Blackman were forced to restrict their collections to the kind of inexpensive medical charms typical of so-called 'folk' cultures. Wellcome did not express 'intense interest' in their findings, as he had before Clarke's travels, nor did the Museum seem to need 'very complete collections of all their fabrications'.[80]

It would be wrong to make sweeping claims for Wellcome's attitude to female researchers. Blackman and Kemp found it difficult to prove their worth, but all women had to work hard for institutional recognition in a male-dominated professional world. Success was exceptional, and brought its own sacrifices. It is interesting that neither Blackman nor Kemp married. It was standard policy at Burroughs Wellcome, and other businesses at the time, for women to resign their jobs on marriage. Although this rule did not affect Blackman or Kemp, two other women who worked on the 'Scientific Staff' at the Museum, Mary Borer and Joan Raymont, were forced to resign, very much against their will, when they wed. Raymont's case was further complicated by the fact that her husband, Hermann Braunholtz, worked at the British Museum. Wellcome and Malcolm agreed that it was 'undesirable that we should have people on our staff who were connected with other museums, so that the knowledge of the work we are doing may become known to them'. Despite their concerns regarding a potential disclosure to the British Museum, Malcolm wrote to Hermann Braunholtz, not Joan, to 'suggest' that she resign her post.[81]

Wellcome undeniably held traditional views. His wife, Syrie, had sometimes found them stifling. But he had formed successful friendships with other independent women. He became a lifelong friend of May French Sheldon, the American traveller known as the 'Lady Stanley', who caused a sensation when she travelled from Mombasa to Mount Kilimanjaro with no white companion in 1891 (her 150 Zanzibari porters and guides apparently counted for little).[82] Wellcome and Henry Stanley had helped to plan her expedition; Burroughs Wellcome had provided tailored medical equipment, and Wellcome had personally designed a palanquin for her (Figure 23). Made of cane, bamboo, and aluminium, with silk fittings, it was beautiful, light, waterproof, and durable, and gave her somewhere to sleep, travel, and store her belongings.[83] Wellcome was also great friends with Genevieve Ward, a successful opera singer, actress, and teacher, who, as a performer, 'was drawn towards resolute and individualistic female characters outside tragedy, ones which pitted her against ruthless men in a clash of wills'.[84] After an early, failed marriage, Ward remained single, toured the world, and carved out an independent and extremely successful career for herself. Wellcome was one of her closest friends.[85]

The 'Scientific Staff' remembered Wellcome as an elderly, slightly eccentric but well-mannered man. They saw him infrequently, but Raymont remembered that 'when he occasionally called in at the Museum he always seemed pleased to see us, and bowed courteously'.[86] A. W. J. Haggis, who joined the Museum late in 1929 as a researcher, also commented on Wellcome's courtesy. 'Always his bearing was that of a man of considerable personal charm, which was enhanced by an extremely strict observance of etiquette, and by his easy and natural politeness which in the later years of his life stood out in refreshing contrast to the tendency of the twentieth century.'[87] But Malcolm did not engender much affection. It was Malcolm who instigated Raymont's dismissal, by drawing Wellcome's attention to her

Mrs. FRENCH SHELDON'S PALANQUIN.

This palanquin was made at Whiteley's for Mrs. French Sheldon, the "Lady Stanley" who is bound for Central Africa, from designs by Mr. Henry S. Welcome (of Messrs. Burroughs & Wellcome, Snow Hill). It is a unique specimen of strong, light, and artistic cane and bamboo work, and Mr. Wellcome must be congratulated on his excellent taste. The palanquin will be carried by four of Mrs. Sheldon's Zanzibari porters.

Figure 23. Mrs French Sheldon's palanquin, designed by Henry Wellcome in 1891.

marriage. Wellcome was more concerned by the possibility that his plans would be 'leaked' to the British Museum; but Malcolm argued that he saw in her an 'indefinable attitude' since her marriage that affected her duties at work.[88] It was Malcolm who worried about Phyllis Kemp's financial competence, and decided to speak to Blackman's brother about Blackman's work. But these attitudes were not unusual. Blackman's misfortune was her heavy reliance on Wellcome as a patron, coupled with his single-mindedness when it came to acquisitions. She hoped to engage him in her academic career, but he was interested in acquisitions. He paid for tangible results, not research support, as his earlier dealings with Sambon and Thompson had indicated. This was brought home to Blackman on one particular occasion towards the end of her association with the Wellcome Historical Medical Museum, and, despite her efforts to communicate directly with Wellcome, the situation was mediated by Malcolm.

Blackman gave a paper at a meeting of the British Association for the Advancement of Science in September 1931. Her talk was illustrated by a selection of tattoo designs, drawn on paper, that she had collected during her time in Egypt. The anthropological exhibits for the meeting were, by coincidence, to be displayed in the Wellcome Historical Medical Museum, so Blackman sent her tattoo designs there. In the months that followed she struggled to get them back. In November she complained to Wellcome, 'I have been to the Museum to fetch them, telephoned, written more than once and telegraphed to have the collection and catalogue returned, but I have not got them yet.' She used the tattoo designs regularly for lecturing, which helped her to raise money—money, she added, that 'simply goes towards the collection which I make for the Wellcome Museum' anyway—and they were not intended for Wellcome's collection. She planned to make another collection of tattoo designs for Wellcome. Hers was a working collection, designed to help her supplement the limited grant Wellcome gave her. She needed more money, and the lectures eased the financial pressure on her family.[89]

Eventually, Malcolm returned her designs, but he sent her a rather formal letter, referring her to the contract she signed in 1927, 'in which you expressly stated that you would collect material for this Museum and for no other institution or person whatever . . . I consider, therefore, that the tattoo designs are our property and I am sending them back to you as a loan.' Furthermore, Malcolm requested written confirmation that the rest of her collection would be sent to the Museum: 'in your recent lecture at the Royal Anthropological Institute it was stated publicly that you had a collection of over two-hundred exhibits. This is in distinct contravention to the terms of your agreement with us.'[90] It is hard to imagine Malcolm writing a letter in these terms to Jeffreys, who was not asked to hand over any private collections as a condition of his work for Wellcome.

Soon after this incident, Wellcome withdrew his funding from Blackman. The exact reason for his decision is unknown. Malcolm referred to the Museum's 'many commitments' and the fact that they had supported her work for 'some considerable time'.[91] Perhaps her reluctance to part with every single thing she owned from Egypt contributed to their decision. Her contractual agreement with Wellcome was not unusual—all Wellcome's employees had to sign contracts promising that they would hand over any objects to the Museum as a condition of their work—but it was the manner of its enforcement that was so relentless. She was paid for her artefacts alone: there could be no gentlemanly understanding between Blackman and Wellcome.

CHAPTER FIFTEEN

THIS INTERNATIONAL
HISTORICAL MUSEUM

One of Wellcome's collectors was given a much freer rein, financially and administratively, than any other during the late 1920s and 1930s. Peter Johnston-Saint, a suave and well-connected ex-army officer, spent more money buying a single batch of letters than Winifred Blackman ever received for an entire field season in Egypt.[1] Between 1927 and 1935, Johnston-Saint went on two or three long tours, of two to five months, every year for Wellcome. He almost always began his travels in France, and frequently moved on to Italy or Spain. He went to Austria, Greece, Germany, Switzerland, Egypt, and the Middle East a number of times. He also visited India and Ceylon (Sri Lanka) on behalf of the Museum. During his earlier trips he spent £100–£200 a month on artefacts; six weeks in France and Italy at the beginning of 1929 saw him spend nearly £1,100 on objects and around £35 a week on travel expenses; during thirteen weeks in the Mediterranean in 1930 he spent £1,900 on acquisitions and £600 on expenses, and a similar trip a year later cost £700 in expenses, and more than £2,300 in purchases.[2] He secured thousands of objects for Wellcome while touring abroad as the Museum's Foreign Secretary. It was the kind of work he had been born to do: hobnobbing with men of influence in the morning and haggling with street vendors in the afternoon.

As a permanent member of Wellcome's staff, Johnston-Saint assumed a position similar in influence to the one Thompson had enjoyed ten years earlier. He was the right man at the right time for Wellcome: his natural self-assurance gave the collecting project stability in the aftermath of Thompson's departure; his efficiency as a buyer kept Wellcome's consumer instincts satisfied; and his enthusiasm for the job countered Malcolm's cautious attitude to acquisitions. Saint's confidence earned Wellcome's trust, and he reaped the rewards as a collector, deciding where he would go, whom he would see, and following his own instincts as a buyer.

Wellcome's Museum had earned a higher profile by the late-1920s, thanks to the Re-opening Ceremony, a number of evening receptions, and an important exhibition in 1927 to celebrate the centenary of Joseph Lister's birth. It was now quite well known on the Continent, and Johnston-Saint proved to be its perfect ambassador. He loved to travel and had a wide social circle, but he was not a pretentious man. He was equally happy talking to the King of Spain, whose wife he had known since childhood, as he was drinking with the locals in a remote tavern in the Sicilian mountains in the company of 'goats, fowls and diminutive asses'. Each of these encounters, incidentally, yielded new accessions for the Historical Medical Museum, to Wellcome's great satisfaction.[3] Both Wellcome and Saint enjoyed, and understood, the finer things in life, but were glad to eschew them when adventure called. Wellcome shared Saint's love for travel, and his journeys through South America as a young man, and more recent visits to Egypt and Sudan, had shown him to be enterprising and resilient, just as Saint was. They were both fond of motor cars. Saint declared that he could 'drive and understand any make of motor car', but he had still been a student at the time of Wellcome's four-wheeled escapades through Europe with his wife in the early 1900s.

Saint had graduated from St John's College, Cambridge, with a degree in history in 1907 and had served in the Indian Army and the Royal Flying Corps during the War (Figure 24). He was a keen athlete and horseman: he had played hockey for Cambridge and polo for his regiment in India, and was an enthusiastic golfer. In his application to the Wellcome Historical Medical Museum he claimed to possess 'a natural practical ability and a love of hard work'.[4] He joined the Museum as Secretary in 1920, and his administrative skills must have proved valuable in the aftermath of Thompson's 'retirement' five years later. Certainly, he seems to have seen an opportunity for his own professional development in the new order of things.

Johnston-Saint made a good impression on Malcolm, who began to rely on him to negotiate for important acquisitions during 1926 and 1927. Saint went on short collecting trips for Malcolm, to Scotland, France, Germany, and Holland. He attended an important sale for the Museum in Frankfurt-am-Main in 1926, acquiring 117 lots from the Kurt Wolff collection of

Figure 24. Photograph of Peter Johnston-Saint, date unknown.

incunabula.[5] When notable auctions came up in London—like the sale of Arthur Evans's collection at Sotheby's in 1927, at which the Museum spent £740 on archaeological artefacts—he assumed the role Thompson once had, viewing the collection, setting price limits, overseeing the Museum's men in action on the day, and taking up the bidding from them when necessary.[6] Meanwhile, Saint put new systems in place for seeking material from scientific institutions and individuals, under Malcolm's direction.[7] He started to gather together a valuable collection of Lister relics during 1926, fraternizing with Lister's family and travelling up to Glasgow to secure furniture and equipment from the Lister ward before it was demolished that year.[8] And Malcolm asked Saint to contact the Pasteur Institute in Paris, to gauge the possibility of acquiring Pasteur relics that could be exhibited in association with the growing Lister collection.[9]

Both Malcolm and Wellcome were struck by Saint's achievements. Malcolm believed that the Museum's connections with British universities were improving and added, 'In this connection, I must say that Captain Johnston Saint is most invaluable, and he is very keen. He has a distinct flair for this kind of work.'[10] Wellcome monitored all from afar: 'It is very gratifying to me to observe . . . the enthusiasm which you and Captain Saint have manifested in securing essential additions to our collections, especially objects associated with Lister.'[11]

It was Saint's ten-day trip to France in May 1927 that confirmed his new status at the Museum. He visited nineteen scholars and doctors during the short tour. His goal was to advance the profile of Wellcome's Museum and encourage donations. He visited scientists in their homes and at their places of work, examined private museums and libraries, and handed out Wellcome Historical Medical Museum guidebooks as gifts. Many of his hosts presented the Museum with artefacts there and then, but the main outcome of his trip was a wealth of information on existing collections, and promises of help for the future. Saint wrote a detailed report, which ran to seven pages, followed by an extra eight pages listing donations, visits, and letters received.[12] Wellcome's response was unusually detailed.

First, I want to express my deep appreciation of this report. It is very clear, concise and comprehensive. France is a field of immense importance to the W.H.M.M., from several points of view, especially in connection with medicine, surgery, anatomy, chemistry, bacteriology, anthropology, etymology, archaeology, folk lore and allied sciences.[13]

Wellcome was brimming over with enthusiasm for Saint's work. Flush with the success of the French trip, Wellcome referred to the Historical Medical Museum in this letter as 'this International Historical Museum'. He now saw fresh opportunities for 'unearthing' an 'immense amount of precious materials' from 'each of the other European nations' by building up long-term relationships with distinguished scientists. His conclusion was unequivocal:

In respect to France this report shows that this field is of special importance to the W.H.M.M., and makes it clear that every one of these openings referred to by Mr. Johnston Saint should be followed up as speedily as possible, consistent with diplomatic handling, according to circumstances in each individual case.

Later that summer, Wellcome drew up a new job description for Johnston-Saint. He would be sent on longer European tours to research the particulars of collectors, scientists, families, and institutions 'who are likely to be helpful in advising and assisting us in obtaining materials of interest', and generally try to promote the Museum's reputation abroad.[14]

Saint became an ambassador. His work would be 'consistent with diplomatic handling', and his job was to implement some unwritten, newly conceived, international policy on behalf of the Museum. Wellcome's language spilled over with political metaphors. Saint's collecting tours were 'missions', and the overall scheme was referred to as 'the mission'. The Museum's recent acquisitions of Lister and Pasteur relics had prompted, according to Wellcome, 'the deep gratification of the French Nation'. And, a 'special clause regarding entertainment', previously unheard of, allowed Saint to host people at the Museum's expense in the hopes of 'diplomatically influencing' them.[15]

All this hyperbole was inspired by Johnston-Saint's newfound talents as a collector, but it was also Wellcome's response to the perceived threat from other American collectors during the 1920s. Saint would lead the Museum's drive against rival bidders, and his task immediately became an urgent one. 'With the large sums of money the Americans are preparing to expend,' Wellcome wrote, 'they are proposing to sweep Europe clean of historical medical material, and they may succeed unless we act quickly and thoroughly.'[16] Malcolm had already asked for directional powers to send Museum representatives to the Continent as soon as important material came up for sale, since so many Americans were interested in objects relating to Pasteur, Jenner, and Lister. During the summer of 1927, he often wrote of the threat from 'the Americans', whose hunger for European collectables was pushing up prices in the sales rooms.[17]

According to Wellcome, intense 'diplomacy' could counter this tide of transatlantic avarice. He hoped to establish productive relationships with collectors in Europe, and recognized that this could take time to achieve. Malcolm had pointed out that personal interviews were far more effective than correspondence when it came to cultivating benefactors.[18] 'It is not possible for a "foreigner" to walk into a distinguished scientist's laboratory and ask for material, but it requires personal cultivation of the individual', he explained.[19] Saint concurred: 'My experience in dealing with these French professors and scientists is that one must approach them in the matter of material gradually; one can accomplish more in a second or third visit than by one visit alone.'[20] But thankfully, as Wellcome pointed out, the French seemed keen to 'aid' them in their mission to save Europe's heritage from America and were grateful that their scientific relics would end up in Britain rather than on the other side of the Atlantic.[21]

Wellcome now framed his appetite for things as a noble act on behalf of his adopted country, which required the assistance of other European nations to succeed. But the theatrical explanations barely hid the real objective of Saint's 'mission', which was nothing new: he was to get as much valuable material for Wellcome as he could for the lowest possible price. 'The main object and purpose of the mission is to secure as free gifts to the Museum all possible relics and other materials connected or associated with the life work of the great scientific research workers and discoverers in the various fields of science.'[22]

This was the other great benefit of a diplomatic approach. If Saint visited his European hosts again and again, occasionally treating them to dinner and nurturing their patronage, he would not only undermine those American collectors who threw their money around so brashly, but he would be more likely to inspire generosity and get the objects themselves cheaply. It appealed to Malcolm's frugality and Wellcome's love for a bargain. Whenever possible, Saint was to obtain artefacts for the Museum 'as free gifts', but he was under orders to pay for things too. The balance between speculative hobnobbing and just getting on and buying things was not easy to pull off. Wellcome's decision to allow Saint funds for hospitality was unusual, and it reflected the special status he was to enjoy as Foreign Secretary, but Wellcome was careful to point out that his expenditure on entertaining must not 'interfere with or materially reduce the funds available for the purchase of materials' for the Museum.[23] A steady stream of new objects was, as ever, the real point of

Wellcome's strategizing, whether he chose to present it as international diplomacy or not.

Saint rose to the challenge that Wellcome had set him with ease. Like Thompson before him, he enjoyed the tactics and strategizing, but he brought to his work an unmistakable air of refinement. He carefully extended his social circle until it led him to the people he was interested in. Here, he writes of his research into Professor Pierre Eugène Marcelin Berthelot, the distinguished French chemist and politician who had died in 1907:

For instance, my acquaintanceship with Professor Matignon originated through Sir William Pope professor of chemistry at Cambridge, who introduced me to Professor Pascal, professor of chemistry at Lille, who passed me on to Professor Lespieau at the Ecole Normale Superieure, and from Professor Lespieau I obtained an introduction to Professor Moureu of the College de France, who introduced me to Professor Matignon who was the colleague of Berthelot. These enquiries all take time and it is only by steadily following up every source that one eventually finds what one is seeking.[24]

No wonder Wellcome was so enthusiastic about Johnston-Saint's new job description. His tours were, in many ways, a natural extension of his social world, allowing him to draw on a privileged set of personal connections. His written reports are littered with the names of European politicians and members of the aristocracy: British ambassadors, governors, and consuls; Spanish dukes and duchesses; cardinals at the Vatican; Indian maharajahs; French princes and counts. They all grace the pages of Johnston-Saint's travel diaries, and they all played their part in his unremitting search for acquisitions.

Saint would sometimes mention, when meeting a potential donor, that he had been honoured to receive a private audience with Pope Pius XI. He brought this up while examining items at a monastic museum in Carthage, during a visit to a furniture shop in Sicily, and when calling at the Royal Monastery of San Lorenzo de El Escorial, near Madrid, and on each occasion he immediately received first class attention and the promise of material for the Museum.[25] He carefully managed all his social networks. He understood that knowing the right people, and keeping them happy, would bring rich rewards. Often the strategy was simple. He promised the director of a museum in Palermo that he would send him foreign stamps, as his family were keen philatelists. He arranged for his colleagues to send out copies of the Museum's handbook to various people he met, as a sign of goodwill, and a reminder, no doubt, to keep its collections ever in mind. He sent flowers to women who were mourning the loss of their eminent husbands.[26] And he

returned to visit the same people regularly, to discuss the current opportunities for acquiring objects.

Much of Saint's time may have been spent nurturing his circle of acquaintances, but this did not stop him buying enormous numbers of artefacts in
shops and markets and through dealers. He enjoyed searching the streets for
bargains just as much as taking academics out for dinner. He acquired
everything from water samples at healing spas, to the remains of a fifteenth-
century drug shop in Damascus, which included taking the ceiling, carved
entrance arch, windows, counter, and fittings.[27] He collected Turkish shoes
made from an old motor tyre; a seventeenth-century bandage-winding
machine from Italy; an eighteenth-century boot-shaped bath equipped with
a furnace (used by a French doctor who suffered from leprosy); the doorway
to a school for training Buddhist monks as doctors in Lhasa; an account of
King Louis XIV's last illness written by one of his doctors at Versailles; and a
single hair from the head of St Catherine of Siena, held in a small piece of
paper sealed with a Cardinal's seal. He bought thousands of manuscripts and
books, votive offerings, paintings of saints, surgical instruments, and old
laboratory apparatus. On some days he would find very little; on other days
he would pack up a number of cases for shipment home.

His collecting work may have taken him to the inner recesses of the
Vatican and the comfort of ambassadorial residences, but it also led him to
explore some rather unsavoury quarters. At Lisieux, in Normandy, where
pilgrims worshipped at the Shrine of Saint Teresa of the Infant Jesus, he
found a house that 'was occupied by a sort of dealer in junk and odds
and ends', but he did not stay long, 'because the stench was so dreadful.
A dreadful old woman with whiskers came to see what I wanted, and
assuredly she did not add to the relief of the situation.'[28] Saint quickly took
his leave, empty handed. But sometimes unpromising surroundings could
harbour precious gems, at least in Johnston-Saint's eyes. While in Sicily, in
the ancient city of Catania, 'in a small hovel next to the Cathedral (St Agatha)
I found a thing that one might look for for years and never come across.
I have not seen one in any museum yet. There is not one in the Museo
National at Rome, nor in the Naples Museum.' What treasure could Saint
have found in this uninspiring environment? Nothing less than 'a Greek terra
cotta ex voto of a trachea'. That is, an old ceramic model of someone's
respiratory tubes. But it was 'almost perfect', and he only paid ten shillings,
even though 'its value is much more than that'. He happily concluded that
the terracotta tracheae was, 'one of the best finds I have had here'.[29]

'It has always been a matter of surprise to me', Saint concluded on a different occasion, 'to find that in some squalid ramshackle shop which resembles more a go-down than a shop, the owner produces most wonderful objects—jewels worth many thousands and objects of art of great beauty and value.'[30] One such establishment was a book shop in Valencia, which he found in March 1928, and, 'for want of a better word', described as 'a junk shop of the first order'.

It was in a narrow dirty street and it was lighted by one gas jet. The proprietor was reclining in a broken wicker chair smoking the stump of a cigar. All around him in the small room, some 12′ × 10′ were piles of rubbish, loose leaves, pamphlets, vellum bound books and such like which you had to walk on indiscriminately.[31]

Rummaging around in the rubbish and papers, Saint unearthed medical books from the sixteenth and seventeenth centuries that were virtually impossible to find in Spain. He was delighted to learn that the proprietor had planned to send these books to the London dealer Maggs Bros. Ltd., so Saint took the opportunity to dispense with the middleman and purchased about 150 titles there and then.

Saint did not limit himself to shops. He visited religious houses, university departments, archaeological excavations, and museums, and often came away with donations or purchases. In Sicily, he decided to take a mule and trek up into the mountains in search of folklore material. At the town of Graniti he stopped for a drink at 'a small and very primitive inn' and found himself in the company of various goats, chickens, and donkeys. But the local livestock did not distract him from noticing a wooden picture hanging on the wall. It was an eighteenth-century ex-voto painting depicting a boy falling from the parapet of a house, which had been made in thanks when prayers for his recovery had been answered (Figure 25). While enjoying his drink, Saint also took a fancy to the bone amulet hanging around the neck of the landlady, which was carved in the shape of a human hand, and a bronze bell worn by 'one of my goat companions' and also designed to ward off the evil eye. However,

The picture was the most important thing to get hold of and at once I saw there was going to be difficulty. Other crones were called into consultation, also an ancient old man with a long beard. The discussion lasted a long time and only L.100 (£1.1.0.) would tempt them to part with it.[32]

After some discussion, Saint managed to get the picture, the bone amulet, the bronze bell, another amulet, and permission to take the lady's photograph

Figure 25. Votive painting depicting a boy falling from a building, acquired by Peter Johnston-Saint in Sicily. WL 44906i.

('which she much resisted') for £1 16s. This was a pittance, considering Saint often parted with £50 or more with little hesitation during his shopping trips. What is more, refreshments were provided for him and his guide free of charge, and, once business was concluded, he was 'piped out of sight by a small urchin on a homemade wooden whistle!'

Saint built up good relationships with European dealers, including the Parisian dealer Victor Degrange and a bookseller in Rouen named Berhard. One of his most important contacts was the firm of Etienne Charavay on Rue de Furstenberg in Paris. The Charavay family specialized in autograph letters, and they sold Saint thousands of letters, pamphlets, and pictures. Saint had discovered Charavay by chance in typical fashion. He was perusing prints in a shop in a Parisian suburb when he overheard two Americans: 'they were talking away when one told the other that so and so, I couldn't catch the name, was hunting for autograph letters and old instruments "surgical" . . . "Oh," says the other, "Charavay in the rue Furstenberg is the man for autograph letters, he's got a pile."' Within minutes Saint had bought his prints, found Charavay's address at the local telephone office, visited, and bought from him a 'large bundle of autograph letters and documents dating from the early 19th century to the present time' including a letter of Pasteur's.[33] Saint became one of Charavay's most loyal clients.

Saint targeted members of the scientific elite in Europe, visiting them repeatedly over the years, gradually building up their trust and benefiting from their familiarity with the local collecting scene. One such person was Albert Nachet, grandson of the famous microscope-maker Camile Sebastien Nachet and heir to his Parisian firm. Nachet microscopes boasted the best quality lenses of all European brands, and many famous nineteenth-century scientists had used them. Saint had noticed the name 'Nachet' inscribed on one of Pasteur's microscopes in the collections at the Institut Pasteur in Lille. He resolved to call at the Nachet headquarters in November 1926 and meet the manufacturers.[34] Albert Nachet had inherited his family business and his father's private collection of early microscopes and books, and he had devoted his time to expanding both interests ever since. He told Johnston-Saint that the collection would be left to his family, but in the meantime he was keen to exchange certain items with Wellcome. Both Saint and Wellcome agreed that this was 'a collection that is worth watching', and Saint was happy to report that Nachet had asked him to visit whenever he was in Paris.[35]

Saint took up the invitation, and inspected Nachet's small but exquisite collection of microscopes more than once. Such was the intensity of Saint's work that he returned to talk to Nachet three times in 1927 and at least twice each year until Albert Nachet's death in April 1930. Nachet was genial, but indecisive when it came to the future of his collection. Although there was no one in his family who was particularly interested in his microscopes, and Nachet was inclined to see his collection kept together in a museum, he would not give any commitment to Saint. In October 1927 Saint learned that 'Mr. Bashford Dean of a New York Museum' had visited the Frenchman in the hope of obtaining the microscopes, but luckily Nachet was determined his microscope collection should remain in Europe.[36]

Nachet was, according to Saint, 'a very difficult man to get any definite decision from',[37] which put Saint in an awkward position, particularly when he had to refer decisions regarding expensive purchases back to London.

If I were given power to negotiate on the spot for odd instruments, I could whip them up or get off with them before he had time to change his mind. At present I cannot clinch with him when I get him red hot. I can only say I must come again. If it should be left to my discretion, I think I could manage things for the benefit of the Museum. At present his mind is like a balance, first it is yes, next minute it is no, and so on.[38]

Saint was initially told he would have to refer decisions on any single item that cost more than £20 to Malcolm, and any single item of more than £100, or any collection of items that cost more than £200, to Wellcome.[39] As time went by, these rules were relaxed a little, and Saint sometimes went over these limits without reference to Malcolm. As early as August 1929, he decided to buy a collection of 400 books from a shopkeeper in Blois for £160, knowing that Malcolm was away from London and any delay would be 'fatal' and he would lose the lot. He had already clarified with Wellcome the best course of action in these situations. 'In a conversation I had a short time ago with Dr. Wellcome, I gathered that on such occasions delay would appear to be dangerous, he would agree to my acting without referring the matter to London.'[40]

Despite some frustrations with Nachet, virtually every time Saint visited the microscope maker he secured some artefacts for the Museum: first, four or five duplicate instruments; then five 'important' microscopes and a collection of twenty-one telescopes and spyglasses. By late 1927 the Museum had thirty-nine of Nachet's microscopes even though Albert had no definite plans for the remaining ninety, or any of his 400–500 books. During 1928 Nachet presented the Museum with a small group of microscopes, including one used by the great natural historian Georges Buffon, and eight original daguerreotypes made by Léon Foucault, the pioneering French scientist and photographer, and dated by him 1844.[41]

Nachet had now decided to write a book, and would not contemplate parting with the rest of his collection until it was completed. Wellcome, avid as ever—'Watch closely the remainder of his collection of microscopes. We must, without fail, secure it.'—offered to publish Nachet's book for him.[42] The following year, when nothing had come of this proposal, Wellcome urged Saint to 'arrange for a good portrait of him in oil—by a skilful artist at a moderate price. Or have him come to London and we can have our artist do the portrait.'[43] Wellcome had, by now, met Nachet and seen his 'marvellous collection of microscopes' for himself and was even more determined to acquire it.[44] Nachet continued to entertain their aspirations by presenting the odd rare pamphlet or clutch of early photographs to the Historical Medical Museum; but he died, in April 1930, without making any definite provision for his valuable collection.[45]

The Museum quickly wired their condolences to the Nachet family.[46] Saint, who was in Florence at the time, called on Nachet's son-in-law, Basil Aicard, on his way through Paris two weeks later.[47] Aicard visited the Wellcome Historical Medical Museum, and Madame Nachet liked the idea of selling her husband's collection to Wellcome, but the price she asked was a prohibitive £8,000. Wellcome could not consider this amount of money for a collection that, although valuable, was relatively small, and the correspondence went cold.[48] Still, the years of Johnston-Saint's patient diplomacy had paid off. Each visit to Nachet had spawned a small, but valuable donation for Wellcome. This was truly a friendship secured by things, and a perfect example of Saint's success as Wellcome's Foreign Secretary.

Saint never became overconfident. He referred difficult decisions back to London, and he knew that Wellcome did not entrust his money to anyone without constant review. Nonetheless, Saint's skill and self-confidence gave him a distinct advantage as a collector, as did his friendship with Wellcome. The two men shared a mutual respect, and Wellcome admired Saint both professionally and personally.[49] In amongst a file of Malcolm's reports there is a telegram from Wellcome dated 1 October 1928. It reads, 'have lost saints introductions and addresses for paris request him send me copies wellcome'.[50] It would be a rather telling role reversal if Peter Johnston-Saint was writing letters of introduction for Henry Wellcome on his travels to France. France had become Saint's most frequent fieldsite: he spoke French fluently, and he knew many of the country's scientists and politicians personally. And Wellcome's early assessment of the French government's gratitude for Saint's work proved correct: in 1934, both Saint and Wellcome were awarded *La Croix de Chevalier de la Légion d'Honneur* for their research into the history of French science; and both men were made *Comendador de la Ordén de la República* in Spain.[51]

Wellcome's pleasure at receiving the *Légion d'Honneur* was said to have been dampened when he heard that Saint, who had made arrangements for the event in Paris, would be honoured at the same ceremony,[52] but these complementary honours symbolized their close working relationship. Wellcome trusted Saint, and increasingly relied on him to steer his collection forward. For twenty-five years, Thompson had held sway over all aspects of the Museum's work, but his rule had gone forever. Hewitt and Malcolm had taken over the management of the Library and the Museum respectively, but it was Johnston-Saint who came to satisfy the insatiable appetite of a man who was, first and foremost, a consumer. Saint was freer from the administrative duties and the burden of cataloguing than his colleagues; collecting became his *raison d'être*. And his relationship with Wellcome seemed more relaxed, perhaps because he had few purely academic aspirations of his own. He showed little interest in writing papers or giving lectures. Instead, he simply relished the opportunity to travel, collect, and work with all the treasures Wellcome acquired.

Saint was the perfect man to promote Wellcome's Museum, because, without any pretension, he was one of Wellcome's greatest admirers. His military background may have instilled in him an unobtrusive loyalty. He shared Wellcome's delight in buying rare things, without asserting his own claims to the credit. He did not push against Wellcome, as others in a similar position might have. He had an easy charm, and he simply enjoyed his work. And in the final years of Wellcome's life, his efficiency kept the Museum staff motivated when the whole project was threatened with collapse. Johnston-Saint loved his work, but his success as a collector unavoidably contributed to mounting disarray back in London during the early 1930s as his were amongst the cases of objects that piled up around the staff. Wellcome was approaching 80 years old, and was often abroad. His interest in the Museum did not diminish, but he was losing his sharp sense of purpose. Meanwhile, Malcolm's reign was quietly disintegrating, as were many of Wellcome's objects, hidden away in storage.

IV. LEGACIES

The steady accumulation of objects—crate by crate, box by box, week after week—set the background rhythm to all Wellcome's relationships with his staff. The hunt for objects united them, and sometimes accentuated their differences, but it always provided the medium through which they could negotiate their relationships. And, as the years went by, the material legacy of all these collaborations began to assert itself. The sheer physical presence of the collection could no longer be ignored. Most of the Museum's staff was based, not in the galleries at Wigmore Street, but on the outskirts of London in Wellcome's main storage warehouse, surrounded by packing cases, trying to keep pace with the onslaught of acquisitions.

For all Wellcome's lofty aspirations, the real work at the Museum was now dominated by the practicalities of collections management. There could be no perfect picture of human history until the thousands of objects he owned had been registered, labelled, conserved, and rendered accessible. In the end, Wellcome was weighed down by the physicality of his intellectual ambitions. He misjudged the time it would take to process his collection, both intellectually and logistically, and his own ability to do so in old age.

Wellcome's collection embodied a belief that ultimately the material world would succumb to the rigours of Western scientific scrutiny; that everything could be contained, known, and understood, if one only had the resources necessary to contain it. But objects are full of ambiguities and entangled histories. They tend to undermine the categories we provide for them, and lead us down unpredictable pathways as we learn from them. Wellcome turned to objects for inspiration and enlightenment, but he underestimated the challenge they would present. It was easier for him to buy more things than attend to those he already had, and he never seems to have admitted to anyone, perhaps not even himself, that the objects he believed he was marshalling were gradually, inexorably, overwhelming him.

CHAPTER SIXTEEN

SHELVE IT

During the final years of his life, Wellcome became increasingly vague. When he was asked to elaborate on his intentions for his business and his research bureau, he was inscrutable. He would simply say, 'My plans exist in my mind like a jig-saw puzzle, and gradually I shall be able to piece it together.'[1] But this illusion of finality—of the puzzle perfected—began to paralyse him. He believed in a lasting picture, and he wanted all the pieces he had gathered together during his life to fit in without gaps or mistakes. When Charles Singer had exclaimed that Wellcome's collection would be dead once it was complete, 'because science was never dead, and would never be complete', Wellcome's response had been 'nonsense'.[2] Did Wellcome really think that he could complete his collection? Did he ever admit his limitations to himself? Did he, during the last few years of his life, see completeness for what it really was: an endlessly receding mirage; a seductive vision that could never be caught?

Perhaps not. Noel Poynter, who joined the Museum as a junior assistant in 1930, remembered that Wellcome

always managed to convey his vision of 'great things' in the future to his staff, and I think others shared my own view that it was this alone which kept us with him, for the appalling working conditions, the irritation and embarrassments of the anonymity and pseudo-secrecy . . . together with the apparently unending task of sorting vast and ever-growing quantities of materials, often made our loyalty seem misguided.[3]

Even in quieter moments, Wellcome betrayed no self-doubt. William Britchford, the Museum's joiner, found himself unexpectedly keeping Wellcome company in 1935. Wellcome, who was not very well, had decided not to open his own house at Gloucester Gate and was staying at the Langham Hotel. Britchford was summoned there to see him.

When I got there Sir Henry asked me how things were going in the museum, etc. and started to tell me what he was going to do in the future and in about five years he would like to do so and so—and he was then eighty-one. Time passed and it got to half past four, when I said to Sir Henry that I thought there was a little job he wanted done, and he said 'It doesn't matter about that. Come and see me tomorrow at the same time, will you?' I did so, and again he talked all of the future. At last, when I asked him what it was he wanted, his secretary produced a suitcase that had a few scratches, which he asked me if I could just cover up, as it looked bad, and said 'Bring it back next week.' I took it back and he carried on talking and then said if I had any time to spare next week could I come again one afternoon, and then I realised that he was a lonely old man and was asking me there just so he could talk to somebody.[4]

Wellcome's private nature left him with few close friends later in life. And, when socializing, his old-fashioned tastes made him into something of a curiosity himself. He continued to give successful dinner parties, and was warmly and widely respected, but his guests were left marvelling at the thirty-six cruets that cluttered the table: 'everyone wondered what they were, but of course everyone had to have their own service.'[5] He had devoted his life to the world of business and the business of collecting, and now these things constituted his future. He could share them most fully with his employees.

Wellcome loved the thought of his finished Museum—he had told Britch-ford before 'of his ambitions for the museum, how it would expand and how he hoped one day to have the biggest private museum in the country'[6]— but he was finding it harder to convert his aspirations into a working strategy. As he approached his eightieth year, he became reluctant to delegate, but less able to reach important decisions alone.[7] As a museum collector, the respon-sibility his material wealth conferred upon him now weighed him down. He could not live up to his own expectations, and by now his collection was a logistical nightmare. Regardless of his hopes for a new Historical Medical Museum in the early 1930s, the challenge had become managerial as much as intellectual. The image Wellcome used, of his mental state manifest as a jigsaw puzzle, was only too true as far as his Museum was concerned. The intellectual achievement was going to be, in reality, a physical one, and the problem was finding enough space and time to piece together his puzzle.

Only a tiny proportion of Wellcome's collection could be shown at the Wigmore Street galleries. By the mid-1920s, he was renting houses and warehouses across London for storage purposes: he owned properties at 8 Stratford Mews, 6 York Mews South, 76 High Street, Marylebone, 5a Bushey Hill Road, 145 Crystal Palace Road, and 4 Stratford Mews, all to keep his collection; he also rented a large old laundry complex and stables at Stanmore and a detached brick warehouse on two floors in Weybridge; he had kept some of his things in storage with Shoolbreds, the department store, for decades, and other objects were housed at the Burroughs Wellcome and Company manufacturing site in Dartford. But there was still not enough space. Thompson does not seem to have been overly concerned about the storage facilities. He surveyed them at the end of 1921 and concluded that 'on the whole everything was all right',[8] but Malcolm had been dismayed when he examined the stores in 1926.

Things were 'close packed up to the ceiling' in many premises and choked the hallways. Malcolm found that packing cases were heaped up, unsupported, sometimes upside-down, their labels were not visible, and 'boxes are dumped anyway, some on their sides, and in general it shows signs of hurry'.[9] But as the acquisitions rolled in, Harry Port, who took charge of the stores in July 1926, was forced to squeeze things in ever more tightly, until it became difficult for anyone to get into the buildings, never mind retrieve the artefacts they were looking for. On one day, in September 1926, forty-one cases of objects and 1,100 spears were transferred to Stanmore, but there was so little room that the spears had to be stacked across the roof rafters.[10] Only narrow gangways were left between the walls of packing cases. Eventually even these alleys were filled.[11] On one occasion, in order to reach something kept in a case at the Marylebone High Street building, Malcolm's staff had to spend two full days moving the surrounding boxes.[12]

The result of the congestion was that no one knew exactly what was in storage. This did not seem to concern Wellcome. He simply bought the same thing again to be sure he had it. One of Wellcome's assistants remembered, 'Because there was no time to catalogue the collection, [we] often bought the same book twice. I'd say, "I'm sure we've got that book already. I remember buying it." He'd say, "Better buy it again to make certain." There simply wasn't time to make a search and check up.'[13]

Cases remained unopened for decades. Many had not been examined since they were first delivered from the salesrooms. In 1927, as the staff began reorganizing the stores, they found themselves opening cases untouched since 1905, when the Museum had been in its infancy and Thompson had led a small team of local buyers.[14] It is hardly surprising that some objects were suffering from neglect after twenty years forgotten. There were problems with damp. The moisture in some of the storerooms was rotting Wellcome's textiles. It stuck photographic negatives together, left pictures mouldy, and rusted boxes of small arms. But little could be done to salvage these things when they were buried deep under a pile of heavy packing cases. Malcolm ordered the doors and windows to be left open at Crystal Palace and Bushey Hill, and the gas fires were kept alight throughout the day in the hopes of drying out the buildings.[15]

All this had begun to worry Wellcome considerably, but his instructions were not altogether helpful. He would become alarmed and demand the impossible:

Do not store pastel pictures, engravings, lithographs or any other pictures printed or painted on paper or any other mountings which are liable to be affected by dampness, in vaults or basements ... All such materials now stored in any of our store houses whether in vaults or basements or otherwise ... should be carefully and critically examined and a very explicit report sent to me. In the future the very greatest possible care should be taken to insure against the storage or placing in any way, anywhere any of the above mentioned items, except in a perfectly dry and safe atmosphere and housing.[16]

Malcolm was well aware of the risks to Wellcome's artefacts, and the staff were doing their best, but there was little they could do until a new, larger, and more manageable storehouse was found. 'Of course, it is impossible for us to examine the stores as they are at present, owing to the congestion', he replied.[17] The Museum staff did not even know what engravings, autographs, paintings and pastels they owned, since 'practically the whole of the pictures and prints have never been dealt with'.[18]

Malcolm's most sensible suggestion—to stop buying large collections until the storage situation could be rectified—was brushed aside.[19] Instead, efforts to find a more suitable warehouse were intensified. Wellcome fired off a cable from abroad: 'extremely urgent advertise immediately rent or purchase make diligent persistent search suitable safe buildings open suburbs more than double capacity all present storehouses consider higher terms suitable premises present scattered buildings wasteful dangerous risk valuable materials wellcome.'[20]

In August 1927, after several months of searching, Malcolm found the Willesden factory.[21] Sandwiched between a road and a railway on an industrial site in north-west London, 9–13 Hythe Road comprised warehouses, outbuildings, yard space, and houses; in all, it would provide around 65,000 square feet of storage space for the Museum (Figure 26). There were offices, and room enough for long trestle tables so that objects could be examined and repaired.[22] So the old machinery was moved out, and new shelves were moved in. An area on the ground floor was bricked up and fitted with fire proof doors, to create secure vaults for valuable objects. Preparations were made to close down the other stores and consolidate their contents at Hythe Road in early 1928.[23] Only the laundry site, nearby at Stanmore, was retained to house Wellcome's 'heavy stone work and wood work'.[24]

Willesden was not a pleasant place to work, but the majority of Wellcome's staff spent their days there. Museum stores are often thought of as dead space—dark, inert places, where things gather dust, hibernating, at best,

Figure 26. Library store of Wellcome Research Laboratories at Willesden, photographed in 1937.

and disintegrating, at worst—and the Willesden store did feel a little like a tomb. The concrete walls and floors were miserable, there was no heating and no kitchen facilities, unpleasant smells from the neighbouring factories saturated the air, and in the winter temperatures barely hovered above freezing. Harry Port and Miss Jones, a secretary, who spent almost all their time at Willesden, had created a relatively cosy office space for themselves with an electric heater and copper kettle, but others had to endure the harsh environment as best they could.[25]

Mr Lambourne, who started work at Willesden in August 1928 and had found his first visit to the stores 'overwhelming', recovered his composure sufficiently to write a damning report on conditions there four months later. 'No convenience is at my disposal at present in the present portion of the building 1. No warmth 2. No gas 3. No solid bench tables 4. No water for cleaning sinks and drain boards 5. No tools, drills or lathe. No electric heating circuit. 6. The concrete floor should be covered in wood.'[26] The situation did not improve much, although the place gradually filled up with odd pieces of furniture: mahogany countertops, leather trunks, velvet and tapestry wing chairs, an oak card index cabinet, typewriters, the odd electric heater, chests, cupboards, and iron-framed tables.[27] In amongst all the packing cases and stacks of disused furniture, this odd assortment must have given Willesden the feel of a long-forgotten auction room, especially as many of the objects had their old lot numbers still attached to them.

Despite the inhospitable environment, many of the Museum's activities went on at Willesden. Things were constantly being delivered, moved around, examined, and packed away again. Harry Port's monthly reports recorded a healthy work rate. His staff often accessioned more than 1,000 objects each month, and sometimes considerably more than 2,000.[28] These objects may not have been on display, but they embodied an intellectual project that was dynamic and ongoing. The stores were a private place, but they were far from inert. Each object had to be unpacked, examined and identified, recorded, wrapped up, and stored away again. Unfortunately, it was impossible to identify many of the objects, because all record of their purpose, age, and origin had been long forgotten. Port and Miss Jones had, Joan Braunholtz later remembered, 'evolved a system and a language of their own' when it came to accessioning. ' "Curious object, use unknown", we were often advised to write or "It has been good". Otherwise it was "shelve it"—when all else failed.'[29]

While this rather haphazard work continued, new objects arrived. The influx of acquisitions was relentless: 'coaches, carriages, perambulators,

African spears, skeletons, porcelain, Japanese netsukes, all arrived [at Willesden] almost daily in huge consignments.'[30] It was not unusual for acquisitions from twenty to forty auction sales to be collected in a month; a small fleet of Ford vans stationed in the yard was ready for despatch. Other arrivals into the stores might include between ten and twenty cases full of acquisitions made privately, or material sent back by Johnston-Saint from his collecting tours.[31] Meanwhile, Wellcome himself was still despatching everything from medicine chests and opium pipes to dolls, armchairs, and items like '4 wooden splitters used for splitting straws for weaving ladies' straw bonnets and hats' (that had cost him six shillings).[32] Besides the reception, processing, and organization of this new material, display cases and other pieces of furniture, including shelving and bookcases, were made and repaired in the workshops at Willesden, and exhibitions, both for the Museum and for the company's trade fairs, were assembled and dismantled.

The workmen and staff who handled the objects in the stores became curatorial experts, although they received little, if any, public acknowledgement. One of the young university graduates Malcolm hired in 1928 remembered working at Willesden with 'Stowe [sic] and Webb who taught me all I know about the actual cleaning of cuneiform tablets and a good deal of other museum techniques'.[33] These men probably knew Wellcome's collection better than anyone. Many of them represented him at auction sales, and they could assess an object's value without any hesitation. Some, like Stow and Bourne, acted as Wellcome's personal assistants and regularly performed maintenance duties at his home in Gloucester Gate. At Willesden, they cleaned and conserved the artefacts in their care. Wellcome employed skilled craftsmen—bookbinders, picture restorers, and joiners—who populated the Willesden workshops, and he often challenged them to innovate. When the ever-enterprising Britchford failed to meet one of Wellcome's demands, he would say 'Leave it for a week or so and then have another try, because once you have found the way to do these things we have it for all time.'

At times he would send for me, tell me what he required, and if I said 'I don't think we could do that' he would put his hand on my shoulder, look me straight in the eyes and say 'You know, I think it could be done if we could find the right man' and then just walk away.[34]

Britchford, a joiner by trade, sometimes wished that Wellcome would employ specialist chemists and technicians for these little projects.

Wellcome worried about conditions in the stores, not out of concern for the well being of his staff, but because of the threat to his objects. The stores had to be dry and well ventilated, and his things kept in waterproof and fireproof containers. He was particularly afraid of fire damage. In 1889, the Burroughs Wellcome chemical works had been completely destroyed by fire. The cause was never determined, but the effects were disastrous and one fireman had been killed. Luckily, much of the firm's equipment and stock had been moved to the new manufacturing premises at Dartford during the preceding months, but Wellcome became quite concerned about fire prevention.[35] When everything had been stored at Willesden, Britchford was called in again, and asked to invent a formula that would make the Museum's packing cases fire resistant. Wellcome himself came in to test Britchford's treatments, taking a lit taper to a series of treated wood shavings, papers, and sticks, before ordering his staff to treat all the packing cases at Willesden with the best solution.[36]

Wellcome's periodic orders to fire-proof and ventilate and evaluate the objects at Willesden cannot have been much appreciated by the staff who worked there every day in the cold and dark surrounded by banks of impenetrable packing cases and faced with heaps of unidentified curiosities waiting to be examined. He seems to have hardly registered the difficulties of the task they faced. His tone betrays his lack of appreciation of the situation he presided over at Willesden. His demands were unrealistic:

Please specially note that fabrics of all kinds, especially costumes such as academic gowns, uniforms, all objects and materials of wool, hair, etc., including shrunken heads, are liable to be attacked and damaged by moths and other destructive insects—more especially when stored in storehouses at Willesden and elsewhere . . . Several times through negligence and want of proper care these have been damaged, notwithstanding our very strict rule for the prevention of such damage. This matter requires the utmost vigilance and periodical inspections, especially in the early spring when moths and other destructive insects begin to 'get busy'.[37]

There was no hope of routine inspections when stacks of boxes had not been opened for twenty years. Wellcome expected his staff to meet his own standards of perfection. When he was not fighting international trademark infringements through the courts, or establishing drug manufacturing plants on the east coast of America for Burroughs Wellcome, he was crouched over small piles of wood shavings with a lit taper testing their chemical properties. Why should his employees not show the same fastidious efficiency? Wellcome was remembered as a demanding employer, but a fair one.

Although he never found it easy to forgive an act which he thought was deliberately opposed to his wishes, failure by an employee to succeed never incensed him if he thought reasonable efforts had been made. Incompetence he could never tolerate, and he detested slovenliness in all its forms. He made great demands of all those who worked for him, but to a rare degree he possessed an extraordinary power to inspire men to give of their best . . . He often worked on to very late hours, oblivious of time, and was apt therefore to make excessive demands upon those of his staff whose presence he needed.[38]

When Wellcome visited Willesden he does not seem to have been particularly concerned by the magnitude of the undertaking his staff faced. On at least one occasion, in 1932, Port could report that 'Sir Henry visited the Willesden and Stanmore stores . . . and expressed his great satisfaction with the progress made at both places.'[39] Other visits raised no comment from Port, and perhaps on these occasions Wellcome did raise concerns, but the bottom line was that the staff could not hope to penetrate the collection at Willesden while Wellcome continued to invest most of his money in new accessions.

Port's men had to field letters from the auction houses complaining that purchases made many months ago had never been collected. A typical letter read,

You seem to take it for granted that we [Sotheby's, in this instance] are ready to store your purchases for you several months after each sale, and leave the matter of payment over until it suits your convenience. We must protest against this assumption on your part, and ask you to pay for and remove your purchases this week.[40]

The auctioneers had long since paid their clients, and needed their warehouses for forthcoming sales, but Port, Wilkins, Stow, and Bourne could hardly keep up with the rate of expansion.

It must have been easier for Wellcome to focus on the constant flow of acquisitions; after all, his objects only became problematic when they were sent—one might say condemned—to storage. *En masse*, the collection posed a mental challenge less apparent amidst the excitement of the acquisition process. Spread out as single purchases, Wellcome's collection seemed meaningful and manageable, as the thrill of each little triumph unfolded; but packed together into a single colossal stack of boxes and cases the collection became a conundrum on a scale that tested his, and Malcolm's, managerial capabilities. Once the objects were hidden from view they became a different kind of monster, both precious and daunting.

The stores at Willesden and Stanmore represented the need to take a final step towards order and synthesis that Wellcome was never able to take. His objects in storage presented him with his opportunity to create the perfect museum and find 'the answer' to human history; the key to completing his jigsaw puzzle of the past. The new storehouse at Willesden not only housed a life's work of financial, intellectual, and emotional commitment, it harboured Wellcome's future as a museum director and educator on a scale never achieved by any individual. The objects there linked Wellcome's past—the intricate, ever-changing story of his restless intellectual interests and enormous purchasing power—with his future and all the hopes he had for establishing a unique museum as a final, lasting, monument to himself.[41] Perhaps the fact that all his artefacts were tightly packed away only heightened their imagined capacity as a vast stockpile of knowledge. Preserving these things added to their value. They were, quite literally, Wellcome's hidden potential. It was a potential that he always claimed he would utilize, and yet he never did.

The pattern of sporadic displays of anxiety combined with long-term neglect suggests that Wellcome recognized the significance of his objects in storage, but could not face up to the intellectual and practical implications they presented. The longer Wellcome kept his collection hidden, the more it grew in size and import, and so the pressure to reveal its significance mounted. The very act of storage reinvented the collection—it became an ever-increasing, unknowably complicated, and mostly hidden, mass of material—and raised the stakes for interpreting and utilizing it. Storage did not mark a neutral passage of time, but intensified the collection's significance.[42] Wellcome was the only person who had coordinated and overseen the development of the collection from its earliest days as a private pursuit. Since then, various contributions from successive curators and agents, encouraged by Wellcome's diversifying interests, had created an impossibly large array of material. With so many people contributing to the collection there was added pressure on Wellcome to coordinate their efforts into a single, intellectual thread.

The Museum's storehouses, in theory, offered Wellcome a space in which he might gather together his life work and interpret it, consider his intellectual ideas, arrange his interests, revitalize his memory, and strengthen his knowledge. In practice, they only added to his burden and paralysis. He did not assert himself within the great stockpile of material he had created. His plan had been to collect on a scale previously unimaginable: countless lives had become entwined with his collection over the years and countless interests and aspirations embodied. The collection, in its persistent disorder, was Wellcome's life in material form. All the mistakes and achievements of the past now had physical mass, and Wellcome had such an affinity for things that he could not disregard any of them. Every thing, he liked to think, had been bought for a purpose, every thing had value, but when every thing was connected to everything else, no clear narrative could ever be carved out. The seriousness with which Wellcome saw his task, even when surrounded by a collection in desperate need of revision, is conveyed in this scene remembered by Britchford:

The man who was in charge of the warehouse we had in Peckham was named Bourne, and one day Sir Henry went to this warehouse and, after looking round, noticed a large kind of tray and said to Bourne 'What's in there?' Bourne replied 'Only bits and pieces.' 'Let me look' said Sir Henry. Bourne took the tray down. Wellcome looked at the contents of the tray and then said 'My life's work and you call it "bits and pieces". Bourne, I'm fed up with you.' Bourne replied 'Sir, I'm fed up with you, too'. So Bourne lost his job as warehouse superintendent but was given another job in the museum, and Mr. Port, who was working at Peckham at the time as a joiner, was then made Superintendent of Stores and Works.[43]

Wellcome could not discount any object, because to do so would have been to undermine his whole ethos as a collector and to question the time and money he had devoted to the project in the past. In a way, it was too late to edit, too late to change course. He believed the material world contained the answers to history's great questions, and that if it could be gathered together in sufficient quantities it would reveal its secrets.

Wellcome was not alone in his philosophy, only in his fervour to put it to the test. Long before the newly professionalized historical sciences, like archaeology and geology, had gained a foothold in university curricula in the early 1900s, objects of all kinds had been thought of as irrefutable facts. Objects had constituted the primary form of data for geologists and archaeologists, palaeontologists, mineralogists, zoologists, and anatomists for decades. In their enthusiasm for evidence that could, quite literally, be mined out of the earth, academics at the turn of the century had talked of 'object lessons' and of collecting as a way of 'marshalling the facts'.[44]

Sir Arthur Keith, at the Historical Medical Museum's Re-opening Ceremony in 1926, had spoken of recent changes in 'the material of history': books and documents no longer held the key to the distant human past; historical stories could be extracted from physical remains, from fossils and tombs and from within 'the crust of the earth'. Here was 'a new way of writing history by deciphering things and not words', and museums opened their doors to that history. Keith explained that museums required great financial invest-ment—in buildings, in the collections they housed, and in those who cared for them—but in return they generated decades of intellectual profit. As Keith elaborated on his theme, the physicality of museums and their aca-demic value became blurred. Curators had to select from their 'great stores', Keith explained, the 'prime pieces of instruction' required to tell a particular story about the past. Museums were concurrently 'repositories of valuable things' and 'engines for the advancement of knowledge'. And, Wellcome had, in his Museum, Keith concluded, offered the student his 'rich and rare stores of knowledge culled from all the countries of the world and from all periods of time'.[45]

Knowing was a kind of skilled apprehension of the physical world: know-ledge, as Wellcome had implied, was one great jigsaw puzzle, and the pieces had to be properly aligned. Museums took the lead in this task, since they had the greatest number of pieces to play with. Wellcome's Museum was indeed a great 'storehouse of knowledge', but his artefacts should have stimulated his mind, not suffocated it. He was so intent on amassing his data that he never managed to complete his picture. When his things arrived at his storehouses, it was a relief: this was a space he ruled over, where his life's work was safe from rival collectors and enquiring academics. But his visits to the stores should have sounded a warning note. Wellcome, even in his seventies, thought there was still plenty of time to organize his collection. He explained his attitude to ageing in a letter to a friend: 'We are all of us as old as we feel and as young as we feel and the best thing for us is to keep on feeling young and not to let anyone convince us that we are old; and when we feel ill the best thing is for us to cut our own acquaintance and forget about our ills.'[46] If only someone could have persuaded Wellcome that he was older than he felt.

In March 1927, Malcolm had informed Wellcome that the Italian Fascist regime had placed an embargo on all archaeological material leaving Italy, and any found in transit would be confiscated. Wellcome had a large amount of Italian museum material in warehouses in Milan owned by Burroughs Wellcome and Company. When Malcolm suggested that these objects should be left for the time being, Wellcome agreed and scribbled down: 'Must leave them at Milan until all these difficulties are past, even if for ten years. Take no risk.'[47] Of course, we now know that Wellcome had died before the ten years had passed. This material was brought back to London in 1932, but Wellcome's comment sums up the role of his stores: they provided a secure, hidden, private space, so inviolable that Wellcome himself never managed to penetrate them. The rows of packing cases serve as a poignant reminder that Wellcome was constantly projecting his work into the future, but he was unable to reach his goal.

CHAPTER SEVENTEEN

INGRAINED HABITS
OF CAUTIOUSNESS

'Since my appointment as Conservator of your Collections,' Saint wrote to Wellcome in November 1935, 'I have endeavoured to evolve some kind of order and system out of the chaos and disorder which it was my misfortune to inherit.'[1] It was a comment on Malcolm's administration. In late 1934, Malcolm resigned as head of Wellcome's Museum (he later became curator at the Horniman Museum). Johnston-Saint took his place and tried valiantly to invest the project with the sense of purpose it had lost along the way (Figure 27). So much for the 'zealous cooperation and efficiency' Malcolm had displayed during his first few months at the Historical Medical Museum.[2] Now, nine years later, 'chaos' seems to have been the word most frequently associated with his contributions to its development. One employee called it 'carefully built chaos'.[3] To one of his former colleagues, Saint gave a similar synopsis of the situation: 'I have inherited a considerable legacy of chaos, but I am gradually getting things straightened out, and I hope that the Museum will function as a Museum ought to, and that its records and routine will be on some kind of logical system.'[4]

Any respect Malcolm might have earned from his colleagues had evaporated. Soon after his departure, one member of staff wrote to a friend of the 'long-drawn-out misery' she had suffered at work, and her optimism now that Johnston-Saint had taken charge.

Life at the W.H.M.M. is looking up under the new régime. After years of disillusionment, one is cautious in hope . . . I can—for the first time in years—look forward

Figure 27. Henry Wellcome photographed with Peter Johnston-Saint, date unknown.

to the day's work with the normal pleasure in a reasonable job, and, at times, real creative zest (which I thought had died in me).[5]

Morale had never been so low. Another member of staff had resigned her position just weeks before Johnston-Saint took command, writing to Malcolm by way of explanation: 'I feel that things have not been satisfactory for some time. There appears to be less and less prospect of improvement in salary, status, or working conditions, and no opportunity to carry out congenial work.'[6] There can be little doubt that Malcolm had failed as a manager. His communication skills were poor; he lacked creativity and authority, and was unable to admit to his limitations; and he had not established a constructive working relationship with Wellcome, who spent much of the time abroad. But, in Malcolm's defence, Wellcome's expectations, which had never been entirely realistic, had become almost impossible to fulfil.

Each of Wellcome's Conservators blamed the last. Johnston-Saint may have inherited a 'legacy of chaos', but Malcolm had tried to rectify past mistakes too. He had scrapped hundreds of inaccurate labels, identified an 'astonishing' number of unregistered objects, refurbished the Museum (and found artefacts in all sorts of unlikely places in the process), restored pictures and objects badly in need of cleaning, and completely reorganized the storage facilities. The truth is that by the time Malcolm succeeded Thompson, Wellcome's collection was already out of hand. A single consignment of objects bought by Wellcome and sent from New York in 1923 brings the magnitude of the challenge into sharp relief. One hundred and twenty numbered cases were despatched on this occasion. Cases 5 to 47 contained books on natural history and scientific subjects, and, together, weighed four tons. Case 48 contained a dozen bottles of preserved fruit. Cases 49 to 79 held 'Natural history specimens and antique Museum specimens' and also had a combined weight of four tons. Cases 82 to 95, weighing more than a ton, held museum specimens, pottery, and plaster casts. The final twenty-five cases, another two tons, contained natural history books, museum specimens, newspapers, and personal effects.[7] This was one amongst a number of deliveries regularly arriving at Wellcome's London storerooms.[8]

An eleven-ton shipment did not happen every week, but neither was it unusual enough to raise any comment from Wellcome's staff. And each instalment contained a bewildering range of things. One delivery, in 1925, included antique mortars and pestles, an old coffee grinder, a barber's basin, wooden toys, postcards, a piece of cotton flannel with Egyptian designs, a pewter bowl, a copper Kabyle hanging lamp, an old Algerian carpet, undershirts, saddle bags, rugs, a Turkish bath gown, a fringed leather satchel, goatskins, and textiles.[9] Battleaxes arrived with maps, and key rings were packed alongside velvet curtains; sponge cloths and teapots, ivory dentures and kaftans, oil paintings and suits, sugar bowls and dolls: the chaos that Saint contended with was Wellcome's chaos first and foremost. It was Wellcome who instructed his staff to buy at every auction sale, and who sponsored collectors to travel for him. Malcolm had been defeated by his sheer acquisitiveness. Saint, at least, benefited from more comfortable surroundings as he and his staff sifted through this jumble, because, after nineteen years, the Museum was no longer housed on Wigmore Street.

The galleries at Wigmore Street had been inadequate for years. Wellcome admitted as much in the early 1920s:

The building now occupied was the only one available at that time and war conditions almost immediately following have rendered it impracticable to secure other premises suitable and adequate for housing the collections. The building temporarily occupied by the Museum is admittedly insufficient in size, and only permits of the exhibition of a comparatively small portion of the objects collected.[10]

Wigmore Street provided 20,000 feet of floor space, but Malcolm thought they needed at least three or four times that amount to have any chance of executing Wellcome's plans. Wellcome agreed that 60,000 to 100,000 feet was required.[11] The Wigmore Street lease was due to end in 1931, and the hunt for a new building, although mentioned in late 1927, began in earnest the following year. Wellcome hoped to find a replacement building within the university-dominated Bloomsbury area of North London.[12]

In March 1928 Malcolm heard from Sir Holburt Waring, Dean of the St Bartholomew's Medical School at the University of London, that the House of Commons was due to consider the allocation of land to the University, and there was a chance that a site might be reserved for Wellcome's Museum, since his 'work with regard to [the] modern development [of museums] was considered as being exceptional'.[13] The choice of site was important to Wellcome because a good location, near to the University of London and the British Museum, would emphasize the academic character of his Museum. But the issue of securing a suitable location dragged on for months. Sir Holburt continued to support Wellcome's interest in the Bloomsbury site; Wellcome later wrote that Waring was 'keenly anxious for the W.H.M.M. to be located near the University Site even though independent of the administration of the U[niversity]; but that he would expect the

Museum to extend facilities to the students, etc., of the University'.[14] Others, however, were aware that the University would expand and, even if it did not require more land straight away, that space would be needed eventually.[15]

It soon became clear that the land would be reserved for the University, and Malcolm's focus shifted. Various possibilities were considered near Baker Street, but these were, according to Malcolm, 'somewhat out of touch with the University area'.[16] In a later letter he relented a little by saying that 'it would not be very difficult for students of the University of London to go' to one of these less convenient sites, but they were not ideal.[17] Enquiries were made about a site at the back of the British Museum and another on Marylebone Road. Wellcome insisted that 'No site south of Russell Square would be suitable for our purpose.'[18] He was determined to secure a place at the academic heart of the city.

Predictably, Wellcome harboured reservations about the nature of the Museum's intended relationship with the University. Malcolm wrote to reassure him, in February 1930, that should the Museum become attached to the University there would be no interference with their 'internal arrangements', but the University authorities would nonetheless be responsible for the curriculum being taught in the Museum. It followed that the Museum's staff would be given academic rank by the University. He mentioned that Holburt Waring was keen to see the Wellcome institutions established as a definite School of the University.[19] As it was, the scheme for University land fell through, and Wellcome decided, instead, to build his own premises on land he already owned along the Euston Road, thus retaining complete control over the Museum's development. Existing buildings at 183–193 Euston Road, which had housed the Wellcome Bureau of Scientific Research and the Wellcome Museum of Medical Science, were cleared in 1930. The new building, named the Wellcome Research Institution, went up in twelve months during 1931 and 1932 (Figure 28). It was an imposing neoclassical edifice designed by Septimus Warwick. It was to house Wellcome's Museum collections—the Museum of Medical Science on the ground floor, and the Historical Medical Museum on the next three floors—with the Wellcome Chemical Research Laboratories and Bureau of Scientific Research, which had taken on a research staff of its own, above.[20]

This building was the physical realization of the original Wellcome Bureau of Scientific Research that Wellcome had announced at the opening of the Historical Medical Exhibition in 1913. For the first time, his museums and laboratories would be housed in the same building, all pushing back the

Figure 28. The Wellcome Research Institute building at 183, Euston Road.

boundaries of knowledge in complementary ways. This was seen as the decisive moment: the climax of all Wellcome's contributions to scientific research and all his collecting work. Although there was not enough space for his Library on the same site (the Library remained 'in purdah' at Willesden[21]), there would be lecture rooms and study rooms, and twice as much laboratory space. Wellcome's vision for scientific research could be brought together for the first time. The Historical Medical Museum had been hidden away on Wigmore Street, where no more than a tenth of the ethnographic collection could be exhibited; now it would be more 'suitably placed' in a grand new building on one of London's main thoroughfares.[22] The foundation-stone for the new building was laid on 25 November 1931, and Lord Moyniham spoke of it as 'a corner-stone of the life-work of the man who had done as much as any man in this or any other country to advance both the science and art of medicine'.[23]

The Euston Road building was completed the following March, and the Wigmore Street Museum was closed five months later. The build had attracted some press attention, and during the summer of 1932 the London

evening newspapers followed developments at Wigmore Street. The removal
of a large museum was not an everyday occurrence. There was a sense of
volatility, almost danger, as Wellcome's staff released his exotic artefacts from
their glass cases and transported them across London:

I have just been watching a squad of aproned workmen dealing with the fetishes and
godlings of the medicine men in a way that would bring some dreadful consequences
on their heads if these grotesque creatures had the power attributed to them by fear
and ignorance—those twins that combine to make superstition. Big-headed, wide-
eyed creatures carved from wood, manikins with flowing hair and sinister, twisted
mouths, things that are half-animal, half-human; I saw the workmen seize all
indifferently, wrap them briskly in torn newspapers, put them between shavings in
packing cases, hammer the nails well home, and take them out to a waiting lorry.[24]

Plans were drafted showing each Wigmore Street exhibit before it was
dismantled, and all the objects were numbered so that they could be
reinstalled in their new home. Vans ferried objects from Wigmore Street to
Euston Road for almost two months. By the end of October, the old building
had been emptied, but one correspondent noted that 'the museum cannot be
completely in order again before the end of this year'.[25] This would prove to
be a serious underestimate. It was not simply a matter of unpacking the boxes
sent from Wigmore Street in their new home, because hundreds of cases were
also being delivered to the new building from Wellcome's storerooms. The
Museum staff spread themselves across the lower floors at Euston Road and
set about unpacking boxes and ranking their contents for exhibition.

This work went on for years. Malcolm began to make arrangements for a
new 'Primitive Hall' and 'Hall showing the Development of Man and Prehistory',[26] but Wellcome, who had lost faith in Malcolm's management
skills, would not allow any decisions to be taken in his absence, and he was
frequently in America. The staff, who could only register and sort objects
roughly, according to their general quality, while awaiting final authorization, began to despair. Any sense of order gradually dissipated, as more and
more objects were produced but no progress was made on the displays.
Perhaps the 'fetishes and godlings' from Wigmore Street had taken unkindly
to their relocation after all.

Wellcome's own frustrations with the situation began to mount. The
Euston Road building presented the opportunity to reorganize the Museum
displays completely. But he was, by now, reluctant to give Malcolm any real
responsibility for the refit. He sent a particularly stern letter in July 1933,

rebuking Malcolm for arranging some of the prehistoric material. 'I told you that I would personally supervise and direct the arrangement of these exhibits and decide the methods of display of all the aforementioned materials.' Wellcome wanted 'all my ethnological, anthropological, archaeological and all other primitive material sorted out, classified, prepared, numbered and catalogued',[27] but nothing could then be done with it until he was present. There was no room for such a huge undertaking; great stacks of objects grew up only to be left in limbo. Still Wellcome insisted that the huge stock-taking exercise must be completed before work on the displays could begin. He wrote to a friend, in 1930,

Sometimes I have wished that I persisted in my original intention to postpone the opening of the Museum until the collections could be properly and completely studied, classified and catalogued, which plan I have rigidly pursued in respect to the Library. However, the Museum is now in a state of evolution, and my plans are being gradually developed in accordance with my original ideas and intentions for constant progress on scientific lines. I anticipate that it will in course of time attain to the high ideas to which I aspire.[28]

Once all the objects had been examined, Wellcome had 'every intention of organizing and arranging [the Museum] himself',[29] but he was now rarely in London. One member of the 'scientific staff', Mary Borer, wrote to Wellcome on her resignation in 1935, 'It is with much disappointment that I leave your service, for, after six and a half years, I have only just had the opportunity of meeting you and discussing plans for the future Museum.'[30] Wellcome had little time for his junior staff, and Malcolm had left them rudderless in an endless sea of things.

The inadequacy of Wellcome's relationship with Malcolm played its part in the Museum's stagnation. Wellcome had issued cautions repeatedly: Malcolm did not structure his letters properly, or give enough detailed information, or express his own opinions, or take the initiative when objects came up for sale. Malcolm repeated himself without offering crucial details, and he constantly made excuses for the slow progress. Wellcome's reprimands only fuelled Malcolm's reticence. He now constantly sought Wellcome's advice, and followed his instructions blindly. His confidence was gradually eroding. His work, and the work of his staff, became mundane and unimaginative. They waited for some initiative, but the initiative never came. A letter from Malcolm to Wellcome in June 1930 is typical:

Progress in the Prehistoric Hall has been rather slow of late and I have been waiting to hear your approval or otherwise of the methods we have been employing. They are certainly sound from the scientific point of view, but the methods of arrangement we are leaving until you return as it would not take long after discussing the problem with you. There are several other little details I would like your advice about concerning this room.[31]

Perhaps Wellcome was struggling with the enormity of the job too, and perhaps it was all too easy, as old age undermined his powers of concentration, for his frustrations to be meted out at Malcolm's door. Wellcome was now in his eighties. His health and stamina were not what they used to be,[32] and the impossibility of the situation at the Historical Medical Museum was only just becoming clear. His concern for detail was beginning to hamper his decision-making:

this policy of careful consideration, seeing a problem from all its angles before coming to a decision, in the early years of the business, did much to place it on its solid foundation. But in later years when the weaknesses of advancing age began to attack him, these ingrained habits of cautiousness developed into a tendency towards procrastination.[33]

Wellcome needed a subtle form of guidance at this time. He needed guidance disguised as confident, reassuring admiration. He needed to feel empowered to make decisions, but Malcolm had never had the self-confidence to provide this support. He tried to fulfil Wellcome's needs by reflecting them, by doing what he was told, with endless assurances that 'Your scheme, therefore, is being complied with in every particular',[34] which were not really assurances at all. This deference simply reflected Wellcome's own limitations back to him.

So in 1935, Malcolm's departure and Johnston-Saint's promotion brought some renewed vigour to the proceedings. Sona Rosa Burstein wrote to a friend that Saint was 'a bit military, perhaps, but the place *needs* it, god knows!' and added that he had 'the honesty to say he does not know, when he doesn't—a refreshing change.—Well, any regime could easily be an improvement on the old.'[35] Saint had already organized a small, temporary exhibition in one of the first floor galleries, illustrating the work of Jean Hyacinthe Vincent, a French bacteriologist. This, he explained to Wellcome, was imperative if they were to continue to attract important donations from medical families, since the Museum had been closed for two years. 'Relatives of great scientists and savants wished to know what was going to happen to valuable material which they intended to present, how it was going to be utilized and in what manner set out for exhibition.' So Johnston-Saint decided, 'it was most desirable to show something concrete, even if it were of only a temporary nature'.[36] However modest this exhibition was, it must have given his colleagues heart to see something on display to show for all their work.

Soon after his promotion, Saint set about recruiting new staff to replace those who had resigned or retired. He even tried to lure back some of the old team, with assurances that things were now 'beginning to go ahead' at the Museum.[37] He set up new systems for registering and re-registering objects from the stores, and reassigned his staff so that they could work together more efficiently. He consulted fellow collectors and colleagues in other museums to determine the best registration system. Display cases and furniture were sent to the carpenter's department to be repaired. There was a feeling of the staff finally pulling together. Even Wellcome's chauffeur, Ashman, was put to work at the Museum in Wellcome's absence. Saint started him 'doing minor repairs to small guns, pistols, revolvers, etc., and cleaning and oiling, where necessary', although he was absent every Saturday morning attending to Wellcome's cars.[38]

Saint also had to try and rectify past mistakes. Recent work on Wellcome's collection of arms had shown that '850 of the originally accessioned entries were either erroneous or without any information whatsoever and required to be corrected and identified'.[39] It was a similar story when they turned their attention to the wooden figures and the coins and medals. But the general disarray, and even decay, proved more daunting than poor documentation. Saint began to organize the Museum's records—'an accumulation of papers, research notes, small drawings, typescript MSS., and the 101 things which we have garnered together from all kinds of sources'—and found that some of the notes dated back to 1898. They were now, according to Saint, being properly filed for the first time.[40] The artefacts themselves had suffered from long years in storage. 'On inspection it was found that practically every piece of statuary and sculpture required cleaning and putting in order, and many of the plinths were badly chipped.'[41] Of seventy-five cases filled with classical artefacts, six were discovered to contain duplicates and 'doubtful' material not suitable for exhibition, and another fifteen had only 'poor specimens and fragments' that were useless.[42] Many of the objects, prints, and paintings unpacked had to be cleaned and repaired. The wooden sculptures from the ethnographic collections needed treatment for worms.[43] And an expert from

South Kensington Museum was called in to rescue the Italian and Greek casts from disintegration.[44]

Saint realized how important it was to have at least some of Wellcome's objects on display. He constantly received enquiries from people hoping to visit the Museum. The ground floor of the Wellcome Research Institution had been assigned to the Wellcome Museum of Medical Science, the separate medical collection that had been established in 1914 and was now under the directorship of Sidney Herbert Daukes. Wellcome did not monitor work at the Museum of Medical Science as closely—it had been established as a collection specializing in tropical disease on the initiative of Andrew Balfour, the first director of the Wellcome Bureau of Scientific Research—and, although the new displays were not completed until 1938, Daukes had already opened them to students and teachers from London's medical schools. He hoped to bring his visitors next door to the Historical Medical Museum and Saint thought this 'most desirable'.[45]

Saint knew it was important for his staff, too, to see that all their efforts would bring reward, and to instil some life into the place. He proposed 'a small general historical medical exhibition in the Hall of Statuary and Gallery' which would be open to visitors. The new Hall of Statuary, on the second floor at Euston Road, was a self-contained space, ideal for a temporary exhibition. Knowing that Wellcome would be uncertain about committing to a exhibition for fear it would detract from the work of refitting the Museum as a whole, Saint stressed that 'such an exhibition would be of an entirely temporary and improvised nature. It could be altered, rearranged or dismantled very quickly and at very short notice.' He tried to reassure Wellcome that installing it 'would in no way interfere with the progress of the ordinary classification and the dealing with the material'.[46] Saint drew up 'several schemes' for the exhibition and staged photographs 'showing the exact appearance of each proposal', and took them on a visit to America in January 1936 to show Wellcome.[47] But Wellcome, as ever, was hesitant to approve anything that could be viewed as a compromise.

Wellcome thought all the staff should be committed to the same goal: completing his Museum as quickly as possible.[48] He was removed from the daily dissatisfactions of his staff, and continued to insist on patience and perfectionism. Work at the Museum was still shrouded in secrecy. No plans or exhibits could be publicized before they were completed in every detail. And Wellcome's stubbornness did not soften: 'once he had embarked upon a project, [he] was not easily persuaded to change his mind.'[49] But Wellcome

Figure 29. The last portrait taken of Henry Wellcome.

was not as strong as he once had been (Figure 29). George Pearson, the General Manager, felt that his 'physical and mental vigour' had been in decline for a few years. He found it harder to concentrate, and his memory was not as sharp. The sense of invincibility that had shaped his ambitions for so long did not diminish, but the more urgent it was to act on his ideas, 'the more difficult it became to express them in the form of concrete proposals'. He was increasingly reluctant to make decisions, but 'the old characteristic of determination to control every detail of the execution of his plans still persisted and prevented him entrusting their development and completion to others so long as he lived'.[50]

Saint's hopes for a temporary exhibition fell prey to this intransigence. Wellcome was caught between his ongoing desire for secrecy, which helped to maintain his perceived authority over the project, and the growing need to authenticate his actions by sharing his work with others.[51] He could not let go, but he could barely cling on any longer. His physical health was deteriorating. He had been suffering from mild arthritis of the spine, painful sinuses, and, more worryingly, intestinal pain. In the spring of 1935, he was admitted, at his own request, to the Mayo Clinic in Rochester, Minnesota, and a few months later he underwent an operation to remove a malignant growth from his abdomen. Wellcome recovered well during the following winter,[52] but Saint now had only a few months to try and piece together his employer's dream of opening 'the biggest private museum in the country'.[53]

Wellcome returned to England in July 1936, but his discomfort had increased considerably, and he was found to be suffering from bladder cancer. This time he faded fast, and died on 25 July. The man who 'never thought he would die' had run out of time.[54] His body was briefly laid in state in the auditorium of the Euston Road building, where his longest-serving staff took their turn to keep guard, amongst them Harry Port, Harry Stow, and John Comins, who had bid for him at the salesrooms for decades and ferried his artefacts across the country.[55] What must have passed through their minds as they left the Museum's overflowing storehouses to watch over Sir Henry's coffin? The funeral was at Golders Green Crematorium on 29 July. It was a simple ceremony: mourners were asked not to bring flowers.

CHAPTER EIGHTEEN

SIR HENRY
WELLCOME IS DEAD

Without Wellcome, the collection lost its driving force, and, almost imme-diately, it began to fragment. Wellcome's successors could not defend such a great, and expensive, material legacy, particularly when most of it was stashed away, out of sight and in a state of disarray. Had Wellcome successfully transformed his collection into a museum during his lifetime no doubt the story would have been different. Once completed, the Wellcome Historical Medical Museum might have provided a service to the public that justified its maintenance in perpetuity. As it was, Wellcome's trustees were faced with thousands of unopened packing cases, many filled with artefacts of unknown provenance and quality. Now that Wellcome's vision could no longer hold this largely impenetrable collection together, practical and financial consid-erations took precedence for the first time and dictated that the collection must be rationalized.

On Wellcome's death, the Wellcome Foundation Ltd, which comprised all his business and research interests, was vested in a board of trustees who were charged with distributing the firm's profits into medical research and the history of medicine.[1] Not only were they liable for huge death duties on Wellcome's assets, including the Museum and Library, but the firm's success was by no means guaranteed in 1936. Wellcome's collecting work, and the building of the Wellcome Research Institution on Euston Road, had put a considerable strain on profits. Communication within the management had been poor for some time, and a number of key research staff left Burroughs Wellcome for competing companies during and after the First World War.

In addition, Wellcome's insistence on protecting the academic credentials of his research laboratories and keeping them separate from business operations had contributed to a decline in product development at Burroughs Wellcome. So the company underwent a phase of restructuring in the decades following Wellcome's death. The result was that during the first twenty years of its existence the Wellcome Trust only distributed £1 million for scientific research.[2]

Wellcome had drawn up his Will in 1932. In it, he transferred all his collections to his trustees to furnish the museums, libraries, laboratories, and other scientific institutions associated with the Wellcome Foundation. He stipulated that an (unspecified) portion of the Foundation's annual profits should be set aside to maintain and expand these museums and libraries, and for research and collecting in the history of medicine and the allied sciences. The museums and libraries should be open to researchers, students, and other interested people. In an informal memorandum to his trustees, which Wellcome signed on the same day as his Will, he expressed his desire that the objects he already owned should be repaired and restored. The memorandum stated that: 'My original Museums and Research Library should be made as complete as possible or practicable'; but went on to assert, 'The rules regulating my Museums, Research Laboratories, Library and Research Institution [are] to be such as my Trustees may deem fit to adopt.'[3]

Wellcome's trustees—two scientists, two lawyers, and an accountant—had little appreciation of his objectives as a collector, and only one of them, Sir Henry Dale, who was Director of the National Institute for Medical Research, had any inside experience of the Wellcome organization.[4] They were concerned by the expense and scale of the collecting operation, and, instead of completing the collections as Wellcome had suggested, they began to economize. In 1937 Johnston-Saint's budget was cut, and the trustees decided that the Museum should concentrate solely on the history of medicine, reining in Wellcome's growing interests in cultural history. In a long letter to the anthropologist and collector Mervyn Jeffreys, who was still shipping crates of ethnographic material to London from Nigeria, Johnston-Saint explained the consequences of Wellcome's death in no uncertain terms. Jeffreys, Saint wrote, must 'close down the collecting entirely'[5] and not send any more objects, as Saint was already overwhelmed with things.

Sir Henry Wellcome is dead and the Museum is now under Trustees. The Trustees have to decide what to do with the vast collections accumulated by Sir Henry during his life time, of which the ethnographical collection is only one of many. Sir Henry seemed to collect everything. The Trustees have decided that we must confine ourselves to the original purpose of the Museum, which was to show the history of medicine and allied sciences throughout the world from prehistoric times. No space is available to show any other collections, even if it was so desired ... so many of Sir Henry's intentions have had to be curtailed, or even abandoned, in order to cope with existing circumstances, that you will, I know, understand the difficult position that I am in.[6]

Saint's expenditure was now 'very definitely limited. I must economise in as many directions as possible.' He could hardly afford to transport Jeffrey's existing packing cases back to London. His organizational skills were no longer focused on putting Wellcome's Museum together; they were aimed at setting apart objects that could be discarded. Artefacts from Wellcome's home were transferred to the Wellcome Research Institution. In amongst the desks, chairs, and bookcases packed up into vans at Gloucester Gate there was a Tunisian settee, a Nigerian stool, and an 'etched gourd'.[7] Was this the same Guatemalan gourd Wellcome had acquired on his travels in South America as a young man? We will never know. These are the final indistinct glimpses of the collection he had kept in his home.

Meanwhile, the Willesden warehouse was assessed and saleable objects were identified. The first auctions took place in 1937. Twenty-seven auction sales were devoted to sections of Wellcome's collection during the course of the following two years. By the outbreak of the Second World War in 1939, a number of Wellcome's statues, masks, musical instruments, animal traps, steam engines, stone tools, medals, china, furniture, textiles, paintings, and books had been sold. Johnston-Saint himself bought some chairs, rugs, and tables from Wellcome's storerooms in August 1939.[8]

So began the long process of dispersal that saw Wellcome's collection scattered around the world again, distributed between libraries and museums and private homes, and sent to hospitals, charities, military units, and churches. It took almost as long to re-home Wellcome's possessions as it had to collect them all together in the first place. During the War, Saint's staff continued to prepare the Museum for opening at Euston Road. In 1939, he reported the completion of nine reconstructions of ancient pharmacies of various types, and ongoing work on an alchemist's laboratory, an Indian drug shop, and a Roman surgeon's house.[9] Meanwhile, cases filled with Wellcome's books were stacked against the windows for protection during air raids.[10] The building, and some artefacts, did suffer damage when Gower

Place was bombed, but the structure was sound and could be repaired. The company's headquarters were not so fortunate. Snow Hill, and the offices Wellcome had taken such a keen interest in designing sixty years earlier, were destroyed in 1941—'The floor, staircases and all the partitions were of wood with lino covering all the floor which no doubt helped the building to burn more easily', one employee recalled[11]—and some staff were moved to Euston Road. In 1946, the Library finally opened for readers in a converted Hall of Statuary: the grand, galleried room that Saint had hoped to fill with a temporary exhibition in the 1930s, but Wellcome had preferred to reserve for his most impressive sculptures, was now filled with bookcases.[12]

Later that year, the Euston Road building became the firm's official headquarters. It was meant to be a temporary arrangement, and the Museum was moved into a Georgian townhouse at Portman Square, but Burroughs Wellcome and Company did not move again until the late 1980s. The Wellcome Research Institution had only hosted a couple of temporary exhibitions before the galleries were transformed into business offices. As one observer commented at the time, 'Sir Henry Wellcome clearly did not erect his classical marble palace on Euston Road to be occupied by clerks and stenographers of his Company.'[13] Although the Library remained in place, 1947 was spent dismantling a nearly completed Museum, and putting many of the artefacts back into storage again. Johnston-Saint retired that year. He had dutifully siphoned off objects for sale, and cleared out the Willesden warehouse. He left in bitter disappointment. He had overseen the break-up of Wellcome's collection, the forced evacuation of the building intended for his Museum, and the gradual dissolution of his own life's work.[14]

In 1939, T. T. Paterson, curator at the Cambridge University Museum of Archaeology and Anthropology, had written to Saint after a visit to Willesden, 'You have one of the finest collections of prehistoric material in the world . . . there are individual collections which are unique, and could not be replaced under any circumstances should they be dispersed as the Trustees would like. For research students these collections are of inestimable value.'[15] The same could have been said of Wellcome's ethnographic collections, his classical antiquities, or his arms collection, which has been described as 'probably the greatest arms collection of all [time]'.[16] In 1945, just one of many sales of Wellcome's arms transformed the purchaser, a London estate agent, into an international arms dealer and his assistant into one of the foremost experts on the history of British firearms. The latter man, Howard Blackmore, spent his free time sorting through his employer's shop, which, at a stroke, became 'crammed with guns, swords, daggers, polearms etc . . . there must have been examples of every kind of weapon devised by man'.[17]

Perhaps Wellcome's collection could only enjoy the space it required to inspire others once it had been divided up, but Johnston-Saint's great sadness was not just to see this extraordinary collection scattered, but to know that many precious artefacts went unrecognized and unprovenanced in the process, as they were sold in bulk, or, worse, sent for scrap. Wellcome had expected his staff to fulfil his aspirations for a research museum. He told his peers that he had made full provision for the future of his collection after his death: there would be collaborations with other scientific bodies and teaching programmes based in the Museum. 'I have made full provision for its continual growth and future expansion. It must never become moribund. I wish to be quite definite on this point . . . all the activities of the Museum will be at the disposal of those interested in the subjects with which the Museum will deal.'[18] But his trustees had different priorities, and Saint retired with little hope of seeing Wellcome's plans realized on the scale he intended.

After the War, the transfer of non-medical material from Willesden entered a new phase.[19] Between 1949 and 1954, ten 'distributions' of ethnographic material were organized at the British Museum (Figure 30). Curators from around the country were invited to choose from hundreds of packing cases. Each representative was allotted a corner of the room in which to stack their pickings. It was not always possible to open the cases, and many curators simply took potluck, only discovering exactly what they had acquired when they got home. A total of 1,300 cases of objects were dispersed in this way. But still, thousands of non-medical artefacts remained. During the 1960s and 70s, Wellcome's Egyptology collections were given away. More than 300 crates of material from ancient Egypt were distributed—Liverpool Museum alone received ninety cases. The British Museum had received the majority of Wellcome's prehistoric artefacts in 1965, but a further two tons, six hundred weight of flint implements, packed in fifty-two cases, were sent to Ulster Museum in 1967. More ethnographic material was dispersed. The University of California Los Angeles received 30,000 anthropological objects in the mid-1960s.[20] Large transfers like these were accompanied by numerous smaller exchanges and auctions over the years.

The dispersal of the Wellcome collection reflected broader trends affecting museums in the twentieth century. Wellcome's notion of a grand museum dealing with the whole history of mankind had become outdated even as his staff worked towards its opening on Euston Road. Wellcome ran out of time

Figure 30. Weapons, spears, and shields from Wellcome's collection laid out in the Duveen Gallery at the British Museum, for selection by

as a collector, but his collection had become 'out of time' in other ways. As he poured more and more money into his acquisitions, the world around him was moving on. By the 1930s the time for great private collections had slipped by and museum collections had become the by-product of research increasingly focused elsewhere.

The museum mission of collecting, classifying, preserving, and displaying objects had been 'self-evident and untroubled' at the turn of the century when Wellcome set about organizing his Historical Medical Museum, but as the century progressed, the analytical methods employed by museum-based scientists were increasingly supplanted by experimental science. Laboratories became the place for cutting-edge scientific research. The very self-contained physicality of museums made them vulnerable to these changes in the intellectual landscape. As university research flourished in laboratories and out in the field, museums 'could easily be marginalized through their relative disengagement from the rough and tumble of intellectual debate'.[21]

The move away from museum research in the first half of the twentieth century was gradual but unremitting. In the natural sciences, 'experimentalism' became hegemonic: 'The ideology here was *command*, not classification; [science became] a manipulative, controlling discipline, practised in laboratories but promising future control in the "real world" of hospitals or factories.'[22] Biologists no longer studied whole animals, but concentrated instead on cells and molecules. Specialist medical institutions began to replace medical museums, and medics now learned their skills while on the rounds in hospital wards. Improvements in photographic technology, and, eventually, computer technology, meant that the collections themselves were no longer essential for teaching purposes. Science students relied increasingly on textbooks and direct observation to learn their trade. In physical anthropology, the study of skeletal remains in museums was superseded by work on genetics, blood groups, and the ecology and physiology of living communities. Physical anthropologists became allied to medical institutions rather than museums.[23]

Changes affected the humanities too. Social anthropologists reacted against the historical perspective of late-nineteenth-century 'social evolutionism', and turned their attention, instead, to the structure and function of societies in the present: most disregarded museums and established their credentials in the field instead. Archaeology moved from an antiquarian interest in rare finds to analysis of the whole excavation 'archive', which was more suited to bulk storage than exhibition. Meanwhile, the history of science became closely affiliated with philosophy and the history of ideas, so historians eschewed the study of objects and visual media in favour of work on literary texts. In short, new generations of scientists and social scientists were trained in university departments rather than museums and were under no obligation to visit the collections cared for by their institutions.[24]

During a growth period for universities, museums failed to keep pace with proliferating specialities in the disciplines they represented. Wellcome's panoramic vision was unsustainable. Gradually, the quest for a universal vision of human diversity gave way, under its own weight, to a myriad of specialist academic discourses. As specialisms spawned further sub-specialisms the space that might have been reserved for expanding museum collections was devoted to classrooms, lecture theatres, libraries, and laboratories instead. Curatorial work became an inconvenience to many academics working in museums, because it increasingly meant taking time away from research work, rather than constituting the research in itself. Large museums, with broad remits, were more suited to generalists who could care for a range of artefacts of different provenance and could identify the relationships that united these collections despite their diversity, but generalists were becoming a rare breed.

And so museums focused more on the needs of the public, because they could offer a broad educational overview more easily than providing for the manifold needs of a new, larger generation of academic researchers. Museums became primarily places for inspiration and illustration. To a certain extent, they came to be seen as collections of 'curios' again, removed from the cutting edge of academic enquiry. They now had to defend themselves against the charge of 'mere antiquarianism'.[25] By the early 1950s, research museums were struggling to find a new identity for themselves while the academic establishment assumed them to be 'dull and not very consequential'. In this atmosphere, an American anthropologist could declare,

Few of the forward steps in the study of culture and society in the last half-century have come about as a result of the description and analysis of museum specimens. Specimens are valuable as ancillary tools for research, for use as illustrative material, but the close perusal of specimens, in itself, has not stimulated and does not now promise to stimulate fruitful research.[26]

His words would surely have mystified and appalled Wellcome.

In addition, the grand classical architecture of many national museums became an embarrassment as the confidence of the British Empire gave way to guilt and introspection regarding the nation's imperial past. The unquestioned assumptions that had established museums as great temples of science—the belief in the forward march of technological progress, the existence of cultural hierarchies, and the objective nature of the empirical data that had shaped Wellcome's collecting project—were placed in their own historical context. Before long, museums had become worthy of study in their own right. They had left a legacy undoubtedly rich, but one that also proved to be deeply troubling in the later twentieth century. Ethnographic museums in particular struggled with their own legacies. The history of their collections was inextricably bound together with colonial histories of appropriation, subordination, and exploitation. The subjects they represented rarely had any say in how they were portrayed.

Whole institutions could now be seen as curiosities rooted in another time, and by the end of the century anthropologists were embarking on fieldwork *in museums*, to study the dynamics of staff politics and the challenges of mounting exhibitions that were both ethical and relevant to modern life. All this contributed to a general unease regarding the role of museums in academic and public life. As institutional funding declined, many believed that 'museums and collections are an expensive luxury that can no longer be afforded'.[27]

Wellcome cannot have foreseen the extent of these transformations, but he may well have recognized that the trend towards academic specialization presented him with a problem as the director of such an ambitious museum. In 1928, he had accepted that 'knowledge at the present day is diverging', but he went on to explain that, in his opinion, 'a research museum is necessary to control, as it were, the developments which are taking place from day to day'. He said that he had collected his artefacts together, 'so that they may be studied in full in the future'.[28] Perhaps he came to see his collection as a bastion of completeness in an intellectual world that was increasingly subdivided. But this reasoning was to die with him. Wellcome's guiding vision of a broad-ranging research museum had become unsustainable by the mid-twentieth century. He had left an enormous material legacy, but few now shared his faith in its cohesive intellectual value. It was not worth the resources required to keep it all together: it could be more useful, and more manageable, once it had been split apart. Time had caught up with Wellcome as a collector, and time had caught up with the collecting tradition to which he belonged.

And so it is that today more than one hundred institutions worldwide look after the objects once collected by Henry Wellcome. A number of them, including Liverpool Museum, were given Wellcome's artefacts to help replenish their collections after the air raids of the Second World War. During the late 1970s and early 80s, the majority of what remained of Wellcome's Historical Medical Museum was transferred to London's Science Museum. The Science Museum received an estimated 100,000 artefacts, including 25,000 surgical instruments alone, from around 165,000 artefacts dealing with the history of medicine and human health, and the remainder was given to other museums.[29] At the Science Museum, Wellcome's collection formed a new department and the basis for two permanent public galleries. Wellcome's library had also been streamlined over the years. Unwanted books had gradually been sold to other institutions and dealers; some were sold to the British Museum library in 1946 to replace volumes destroyed in the War. But the Wellcome Foundation, later the Wellcome Trust, retained the bulk of its founder's extensive library as well as an important iconographic collection of paintings, prints, and photographs. Today, the Wellcome Library houses over 600,000 books and journals, thousands of manuscripts and extensive historical archives, and more than 100,000 pictures.

The building on Euston Road did not immediately become the research institution Wellcome had planned. The Library and the firm's offices lived there side by side for many years, while, elsewhere, the layers of Wellcome's collection were progressively shed. The Historical Medical Museum, in reduced form, had moved back into the building in 1954 and stayed until the late 1970s. Space for displays and staff offices gradually increased during this period, and a number of successful temporary exhibitions were mounted. Cataloguing and research continued at the Museum, publications were issued, and, during the 1970s, a diploma in the history of medicine was established. Nevertheless, the trustees decided to focus their resources on medical research, and, while the Library remained *in situ*, the Museum collections were sent to the Science Museum. As the objects moved out, a new collaboration was formalized between the Wellcome Institute and University College London, creating a joint Academic Unit. Members of staff at the Institute became honorary lecturers at University College; more academic staff were recruited; and pre-clinical medical students could take a one-year undergraduate course in the history of medicine. Lectures, seminars, and symposia were gradually established, and the Library, still housed in the Euston Road building, enjoyed more space and funding.[30]

By the turn of the twenty-first century, the Wellcome Trust had begun to attend to its museological roots again. It funded the Science Museum's new

Wellcome Wing in London, which opened in 2000, and, three years later, an exhibition was held at the British Museum to celebrate 150 years since Wellcome's birth. *Medicine Man: The Forgotten Museum of Henry Wellcome* reunited 700 objects from Wellcome's collection, loaned by a number of different institutions. Although only a tiny fraction of the collection could be displayed, the exhibition celebrated the breadth of Wellcome's interests in human health. Later that same year, 2003, a permanent Wellcome Trust Gallery opened at the British Museum, housing an exhibition called *Living and Dying*, which investigates a range of cultural responses to sickness, sorrow, and misfortune: two lengths of 14,000 prescription tablets, the average number prescribed to a British individual in the course of their lifetime, are arranged alongside a Bolivian dance mask, a spirit board from Papua New Guinea, and other artefacts from around the world.

In 2007, Wellcome Collection opened in the refurbished Wellcome Building on Euston Road. After years of isolation, the Library now dominates the enterprise and occupies two floors in the building, but three exhibition spaces display scientific technology, modern art, and cultural artefacts in juxtaposition. Only a small number—around 300—of the objects Wellcome collected are on display, but books, pictures, and artefacts are all housed together. Wellcome Collection aims to explore health from different perspectives, through art, science, philosophy, commerce, industry, and spirituality. And, in an echo of Wellcome's own declaration that his collection should be an academic resource, the show is aimed at adults rather than children. And a members' club organizes lectures and social events in the hope that those 'with a keen interest in medicine, life, and art'[31] will come together to discuss their ideas.

Wellcome's hopes for a panoramic vision of the past proved impossible to fulfil on the scale he had envisaged. Progress towards his stated aim, of establishing an international research collection, could only come after his death, when the project was taken from his grasp and heavily rationalized. The results are necessarily more modest than Wellcome had anticipated. He had wanted to conjure the world in microcosm, and had worked towards a continuous display that would reveal the whole history of the human past, and establish himself as author of it all. He lived, like so many collectors, at 'that pivotal point where man finds himself rivalling god and teeters between mastery and madness',[32] for his own power to follow his interests had become his downfall; his unchecked consumer instincts cluttered his aspirations. His death provided the limitations that the project had needed all along, and he had not been able to assert: practicalities were prioritized for the first time, and Wellcome's plans were cut down to size. As Saint had explained to Jeffreys, there was no other way to cope in the circumstances. No single person could complete the picture Wellcome had envisaged.

Wellcome is remembered as a pioneering businessman and a patron of scientific research. His collection has, until recently, remained in the shadows. His name is inextricably tied to the work of the Wellcome Trust, which has become the United Kingdom's largest non-governmental source of funds for biomedical research and runs a number of grant schemes in the history of medicine. But the Trust's status has been relatively recently earned. During the 1960s, the majority of the firm's profits were reinvested in the business, which did not fully recover its strength and innovative reputation until the 1970s. Still, the Trust awarded nearly £6 million in medical research grants during the 1960s; by the early 1990s it was disbursing more than £100 million a year for research, and, at the time of writing, that figure had grown to £650 million. Although it owes its existence to Henry Wellcome, the Trust's success is as much due to the achievements of his successors in the twentieth century.[33]

In any case, Wellcome's posthumous reputation has been little influenced by his efforts as a collector. He failed to finish his Historical Medical Museum, and, for his trustees, the collection became a burden rather than a resource. His friend and colleague, Henry Dale, who had been a great admirer of Wellcome and became chairman of his trustees, nonetheless had reservations about his motivations. In 1941 he admitted, although he later qualified his words, that 'Wellcome, in some respects, was a flamboyant poseur, who wasted on hobbies and a gigantic advertising money which ought to have gone to assure the future of his business, and our Trust.'[34] This is an understandable gripe, given that Dale was faced with tons of objects that had to be thrown out and tons more that needed classifying and re-homing, but it reveals Dale's prejudices as well as the enormous challenges he faced while trying to put Wellcome's affairs in order. Wellcome is to blame for the fact that his collection was untenable, but his successors found it difficult to identify with his vision in part because they were from a different generation. It is hardly surprising that Wellcome's personal legacy was established despite his collecting interests rather than because of them. It may not have been what Wellcome wanted, but it was a sign of the times. He died a few years before the Second World War and the ensuing dissolution of the British Empire: the world had moved on, and Wellcome's vast collection was cut adrift in its wake.

Yet things endure. Wellcome had asked that his collection be made available for research, and although the thousands of treasures sifted from his warehouses were not all homed together, today they can be found, and consulted, in collections throughout Britain and beyond. Many artefacts that, for decades, had not received the attention they deserved are now exhibited to the public every day, and, notwithstanding the numerous individual items that are precious in their own right, Wellcome's interdisciplinary perspective, which so confounded his trustees, remains the collection's great strength. This is particularly true at the Wellcome Library, where his manuscripts, prints, drawings, books, paintings, photographs, and documents of all genres and provenance can be studied together. Things, like votive paintings and recipe books, that other collectors passed over, are well represented in Wellcome's collection, and his boundless curiosity has fuelled a proliferation of research agendas in recent decades. Wellcome's scholarly objectives meant that he was not easily swayed by fads or conventions, and his comprehensive vision of the past, which pushed at the boundaries of disciplines like anthropology and the history of medicine, is now reaping rewards. There is no doubt that Wellcome's acquisitiveness continues to haunt the work of caring for his objects—many of his possessions, dispersed around the country, still await proper cataloguing—but today, more of his artefacts are available to the public than ever before.

CHAPTER NINETEEN

HONOUR TO WHOM
HONOUR IS DUE

Wellcome was a self-made man: born into nothing, he died a millionaire. He lived out the 'rags to riches' success story that has long been a biographical classic. With his partner, Silas Burroughs, he mastered the pharmaceuticals market, and helped to transform the way in which health was promoted and transacted at the turn of the past century. His opportunities were conferred on him by the capitalist system, and his achievements have been measured within that sphere. Indeed, the philosophical implications of capitalism not only guaranteed Wellcome's status as a 'great man', they secured his objectives as a museum collector, and sustained the life-writing tradition through which he would later be known.

The forces of capitalism have shaped specific kinds of subjects: intentional individuals, self-contained and with free will, who are held accountable for their actions, whose internal states, beliefs, and desires are thought to determine those actions, and who have rights, to trade, and to own land and goods. Wellcome's career path was constituted by the same cultural forces that have shaped perceptions of the self in capitalist societies, and have likewise shaped the history of biography as a genre. 'Without notions of personal uniqueness in culture, biography is out of a job.'[1] Biography takes as its baseline an independent agent, a subject who is self-sufficient, distinctive, coherent, and set apart from the social and material world that provides a context for their actions.

According to this worldview, the material world constitutes an objective reality of inert things, which are separate from the thinking human subject.

People and things are constituted in opposition to each other. Things can represent people's mental states, but they are always subordinate. Things can be organized, and possessed, and exchanged, and used as evidence, and shown off, but it is always humans who are active, while the material world they interact with remains passive. The Western collecting tradition—and in particular the classificatory collection typical of the late nineteenth century— is an expression of this worldview. Capitalism not only fuelled collecting in practical terms, through the explosion of consumer goods and global trade networks that brought collectors into ever greater contact with the makers and sellers of the artefacts that interested them, it provided philosophical validation for the whole collecting tradition. Individual enterprise and a proprietorial attitude towards the world were encouraged, and collecting things became a noble pursuit.[2]

Wellcome's success as a businessman and his exploits as a collector are two, parallel manifestations of the same value system. He made his money selling things, and the process of acquiring things structured his broader interactions with the world around him. He navigated the commercial world for business and for pleasure, and for intellectual enlightenment. In the late nineteenth century, through the collecting tradition, knowledge too became commoditized. The material world presented an external, objective reality that could be possessed, both physically and intellectually. A collection represented its maker's efforts to understand the world, so that understanding was, at one level, a celebration of human mastery over material things. Things did not simply demonstrate knowledge, they were knowledge. Wellcome approached knowledge in this way, as something that could be owned, exchanged, and accrued in physical form. When he first opened his Historical Medical Museum his intention had been 'to place before the profession, in a collected form, all the information [he had] obtained'.[3] His Museum consisted of information in collected form. Things were his intellectual capital, and he accumulated historical data as no one has before or since.

In the hands of a man of such wealth and determination, the implications of this belief that information was available in object form were numerous. For a start, it meant that other people could collect things for Wellcome without compromising his intellectual rights. Knowledge could be bought, so you could pay other people to buy it for you. New information could simply be handed over at the end of the day. And buying things made the pursuit of knowledge into a game. To achieve his goals, Wellcome had to maximize his opportunities for acquisition and outwit his rivals, whether they were dealers, tradesmen, or fellow collectors. His intellectual project became a sport of strategy, skill, and luck, as he played the antiquities market for scholarly profit. Wellcome monitored every twist and turn of the plot apprehensively—scribbling 'I am very anxious to get this', 'follow up', 'don't let any of these good things slip away', 'don't lose them' to his staff—but his apprehension must have added to the thrill of victory when it came. He could take pleasure in the catalogue of triumphs, large and small, each faithfully reported by his staff, that guaranteed his position as one of the most dominant collectors ever seen. Finding out about the world in this way doubled as an exercise in self-congratulation. Wellcome was the hero of his own collecting narrative, and his ultimate prize would be acceptance within the academic community. But this kind of scholarship had more in common with the business world than with academic work.

For Wellcome, learning about the world meant galvanizing resources. It required money, a competent team of employees, and substantial premises to stockpile the data as it accumulated. He could collect more than other people because he had the wealth, the determination, and the management skills to do so. His intellectual venture became a job. Some of Wellcome's staff devoted their whole careers to expanding his collection, and once he had established effective systems of acquisition it became very difficult to stop them. Before long, it was easier for Wellcome to buy things than to refuse them. The collection emerged piecemeal, through thousands of relatively small transactions all over the world, so there was little reason for him to circumscribe the process. He admitted that it made little sense to turn a thing down, even if it was over-priced, if it was worth more to him than the money it cost to buy. The organization he had created developed a rhythm of its own: Wellcome became a part of his own collecting machine.

This kind of intellectual work also appealed to Wellcome's sense of style and flair for showmanship. Information in material form was ideal for showing off. It is no coincidence that nineteenth-century museums shared much of their heritage with commercial institutions, like department stores and trade fairs, and entertainment venues, like theatres, panoramas, and zoos. Burroughs Wellcome and Company had profited from an emphasis on quality and design, and established a reputation for innovative trade exhibits. In a similar way, Wellcome's Museum was designed to impress as much as to inspire. He collected scientific relics to 'hand down to posterity the names of those who in the course of time might be forgotten, thus rendering honour to whom honour is due',[4] but no eponymous project of this scale is undertaken without an eye to personal glory. Wellcome tried to collect his way into the ranks of scientists and scholars he sought to memorialize, but his stated aim, to provide a research museum for the academic community, sat uneasily with his desire to keep the credit for the collection for himself.

Wellcome believed that his academic venture—fuelled largely by his business acumen—was something that could be accomplished. It promised both success and completion. This notion of accomplishment drove him to collect more and more, but the nearer he got to completing his collection, the further away the finished product became, because neither knowledge nor a collection can be finished. Academic research cannot be concluded, or achieved, or perfected. There is always more to know, and there is always more to buy. This is the twist in the tale: Wellcome's collection was rooted in the defining dualism of late-nineteenth-century capitalist confidence— that things are passive while people are active, so that with the right procedures the world can be possessed and known—but it also proves that dualism to be a limited model for human experience. Wellcome thought he could master the material world and marshal it for all to see, but in actual fact the material world gradually mastered him. His collection, like many collections in this regard, subverted the very ideological principles that created it, and Wellcome, quite simply, got carried away by it all.

Material things are not merely representative or contextual, they are formative.[5] Objects play a vital part in transforming and establishing people's intentions: a person cannot exist beyond the material world through which they must act and interact. Clothes, buildings, furniture, vehicles, computers, all link us in ways that would not be possible otherwise, and all give definition to our interactions. Wellcome's collection was never a straightforward representation of his mental state. It emerged through his relationships with others, and his relationships with others emerged through his collection. The collection was happening all around him. Both collector and collection were mutually constituted: one did not exist beyond the other.[6] The collection was not just an illustration of Wellcome's life, it was a way of life for him. As one of his staff members explained, Wellcome 'was one of those who find the journey more interesting than the end'[7]; and it was too easy to be distracted by—to be shaped by—all the people, places, and stories he discovered along the way.

So Wellcome never perfected his great puzzle. And perhaps this is an appropriate end to the story after all, because it is a reminder that lives are lived incomplete, and that a person's experiences are far more messy than the narratives they inspire. Collecting is an open-ended enterprise, and Wellcome's attitude to his collection is full of ambiguities. He claimed to be striving for historical accuracy, but perhaps he was simply driven by a desire to outdo his competitors in the antiquities market. He declared that his Museum was a philanthropic gesture, but he recognized that it would promote his business interests. He saw his work as a contribution to the world of scientific research, but he never managed to share it with the academics he professed to serve. He collected to safeguard the world's heritage for the benefit of future generations, but he was also securing his own legacy as a patron of research. Wellcome's collection was both a generous gesture and a selfish indulgence. Part science, part obsession, part research, part entertainment, part benefaction, part self-promotion: Wellcome's great Historical Medical Museum was always more of a fantasy than a reality.

Maybe, in his final years, Wellcome allowed himself to feel a little bemused by his inability to conquer his museum collection. It is difficult to know whether his failure to open his Museum stemmed from a fear of finality or from a steadfast faith in the future. Did he ever acknowledge the power the material world had over him? Did he fail to finish his Museum because he underestimated that power, or because he was too beholden to it? In the end, he took too much upon himself. He had created a material legacy of astonishing proportions, but he could not galvanize the team of people necessary to control it. In order to secure his legacy as a collector, he had to share it, and this was something he could not bring himself to do. His efforts to reserve the honours for himself gradually defeated him. Even 'great' lives rest upon collaboration, and trust, and compromise, and luck. Wellcome was happy to delegate the practical work of seeking out and acquiring interesting artefacts—his intellectual capital—but he could neither bring himself to rely on others to help interpret it, nor muster the energy or confidence to do it alone. His success in the business of collecting only compounded his difficulties when it came to elucidating his work.

On 30 July 1936, the day after Sir Henry Wellcome's funeral at Golders Green Crematorium, Peter Johnston-Saint despatched a memo to George Pearson, the company's General Manager:

At 4 p.m. on July 29th, I received from Mr Kenyon the urn containing the ashes of Sir Henry Wellcome. This is a plain bronze urn measuring 11½ ins. long by 7½ ins.

broad by 8 ins. high. I have placed this urn in the West Strong Room on a small table and have attached a small label bearing the following words: 'Urn containing the ashes of H.S.W.' which is, I think, what you suggested. Access to this Strong Room is forbidden without permission from me.[8]

So it was that Wellcome was interred—urn carefully measured and recorded—alongside some of his most precious belongings, within his own Museum, complete with descriptive label. The urn was eventually forgotten about and it was not until February 1987 that Wellcome's ashes were buried in the churchyard of St. Paul's Cathedral and a plaque placed in his memory in the crypt. For fifty years, the collection Wellcome had dedicated his life to assembling served as his resting place after death. He had created a collection to endure through the generations, as a gift to scholarship, and in a bid for distinction. The collection promised Wellcome immortality, but it also reduced him down to size. Perhaps it is fitting that his ashes were forgotten in the maelstrom of his possessions before being properly recognized and commemorated decades later. In the end, Wellcome was just one part of the collection that consumed him; it was the things, the infinite things, that lived on to tell their tales.

NOTES

Unless otherwise stated, citations refer to the Wellcome Archives (WA) and the Wellcome Foundation archive (WF) at the Wellcome Library, London.

Chapter 1. Quite indescribable disorder

1. P. Johnston-Saint (1943) 'Report on the steps which have been taken to dispose of surplus material in the stores, and the present position with regard to collections at Willesden and the Wellcome Research Institute', WA/HMM/TR/Eth/A.1
2. Russell (1986).
3. Artefacts from the Wellcome Collection are illustrated in Allan (2003), Arnold and Olsen (2003), and Gould (2007).
4. Letter from William Britchford to Mr Faulder, 19 April 1975, WA/HSW/PE/C.23.
5. Clifford (1978), 47.

Chapter 2. Herewith please find three rolls of chocolate foil

1. Wellcome to Burroughs, 6 September 1881, WF/E/01/01/01.
2. 'Private Collection W.', WA/HMM/CM/Lis.2. Although this list is undated, it includes items Wellcome acquired before he left America in 1880 and their origins are consistent with his travel itinerary during the late 1870s.
3. See previous note.
4. Wellcome to Frank Elwell, 11 July 1883; to Dudley Shaw and Co., 3 August 1887; and to Mr Adams, Joe Paul and Frank J. Francis, 4 August 1887, WF/E/01/01/01. Wellcome to C. H. Woodward, October 1888, WF/E/01/01/02. Wellcome to E. Cooper and R. Borthwick, 9 April 1895; letters to Captain Pelham, November 1895 and October 1896, WF/E/01/01/03.
5. Quoted in Tuner (1980), 38–9.
6. Royal Commission on National Museums and Galleries, Minutes of Evidence (1929), 105, WA/HSW/OR/L.5.
7. Wellcome to Burroughs, 6 September 1881, WF/E/01/01/01.
8. Cohen (2006), 134. See also 32–4 and 124–5.
9. Loftie (1876). See also Edis (1881) and Herrmann (1999).
10. See Church (2005, 2006).

11. 'Reports and Analyses and Descriptions of New Inventions in Medicine, Surgery, Dietetics, and the Allied Sciences', *British Medical Journal* 91 (25 July 1885), 155.

12. Reminiscences of Burroughs Wellcome and Co., by Mr Warden, WF/M/H/07/04.

13. Church (2005).

14. Reminiscences by E. W. Garnham, Head of the Construction Department, Burroughs Wellcome and Co., 17 October 1947, WF/M/H/07/01.

15. *Chemist and Druggist* 32 (28 January 1888), 104–6. See also drawings of the Burroughs Wellcome and Co. head office at Snow Hill, 1883–1900, WF/CA/P/01.

16. *Chemist and Druggist* 32 (28 January 1888), 104–6.

17. S. M. Burroughs to Wellcome, 14 February 1894, Burroughs's Personal Letter Book. The letter dates to a time when Burroughs's relationship with Wellcome was strained—both accused the other of incurring undue expenses—and Burroughs complains about Wellcome's spending habits stretching back to the early 1880s. He states that during the Spanish trip Wellcome 'debited the firm with £3 per day or more'. My thanks to Julia Sheppard for showing me this letter.

18. See Church and Tansey (2007), 46.

19. Wellcome to Burroughs, 29 June 1883, WF/E/01/01/01.

20. Ibid. 9 July 1885.

21. Stanley (1891 [2001]), 37.

22. Quoted in 'Memo to Management', 25 February 1902, WA/HMM/CM/Lis/1.

23. Wellcome to H. F. Johnson, 18 October 1901, WA/HSW/CO/Bus/A.5.

24. Ibid.

25. Reminiscences by Garnham, 17 October 1947, WF/M/H/07/01.

26. Wellcome's comments on H. F. Johnson's report dated 4 September 1901, WA/HSW/CO/Bus/A.4.

27. Wellcome to H. A. D. Jowett, 19 September 1928, WA/HMM/CO/Sai/A.4.

28. See *'Tabloid' A Brief Medical Guide for Explorers, Missionaries, Travellers, Colonists, Planters and Others* (London: Burroughs Wellcome and Co., n.d.).

29. 'Rough memo book of goods received from Mr Wellcome from the Continent', WA/HMM/CM/Lis/1.

30. Symons (1998), 111.

31. Needham (2001), 190.

32. A. B. Inglis, 27 November 1980, WA/HSW/PE/C.23.

33. Wellcome's comments on H. F. Johnson's report dated 4 November 1901, WA/HSW/CO/Bus/A.6.

34. H. F. Johnson to Wellcome, 18 and 24 October 1901, WA/HSW/CO/Bus/A.5. An Egyptian winged sun was later carved above the door to the Wellcome Research Institution at 183, Euston Road.

35. Ibid. 8 November 1901, WA/HSW/CO/Bus/A.6.

36. Wellcome to Kenneth Campbell, 29 March 1899, WF/E/01/01/07.

37. Burroughs Wellcome and Co., Museum and Exhibition Guard Book, WF/M/GB/29/28.
38. Burroughs was travelling abroad from October 1881 until March 1884.
39. 'Fifty-fourth Annual Meeting of the British Medical Association held in Brighton, August 10th, 11th, 12th and 13th, 1886: The Annual Museum', *British Medical Journal*, 1340 (4 September 1886), 454.
40. Ibid.
41. Wellcome to Julian Price, 8 April 1895, WF/E/01/01/03.
42. A. W. J. Haggis, quoted in Rhodes James (1994), 222. See also Reminiscences of Burroughs Wellcome and Co., by Mr Warden, WF/M/H/07/04.
43. Memo from M.G.S. to E.C.B., 1 May 1940, WA/HSW/PE/C.6. See other memos, and Linstead's 'Chronological List of Photographs of some Exhibits of Burroughs Wellcome and Co. and the Institutions of the Wellcome Foundation Ltd.', in this folder for Wellcome's role in preparing exhibitions.
44. Royal Commission on National Museums and Galleries, Minutes of Evidence (1929), 105, WA/HSW/OR/L.5.
45. 'The Life of Sir Henry Wellcome', *The Times*, 25 August 1953.
46. Wellcome to W. J. Davy, 18 September 1903, WF/E/01/01/07. The word 'museum' did not have the definite meaning it carries today, but could be used to describe any group of objects, whether in a public exhibit, in a private home, or in business offices. Wellcome did not regularly refer to his collection as a 'museum' in the sense that we would understand it—that is, as the 'Wellcome Historical Medical Museum'—until 1912, shortly before it opened the following year.

Chapter 3. A very full and complete volume

1. A visitor to Burroughs Wellcome and Co., 21 July 1893, quoted in Church and Tansey (2007), 75.
2. Wellcome to Mary Curtis Wellcome, 9 April 1880, WA/HSW/FP/E.6.
3. Briggs (1990), 91. On Lever and his collection, see Morris (1992a).
4. The most comprehensive assessment of Wellcome's relationship with Burroughs to date can be found in Church and Tansey (2007), Chapter 4.
5. Wellcome to Mary Curtis Wellcome, 12 June 1896, WA/HSW/FP/E.7.
6. Ibid. 17 December 1889, WA/HSW/FP/E.7.
7. Ibid. 4 October 1895, WA/HSW/FP/E.7.
8. Tansey (1989).
9. Wellcome's work in Sudan is discussed further in Chapter 4.
10. Tansey (2002), 412.
11. See discussion in Chapter 11.

12. Tansey (2002); Rhodes James (1994), 278–89; Church and Tansey (2007), Chapter 16.

13. Church and Tansey (2007), 76 and 182.

14. This application was rejected, and Wellcome did not succeed in registering his laboratories until 1901. See brief discussion in Chapter 10, and Church and Tansey (2007), 170–5.

15. This quotation and those in the following two paragraphs are taken from Wellcome's letter to Friedrich Hoffmann, 27 July 1896, WF/E/01/01/03.

16. Wellcome to G. Norman Douglas, 20 May 1896, WF/E/01/01/03.

17. Gosden and Larson (2007), 53–9.

18. This quotation and those in the following two paragraphs are taken from Wellcome's letter to Friedrich Hoffmann, 27 July 1896, WF/E/01/01/03.

19. Schütze (1993); Symons (2004).

20. Thompson to Wellcome, 8 November 1896, WA/HSW/CO/Gen/H.19.

21. Ibid. 9 December 1896, WA/HSW/CO/Gen/H.19.

22. Ibid. 10 May 1897, WA/HSW/CO/Gen/H.19.

23. *Receits of phisick and chirurgery 'The Lady Ayscough Booke Anno Domini 1692'*, Wellcome Trust Library, MS.1026. This is the first recorded purchase by Thompson for the Wellcome Collection.

24. Thompson to Wellcome, 22 June 1898, WA/HSW/CO/Gen/J.18.

25. Ibid. 24 March 1899, WA/HSW/CO/Gen/K.19.

26. Burroughs Wellcome and Co. to Thompson, 29 November 1899, WF/E/03/03.

27. See Thompson to Wellcome, 18 May and 1 July 1899, WA/HSW/CO/Gen/L.20; H. F. Johnson to Thompson, 1 August 1899, WF/E/01/01/07.

28. Burroughs Wellcome and Co. to Thompson, 18 December 1899, WF/E/03/03.

29. Wellcome to R. Hovendon, 9 November 1900, WF/E/01/01/07. Wellcome to the Librarian at Salisbury Cathedral, 4 September 1903, WF/E/01/01/07.

30. H. F. Johnson to Wellcome, 10 January 1902, WA/HSW/CO/Bus/A, and other correspondence regarding Thompson's work in this file.

31. Thompson to Wellcome, 16 July 1898, WA/HSW/CO/Gen/J.18. Original emphasis.

32. Wellcome to George Wagner, 8 May 1905, WF/E/01/01/08.

Chapter 4. The ideal of my heart

1. Congratulatory letters to Wellcome, June and July 1901, WA/HSW/MD/A.1.

2. Jephson to Wellcome, 4 June 1901, WA/HSW/MD/A.1.

3. Henry Nisbet to Wellcome, 4 June 1901, WA/HSW/MD/A.1.

4. Rhodes James (1994), 254.

5. H. F. Johnson to Wellcome, 6 June 1901, WF/E/01/01/05.

6. Wellcome to Kitchener, 26 November 1898, WA/HSW/CO/Ind/A.3.

7. Quoted in Haggis (1942), 356.

8. Rhodes James (1994), 254.

9. See D'Arcy (1999).

10. Typescript of Wellcome's interview by the Royal Commission on National Museums and Galleries in 1928, WA/HSW/OR/L.1.

11. D'Arcy (1999), 116.

12. Wellcome to Balfour, 29 July 1903, WF/E/01/01/06.

13. See letters from H. F. Johnson to Wellcome Club and Institute staff on 22 July 1901, and 31 May, 17 July, 24 August, and 3 September 1903, WF/E/01/01/05–07.

14. Two lists of items 'Brought to Snow Hill by Mr Wellcome from the Hotel Russell, 20 January 1903', WA/HMM/CM/Lis/1.

15. Wellcome (1912), 263.

16. For the history of collecting in Egypt, see Jasanoff (2005).

17. Letters from Wellcome to Frederick Treves and others, December 1901, WF/E/01/01/06.

18. See Gould (1981), Jorion (1982), Quigley (2001).

19. Letters from Wellcome, November and December 1901, WF/E/01/01/06.

20. Wellcome to Petrie, 18 December 1902, and duplicate letters to other correspondents during December 1902 and January 1903, WF/E/01/01/06.

21. Rough memo book of goods received from Mr Wellcome from the Continent 1901–8, WA/HMM/CM/Lis/1.

22. H. F. Johnson to Wellcome, 9 October 1901, WA/HSW/CO/Bus/A.5. See also correspondence from Johnson during 1901 dated 5 October, 7 and 30 November, and 20 December, WA/HSW/CO/Bus/A.5–A.7.

23. Syrie Wellcome to A. C. Fletcher, 14–16 August 1910, WA/HSW/MD/B.1.

24. Syrie Wellcome to Henry Wellcome, 6 August 1910, WA/HSW/MD/B.1.

25. Extracted from letters by Wellcome to Curtis, 24 August 1910; to Dorothy Stanley, 28 July 1910; and to Robert Lansing, August 1910, WA/HSW/MD/B.2.

26. Maurice Waller to Wellcome, 11 August 1910, WA/HSW/MD/B.2.

27. See Rhodes James (1994), 295–6.

28. Wellcome to Burroughs, 13 March 1883, quoted in Haggis (1942), 315.

29. The main sources of information on the Wellcome marriage are Haggis (1942) and Rhodes James (1994). See also McKnight (1980).

30. Dorothy Stanley to Wellcome, 20 July 1910, WA/HSW/MD/B.2. Original emphasis.

31. Wellcome to Mrs Jephson, 8 June 1910, and Curtis, 24 August 1910, WA/HSW/MD/B.2.

32. Wellcome to Dorothy Stanley, 28 July 1910, WA/HSW/MD/B.2.

33. Wellcome to Curtis, 24 August 1910, WA/HSW/MD/B.2.

34. Early pamphlet, 'Historical Exhibition of Rare and Curious Objects relating to Medicine, Chemistry, Pharmacy and the Allied Sciences', probably dating to 1905, WA/HMM/PB/Han/1.

35. Haggis (1942), 404.

36. Motor tour to Spain and Portugal, 1907, WA/HSW/PE/A.14. Wellcome's motor tours are discussed further in Chapter 8.

37. These, and quotations by Syrie in the following paragraphs, are taken from her letter to Fletcher, 14–16 August 1910, WA/HSW/MD/B.1.

38. Deed of Separation between H. S. Wellcome and G. M. S. Wellcome, 2 September 1910, WA/HSW/MD/B.3.

39. Syrie to Fletcher, 2 January 1911 and further undated letters, and to Wellcome on 12 November 1911 and 8 July 1913, WA/HSW/MD/B.2.

40. Syrie to Fletcher, 14–16 August 1910, WA/HSW/MD/B.1.

41. Wellcome to Robert Lansing, August 1910, WA/HSW/MD/B.1.

42. Wellcome (1912 [1949]), 263–4.

43. Addison (1949). And see also typescript of Wellcome's interview by the Royal Commission on National Museums and Galleries in 1928, WA/HSW/OR/L.1.

44. Wellcome to J. S. Uribe, 6 February 1917, quoted in Haggis (1942), 434.

45. Rhodes James (1994), 315.

46. Wellcome (1912 [949]), 265.

47. Crawford (1955), 97.

48. Syrie launched her interior design business in Baker Street in 1922, and later opened shops in New York, Chicago, Palm Beach, and Los Angeles. She became famous for her minimalist 'white-on-white' designs (perhaps, as Ross McFarlane at the Wellcome Trust pointed out to me, this was partly a rebellion against Wellcome's stocks of antiques). Syrie met Somerset Maugham in 1913, and, two years later, they had a daughter, Liza, in Rome. Wellcome divorced her in 1916, and she married Maugham the following year, but their marriage was unhappy and ended in divorce. She died in 1955. See Hoare (2004); Fisher (1978).

49. Quoted in Cohen (2006), 159–60.

Chapter 5. An historical exhibition of rare and curious objects

1. Church and Tansey (2007), 105. The firm's net profits fell below £40,000 in only one year between 1906 and 1913. Wellcome's personal finances are impossible to track in detail, but in the ten years from 1905 to 1914 he withdrew from the firm an average of £22,581 per annum. This includes a low of £8,504 in 1905 and a high of £46,843 in 1914, by which time his Sudan excavations had become an enormous financial commitment (Church and Tansey (2007), 280).

2. Early pamphlet, 'Historical Exhibition of Rare and Curious Objects relating to Medicine, Chemistry, Pharmacy and the Allied Sciences', possibly dating to 1905, WA/HMM/PB/Han/1.

3. Printed circulars were specifically directed towards nurses, veterinary surgeons, missionaries, and medics. The earliest circulars were addressed from Snow Hill and recipients included people on Burroughs Wellcome's client lists. See WF/M/GB/01/06.

4. WA/HMM/CO/Ear/1047. See also Symons (1993), 5.

5. H. F. Johnston to the Portman Rooms, 12 January 1904, WF/E/01/01/07. Letters from Thompson to various venues in 1905, WA/HMM/CO/Sub/120.

6. 'Historical Exhibition of Rare and Curious Objects', WA/HMM/PB/Han/1.

7. Wellcome to David Hooper, 6 January 1904, WF/E/01/01/07.

8. 'Historical Exhibition of Rare and Curious Objects', WA/HMM/PB/Han/1.

9. Standard letters were sent to people stationed abroad, see WF/M/GB/01/06.

10. 'Historical Exhibition of Rare and Curious Objects', WA/HMM/PB/Han/1.

11. Wellcome to Friedrich Hoffmann, 27 July 1896, WF/E/01/01/03.

12. Wellcome to David Hooper, 6 January 1904, WF/E/01/01/07.

13. Wellcome to Brunton, 16 January 1904, WF/E/01/01/07.

14. 'Historical Exhibition of Rare and Curious Objects', WA/HMM/PB/Han/1.

15. Wilkinson (2002), 570.

16. Wellcome to Sambon, 12 December 1903, WF/E/01/01/07.

17. Notebook, 'Foreign Purchases, 1904–1910', WA/HMM/FI/Hme/1.

18. Thompson's early letters and reports, WA/HMM/CO/Ear and WA/HMM/RP/Tho/1.

19. 'List of Goods purchased for H. M. E. and stored at C. P.', WA/HMM/FI/Hme/2.

20. See correspondence with James Shoolbred and Co. regarding accounts and insurance for storage facilities, WF/E/01/01/03.

21. WA/HMM/RP/Tho/1.

22. WA/HMM/RP.

23. Haggis (1942), 510.

24. See Thompson reports, 26 March and 7 and 28 May 1907, WA/HMM/RP/Tho/1.

25. Extracted from reports dated 4, 11, and 18 February and 18 and 26 March 1907, and 28 February 1908, WA/HMM/RP/Tho/1.

26. Thompson to Wellcome, 22 December 1908, WA/HMM/RP/Tho/1.

27. Reminiscences of Henry Wellcome, by Mr Warden, WF/M/H/07/04.

28. Thompson to Wellcome, 22 December 1908, WA/HMM/RP/Tho/1.

29. Thompson to Wellcome, 5 January 1909, WA/HMM/RP/Tho/2. See also Wellcome Historical Medical Museum (1913), 110.

30. Wellcome to Thomas Fraser, 16 August 1904, WF/E/01/01/08.

Chapter 6. Excuse me Mr Treve

1. Thompson to Wellcome, 27 January 1899, WA/HSW/CO/Gen/K.19.
2. Haggis (1942), 510. Letters and messages from Wellcome to his Museum staff testify to his personal involvement in the acquisition process, when time and money allowed. See, for example, Harry Stow's staff file, WA/HMM/ST/Lat/A.204, and Harry Port's staff file, WA/HMM/ST/Lat/A.175.
3. Symons (1998), 111.
4. Herrmann (1980), 64 and 70–84.
5. McGregor (1997), 8.
6. Ibid. 22.
7. Herrmann (1999), 343.
8. Allingham (1924), 74 and 83.
9. Herrmann (1980), 92. See also Symons (1998), 120. Osler was consulted during preparations for the opening ceremony of the Wellcome Historical Medical Museum in 1913, and was an early admirer of Wellcome's collection. See Thompson reports, 21 November 1912 and 27 February 1913, WA/HMM/RP/Tho/6 and 7.
10. Freeman and Freeman (1990), 41–2 and 49.
11. Marks (1983), 117–18 and 129.
12. Symons (2004).
13. WA/HMM/ST/Lat/A.28 and A.204.
14. Wellcome to Thompson, May 1918, WA/HMM/RP/Tho/13.
15. Wellcome to a Burroughs Wellcome representative, 29 January 1903, WF/E/01/01/06.
16. Wellcome to Robert Lansing, 7 September 1903, WF/E/01/01/07.
17. See above n. 9. Osler, represented by Quaritch, bid against Wellcome at the sale of Frank Payne's Library at Sotheby's in 1911. Symons (1998), 120.
18. Wellcome's tactics may have been more successful abroad. In the late 1920s, on the second day of the sale of the Pareyn Collection from the Belgian Congo, the Belgian authorities were alarmed to find that every single lot had been bought by two unknown men called Willis and Stowe. Proceedings were suspended while enquiries were made regarding their identity and credit. The replies came back: 'Willis'—Henry Wellcome, 'Stowe'—a porter, and their credit—'unlimited'. Skinner (1984), 40–1.
19. Ettinghausen (1966), 64. See also Symons (1993), 5.
20. Thompson report, 17 April 1907, WA/HMM/RP/Tho/1.
21. Thompson report, 30 November 1908, WA/HMM/RP/Tho/1.
22. No more information about the head has survived.
23. Thompson report, 12 January 1907, WA/HMM/RP/Tho/1.
24. Ibid.

25. Thompson reports, 9 November and 16 December 1908, WA/HMM/RP/Tho/1.
26. Stow, Bourne, and their co-workers received little more than £2 a week before 1920. See WA/HMM/ST/Lat/A.28 and A.204.
27. Purchases from Stevens, Thompson report, 13 November 1909, WA/HMM/RP/Tho/2.
28. These figures were calculated using data compiled from a series of accounting ledgers, WA/HMM/FI/Pur/1–10, that list Museum material acquired at auction houses, primarily in London, between 1907 and 1936. The Museum's accounts are complicated, with many overlapping systems of records, so the numbers here should be seen as a general guide rather than a definitive analysis.
29. Thompson report, 5 January 1909, WA/HMM/RP/Tho/2. At the time of his death, Wellcome's surgical instrument collection numbered some 25,000 items; see Wright (1984), 24.
30. Haggis (1942), 512.
31. Typescript of Wellcome's interview by the Royal Commission on National Museums and Galleries in 1928, WA/HSW/OR/L.1.
32. Ibid. WA/HSW/OR/L.2.
33. Lane Fox [Pitt Rivers] (1868), 143.
34. Lane Fox [Pitt Rivers] (1875b), 24.
35. On the Victorian perception of progress, see Bowler (1989) and Bennett (2004).
36. Skinner (1986).
37. Early pamphlet, 'Historical Exhibition of Rare and Curious Objects relating to Medicine, Chemistry, Pharmacy and the Allied Sciences', probably dating to 1905, WA/HMM/PB/Han/1.
38. Wellcome Historical Medical Museum (1926), 6–7.
39. Skinner (1986), 395. Wellcome (1887), 151–3.
40. Typescript of Wellcome's interview by the Royal Commission on National Museums and Galleries in 1928, WA/HSW/OR/L.2.
41. Lane Fox [Pitt Rivers] (1875a), 302.
42. Lane Fox [Pitt Rivers] (1875b), 41.
43. Lane Fox [Pitt Rivers] (1875c).
44. Wellcome (1912, 1914).
45. 'Sir Henry Wellcome Inventor Of "Tabloids" ', in *The Times*, 27 July 1936.
46. Haggis (1942), 406.
47. Thomas Barlow, quoted in Wellcome Historical Medical Museum (1926), 39.
48. Smith (1989), 51–66.

Chapter 7. Fellow feeling as a collector

1. Davidson correspondence, 1904–11, WA/HMM/CO/Hme/14.
2. Davidson to Wellcome, 15 March 1909, WA/HMM/CO/Hme/14. Thompson to Wellcome, 26 April 1909, WA/HMM/RP/Tho/2.

3. Davidson (1906, 229) wrote, 'The collecting of Bell-Metal Mortars may perhaps be considered rather a deviation from the path of the connoisseur, but as these implements of a byegone [*sic*] age are now becoming rare, some particulars of a collection and also a few sidelights on the history of mortars may be of interest.' See also Hemming (1929).

4. See *The Chemist and Druggist*, 28 June 1913, 64.

5. Davidson to Wellcome, 15 March 1909, WA/HMM/CO/Hme/14.

6. Thompson to Wellcome, 26 April 1909, WA/HMM/RP/Tho/2.

7. Correspondence dated 14 April and 11, 12, 19, and 20 May 1909, WA/HMM/CO/Hme/14.

8. Correspondence dated 22 April, 2 November, and 7 November 1910, WA/HMM/CO/Hme/14.

9. Thompson to Wellcome, 18 and 25 November 1910, WA/HMM/RP/Tho/4.

10. Davidson to Wellcome, 29 June 1911, WA/HMM/CO/Hme/14.

11. Thompson to Wellcome, 21 and 26 April 1909, WA/HMM/RP/Tho/2.

12. Memo to J. Macvie Hill, 11 October 1910, WA/HMM/CO/Hme/14.

13. Thompson to Wellcome, 18 and 25 November 1910, WA/HMM/RP/Tho/4.

14. Quoted in Pearce et al. (2002), 87.

15. Larsen (1996), 363–4.

16. Quoted in Wainwright (1989), 287.

17. Larsen (1996), 361.

18. See Greenhalgh (1988).

19. McGregor (1997), 22.

20. Quoted in Hudson (1975), 63.

21. Hermann (1999), 17–18.

22. Thompson to Wellcome, 4 February 1907, WA/HMM/RP/Tho/1.

23. Thompson to Wellcome, 7 May 1907, WA/HMM/RP/Tho/1.

24. Thompson to Wellcome, 15 April, 4 and 15 May 1925, WA/HMM/RP/Tho/15.

25. Thompson to Wellcome, 18 December 1908, 5 January and 21 April 1909, WA/HMM/CM/Col/37.

26. Thompson to Wellcome, 13 January 1911, WA/HMM/RP/Tho/5.

27. I have been unable to find this letter in the archive, but it is quoted at http://www.dursley-pedersen.net/mp_bio.html in an article, 'Mikael Pedersen of Marbjerg, Denmark' by Finn Wodschow. Given Wodschow's comments, and the writing style, it must have been written by Thompson.

28. Wellcome's notes on Thompson's report, 2 December 1910. WA/HMM/RP/Tho/4.

29. Rhodes James (1994), 271.

30. Thompson to Wellcome, 13 January 1911, WA/HMM/RP/Tho/5.

31. Thompson to Wellcome, 2 December 1910, WA/HMM/RP/Tho/4.

32. Thompson to Wellcome, 13 January 1911, WA/HMM/RP/Tho/5.
33. Thompson to Wellcome, 24 February 1911, WA/HMM/RP/Tho/5.
34. Thompson to Wellcome, 17 March 1911, WA/HMM/RP/Tho/5.
35. Thompson to Paira Mall, 16 June 1911, WA/HMM/CO/Ear/560.
36. The 1895 exhibition was noted in *The Times*, 2 August 1895, and in scholarly journals, including *Science*, 30 August 1895.
37. Sambon (1895).
38. Thompson to Wellcome, 18 November 1910, WA/HMM/RP/Tho/4.
39. Wellcome to Sambon, 15 and 16 January 1904, WA/HMM/Co/Ear/842.
40. The story of the sale was reported to Wellcome by Thompson, 18 November 1910, WA/HMM/RP/Tho/4.
41. Wellcome wrote, for example, on 15 May 1930, 'Special care should be taken of the oriental rugs which I have from time to time loaned to the Museum on special occasions.' WA/HMM/RP/Mal/6.
42. 'An inventory and valuation of the furniture and effects at the Wellcome Historical Medical Museum No. 183 Euston Road, London, N.W.1.' Allsop and Co., WA/HSW/LE/E.10.
43. W. Britchford to J. Symons, 16 August 1985, WA/HSW/PE/C.23.
44. See H. Port reports, WA/HMM/RP/Sta/12; H. Stow staff file, WA/HMM/ST/Lat/A.204; and staff memoranda, WA/HMM/ST/EAR/B.1.
45. Undated memo on cats, WA/HMM/CO/Sai/A.5.
46. Johnston-Saint to Wellcome, 22 August 1935, WA/HMM/RP/Jst/B.24.
47. Wellcome to Mary Curtis Wellcome, March 1894, WA/HSW/FP/E.7.

Chapter 8. The whole of India should be ransacked

1. Wellcome (1880), 820.
2. Typed notes accompanying a print, 'A Bridge over the Guaillabamba, Ecuador', WA/HSW/CO/Ind/B.3.
3. Wellcome to Mary Curtis Wellcome, 8 May 1881, WA/HSW/FP/E.7.
4. See Rhodes James (1994), 145.
5. 'The Pharmaceutical Aviary', in *Chemist and Druggist*, 2 June 1900, 926.
6. Church and Tansey (2007), 87 and 263.
7. Additional reminiscences by E. W. Garnham, Head of the Construction Department, Burroughs Wellcome and Co., 27 October 1947, WF/M/H/07/01.
8. Plans and Wellcome's motor tours 1907–9, WA/HSW/PE/A.14.
9. Conway (1914), 107.
10. Wellcome's motor tours 1907–9, WA/HSW/PR/A.14.
11. Additional reminiscences by Garnham, WF/M/H/07/01.
12. Ibid.

13. Church and Tansey (2007), 460. In later years, Wellcome's business corres-
    pondence either declined or has not survived.
14. Quoted in Marks (1983), 77.
15. Quoted in Rhodes James (1994), 270.
16. Ibid.
17. 'Notes from letter to Dr Power from Dr Hoffmann, of Leipzig', WA/HSW/
    CO/Gen/G.8.
18. Ibid.
19. Wellcome's response to Thompson's report dated 1 May 1918, WA/HMM/RP/
    Tho/13.
20. Wellcome's response to Malcolm's report dated 28 November 1927, WA/
    HMM/RP/Mal/3; Wellcome to Malcolm, 1 August and 6 September 1929,
    WA/HMM/RP/Mal/5.
21. Wellcome to Malcolm, 16 December 1929, WA/HMM/RP/Mal/5.
22. Thompson to Mall, 21 June 1911, WA/HMM/CO/Ear/560.
23. Sambon to Thompson, 20 April 1904, WA/HMM/CO/Ear/842.
24. Ibid. 5 May 1904.
25. Ibid. 23 May 1905.
26. Ibid. 20 April 1904.
27. Mall to Thompson, 26 April and 21 July 1911, WA/HMM/CO/Ear/560. Mall
    was hampered by a local outbreak of plague again in 1918 along the banks of the
    river Beas. He suffered from malaria twice in 1912, and again in 1915 and 1920,
    WA/HMM/CO/Ear/561–7.
28. Mall to Thompson, 21 May 1911, WA/HMM/CO/Ear/560.
29. Mall to Thompson, 17 January 1912, WA/HMM/CO/Ear/561.
30. Thompson to Mall, 12 July and 10 October 1912, 12 August 1915, and 28 August
    1912, WA/HMM/CO/Ear/561 and 563.
31. Thompson to Wellcome, 6 Nov 1909, WA/HMM/RP/Tho/2; and Mall to
    Thompson, 14 November 1912, WA/HMM/CO/Ear/561.
32. See WA/HMM/CO/Ear/842–4.
33. Sambon to Wellcome, 15 March 1909, WA/HMM/CO/Ear/843.
34. George Pearson to Joseph Collett Smith, 6 March 1912, WA/HMM/CO/Ear/844.
35. Thompson's report on a meeting of the pellagra committee, 20 March 1912,
    WA/HMM/CO/Ear/844.
36. Notes by Thompson, July 1911, WA/HMM/CO/Ear/844.
37. Sambon to Thompson, 27 May 1912, WA/HMM/CO/Ear/844.
38. Sambon to Wellcome, 15 March 1909, WA/HMM/CO/Ear/843.
39. Ibid. See also 21 December 1905, WA/HMM/CO/Ear/842.
40. Undated draft letter from Wellcome to Sambon, possibly early 1912, WA/
    HMM/CO/Ear/844.

41. Examples of the standard Burroughs Wellcome and Co. employment contract used for Museum staff can be found in individual staff files under WA/HMM/ST/Lat.

42. Church and Tansey (2007), 83 and 38–9.

43. See above, n. 41.

44. Museums Association, 'Code of Ethics for Museums' (2008), clause 2.15.

45. Wellcome to Brown, 4 January 1899, WF/E/01/01/04. Original emphasis.

46. In contrast, Wellcome encouraged publishing and collaborative research amongst the scientists working in his research laboratories, as will be discussed in Chapter 12.

47. Sambon to Wellcome, 15 September 1909, WA/HMM/CO/Ear/843.

48. 'Notes from letter to Dr Power from Dr Hoffmann, of Leipzig', WA/HSW/CO/Gen/G.8.

49. Thompson to Mall, 2 September 1914, WA/HMM/CO/Ear/563.

50. See Thompson to Mall, 31 October 1913, WA/HMM/CO/Ear/562. In contrast, Mall's monthly purchase allowance was £75; should he need to spend more he had to cable for permission (see WA/HMM/CO/Ear/561). Mall's ethnicity may have counted against him when it came to remuneration. Thompson had drawn on racial stereotypes when first describing Mall's qualifications in a letter to Wellcome in 1909: Mall was, 'a man of highly strung, artistic temperament, and like most Hindoos, something of a mystic' who must be 'carefully handled'. And when it came to discussing his wages, Wellcome warned, 'the cost [of living] to Europeans is much more than to natives [in India]. I think you have allowed him too much for a native', adding, 'of course he must live properly' (29 December 1909 and 20 January 1911, WA/HMM/RP/Tho/2). Sambon had been paid 200 guineas for six months work in 1904 (Wellcome to Sambon, 12 December 1903, WF/E/01/01/07).

51. Mall to Thompson, 27 December 1922, WA/HMM/CO/Ear/568.

52. Thompson to Mall, 10 October 1924, WA/HMM/CO/Ear/568.

Chapter 9. An impossible man to deal with

1. Mall to Thompson, 9 May 1911, and Wellcome's notes to Thompson, WA/HMM/CO/Ear/560.

2. Wellcome to Malcolm, 11 February 1928, WA/HMM/RP/Mal/4.

3. Thompson to Wellcome, 2 March 1919, WA/HMM/RP/Tho/13.

4. Johnston-Saint report, 16 November 1928, WA/HMM/RP/Jst/B.2.

5. Sambon to Thompson, 11 February 1912, WA/HMM/CO/Ear/844.

6. Thompson offered to buy Gorga's 'Roman surgical instruments' and 'interesting bottles, one for ice, others for liquid or aerated liquid' on 23 February 1912.

The objects Gorga said he would loan for Wellcome's Exhibition never arrived (WA/HMM/CM/Col/47).

7. Ibid.

8. Thompson to Wellcome, 28 January 1915, WA/HMM/RP/Tho/9.

9. Gorga to Thompson, 8 November 1915, WA/HMM/CM/Col/47.

10. Thompson's correspondence with Amoruso can be found in WA/HMM/ST/Ear/A.2.

11. Amoruso to Thompson, 17 December 1915 and 20 February 1916, WA/HMM/ST/Ear/A.2.

12. Amoruso remained in Italy after the War. Although he undertook a little informal collecting for Wellcome, he did not return to his post at the Wellcome Historical Medical Museum.

13. Thompson to Wellcome, 16 and 23 February 1919, WA/HMM/RP/Tho/13.

14. Ibid. 23 February and 2 March 1919.

15. Ibid. 2 March 1919.

16. Davidson to Wellcome, 12 and 20 May 1909, WA/HMM/CO/Hme/14.

17. See Pearce (1995), 175–6 and 235–6.

18. Thompson to Wellcome, 13 December 1921, and Wellcome's notes in reply, WA/HMM/RP/Tho/13.

19. Thompson to Wellcome, 14 March 1922, WA/HMM/RP/Tho/14.

20. Sambon to Thompson, January 1922, WA/HMM/CM/Col/47.

21. The American opened negotiations in March 1921 and they had come to an understanding by the end of the year. Gorga to Sambon, 31 December 1921, WA/HMM/CM/Col/47.

22. 'The Edward C. Streeter Collection of Weights and Measures: Cushing/Whitney Medical Library, Yale University', http://www.isasc.org/Streeter/background.htm, retrieved 11 December 2007; 'Leroy Crummer, M.D.', *Bulletin of the Medical Library Association* 22:3 (1934), 169–70; 'Leroy Crummer', *American Heart Journal* 9:3 (1934), 418.

23. Crummer to Thompson, 28 October 1922, and further correspondence, WA/HMM/CO/Alp/165.

24. Wellcome to Thompson, 13 April 1923, and Thompson's reply, 24 April 1923, WA/HMM/RP/Tho/14.

25. Cannon (1941).

26. See WA/HMM/CO/Ear/913 and WA/HMM/CO/Chr/A.95.

27. Thompson to Wellcome, 14 May 1923, WA/HMM/RP/Tho/14.

28. Cushing's library later contributed to the foundation of the Medical Historical Library at Yale, and, along with Streeter's collection of weights and measures, it now forms part of the Harvey Cushing/John Hay Witney Medical Library at the University.

29. Thompson to Wellcome, 14 May 1923, WA/HMM/RP/Tho/14.
30. Ibid. 24 April 1923.
31. Ibid. 12 June 1923, and Wellcome's notes in reply.
32. Ibid. 10 December 1923.
33. Ibid. 9 and 24 January 1924.
34. Ibid. 24 January and 12 February 1924.
35. Robert C. Witt, 'The Nation and its Art Treasures' (1911), quoted in Herrmann (1999), 374.
36. Royal Commission on National Museums and Galleries, Minutes of Evidence (1929), 109, WA/HSW/OR/L.5.
37. Wellcome to Malcolm, 19 August 1927, WA/HMM/RP/Jst/B.1.
38. Wellcome's notes on Malcolm's report dated 3 September 1927, WA/HMM/RP/Mal/3.
39. Malcolm to Wellcome, 15 November 1927, WA/HMM/RP/Mal/3.
40. Ibid. 5 July 1927.
41. Malcolm to Wellcome, 17 April 1928, WA/HMM/RP/Mal/4.
42. Johnston-Saint report, 16 November 1928, WA/HMM/RP/Jst/B.2.
43. Johnston-Saint report, 21 January 1929, WA/HMM/RP/Jst/B.3.
44. Johnston-Saint report, 7 April 1930, WA/HMM/RP/Jst/B.6.
45. Johnston-Saint report, 26 March 1931, WA/HMM/RP/Jst/B.8.
46. Johnston-Saint report, 6 November 1929, WA/HMM/RP/Jst/B.4.
47. Johnston-Saint report, 10 March 1930, WA/HMM/RP/Jst/B.6.
48. Sambon to Thompson, January 1922, WA/HMM/CM/Col/47.
49. Cushing to Thompson, 14 November 1925, WA/HMM/CO/Alp/169.
50. Streeter to Thompson, 25 May 1923, WA/HMM/CO/Chr/A.95. And 14 November 1921, WA/HMM/CO/Ear/931.
51. Streeter to Thompson, 2 March 1921, WA/HMM/CO/Ear/931. Streeter's comments were addressed to Wellcome.
52. Malcolm to Wellcome, 21 March 1927, WA/HMM/RP/Mal/2.

Chapter 10. The finest historical medical museum in the world

1. Royal Commission on National Museums and Galleries, Minutes of Evidence (1929), 106, WA/HSW/OR/L.5. Wellcome also explained in a letter to Fielding H. Garrison that he had been persuaded to open the exhibition on a temporary basis before he was ready, and when the exhibition closed, he had been 'prevailed upon (contrary to my own inclinations and settled plans) to keep the Museum open, permanently' (see Haggis (1942), 538–9). In fact, he announced that the Museum would become a permanent institution at the Opening Ceremony in June 1913.

2. Thompson to Wellcome, 18 February 1910, WA/HMM/RP/Tho/4.

3. 'International Medicine', *The Times*, 4 August 1913, 7.

4. Henry Wellcome, quoted in Wellcome Historical Medical Museum (1926), 45.

5. H. M. Walbrook, 'A Collection of Witchcraft and Science', *The Bazaar*, 5 April 1930, WA/HMM/PR/1. The displays were relatively little changed over the years, and I have drawn on press reports of various dates in this chapter.

6. Successive editions of *The Handbook of the Historical Medical Museum*, first published in 1913 (later the *Guide to the Wellcome Historical Medical Museum*), describe the contents of the rooms, WA/HMM/PB/Han.

7. *Manchester Guardian*, undated press clipping, 1914, WA/HMM/PR/1.

8. *African World*, 28 June 1928, WA/HMM/PR/1.

9. *Daily Chronicle*, 23 October 1926, WA/HMM/RE/B.7.

10. Edward C. Forbes, in *American Druggist*, December 1930, WA/HMM/PR/1.

11. Wellcome Historical Medical Museum (1927), 75.

12. See Thompson to Wellcome, 18 March 1913, WA/HMM/RP/Tho/7.

13. Thompson to Wellcome, 1 May 1913, and Wellcome's comments, WA/HMM/RP/Tho/7.

14. Henry Wellcome, quoted in Wellcome Historical Medical Museum (1926), 46.

15. Royal Commission on National Museums and Galleries, Minutes of Evidence (1929), 104, WA/HSW/OR/L.5.

16. *The Nation*, 23 October 1926, WA/HMM/RE/B.7.

17. *The Amateur Photographer*, 8 April 1931, WA/HMM/PR/1.

18. Typescript translation of 'Foreign Matters', Danish article, WA/HMM/PR/1.

19. *Pearson's Weekly*, 13 December 1930, WA/HMM/PR/1.

20. Walbrook, 'A Collection of Witchcraft and Science'.

21. *Evening Standard*, 30 Jan 1930, WA/HMM/PR/1.

22. Wellcome, quoted in Wellcome Historical Medical Museum (1926), 46.

23. Wellcome Historical Medical Museum (1920), 6.

24. Ibid.

25. Wellcome Historical Medical Museum (1913), 13–4. See Malcolm to Wellcome, 25 May 1926, WA/HMM/RP/Mal/1.

26. Wellcome Historical Medical Museum (1913), 7.

27. Bennett (2004), 72–7.

28. Skinner (1986), 398.

29. Wellcome to Malcolm, 31 August 1926, quoted in Skinner (1986), 399.

30. Hill (2007), 68–9.

31. *The Westminster Gazette*, 25 June 1913, WA/HMM/RE/A.3.

32. *The Evening News*, 7 March 1929, WA/HMM/PR/1.

33. *Journal of the Chartered Society of Massage and Medical Gymnastics*, July 1927, WA/HMM/PR/1.

34. Symons (1993), 13.
35. See WA/HMM/CO/Ear/1048 and 1053.
36. Historical Medical Museum Visitors' Book, 1913–28, WA/HMM/VI/A.2.
37. Royal Commission on National Museums and Galleries, Minutes of Evidence (1929), 107, WA/HSW/OR/L.5. Asa Briggs (1988, 42) notes that the common belief in a 'criminal class' ensured locks were 'among the most important categories of Victorian things'. And many collectors were interested in locks and keys. 'Indeed, some of their critics suggested that they and criminals had certain features in common, notably the desire to possess something not your own and the will to realize it.'
38. Royal Commission on National Museums and Galleries, Minutes of Evidence (1929), 104, WA/HSW/OR/L.5.
39. Wellcome to Malcolm, 28 August 1926, WA/HMM/RP/Mal/1. In an internal memo referring to this point, Mr Linstead, head of the Burroughs Wellcome advertising department, wondered whether Malcolm still felt that the idea of a 'sequence map' should be abandoned, hinting at a point of disagreement between Wellcome and Malcolm.
40. *Evening News*, London, 4 December 1928, WA/HMM/PR/1.
41. Visitor figures for Wellcome's Museum can be found in the general Museum reports from 1918, WA/HMM/RP/HMM/1 and 2. See also Malcolm's review for 1920–7 in his 1927 Annual Report, WA/HMM/RP/Mal/3. For comparison with other museums, see Alberti (2002), 305; Alberti (2007), 377; Flanders (2006), 405; Hill (2005), 126; Kehoe (2004), 505; and Sheets-Pyenson (1986).
42. See WA/HMM/CO/Sub/120, and Thompson to Wellcome, 14 December 1909, WA/HMM/RP/Tho/3 and 19 January 1910, WA/HMM/RP/Tho/4.
43. WA/HMM/CO/Ear/1047.
44. See, for example, Wellcome to Colonel Brereton, early 1921, WA/HMM/RP/Tho/13.
45. Church and Tansey (2007), 432–3. Church and Tansey include a table of annual Library and Museum expenditure, 1919–37. Wellcome spent significantly more on his Museums than his Library during this period, and from 1928 to 1935 the total amount never fell below £28,000 and reached a peak of £72,000.
46. Thompson to Wellcome, 30 May and 25 July 1917, WA/HMM/RP/Tho/10, and 1 November 1923, WA/HMM/RP/Tho/14.
47. In November 1927, Pearson expressed his concern that Museum publications funded by the company were handicapping business publications and advertising (Church and Tansey (2007), 433).
48. Correspondence in WA/HMM/CO/Ear/1046.
49. Correspondence in WA/HMM/CO/Ear/114 and 115. See also Thompson to Wellcome, 18 and 26 March 1907, WA/HMM/RP/Tho/1.

50. There are various references to Burroughs Wellcome representatives buying, picking up, and storing objects for the collection in Thompson's correspondence throughout the 1900s–20s. In December 1911, he referred to the firm's representative in Palestine who had been 'very carefully coached for H[istorical] M[edical] E[xhibition] purposes' and had bought an old midwifery chair in Aleppo, WA/HMM/RP/Tho/5. In January 1918, Wellcome wrote, 'In regard to the firm's representatives negotiating for objects like the turquoise blue bottles at Gloucester, such representatives will need very careful coaching, otherwise they will excite the cupidity on account of BW&Co of the owner, and fancy prices may be demanded' (WA/HMM/RP/Tho/11).

51. Sending Burroughs Wellcome medicine cases in exchange for artefacts cases was routine and is frequently referred to in correspondence from the 1900s to the 1930s. See Knight (2004), chapter 11; Hill (2006), 373–6.

52. See, for example, Mall to Thompson, 9 May 1911, and Thompson's reply, 29 May 1911, WA/HMM/CO/Ear/560.

53. Correspondence in WA/HMM/CO/Ear/114 and 115.

54. W. Britchford to Mr Faulder, 29 April 1975, WA/HSW/PE/C.23.

55. Wellcome to Mr Holmes, December 1903, quoted in Rhodes James (1994), 264.

56. Wellcome to Colonel Brereton, early 1921, WA/HMM/RP/Tho/13.

57. Thompson to Wellcome, 24 January 1924, WA/HMM/RP/Tho/14.

58. Malcolm to Wellcome, 24 September 1926 and 21 March 1927, WA/HMM/RP/Mal/1.

59. Henry Wellcome, quoted in Wellcome Historical Medical Museum (1926), 46.

60. Church and Tansey (2007), 175.

61. Ibid. 180.

62. Ibid. 179, 213, 294, and 302.

63. A. A. Tindall to Wellcome, 4 January 1926, and Wellcome's reply, 4 January 1926, WA/HSW/LE/E.1.

64. Rhodes James (1994), 44.

65. Haggis (1942), 411.

66. Ibid. 341.

67. *Aberdeen Evening Express*, 16 October 1926. WA/HMM/RE/B.7. Other papers, including the *Newcastle Chronicle*, the *Shields Daily Guardian*, and the *Manchester Dispatch*, also ran this article.

Chapter 11. When the whole is complete, it will be an exact facsimile of the original

1. *The Times*, 25 July 1917, 9.

2. Thompson to Wellcome, 30 May and 13 July 1917, WA/HMM/RP/Tho/10.

3. Ibid. 25 July 1917.
4. Ibid.
5. *The Times*, 25 July 1917, 9. See also Waywell (1986), 65. Thompson mentioned Selfridge's intention to house the statues at Highcliffe, 31 August 1917, WA/HMM/RP/Tho/10.
6. *The Times*, 25 July 1917, 9; Waywell (1986), 65.
7. Waywell (1986), 66, 69, 71.
8. Behrman (1952), 117.
9. Nasaw (2001), 295.
10. Swanberg (1961), 430 and 551–2.
11. Morris (1992a); Kidson (1992), 208.
12. Morris (1992b).
13. Schupbach (2003a).
14. Schupbach (1989, 2003a).
15. Principe and DeWitt (2002), 13. For Wellcome's collection of 'Alchemist' paintings, see Schupbach (2003b).
16. Schupbach (1989), 14.
17. Principe and DeWitt (2002), 10.
18. See Sambon to Thompson, 6 April 1906, WA/HMM/CO/Ear/843; 20 April 1904, WA/HMM/CO/Ear/842; and 11 February 1912, WA/HMM/CO/Ear/844. See also Wilkinson (2002).
19. Thompson to Wellcome, 21 June 1910, WA/HMM/RP/Tho/4.
20. Ibid. 16 December 1910.
21. Ibid. 28 January 1910.
22. Ibid. 9 February 1909.
23. Ibid. 12 April 1909.
24. Ibid. 11 January 1910.
25. Ibid.
26. Ibid.
27. Thompson to Wellcome, 30 May 1911, WA/HMM/RP/Tho/5.
28. Letter from William Britchford to Mr Faulder, 19 April 1975, WA/HSW/PE/C.23.
29. Thompson to Wellcome, 28 January 1910, WA/HMM/RP/Tho/4.
30. H. C. Barlow to Malcolm, 6 February 1926, WA/HMM/CO/Chr/D.45.
31. Theodore Gaster to John Symons, 26 December 1981, WA/HMM/ST/Lat/A.4. Armand Lacaille was the Museum's archaeologist from 1928 until his retirement in 1959. See Symons (1993), 21 and 41.
32. Pilbeam (2003), 171–4.
33. Louis Tussaud to Wellcome, 15 March 1897, WA/HSW/CO/Gen/G.19.

34. John Tussaud to Wellcome, 15 September 1897, WA/HSW/CO/Gen/H.19, and Wellcome to John Tussaud, 2 August 1900, WF/E/01/01/05.
35. Victor Tussaud to Wellcome, undated, WA/HSW/CO/Gen/K.19.
36. Pilbeam (2003), 223.
37. Schwartz (1995).
38. Altick (1978).
39. Hill (2005), 111–20.
40. For a parallel discussion of the Wellcome Historical Medical Museum in this context, see Hill (2007), 73–7.
41. Reinarz (2005), 426.
42 Bates (2008).
43. Ibid. 2.
44. Wellcome to E. W. Bligh, 19 July 1913, WA/HMM/CO/Ear/1048.
45. Alberti (2007), 372, 292–3.
46. Royal Commission on National Museums and Galleries, Minutes of Evidence (1929), 107, WA/HSW/OR/L.5. See Chapter 10 for press descriptions. For the irrepressibility of museum visitors see Alberti (2007).
47. Millenson (2001).
48. Haskell and Penny (1981), 122; Connor (1989), 227–8.
49. See Harrod (1985).
50. Quoted in Connor (1989), 214.
51. Thompson to Wellcome, 31 August and 9 October 1917, WA/HMM/RP/Tho/10. The work was done by D. Brucciani and Co. Ltd. See also Waywell (1986), 70.
52. Thompson to Wellcome, 31 August and 9 October 1917, WA/HMM/RP/Tho/10.
53. Wellcome went on to buy a marble Aesculapius, which was exhibited on the staircase in the Wellcome Building, Euston Road, in the early 1930s.
54. Schupbach (1989), 20.
55. Bennett (2004), 76–7, 162–7.

Chapter 12. This is the History of Medicine

1. Typescript notes for Wellcome's evidence to the Museums and Galleries Commission (December 1928), WA/HSW/OR/L.1.
2. Duggan (1981), 29; Wellcome Foundation Ltd (1964). The Museum of Tropical Medicine and Hygiene was renamed the Wellcome Museum of Medical Science in 1924.
3. Members of Wellcome's excavation team in Sudan were refused permission to publish their findings until an official report had been produced. Wellcome also prevented the publication of any chance archaeological discoveries in the

surrounding region in case they fell within his geographical remit, establishing a 'veil of secrecy' around the whole Sudanese enterprise. The excavations were not published until 1949. See Addison (1949), 9; and Thompson to Wellcome, 20 May 1913, WA/HMM/RP/Tho/7.

4. Church and Tansey (2007), 214.

5. Ibid. 201, 288.

6. Ibid. 296, 469.

7. Norman Moore, quoted in Wellcome Historical Medical Museum (1926), 26 and 37.

8. Thomas Barlow, quoted ibid. 39.

9. Symons (1993), 14–16. Between 1920 and 1925, library and museum expenditure hovered at between £3,000 and £5,000 (the Gorga acquisition pushed the total for 1924 up to £12,000). It was not until the late 1920s that Wellcome started spending larger amounts, usually more than £30,000 each year, on his Museum and Library. See Church and Tansey (2007), 432.

10. Barnard to Thompson, 8 March 1919, quoted in Symons (1993), 55 n. 26.

11. Wellcome's secretive attitude is discussed in Chapter 13.

12. Wellcome sometimes referred to Thompson as 'the late Curator' after his resignation.

13. Wellcome to Thompson, 1 December 1911, WA/HMM/RP/Tho/5.

14. Thompson (1912).

15. Thompson (1897, 1898, 1899), and Creswick J. Thompson (1899).

16. Burroughs Wellcome and Co. to Thompson, 18 December 1899, WF/E/03/03.

17. Thompson (1919, 1920, 1921, 1923).

18. My thanks to John Symons for sharing the details of Thompson's resignation. See also Symons (1993), 18.

19. See WA/HMM/RP/Tho/14 and WA/HMM/RP/HMM/1.

20. Symons (1993), 18.

21. Malcolm to Herbert Bolton, 10 October 1925. Uncatalogued papers relating to L. W. G. Malcolm. My thanks to John Symons for showing me these letters.

22. Skinner (1986), 397.

23. Thompson to Wellcome, regarding the Burroughs Wellcome book *Anaesthetics Ancient and Modern*, 4 February 1907. WA/HMM/RP/Tho/1.

24. *Museums Journal* (1946), 174. See also Tuchscherer (1999), 57 and 62–3.

25. Quoted in Skinner (1986), 397.

26. Wellcome to Malcolm, 14 August 1926, WA/HMM/RP/Mal/1.

27. Correspondence between Wellcome and Spielmann, WA/HMM/RP/Mal/6.

28. Wellcome to Malcolm, 14 August 1926, WA/HMM/RP/Mal/1.

29. Malcolm to Wellcome, 3 September 1926, WA/HMM/RP/Mal/1.

30. Ibid. 25 May 1926.

31. Wellcome to Malcolm, 16 December 1929, WA/HMM/RP/Mal/5.
32. Wellcome's notes on Malcolm's report dated 9 January 1930, WA/HMM/RP/Mal/6.
33. Wellcome to Malcolm, 26 January 1930, WA/HMM/RP/Mal/6, and 29 January 1930, WA/HMM/RP/Mal/7. Malcolm to Wellcome 11 February and 8 April 1930, WA/HMM/RP/Mal/7.
34. Malcolm to Wellcome, 21 March 1927, WA/HMM/RP/Mal/2.
35. Keith (1950), 356.
36. Ibid.
37. Keith (1926).
38. Power, quoted in Wellcome Historical Medical Museum (1926), 65.
39. Wellcome to Malcolm, 16 December 1929, WA/HMM/RP/Mal/5.
40. Power, quoted in Wellcome Historical Medical Museum (1926), 65.
41. Underwood (2004). See 'Exhibitions and Functions', in 'W.H.M.M. Records', a bound typescript by A. L. Dean, for Singer's talk on 'Ancient Greek Surgery' at the Museum in 1921.
42. John Symons, personal communication.
43. Johnston-Saint report, 25 February 1927, WA/HMM/RP/Mal/2.
44. Malcolm to Wellcome, 21 March 1927, WA/HMM/RP/Mal/2.
45. Ibid.
46. Ibid.
47. Wellcome explained the limitations at Wigmore Street in a letter to Colonel Brereton in early 1921, WA/HMM/RP/Tho/13. See also Chapter 17.
48. Typescript notes for Wellcome's evidence to the Museums and Galleries Commission, December 1928, WA/HSW/OR/L.1.
49. Wellcome to Malcolm, 4 January 1930, WA/HMM/RP/Mal/6.
50. Wellcome to Malcolm, 29 May 1928, WA/HMM/RP/Mal/4.
51. Haggis (1942).
52. Wellcome's notes on Malcolm's report dated 1 March 1927, WA/HMM/RP/Mal/2.
53. Malcolm to Wellcome, 14 April 1927, WA/HMM/RP/Mal/2.
54. The words are Malcolm's: Malcolm to Wellcome, 29 October 1926, WA/HMM/RP/Mal/1.
55. Wellcome's notes on Malcolm's report dated 3 September 1927, WA/HMM/RP/3.
56. Church and Tansey (2007), 432.
57. Barnard to Thompson, 8 March 1919, quoted in Symons (1993), 55 n. 26.
58. See discussion of Malcolm's tenure in Chapter 13.
59. Wellcome's notes on Malcolm's report dated 21 March 1927, WA/HMM/RP/Mal/2.

Chapter 13. All tied up in knots

1. *Museums Journal* (1946), 174. See also Tuchscherer (1999), 57 and 62–3.
2. Malcolm to Herbert Bolton, 10 October 1925. Uncatalogued papers relating to L. W. G. Malcolm. My thanks to John Symons for showing me these letters.
3. Malcolm to Herbert Bolton, 20 August 1925. See previous note.
4. Malcolm to Wellcome, 25 February and 11 March 1927, WA/HMM/RP/Mal/2.
5. Malcolm to Wellcome, 10 February 1926, WA/HMM/RP/Mal/1.
6. Malcolm to Wellcome, 31 May 1927, WA/HMM/RP/Mal/2, and 9 August 1927, WA/HMM/RP/Mal/3.
7. Malcolm to Wellcome, 3 April 1928, WA/HMM/RP/Mal/4.
8. Malcolm to Wellcome, 22 March 1927, WA/HMM/RP/Mal/2.
9. Malcolm to Wellcome, 16 March and 20 April 1926, WA/HMM/RP/Mal/1.
10. Wellcome to Malcolm, 7 May 1927, WA/HMM/RP/Mal/2.
11. Rhodes James (1994), 22.
12. Wellcome, suffering from exhaustion and on orders to rest, had travelled to Maine in 1886. While there, 'he camped, canoed, hunted and began writing *The Story of Metlakatla*'. The book received a lot of publicity and sold well, but it was biased and got mixed reviews. Wellcome led Duncan's campaign for protection from the US government, organizing meetings, speeches, committees, and fund-raising. He helped Duncan again, financially and politically, in 1916. They remained friends until Duncan's death in 1918. See Murray (1985), and Rhodes James (1994), 146–51 and 333.
13. See Chapter 2.
14. 'List of Goods purchased for H. M. E. and stored at C. P.', WA/HMM/FI/Hme/2.
15. Kehoe (2004), 505.
16. Typescript notes for Wellcome's evidence to the Museums and Galleries Commission, December 1928, WA/HSW/OR/L.1.
17. Ibid.
18. Malcolm to Wellcome, 10 February 1926, WA/HMM/RP/Mal/1.
19. Malcolm to Wellcome, 25 February 1927, WA/HMM/RP/Mal/2.
20. Wellcome's notes on Malcolm's report dated 25 February 1927, WA/HMM/RP/Mal/2.
21. Malcolm to Wellcome, 10 May 1927, WA/HMM/RP/Mal/2.
22. Ibid. 29 March 1927.
23. Ibid. 10 May 1927.
24. Wellcome to Malcolm, 23 May 1927, WA/HMM/RP/Mal/2.
25. Malcolm began working on the Folklore Exhibition in September 1927. See WA/HMM/RP/Mal/3.

26. The Royal Anthropological Institute met at the Museum on 24 May 1927, and the Folk-Lore Society on 12 October 1927 and 19 September 1928. See 'Exhibitions and Functions', in 'W.H.M.M. Records', a bound typescript by A. L. Dean at the Wellcome Library.

27. 'Notes for consideration and discussion in reference to the proposed co-operation between the Royal Anthropological Institute and the Wellcome Historical Medical Museum', WA/HMM/CO/Wel/E.4.

28. See Malcolm to Wellcome, 31 May 1927, WA/HMM/RP/Mal/2.

29. Waldron (2000), 382–6. Malcolm's correspondence with Elliot Smith, WA/HMM/CO/Chr/C.37, D.40 and G.31.

30. Johnston-Saint to Wellcome, 17 June 1927, WA/HMM/RP/Jst/B.1.

31. Wellcome's notes on Malcolm's report dated 25 February 1927, WA/HMM/RP/Mal/2.

32. Wellcome's notes on Malcolm's report dated 1 March 1927, WA/HMM/RP/Mal/2.

33. Wellcome's notes on Malcolm's report dated 3 January 1928, WA/HMM/RP/Mal/4.

34. Wellcome's notes on Malcolm's report dated 3 September 1927, WA/HMM/RP/Mal/3. See discussion in Chapter 12.

35. Malcolm to Wellcome, 25 April 1930, WA/HMM/RP/Mal/7.

36. Wellcome's notes on Malcolm's report dated 11 November 1927, WA/HMM/RP/Mal/3.

37. Between 1927 and 1930, receptions were held for the International Society of Medical Hydrology, the *Association des Anatomistes*, the Royal Anthropological Institute, the African Society, the Folk-Lore Society, the King Edward's Hospital Fund for London, the International Congress of Military Medicine and Pharmacy, the Egypt Exploration Society, and the Psychiatry Section of the Royal Society of Medicine. In 1932 various receptions were held in conjunction with the Centenary Meeting of the British Association for the Advancement of Science, and again the following year for the Centenary of the British Medical Association. See above, n. 26.

38. Muensterberger (1994), 3 and 40–3.

39. Malcolm to Wellcome, 16 August 1926, WA/HMM/RP/Mal/1. Malcolm first commented on the lack of storage space in April 1926 and continued to raise concerns throughout 1927. See Chapter 16.

40. 'Report on Mr. Malcolm's trip to America, November–December 1926', WA/HMM/RP/Mal/1.

41. Reminiscences of Henry Wellcome by Mr Warden, WF/M/H/07/04.

42. Wellcome to Malcolm, 18 March 1927, WA/HMM/RP/Mal/2.

43. Ibid. 7 May 1927.

44. Ibid. 11 March 1927; 3 September 1927, WA/HMM/RP/Mal/3; 11 February 1928, WA/HMM/RP/Mal/4; 1 August, 6 September, and 24 November 1929, WA/HMM/RP/Mal/5.
45. Malcolm wrote, on 11 November 1927, 'it is sometimes impossible to give you all the information and material for which you ask,' adding, by hand, 'as I do not have it', WA/HMM/RP/Mal/3.
46. Malcolm to Wellcome, 22 April 1927, WA/HMM/RP/Mal/2.
47. Malcolm to Wellcome, 1 March 1928, WA/HMM/RP/Mal/4.
48. Ibid. 1 May 1928.
49. Wellcome to Malcolm, 29 November 1927, WA/HMM/RP/Mal/3.
50. Wellcome to Malcolm, 11 February 1928, WA/HMM/RP/Mal/4.
51. Wellcome to Malcolm, 16 December 1929, WA/HMM/RP/Mal/5.
52. Malcolm to Wellcome, 9 January 1930, WA/HMM/RP/Mal/6.
53. Wellcome to Malcolm, 7 February 1930, WA/HMM/RP/Mal/6.
54. Malcolm to Wellcome, 5 March 1930, WA/HMM/RP/Mal/7. Church and Tansey (2007), 432–3.
55. Malcolm to Wellcome, 25 May 1926, WA/HMM/RP/Mal/1.
56. Ibid. 29 October 1926.
57. See discussion in Chapter 16.
58. Symons (1993), 20–1.
59. Joan Braunholtz, 'Some Recollections 1928–32', 29 July 1985, WA/HMM/ST/Lat/A.29.
60. Ibid.
61. Theodore Gaster to John Symons, 26 December 1981, WA/HMM/ST/Lat/A.4.
62. Braunholtz, 'Some Recollections 1928–32'.
63. Johnston-Saint to Beaumont Albany Fetherston-Dilke, WA/HMM/ST/Lat/A.63.
64. Notification of Leaving for Ashley Montague, WA/HMM/ST/Lat/A.4.
65. Theodore Gaster to John Symons, 26 December 1981, WA/HMM/ST/Lat/A.4.
66. Malcolm to Wellcome, 22 October 1929, WA/HMM/RP/Mal/5.
67. Ashley Montagu to John Symons, 2 December 1981, WA/HMM/ST/Lat/A.4.
68. Malcolm to Wellcome, 25 April 1927, WA/HMM/RP/Mal/2.
69. Braunholtz, 'Some Recollections 1928–32'.
70. Malcolm to Wellcome, 29 March 1927, WA/HMM/RP/Mal/2.
71. Ibid. 31 May 1927.
72. Malcolm to Wellcome, 13 December 1927, WA/HMM/RP/Mal/3.
73. Malcolm to Wellcome, 1 May 1928, WA/HMM/RP/Mal/4.
74. Braunholtz, 'Some Recollections 1928–32'.
75. Ibid.

76. Hewitt to Malcolm, 7 July 1926, WA/HMM/RP/Mal/1. Annual Report for the Library, 1927, WA/HMM/RP/Mal/3.
77. Malcolm to Wellcome, 3 September 1926, WA/HMM/RP/Mal/1.
78. Malcolm to Wellcome, 22 April 1927, WA/HMM/RP/Mal/2. Johnston-Saint oversaw the disposal of the building material from the Lister Ward after Wellcome's death. Johnston-Saint, 1943 report, WA/HMM/TR/Eth/A.1.
79. Malcolm to Wellcome, 3 April 1928, WA/HMM/RP/Mal/4.

Chapter 14. We need very complete collections of all their fabrications

1. Malcolm to Wellcome, 10 May 1927, WA/HMM/RP/Mal/2.
2. See Kuklick (1997); Gosden and Larson (2007).
3. This new generation was led by B. Malinowski, A. R. Radcliffe-Brown, and E. E. Evans-Pritchard.
4. Young (2004); Stocking (1992), 40–59.
5. Typescript of Wellcome's interview by the Royal Commission on National Museums and Galleries in 1928, WA/HSW/OR/L.2.
6. See Ikram (2000); Hopkins (2003). Blackman's papers are kept in Liverpool University Library, Special Collections and Archives. *The Fellahin of Upper Egypt* remains a standard work to this day, admired for the quality of the research and its engaging style.
7. Malcolm to Wellcome, 24 January 1927, WA/HMM/RP/Mal/2.
8. Blackman to Wellcome, 12 November 1926, WA/HMM/CM/Col/12.
9. Wellcome's comments on Malcolm's report dated 24 January 1927, WA/HMM/RP/Mal/2.
10. Ibid. 4 February 1927. Blackman to Malcolm, 6 February 1927, WA/HMM/CM/Col/12.
11. For example, Jeffreys and Clarke, who are discussed later in this chapter.
12. Details of Blackman's financial circumstances, and her efforts to find full-time employment, can be found in her family correspondence, kept in Liverpool University Library, Special Collections and Archives.
13. Blackman to Malcolm, 14 March 1927, WA/HMM/CM/Col/12.
14. Ibid. 20 July 1927. Details of the collection can be found in the same file.
15. Ibid. 20 June 1927.
16. Malcolm to Blackman, 12 October 1927, WA/HMM/CM/Col/12.
17. Blackman to Malcolm, 19 November 1927, WA/HMM/CM/Col/12.
18. Malcolm to Wellcome, 11 November 1927, WA/HMM/RP/Mal/3.
19. Malcolm to A. M. Blackman, 22 December 1927, WA/HMM/CM/Col/12.
20. Malcolm to Wellcome, 10 January 1928, WA/HMM/RP/Mal/4.

21. Wellcome to Malcolm, 5 January 1928, WA/HMM/RP/Mal/4. See also Blackman's correspondence with Malcolm, January 1928, WA/HMM/CM/Col/12.

22. Blackman to Malcolm, 9 February 1928, WA/HMM/CM/Col/12.

23. Ibid. 16 January 1928.

24. Ibid. 17 July 1928.

25. Malcolm to Wellcome, 23 July 1929, WA/HMM/RP/Mal/5.

26. Blackman to Malcolm, 31 May 1929, WA/HMM/CM/Col/12.

27. Ibid. 21 July 1929.

28. Blackman first mentioned buying musical instruments and costumes in 1929, but Wellcome refused her offers in 1933, WA/HMM/CM/Col/12.

29. See WA/HMM/ST/Lat/A.123, which includes Malcolm's testimonial for Kemp, 5 January 1931.

30. See Malcolm's report for 9 January, Wellcome's cable dated 23 January, WA/HMM/RP/Mal/6. See also WA/HMM/RP/Kem/1.

31. Malcolm to Kemp, 28 March 1930, WA/HMM/RP/Kem/1.

32. Ibid. 3 March 1930.

33. Ibid. 28 March 1930.

34. Kemp to Malcolm, 29 March 1930, WA/HMM/RP/Kem/1.

35. Kemp report, 24–9 March 1930, WA/HMM/RP/Kem/1.

36. Malcolm to Kemp, 8 April 1930, WA/HMM/RP/Kem/1.

37. Kemp to Malcolm, 11 April 1930, and Malcolm's comments in reply, WA/HMM/RP/Kem/1.

38. Malcolm's comments on Kemp's report dated 12 May 1930, WA/HMM/RP/Kem/1.

39. Kemp to Malcolm, 13 April 1930, WA/HMM/RP/Kem/1.

40. See Kemp's reports, WA/HMM/RP/Kem/1.

41. Kemp to Malcolm, 1 May 1930, WA/HMM/RP/Kem/1.

42. Kemp to Malcolm, 13 April 1930, and Malcolm's comments in reply, WA/HMM/RP/Kem/1.

43. Kemp to Dean, 1 May 1930, WA/HMM/RP/Kem/1.

44. Malcolm to Wellcome, 9 August 1929, WA/HMM/RP/Mal/5.

45. Wellcome to Malcolm, 6 September 1929, WA/HMM/RP/Mal/5.

46. Wellcome cable to Malcolm, 18 August 1929, WA/HMM/RP/Mal/5.

47. Malcolm to Wellcome, 27 August 1929, WA/HMM/RP/Mal/5.

48. See WA/HMM/CO/Alp/137. Clarke to Malcolm, 12 April 1930, WA/HMM/CO/Alp/137. Wellcome had received an honorary doctorate (LLD) from Edinburgh University in 1928.

49. Clarke to Malcolm, 3 December 1929, WA/HMM/CO/Alp/137.

50. Malcolm to Clarke, 2 January 1930, WA/HMM/CO/Alp/137.

51. 'Statement of a/c with Dr Wellcome's Historical Research Museum', December 1929, WA/HMM/CO/Alp/137.

52. Clarke to Malcolm, 29 April 1930, WA/HMM/CO/Alp/137.
53. Malcolm to Wellcome, 4 March 1930, WA/HMM/RP/Mal/7.
54. Ibid. 8 April 1930.
55. See Malcolm to Wellcome, 27 May 1930, WA/HMM/RP/Mal/6.
56. Wellcome's comments on Malcolm's report dated 9 January 1930, WA/HMM/RP/Mal/6.
57. Ibid. 13 May 1930.
58. As quoted in Malcolm to Clarke, 2 January 1930, WA/HMM/CO/Alp/137.
59. Jeffreys and Malcolm met to discuss his collecting venture in February 1926 (see Jeffreys to Malcolm, 6 March 1926, WA/HMM/RP/Mal/1). In May, Jeffreys checked the accuracy of some of the Nigerian displays in the Museum (see Malcolm to Wellcome, 25 May 1926, WA/HMM/RP/Mal/1).
60. Jeffreys to Malcolm, 11 April 1926, WA/HMM/CO/Chr/C.14.
61. Malcolm to Jeffreys, 12 April 1926, WA/HMM/CO/Chr/C.14.
62. Jeffreys to Johnston-Saint, 9 April 1938, and internal memo by Dean, 18 January 1939, WA/HMM/CO/Chr/J.110.
63. Internal memo by Dean, 18 January 1939, WA/HMM/CO/Chr/J.110.
64. Ibid.
65. See for example, Jeffreys to Malcolm, 26 September and 14 November 1932, WA/HMM/CO/Chr/J.110.
66. Jeffreys to Malcolm, 15 January 1932, WA/HMM/CO/Chr/J.110.
67. See Jeffreys to Dean, 26 May 1935, WA/HMM/CM/Lis/14. Jeffrey's initial agreement stipulated that 'In consideration of my agreeing to purchase, pack, ship, etc. such material the Museum would allow me to have prints and or slides of any of the material secured by me. The copyright of such prints and slides to remain with the Museum. Any proceeds received by me through the publication or exhibition of such prints or slides to be my personal property' (Jeffreys, 28 January 1939, WA/HMM/CO/Chr/J.110).
68. See Jeffreys to Malcolm, 30 March 1932, WA/HMM/CO/Chr/J.110.
69. See Malcolm to Jeffreys, 5 March 1932, and Jeffreys, 31 January and 9 June 1932, WA/HMM/CO/Chr/J.110.
70. See Jeffreys to Johnston-Saint, 4 September 1936, WA/HMM/CO/Chr/J.110.
71. Ibid. 4 November 1936, WA/HMM/CM/Col/58.
72. Ibid. 4 September 1936, WA/HMM/CO/Chr/J.110.
73. Malcolm to Wellcome, 3 May 1932, WA/HMM/RP/Mal/8.
74. Internal memo on the Jeffreys Collection, WA/HMM/CM/Col/58.
75. Notes by Jeffreys, 28 January 1939, WA/HMM/CO/Chr/J.110. The Jeffreys Collection and the Blackman Collection were transferred to the Pitt Rivers Museum after Wellcome's death. A portion of the Blackman Collection went to the British Museum.

76. Ikram (2000).

77. Blackman to her sister, Elsie, 18 February 1923, D.84/1/34, Liverpool University Library, Special Collections and Archives.

78. See Coombes (1994).

79. See Colls and Dodd (1986), Kumar (2003), Samuel (1998).

80. Wellcome to Malcolm, 6 September 1929, WA/HMM/RP/Mal/5.

81. Report on the resignation of Joan Braunholtz (née Raymont), WA/HMM/ST/Lat/A.29. Borer's resignation is detailed in WA/HMM/ST/Lat/A.26.

82. Boisseau (2004), 88–91.

83. Rhodes James (1994), 133–7 and 178–83.

84. Emeljanow (2004).

85. Rhodes James (1994), 98.

86. Joan Braunholtz, 'Some Recollections 1928–32', 29 July 1985, WA/HMM/ST/Lat/A.29.

87. Haggis (1942), 590.

88. Report on Braunholtz's resignation by Malcolm, 19 November 1932, WA/HMM/ST/Lat/A.29.

89. Blackman to Wellcome, 14 November 1931, WA/HMM/CM/Col/12.

90. Malcolm to Blackman, 2 November 1931, WA/HMM/CM/Col/12.

91. Ibid. 30 August 1932.

Chapter 15. This International Historical Museum

1. The most Blackman was given by Wellcome for a single field season was £250 (WA/HMM/CM/Col/12). Johnston-Saint rarely spent more than this in one transaction, and never without prior agreement from Wellcome, but it did happen. In September 1930 he bought ninety-nine letters by Madame de Maintenant, from the Parisian dealer Charavay, for £390 (WA/HMM/RP/Jst/B.7). The following February, again in Paris, he acquired a collection of Pasteur's letters for £320, together with a further miscellaneous collection of letters for £124, from the dealer Degrange (WA/HMM/RP/Jst/B.8). Most of Johnston-Saint's purchases cost less than £10, but he occasionally spent £40 or £50 in a single transaction.

2. See WA/HMM/RP/Jst/B.1, B.3, and B.6, and a letter from Johnston-Saint to Malcolm, 21 December 1931, WA/HMM/ST/Lat/A.115.

3. Johnston-Saint met with the King more than once by chance—once in Cairo in 1932, when he found 'that the King of Spain with his suite was having tea at the hotel' and they spoke about the Museum (WA/HMM/RP/Jst/B.10), and, on another occasion they were on the same boat from Naples, the King was bound for Khartoum and Johnston-Saint was on his way to Bombay (WA/HMM/RP/Jst/B.24). The King was interested in the Museum's work, and had visited in

1931. Johnston-Saint's visit to the Sicilian village in February 1929 is discussed later in this chapter.

4. Peter Johnston-Saint's curriculum vitae, WA/HMM/ST/Lat/A.115.

5. Symons (1993), 19. See also Johnston-Saint reports, WA/HMM/RP/Jst/B.1.

6. Johnston-Saint report, 12 July 1927, WA/HMM/RP/Jst/B.1.

7. Malcolm to Wellcome, 25 May 1926, WA/HMM/RP/Mal/1.

8. Ibid. 12 May and 8 June 1926. 'Report of the Result of Captain Johnston-Saint's visit to Glasgow re. Lister Material. 18 May 1926', WA/HMM/RP/Jst/B.1.

9. Malcolm to Wellcome, 8 June 1926, WA/HMM/RP/Mal/1.

10. Ibid. 15 June 1926.

11. Wellcome to Malcolm, 14 August 1926, WA/HMM/RP/Mal/1.

12. 'Johnston-Saint's visit to Paris 17th–27th May 1927', WA/HMM/RP/Jst/B.1.

13. Wellcome to Malcolm, 11 June 1927, WA/HMM/RP/Jst/B.1.

14. Wellcome to Pearson, 19 August 1927, WA/HMM/RP/Jst/B.1.

15. Ibid.

16. Ibid.

17. See discussion in Chapter 9, and WA/HMM/RP/Mal/2.

18. Malcolm to Wellcome, 29 April 1927, WA/HMM/RP/Mal/2.

19. Ibid. 3 January 1928, WA/HMM/RP/Mal/4.

20. Johnston-Saint report, 23 June 1927, WA/HMM/RP/Jst/B.1.

21. Wellcome to Pearson, 19 August 1927, WA/HMM/RP/Jst/B.1.

22. Underlined by Wellcome; ibid.

23. Ibid.

24. Johnston-Saint report, 23 June 1927, WA/HMM/RP/Jst/B.1.

25. Johnston-Saint reports, 4, 7, and 22 February 1929, WA/HMM/RP/Jst/B.3; and 25 October 1929, WA/HMM/RP/Jst/B.4.

26. For example, Johnston-Saint reports, 30 January, 13 February, 25 March, 14 June 1929, WA/HMM/RP/Jst/B.3 and B.4.

27. There are numerous examples of Johnston-Saint acquiring bottles of water 'which can be added to our collection of waters from other sources' (1 February 1929, WA/HMM/RP/Jst/B.1), recorded throughout his reports. The 'Arabian drug shop' was bought for £100 on 19 January 1932, WA/HMM/RP/Jst/B.10.

28. Johnston-Saint report, 30 July 1929, WA/HMM/RP/Jst/B.4.

29. Ibid. 6 February 1929, WA/HMM/RP/Jst/B.3.

30. Ibid. 10 February 1934, WA/HMM/RP/Jst/B.17.

31. Ibid. 1 March 1928, WA/HMM/RP/Jst/B.2.

32. Ibid. 5 February 1929, WA/HMM/RP/Jst/B.3.

33. Ibid. 7 December 1927, WA/HMM/RP/Jst/B.1.

34. Ibid. 23 November 1926. Thompson had also been in touch with Nachet in July 1920 and discussed exchanging or selling some microscopes with him, but they did not reach an agreement (WA/HMM/CM/Col/72).

35. Johnston-Saint report, 11 June 1927, WA/HMM/RP/Jst/B.1.
36. Ibid. 8 October 1927.
37. 'General Report on Johnston-Saint tour 5 Oct–13 Dec 1927', WA/HMM/RP/Jst/B.1.
38. Quoted in Malcolm to Wellcome, 10 October 1927, WA/HMM/RP/Mal/3.
39. Wellcome to Pearson, 19 August 1927, WA/HMM/RP/Jst/B.1.
40. Johnston-Saint report, 28 August 1929, WA/HMM/RP/Jst/B.4.
41. Ibid. 5 December 1927, 'General Report on Johnston-Saint tour 5 Oct–13 Dec 1927', WA/HMM/RP/Jst/B.1; and Johnston-Saint report 20 October 1928, WA/HMM/RP/Jst/B.2. See also WA/HMM/CM/Col/72.
42. Johnston-Saint reports, 21 January and 20 October 1928, and Wellcome's comments on them, WA/HMM/RP/Jst/B.2.
43. Wellcome's comments on Johnston-Saint's report dated 6 June 1929, WA/HMM/RP/Jst/B.4.
44. Wellcome to Nachet, 8 October 1928, WA/HMM/CM/Col/72.
45. Johnston-Saint report, 20 April 1930, WA/HMM/RP/Jst/B.6.
46. See cable from Wellcome to Malcolm, 12 April 1930, WA/HMM/CM/Col/72; and cable from Malcolm to Johnston-Saint, 14 April 1930, WA/HMM/RP/Jst/B.6.
47. Nachet's widow, whom Johnston-Saint had hoped to see, was not in Paris at the time. Johnston-Saint report, 28 and 30 April 1930, WA/HMM/RP/Jst/B.6.
48. Correspondence between Johnston-Saint and Aicard, May to August 1930, WA/HMM/CM/Col/72.
49. See Reed (1986), 19.
50. WA/HMM/RP/Mal/4.
51. See Symons (1993), 23.
52. A. B. Inglis, reminiscences, 27 November 1980, WA/HSW/PR/C.23.

Chapter 16. Shelve it

1. Notes by A. W. J. Haggis of a conversation with George Pearson, 12 December 1940, quoted in Rhodes James (1994), 357.
2. Malcolm to Wellcome, and Wellcome's notes in reply, 21 March 1927, as discussed in Chapter 12, WA/HMM/RP/Mal/2.
3. F. N. L. Poynter, report to the Trustees, 1964, quoted in Rhodes James (1994), 365.
4. Letter from William Britchford to Mr Faulder, 19 April 1975, WA/HSW/PE/C.23.
5. Leslie Matthews, *Wellcome Foundation News*, 1973, quoted in Rhodes James (1994), 355. In amongst the furniture moved from Wellcome's home after his death were ten butler's trays and stands. See WA/HMM/CO/Sai/A.34.

6. Letter from William Britchford to Mr Faulder, 19 April 1975, WA/HSW/PE/C.23.

7. Notes by A. W. J. Haggis of a conversation with George Pearson, 12 December 1940, quoted in Rhodes James (1994), 357.

8. Thompson to Wellcome, 13 December 1921, WA/HMM/RP/Tho/13.

9. Malcolm to Higginson, 3 July 1926, WA/HMM/ST/Lat/A.102.

10. Stanmore reports, 18 September 1926, WA/HMM/CO/Chr/D.45.

11. Malcolm to Wellcome, 11 November and 13 December 1927, WA/HMM/RP/Mal/3.

12. Malcolm to Wellcome, 20 April 1926, WA/HMM/RP/Mal/1.

13. Leslie Matthews, *Wellcome Foundation News*, 1973, quoted in Rhodes James (1994), 356.

14. Malcolm to Wellcome, 5 July 1927, WA/HMM/RP/Mal/3.

15. See Wellcome to Malcolm, 10 June 1927, WA/HMM/RP/Mal/2, and Malcolm to Wellcome, 5 July and 3 September 1927, WA/HMM/RP/Mal/3, and 3 April 1928, WA/HMM/RP/Mal/4.

16. Wellcome to Malcolm, 10 June 1927, WA/HMM/RP/Mal/2.

17. Malcolm to Wellcome, 5 July 1927, WA/HMM/RP/Mal/3.

18. Ibid. 9 August 1927.

19. Malcolm to Wellcome, and Wellcome's reply, 5 August 1927, WA/HMM/RP/Mal/3.

20. Wellcome to Malcolm, 14 August 1927, WA/HMM/RP/Mal/3.

21. Malcolm first viewed the Willesden site in August and decided upon it in October, WA/HMM/RP/Mal/3.

22. Malcolm to Wellcome, 8 October 1927, WA/HMM/RP/Mal/3.

23. Malcolm took possession of 9–13 Hythe Road in January 1928. Alterations took place in February, and the first material was transferred in March. By April, staff were 'unloading Crystal Palace at a rate of two wagon loads a day', and by early May, Weybridge, 4 Stratford Mews, and Crystal Palace had all been cleared. The building allocated to the Library had to be re-roofed, in October 1929, but by November most of the staff were organizing the collection at Willesden (WA/HMM/RP/Mal/4 and 5).

24. Malcolm to Wellcome, 8 October 1927, WA/HMM/RP/Mal/3.

25. See Joan Braunholtz, 'Some Recollections 1928–32', 29 July 1985, WA/HMM/ST/Lat/A.29, and WA/HSE/LE/E.14.

26. Lambourne report, 13 December 1928, WA/HMM/ST/Lat/A.131.

27. 'Valuation of certain furniture and effects at the Wellcome Foundation Store, 9/13 Hythe Road, Willesden, N.W.10.', WA/HSW/LE/E.14.

28. Port reports, 1929–1940, WA/HMM/RP/Sta/12.

29. Braunholtz, 'Some Recollections 1928–32'. Original emphasis.

30. Ibid.
31. Port reports, 1929–1940, WA/HMM/RP/Sta/12.
32. Loose lists of Wellcome's purchases, WA/HMM/CM/Lis/2.
33. Theodore Gaster to John Symons, 26 December 1981, WA/HMM/ST/Lat/A.4.
34. Letter from William Britchford to Mr Faulder, 19 April 1975, WA/HSW/PE/C.23.
35. See Rhodes James (1994), 171. Wellcome repeatedly voiced concerns about fireproofing during the search for a replacement store in late 1927 and 1928 (WA/HMM/RP/Mal/4).
36. Letter from William Britchford to Mr Faulder, 19 April 1975, WA/HSW/PE/C.23.
37. Wellcome to Malcolm, 15 May 1930, WA/HMM/RP/Mal/6.
38. Haggis (1942), 584–5.
39. Port report, October 1932, WA/HMM/RP/Sta/12.
40. Sotheby to Webb, 22 April 1929, WA/HMM/CO/Chr/F.33. See also, for example, letters dated January and February 1929 in the same file, and letters dated June 1926 in WA/HMM/CO/Chr/C.37.
41. See Pearce (1995), 243 and 250.
42. Van Beek (1990), 33. See also Hendon (2000).
43. Letter from William Britchford to Mr Faulder, 19 April 1975, WA/HSW/PE/C.23. Wellcome was knighted by George V on 26 February 1932.
44. See Gosden and Larson (2007).
45. Keith (1926).
46. Wellcome to J. Ferreira, 6 September 1922, HSW/CO/Ind/A.2.
47. Malcolm to Wellcome, 1 March 1927, WA/HMM/RP/Mal/2.

Chapter 17. Ingrained habits of cautiousness

1. Johnston-Saint to Wellcome, 8 November 1935, WA/HMM/RP/Jst/B.24.
2. Wellcome to Malcolm, 7 May 1927, WA/HMM/RP/Mal/2, quoted in Chapter 13, n. 10.
3. Sona Rosa Burstein to Beatrice Blackwood, 6 February 1936. Pitt Rivers Museum manuscript collections, Beatrice Blackwood papers, uncatalogued material 'Music'.
4. Johnston-Saint to Jean Robertson, 16 December 1935, WA/HMM/ST/Lat/A.186.
5. Burstein to Blackwood, 6 February 1936.
6. Marjorie Rainsford-Hannay to Malcolm, 27 September 1934, WA/HMM/ST/Lat/A.96.
7. '1st New York Consignment', 30 August 1923, WA/HMM/CM/Lis/3.
8. See Port reports, 1929–40, WA/HMM/RP/Sta/12, and discussion in Chapter 16.
9. 'Sahara Collection', 1925, WA/HMM/CM/Lis/3.
10. Wellcome to Colonel Brereton, early 1921, WA/HMM/RP/Tho/13.

11. Malcolm to Wellcome, and Wellcome's comments, 9 January 1930, WA/HMM/RP/Mal/6.

12. See typescript of Wellcome's interview by the Royal Commission on National Museums and Galleries in 1928, WA/HSW/OR/L.1.

13. Malcolm to Wellcome, 1 March 1928, WA/HMM/RP/Mal/4.

14. Wellcome to Malcolm, 6 February 1930, WA/HMM/RP/Mal/6.

15. Malcolm to Wellcome, 23 July and 4 October 1929, WA/HMM/RP/Mal/5.

16. Malcolm to Wellcome, 4 October 1929, WA/HMM/RP/Mal/5.

17. Ibid. 19 November 1929.

18. Malcolm to Wellcome, and Wellcome's comments, 9 January 1930, WA/HMM/RP/Mal/6.

19. Malcolm to Wellcome, 25 February 1930, WA/HMM/RP/Mal/7. Given Malcolm's earlier plans to establish the Museum as a centre for teaching and scholarship, and his attempt to reach a formal arrangement with Fellows of the Royal Anthropological Institute, these plans must have been attractive to him.

20. Symons (1993), 22 and 25. See also Church and Tansey (2007), 290–1.

21. Symons (1993), 26.

22. 'Sir Henry Wellcome Inventor of "Tabloids" ', *The Times*, 27 July 1936.

23. Wenyon (1936), 234.

24. Howard Spring, in the *Evening Standard*, 5 August 1932, WA/HMM/PR/1.

25. *Edinburgh Evening News*, 25 October 1932, WA/HMM/PR/1.

26. Malcolm to Wellcome, 26 May 1933, WA/HMM/RP/Mal/9. Plans for a 'Prehistoric Hall', to precede the Hall of Primitive Medicine, had begun in 1929, while the Museum was still at Wigmore Street. The room was designed to illustrate the geological periods before life on earth, the evolution of life and disease, and the development of man through prehistoric times. The displays were to chart 'the many quaint imaginary conceptions of the various peoples of the world' regarding chaos and creation (Wellcome to Malcolm, 30 July 1929, WA/HMM/RP/Mal/5). The Prehistoric Room would also show that 'directly life appeared, disease made its appearance also', and both Wellcome and Malcolm thought it would be 'the most progressive exhibition of this kind which has ever been attempted' (Malcolm to Wellcome, 9 August and 3 December 1929, WA/HMM/RP/Mal/5).

27. Wellcome to Malcolm, 4 July 1933, quoted in Turner (1980), 55. The original letter has since been lost.

28. Wellcome to Fielding H. Garrison, quoted in Haggis (1942), 539.

29. Wenyon (1936), 234.

30. Borer to Wellcome, 22 July 1935, WA/HMM/ST/Lat/A.26. Borer had to resign on marriage, see Chapter 14.

31. Malcolm to Wellcome, 17 June 1930, WA/HMM/RP/Mal/7.
32. See Rhodes James (1994), 357, 368–9.
33. Haggis (1942), 587.
34. Malcolm to Wellcome, 9 August 1929, WA/HMM/RP/Mal/5.
35. Burstein to Blackwood, 6 February 1936.
36. Johnston-Saint to Wellcome, 10 July 1934, WA/HMM/RP/Jst/B.24.
37. Johnston-Saint to Rainsford-Hannay, 12 November 1935, WA/HMM/ST/Lat/A.96.
38. Johnston-Saint to Wellcome, 25 October 1935, and see other Johnston-Saint reports for 1935, WA/HMM/RP/Jst/B.24.
39. Johnston-Saint to Wellcome, 8 August 1935, WA/HMM/RP/Jst/B.24.
40. Ibid. 6 December 1935.
41. Ibid.
42. Ibid. 15 April 1936.
43. Ibid. 25 October 1935.
44. Ibid. 8 November 1935.
45. Wellcome Foundation Ltd (1964), 5–6. Johnston-Saint to Wellcome, 18 October 1935, WA/HMM/RP/Jst/B.24.
46. Johnston-Saint to Wellcome, 18 October 1935, WA/HMM/RP/Jst/B.24.
47. Ibid. 24 January 1936.
48. Symons (1993), 28. Johnston-Saint did organize an exhibition of Museum material for the 10th International Congress of the History of Medicine in Madrid in 1935.
49. Reminiscences of Henry Wellcome, by Mr Warden, WF/M/H/07/04.
50. Notes by A. W. J. Haggis of a conversation with George Pearson, 12 December 1940, quoted in Rhodes James (1994), 357.
51. Hendon (2000), 49.
52. Rhodes James (1994), 369–70.
53. Letter from William Britchford to Mr Faulder, 19 April 1975, WA/HSW/PE/C.23, quoted in Chapter 16.
54. Ibid. quoted in Chapter 1.
55. A. L. Dean to Stow, Comins, and Port, August 1936, WA/HMM/ST/Lat/A.204, A.43 and A.175.

Chapter 18. Sir Henry Wellcome is dead

1. See Symons (1993), 28–31.
2. See Church and Tansey (2007), 453–74, 484–90; Hall and Bembridge (1986); Rhodes James (1994), 371–85.
3. Last Will and Testament, 29 February 1932, WA/HSW/LE/E.2; 'Memorandum of my policy and aims for the guidance and assistance of my Trustees', PP/WDP/G/2/2.

4. Symons (1993), 28.

5. Johnston-Saint to Jeffreys, 3 March 1938, WA/HMM/CO/Chr/J.110.

6. Ibid. 11 May 1938.

7. WA/HMM/CO/Sai/A.34.

8. 'Valuation and Sale of Material', WA/HMM/CO/Sub/137.

9. Hall and Bembridge (1986), 49.

10. Symons (1993), 32.

11. Percy Gamben, 28 July 1975, WF/M/H/07/02.

12. Symons (1993), 32–6.

13. J. F. Fulton, quoted ibid. 37.

14. Harry Port, head of Wellcome's stores, also retired in 1947.

15. Hall and Bembridge (1986), 33.

16. Blackmore (1995), 34.

17. Ibid. 38.

18. Typescript of Wellcome's interview by the Royal Commission on National Museums and Galleries in 1928, WA/HSW/OR/L.1.

19. For details of the Collection's dispersal, see Russell (1986).

20. For details of the UCLA transfer see Hill (2006b).

21. Bennett (1997), 30.

22. Pickstone (1994), 131; original emphasis.

23. Boylan (1999), 51; and Reinarz (2005), 435.

24. Boylan (1999), 51; and Mosley (2007), 290–1.

25. Bennett (1997), 30.

26. Mandelbaum (1953), 756.

27. Boylan (1999), 52.

28. Typescript of Wellcome's interview by the Royal Commission on National Museums and Galleries in 1928, WA/HSW/OR/L.1.

29. Wright (1984), 24.

30. Symons (1993), 42 and 44–50.

31. http://www.wellcomecollection.org/WTD027247.htm, accessed April 2008.

32. Elsner and Cardinal (1994), 6.

33. See n. 2.

34. Hall and Bembridge (1986), 17.

Chapter 19. Honour to whom honour is due

1. Clifford (1978), 43.

2. Pearce (1995), 39 and 111.

3. Leaflet, 'Historical Exhibition of Rare and Curious Objects relating to Medicine, Chemistry, Pharmacy and the Allied Sciences to be held in London, 1913', WA/HMM/PB/Han/5.

4. Early pamphlet, 'Historical Exhibition of Rare and Curious Objects relating to Medicine, Chemistry, Pharmacy and the Allied Sciences', probably dating to 1905, WA/HMM/PB/Han/1.

5. Much has been written by anthropologists regarding the formative role objects play in social life and identity construction. See, for example, Gell (1998), Hoskins (1998), Latour (1993), LiPuma (2000).

6. For the relationship between collector and collection, see O'Hanlon (1993), Schindlbeck (1993), O'Hanlon and Welsch (2000), Gosden and Knowles (2001).

7. F. N. L. Poynter, report to the Trustees, 1964, quoted in Rhodes James (1994), 365.

8. Johnston-Saint to Pearson, 30 July 1936, WA/HMM/CO/Sai/A.102.

BIBLIOGRAPHY

Addison, F., *The Wellcome Excavations in the Sudan*, vol. 1 (Oxford: Oxford University Press, 1949).

Alberti, S. J. M. M., 'Placing Nature: Natural History Collections and Their Owners In Nineteenth Century Provincial England', *British Journal for the History of Science*, 35 (2002), 219–311.

—— 'The Museum Affect: Visiting Collections of Anatomy and Natural History', in A. Fyfe and B. Lightman (eds), *Science in the Marketplace: Nineteenth-Century Sites and Experiences* (London: Harvard University Press, 1978).

Allan, N. (ed.), *Pearls of the Orient: Asian Treasures of the Wellcome Library* (London: Serindia Publications, 2003).

Allingham, E. G., *The Romance of the Rostrum* (London: H. F. and G. Witherby, 1924).

Altick, R. D., *The Shows of London* (London: Harvard University Press, 1978).

Arnold, K. and D. Olsen (eds), *Medicine Man: The Forgotten Museum of Henry Wellcome* (London: British Museum Press, 2003).

Bates, A. W., ' "Indecent and Demoralising Representations": Public Anatomy Museums in Mid-Victorian England', *Medical History*, 52 (2008), 1–22.

Bennett, J. A., 'Museums and the Establishment of the History of Science at Oxford and Cambridge', *British Journal of the History of Science*, 30 (1997), 29–46.

Bennett, T. *Pasts beyond Memory: Evolution, Museums, Colonialism* (London: Routledge, 2004).

Behrman, S. N., *Duveen* (London: Hamish Hamilton, 1952).

Blackmore, H. L., 'The Wellcome Collection: A Look Back at the Largest Arms Collection of All Time', *Man at Arms*, 5 (1995), 34–9.

Boisseau, T. J., *White Queen: May French-Sheldon and the Imperial Origins of American Feminist Identity* (Bloomington: Indiana University Press, 2004).

Bowler, P. J., *The Invention of Progress: The Victorians and the Past* (Oxford: Basil Blackwell Ltd, 1989).

Boylan, P. J., 'Universities and Museums: Past, Present and Future', *Museum Management and Curatorship*, 18 (1999), 43–56.

Briggs, A., *Victorian Things* (London: B. T. Batsford, 1988).

—— 'Samuel Smiles: The Gospel of Self-Help', in G. Marsden (ed.), *Victorian Values* (London: Longman, 1990).

Cannon, W. B., 'Harvey (Williams) Cushing 1869–1939', *Obituary Notices of Fellows of the Royal Society*, 3/9 (1941), 276–90.

Church, R., 'The British Market for Medicine in the Late Nineteenth Century: The Innovative Impact of S. M. Burroughs and Co.', *Medical History*, 49 (2005), 281–98.

—— 'Trust, Burroughs Wellcome and Co. and the Foundation of a Modern Pharmaceutical Industry in Britain, 1880–1914', *Business History*, 43 (2006), 376–98.

—— and E. M. Tansey, *Burroughs Wellcome and Co.: Knowledge, Trust, Profit and the Transformation of the British Pharmaceutical Industry, 1880–1940* (Lancaster: Crucible Books, 2007).

Clifford, J., ' "Hanging Up Looking Glasses at Odd Corners": Ethnobiographical Prospects', in D. Aaron (ed.), *Studies in Biography* (London: Harvard University Press, 1978).

Cohen, D., *Household Gods: The British and Their Possessions* (New Haven: Yale University Press, 2006).

Colls, R. and P. Dodd (eds), *Englishness: Politics and Culture 1880–1920* (London: Croom Helm, 1986).

Connor, P., 'Cast Collecting in the Nineteenth Century: Scholarship, Aesthetics, Connoisseurship', in G. W. Clarke (ed.), *Rediscovering Hellenism* (Cambridge: Cambridge University Press, 1989).

Conway, M., *The Sport of Collecting* (London: T. Fisher Unwin, 1914).

Coombes, A., *Reinventing Africa: Museums, Material Culture and Popular Imagination* (New Haven: Yale University Press, 1994).

Crawford, O. G. S., *Said and Done: The Autobiography of an Archaeologist* (London: Weidenfeld and Nicholson, 1955).

D'Arcy, P. F., *Laboratory on the Nile: A History of the Wellcome Tropical Research Laboratories* (London: Pharmaceutical Products Press, 1999).

D'Souza, A., 'The Accidental Collector: A Portrait of Dr. Gachet—"Cezanne to Van Gogh: The Collection of Doctor Gachet" Traveling Exhibition', *Art in America*, 87 (1999).

Davidson, D., 'Bell-Metal Mortars', *The Connoisseur*, 15 (1906), 229–34.

Duggan, A. J., 'A Brief History of the Wellcome Museum of Medical Science', *Transactions of the Royal Society of Tropical Medicine and Hygiene*, 75 (1981), 29–31.

Edis, R. W., *Decoration and Furniture of Town Houses. A Series of Cantor Lectures Delivered before the Society of Arts, 1880, Amplified and Enlarged* (London: C. Kegan Paul and Co., 1881).

Elsner, J., and R. Cardinal (eds), *The Cultures of Collecting* (London: Harvard University Press, 1994).

Emeljanow, V., 'Ward, Dame (Lucy) Genevieve Teresa (1837–1922)', *Oxford Dictionary of National Biography* (Oxford: Oxford University Press, 2004).

Available at URL:http://www.oxforddnb.com/view/article/39386, accessed 12 May 2008.

Ettinghausen, M., *Rare Books and Royal Collectors: Memoirs of an Antiquarian Bookseller* (New York: Simon and Schuster, 1966).

Fisher, R. B., *Syrie Maugham* (London: Duckworth, 1978).

Flanders, J., *Consuming Passions: Leisure and Pleasure in Victorian Britain* (London: Harper Perennial, 2006).

Freeman, A., and J. I. Freeman, *Anatomy of an Auction: Rare Books at Ruxley Lodge, 1919* (London: The Collector, 1990).

Gell, A., *Art and Agency: An Anthropological Theory* (Oxford: Clarendon Press, 1998).

Gosden, C., and C. Knowles, *Collecting Colonialism: Material Culture and Colonial Change* (Oxford: Berg, 2001).

—— and F. Larson, *Knowing Things: Exploring the Collections at the Pitt Rivers Museum* (Oxford: Oxford University Press, 2007).

Gould, S. J., *The Mismeasure of Man* (New York: Norton, 1981).

Gould, T. (ed.), *Cures and Curiosities: Inside the Wellcome Library* (London: Profiles Books, 2007).

Greenhalgh, P., *Ephemeral Vistas: The Expositions Universelles, Great Exhibitions and World's Fairs, 1851–1939* (Manchester: Manchester University Press, 1988).

Hall, A. R., and B. A. Bembridge, *Physic and Philanthropy: A History of the Wellcome Trust 1936–1986* (Cambridge: Cambridge University Press, 1986).

Haggis, A. W. J., *The Life and Work of Sir Henry Wellcome*, unpublished manuscript (London: Wellcome Library, 1942).

Harrod, T., 'The Cast Courts at the Victoria and Albert Museum', *Burlington Magazine*, 127:983 (1985), 110–11.

Haskell, F., and N. Penny, *Taste and the Antique: The Lure of Classical Sculpture 1500–1900* (New Haven: Yale University Press, 1981).

Hemming, A. G., 'Dated English Bell-Metal Mortars', *The Connoisseur*, 38 (1929), 158–66.

Hendon, J. A., 'Having and Holding: Storage, Memory, Knowledge, and Social Relations', *American Anthropologist*, 102 (2000), 42–53.

Herrmann, F., *Sothebys: Portrait of an Auction House* (London: Chatto and Windus, 1980).

—— *The English as Collectors: A Documentary Sourcebook*, 2nd edn (New Castle, DE: Oak Knoll Press, 1999).

Hill, J., 'Globe-Trotting Medicine Chests: Tracing Geographies of Collecting and Pharmaceuticals', *Social and Cultural Geography*, 7 (2006a), 365–84.

—— 'Travelling Objects: The Wellcome Collection in Los Angeles, London and Beyond', *Cultural Geographies*, 13 (2006b), 340–66.

Hill, J. 'The Story of the Amulet: Locating the Enchantment of Collections', *Journal of Material Culture*, 12 (2007), 65–87.

Hill, K., *Culture and Class in English Public Museums 1850–1914* (Aldershot: Ashgate, 2005).

Hoare, P., 'Maugham (Gwendoline Maud) Syrie (1879–1955)', *Oxford Dictionary of National Biography* (Oxford: Oxford University Press, 2004). Available at URL: http://www.oxforddnb.com/view/article/40189, accessed 17 Jan 2008.

Hopkins, N. S., 'W. S. Blackman and Anthropological Research', in N. S. Hopkins (ed.), *Upper Egypt: Life along the Nile* (Århus: Moesgård Museum, 2003).

Hoskins, J., *Biographical Objects: How Things Tell the Stories of People's Lives* (London: Routledge, 1998).

Hudson, K., *A Social History of Museums: What the Visitors Thought* (London: MacMillan Press, 1975).

Ikram, S., 'Introduction', in W. Blackman (ed.), *The Fellahin of Upper Egypt*, 2nd edn (Cairo: American University in Cairo Press, 2000).

Jasanoff, M., *Edge of Empire: Lives, Culture, and Conquest in the East 1750–1850* (New York: Vintage, 2005).

Jorion, P., 'The Downfall of the Skull', *RAIN* 48 (1982), 8–11.

Keith, A., 'What Should Museums Do for Us?', in Wellcome Historical Medical Museum, *Guide to the Wellcome Historical Medical Museum, 54a, Wigmore Street, London, W.* (1926), 49–61.

—— *An Autobiography* (London: Watts, 1950).

Kehoe, E., 'Working Hard at Giving It Away: Lord Duveen, the British Museum and the Elgin Marbles', *Historical Research*, 77 (2004), 503–19.

Kidman, A., 'Lever and the Collecting of Eighteenth-Century British Paintings', *Journal of the History of Collections* 4 (1992), 201–9.

Knight, F., 'The Collection of a Lifetime: Creating Henry Wellcome's Historical Medical Museum', DPhil thesis, University of Oxford, 2004.

Kuklick, H., *The Savage Within: The Social History of British Anthropology, 1885–1945* (Cambridge: Cambridge University Press, 1991).

Kumar, K., *The Making of English National Identity* (Cambridge: Cambridge University Press, 2003).

Lane Fox [Pitt Rivers], A. H., 'Primitive Warfare. Part II', *Journal of the Royal United Services Institute*, 12 (1868), 399–439, rpt. in J. L. Myers (ed.), *The Evolution of Culture and Other Essays* (Oxford: Clarendon Press, 1906).

—— 'On the Principles of Classification Adopted in the Arrangement of His Anthropological Collection, Now Exhibited in the Bethnal Green Museum', *Journal of the Anthropological Institute of Great Britain and Ireland*, 4 (1875a), 293–308.

—— 'On the Evolution of Culture', *Proceedings of the Royal Institution*, 7 (1875b), 496–520, rpt. in J. L. Myers (ed.), *The Evolution of Culture and Other Essays* (Oxford: Clarendon Press, 1906).

—— 'On Early Modes of Navigation', *Journal of the Anthropological Institute of Great Britain and Ireland*, 4 (1875c), 399–437.

Latour, B., *We Have Never Been Modern* (London: Harvard University Press, 1993).

LiPuma, E., *Encompassing Others: The Magic Of Modernity in Melanesia* (Ann Arbor: University of Michigan Press, 2000).

Loftie, W. J., *A Plea for Art in the House with Special Reference to the Economy of Collecting Works of Art, and the Importance of Taste in Education and Morals* (London: MacMillan, 1876).

MacGregor, A., 'Collectors, Connoisseurs and Curators in the Victorian age', in M. Caygill and J. Cherry (eds), *A. W. Franks: Nineteenth-Century Collecting and the British Museum* (London: British Museum Press, 1997).

McKnight, G., *The Scandal of Syrie Maugham* (London: W. H. Allen, 1980).

Mandelbaum, D. G., 'University Museums', *American Anthropologist*, ns, 55 (1953), 755–9.

Marks, R., *Burrell: A Portrait of a Collector. Sir William Burrell 1861–1958* (Glasgow: Richard Drew, 1983).

Millenson, S. F., *Sir John Soane's Museum* (Ann Arbor: UMI Research Press, 2001).

Morris, E., 'Introduction to Art and Business in Edwardian England: The Making of the Lady Lever Art Gallery', *Journal of the History of Collections*, 4 (1992a), 169–73.

—— 'Advertising and the Acquisition of Contemporary Art', *Journal of the History of Collections*, 4 (1992b), 195–200.

Mosley, A., 'Objects, Texts and Images in the History of Science', *Studies in History and Philosophy of Science Part A*, 38 (2007), 289–302.

Muensterberger, W., *Collecting: An Unruly Passion* (London: Princeton University Press, 1994).

Murray, P., *The Devil and Mr Duncan* (Victoria, BC: Sono Nis Press, 1985).

Nasaw, D., *The Chief: The Life of William Randolph Hearst* (Boston: Mariner Books, 2001).

Needham, P., 'William Morris's "Ancient Books" at Sale', in R. Myers, M. Harris, and G. Mandelbrote (eds), *Under the Hammer: Book Auctions since the Seventeenth Century* (New Castle, DE: Oak Knoll Press, 2001).

O'Hanlon, M., *Paradise: Portraying the New Guinea Highlands* (London: British Museum Press, 1993).

—— and R. L. Welsch (eds), *Hunting the Gatherers: Ethnographic Collectors, Agents and Agency in Melanesia, 1870s–1930s* (Oxford: Berghahn Books, 2000).

Pearce, S. M., *On Collecting: An Investigation into Collecting in the European Tradition* (London: Routledge, 1995).

—— R. Flanders, M. Hall, and F. Morton, *The Collector's Voice*, vol. III: *Imperial Voices* (Aldershot: Ashgate, 2002).

Pickstone, J. V., 'Museological Science? The Place of the Analytical/Comparative in Nineteenth-Century Science, Technology and Medicine', *History of Science*, 32 (1994), 111–38.

Pilbeam, P., *Madame Tussaud and the History of Waxworks* (London: Hambledon and London, 2003).

Prescott, G. M., 'Gachet and Johnston-Saint: The Provenance of van Gogh's "L'Homme à la Pipe"', *Medical History*, 31 (1987), 217–24.

Principe, L. M., and L. DeWitt, *Transmutations: Alchemy in Art. Selected Works from the Eddleman and Fisher Collections at the Chemical Heritage Foundation* (Pennsylvania: Chemical Heritage Foundation, 2002).

Quigley, C., *Skulls and Skeletons: Human Bone Collections and Accumulations* (North Carolina: McFarland, 2001).

Reed, N., 'Mounteney', *Wellcome Journal*, 1:6 (1986), 16–19.

Reinarz, J., 'The Age of Museum Medicine: The Rise and Fall of the Medical Museum at Birmingham's School of Medicine', *Social History of Medicine*, 18 (2005), 419–37.

Rhodes James, R., *Henry Wellcome* (London: Hodder and Stoughton, 1994).

Russell, G., 'The Wellcome Historical Medical Museum's Dispersal of Non-medical Material, 1936–1983', *Museums Journal*, 86(suppl.) (1986), 3–36.

Saltzman, C., *Portrait of Dr. Gachet: The Story of a Van Gogh Masterpiece, Money, Politics, Collectors, Greed, and Loss* (London: Penguin, 1998).

Sambon, L., 'Donaria of Medical Interest in the Oppenheimer Collection of Etruscan and Roman antiquities', *British Medical Journal*, 2 (1895), 146–50, 216–19.

Samuel, R., *Island Stories: Unravelling Britain* (London: Verso, 1998).

Schindlbeck, M., 'The Art of Collecting: Interactions between Collectors and the People They Visit', *Zeitschrift fur Ethnologie*, 118 (1993), 57–67.

Schupbach, W., *The Iconographic Collections of the Wellcome Institute for the History of Medicine London* (London: Wellcome Institute for the History of Medicine, 1989).

—— 'Kunst in der Sammlungen der Wellcome Trusts. Art in the Wellcome collection', in *Medizin & Kunst; Medicine & Art* (Isernhagen: Meduna Arzneimittel, 2003a).

—— 'An (al)chemist restored', *Friends of the Wellcome Library and Centre Newsletter*, 31 (2003b), 6–8.

Schütze, S. K., *Friedrich Hoffmann (1832–1904) and the 'Pharmaceutische Rundschau': A Contribution to the History of American Pharmacy* (Frankfurt: Peter Lang, 1993, tr. 2002).

Schwartz, V. R., 'Museums and Mass Spectacle: The Musée Grévin as a Monument to Modern Life', *French Historical Studies*, 19 (1995), 7–26.

Sheets-Pyenson, S., 'Cathedrals of Science: The Development of Colonial Natural History Museums during the Late Nineteenth Century', *History of Science*, 25 (1986), 279–300.

Skinner, G., 'The Surgical Instrument Collection of the Wellcome Museum', in B. Bracegirdle (ed.), *Proceedings of the Second Symposium of the European*

Association of Museums of the History of Medical Sciences (Paris: Fondation Marcel Merieux, 1984).

—— 'Sir Henry Wellcome's Museum for the Science of History', *Medical History*, 30 (1986), 383–418.

Smith, C. W., *Auctions: The Social Construction of Value* (New York: Free Press, 1989).

Stanley, H. M., *In Darkest Africa, or, the Quest, Rescue and Retreat of Emin Pasha, Governor of Equatoria* (Santa Barbara: Narrative Press, 1891 [2001]).

Stocking, G. W., 'The Ethnographer's Magic: Fieldwork in British Anthropology from Tylor to Malinowski', in G. W. Stocking (ed.), *The Ethnographer's Magic and Other Essays in the History of Anthropology* (Madison: University of Wisconsin Press, 1992).

Swanberg, W. A., *Citizen Hearst* (New York: MacMillan, 1962).

Symons, J., *Wellcome Institute for the History of Medicine: A Short History* (London: Wellcome Trust, 1993).

—— 'These Crafty Dealers: Sir Henry Wellcome as a Book Collector', in R. Myers and M. Harris (eds), *Medicine, Mortality and the Book Trade* (Folkestone: St Paul Bibliographies, 1998).

—— 'Thompson, Charles John Samuel (1862–1943)', *Oxford Dictionary of National Biography* (Oxford University Press, 2004). Available at URL:http://www.oxforddnb.com/view/article/70781, accessed 17 Jan 2008.

Tansey, E. M., 'The Wellcome Physiological Research Laboratories 1894–1904: The Home Office, Pharmaceutical Firms and Animal Experiments', *Medical History*, 33 (1989), 1–41.

—— 'Medicines and Men: Burroughs Wellcome and Co. and the British Drug Industry before the Second World War', *Journal of the Royal Society of Medicine*, 95 (2002), 411–16.

Thompson, C. J. S., *The Chemist's Compendium for Pharmacists, Chemists, and Students* (London: Whittaker, 1896).

—— *The Mystery and Romance of Alchemy and Pharmacy* (London: Scientific Press, 1897).

—— *Notes on Pharmacy and Dispensing for Nurses* (London: Scientific Press, 1898).

—— *Poison Romance and Poison Mysteries* (London: Scientific Press, 1899).

—— 'Henry Hill Hickman: A Forgotten Pioneer of Anaesthesia', *British Medical Journal*, 2676 (1912), 843–5.

—— *The Story of 'Holmleigh' Auxiliary Military Hospital, Harrow on the Hill, by the Commandant* (London: Bale and Danielsson, 1919).

—— *Roman Oculists' Medicine Stamps and Collyria* (London: Wellcome Museum, 1920).

—— *Rules of Health Prescribed for an English Queen in the Fourteenth Century* (London: Wellcome Historical Medical Museum, 1921).

Thompson, C. J. S., *Massage in Antiquity and its Practice in Ancient Greece and Rome* (London: Wellcome Historical Medical Museum, 1923).

Thompson, C. J., *Zorastro: A Romance* (London: Greening and Co., 1899).

Tuchscherer, K., 'The Lost Script of the Bagam', *African Affairs*, 98 (1999), 55–77.

Turner, H., *Henry Wellcome: The Man, His Collection and His Legacy* (London: Wellcome Trust and Heinemann, 1980).

Underwood, E. A., 'Singer, Charles Joseph (1876–1960)', *Oxford Dictionary of National Biography* (Oxford University Press, 2004). Available at URL:http://www.oxforddnb.com/view/article/36110, accessed 12 Jan 2007.

van Beek, G., 'The Rites of Things: A Critical View of Museums, Objects and Metaphors', *Etnofoor*, 3 (1990), 26–44.

Wainwright, C., *The Romantic Interior: The British Collector at Home, 1750–1850* (New Haven: Yale University Press, 1989).

Waldron, H. A., 'The Study of the Human Remains from Nubia: The Contribution of Grafton Elliot Smith and His Colleagues to Palaeopathology', *Medical History*, 44 (2000), 363–88.

Waywell, G. B., *The Lever and Hope Sculptures: Ancient Sculptures in the Lady Lever Art Gallery, Port Sunlight and a Catalogue of the Ancient Sculptures Formerly in the Hope Collection, London and Deepdene* (Berlin: Gebr. Mann Verlag, 1986).

Wenyon, C. M., 'Henry Solomon Wellcome 1853–1936', *Obituary Notices of Fellows of the Royal Society 1936–1938*, 2 (1936), 229–38.

Wellcome Foundation Ltd., *The Wellcome Museum of Medical Science 1914–1964: An Account of its Development, Content and Techniques Compiled and Illustrated by Members of the Staff* (London: Wellcome Foundation, 1964).

Wellcome, H. S., 'A Visit to the Native Cinchona Forests of South America', *Proceedings of the American Pharmaceutical Association Annual Meeting*, 27 (1880), 814–30.

—— *The Story of Metlakahtla* (London: Saxon, 1887).

—— 'Remains of Primitive Ethiopian Races Discovered in the Southern Sudan', (1912), rpt. in F. Addison, *The Wellcome Excavations in the Sudan*, vol. I (London: Oxford University Press, 1949).

—— 'Graeco-Roman Surgical Instruments Represented in Egyptian Sculpture', *XVIIth International Congress of Medicine, London, 1913, Section XXIII History of Medicine* (London: Henry Frowde, Hodder and Stoughton, Oxford University Press, 1914).

Wellcome Historical Medical Museum, *Handbook of the Historical Medical Museum Organised by Henry S. Wellcome, 54a, Wigmore Street, London, W.* (London: Wellcome Historical Medical Museum, 1913).

—— *Handbook to the Wellcome Historical Medical Museum Founded by Henry S. Wellcome, 54a, Wigmore Street, London, W.* (London: Wellcome Historical Medical Museum, 1920).

—— *Guide to the Wellcome Historical Medical Museum, 54a, Wigmore Street, London, W.* (London: Wellcome Historical Medical Museum, 1926).

—— *The Wellcome Historical Medical Muesum, 54a, Wigmore Street, London, W.* (London: Wellcome Historical Medical Museum, 1927).

Wilkinson, L., 'A. J. E. Terzi and L. W. Sambon: Early Italian Influences on Patrick Manson's "Tropical Medicine", Entomology, and the Art of Entomological Illustration in London', *Medical History*, 46 (2002), 569–79.

Wright, D. W., 'The Transfer of the Wellcome Collections to the Science Museum, 1977–1983', in B. Bracegirdle (ed.), *Proceedings of the Second Symposium of the European Association of Museums of the History of Medical Sciences* (Paris: Fondation Marcel Merieux, 1984).

Young, M., *Malinowski: Odyssey of an Anthropologist 1884–1920* (New Haven: Yale University Press, 2004).

INDEX

Mellon, Andrew William 137, 164
Metropolitan Museum, New York 177
Mockler, Frederick 101
Mond, Alfred 163
Moore, Norman 144
Morgan, John Pierpont 85, 137, 164
Morris, William, library of 19, 78
Museum of Fine Arts, Boston 177

Nachet, Albert 238–40
Natural History Museum, London 49
Neues Museum, Berlin 177

Oppenheimer Collection 103–4
Osler, William 79, 82

Pasteur, Louis 231, 232, 238
Pearson, George 22, 206, 288
Pedersen, Mikael 100–2, 107
Pender Davidson, D. 207
Petrie, William Matthew Flinders 50, 64, 202
Pitt Rivers Museum, Oxford 34–5, 88, 181, 199, 213–14
Pitt Rivers, Augustus Henry Lane Fox 88–90, 152, 178, 212
plaster casts 171, 176–8
Port, Harry 105, 247, 250, 253, 270
Power, D'Arcy 184–5, 187, 188–9
Power, Frederick 114
Poynter, Noel 245

Raymont, Joan, see Braunholtz, Joan
replicas 171–3, 178–9
relics 161, 171, 175, 231, 232, 233, 286
Rockefeller, John D. 85
Rolleston, Humphry 140, 187, 188, 191
Royal Anthropological Institute 188, 200–1
Royal College of Surgeons 49, 150, 187
Royal Commission on Museums and Galleries 155, 199
Royal Society of Medicine 184, 18, 190
Russell, George W. E. 59

Saint, Peter, see Johnston-Saint, Peter
St Louis World's Fair (1904) 24, 94
Sambon, Louis 76, 103–4, 129, 134, 139, 181, 183, 226

pellagra research 120–1
travels 68, 113, 117, 119, 167
relationship with Wellcome 119–21, 124–5
Science Museum, London 3, 280
Second World War 31, 273–4, 280, 282
Selfridge, Gordon 163, 165, 177
Sheldon, May French 108, 225
Shirreff, F. G. 181
Shoolbred's department store 70, 247
Singer, Charles 182, 190–1, 193–4, 197, 245
Smiles, Samuel 29
Smithsonian Institution 49, 84
Soane, John 176–177
Sotheby's, auction house 1, 19, 71, 77–9, 183, 205, 231, 253
South Kensington Museum 88, 177, 199
Spencer, Herbert 88
Spielmann, Marion Harry 186
Stanley, Dorothy 53
Stanley, Henry 17, 22, 108, 225
Stevens, J. C., auction house 79 83–4, 125, 144, 172, 183
storage 1–2, 70–1, 206–7, 247–57, 267, 274
Stow, Harry 81–2, 84, 105, 138, 251, 253, 270, 297 n. 18
Streeter, Edward 134–6, 139–40
Sudan 30, 46–9, 90, 109, 160, 180, 229
  Jebel Moya excavations 58–9, 144, 202, 208, 309 n. 3
Sudlow, Robert 13, 27

Teniers, David, the Younger 165–166
Terzi, Aleardo 167
Thompson, Charles John Samuel 20, 50, 91, 105, 106, 226, 260
  early work for Wellcome 35–42, 67–9, 15
  as an author 35–6, 40–1, 180, 183–4, 186
  travels 36, 68, 113, 130–3, 137
  at auctions 77–87, 91–2, 162–3, 165, 166, 297 n. 18
  and private collectors 93–104, 129–37
  report writing 71–2, 115–16, 185, 203
  supervises collecting agents 119–20, 125
  supervises illustrators 167–70, 172
  manages the Museum 67–9, 71–6, 143–4, 148–9, 154–8, 172, 177–8, 181, 247
  resignation 182–9, 190, 193, 197, 198, 228–9